CANADIAN SOCIALISM

ESSAYS ON THE CCF-NDP

Alan Whitehorn

D1555395

Toronto **OXFORD UNIVERSITY PRESS** 1992

Oxford University Press, 70 Wynford Drive, Don Mills, Ontario M3C 1J9

Toronto Oxford New York Delhi
Bombay Calcutta Madras Karachi Kuala Lumpur
Singapore Hong Kong Tokyo Nairobi Dar es Salaam
Cape Town Melbourne Auckland

and associated companies in
Berlin Ibadan

This book is printed on permanent (acid-free) paper

Canadian Cataloguing in Publication Data
Whitehorn, Alan
　Canadian socialism

Includes bibliographical references and index.
ISBN 0-19-540695-8

1.　Co-operative Commonwealth Federation.　2.　New
Democratic Party.　3.　Socialism — Canada.
4.　Canada — Politics and government — 20th century.
I. Title

JL197. N4W5　1992　　　324.27107　　　C92-093136-7

Design by Heather Delfino

CONTENTS

ACKNOWLEDGEMENTS

It would have been impossible to complete a work of so many years on a party involving hundreds of thousands of members without the assistance and sound advice of many persons. Among the multitude of people who have helped in the long birth of this book are the following who graciously consented to interviews: T.C. Douglas, David Lewis, Ed Broadbent, and Audrey McLaughlin; NDP federal secretaries Terry Grier, Cliff Scotton, Robin Sears, Mary Ellen McQuay, Dennis Young, Gerry Caplan, Bill Knight, and Dick Proctor; Ontario NDP leaders Ted Jolliffe, Donald MacDonald, Stephen Lewis, Mike Cassidy, and Bob Rae; and several provincial/territorial leaders, including Elizabeth Weir, Alexa McDonough, and Tony Penikett.

Over the years I have had the good fortune to receive helpful information from a multitude of CCF-NDP activists and staff members, including Rosemarie Bahr, Ken Bryden, Anne Carroll, Ed Dale, Anita Devillez, Marion Dewar, Patrick Donahue, Hania Fedorowicz, Anna Rae Fishman, Eugene Forsey, Diane Gibeault, Judy Giroux, Brian Harling, Sandra Houston, Wendy Hughes, Shirley Johnson, Kalmen Kaplansky, Audrey Kari, Pat Kerwin, Carlyle King, Stanley Knowles, Carmel Bélanger, Michael Lewis, Julie Mason, Lynn McDonald, Brian McKee, Tommy McLeod, George Nakitsas, Joan Neal, Terry O'Grady, Michael Oliver, Abby Pollonetsky, Keith Reynolds, Gillian Sandman, Frank Scott, Gerry Scott, Janet Solberg, Leslie Turnbull, Judy Wasylycia-Leis, Gail Whelan-Enns and Arlene Wortsman. There are a great many others, and no doubt I've inadvertently omitted a few. To them and to all those who have filled out my survey questionnaires at NDP conventions over the years, a grateful thank-you.

Pollsters are increasingly an important factor in Canadian politics, and I wish to thank Lorne Bozinoff, Donna Dasko, Vic Fingerhut and Dave Gotthilf for providing access to some of their data.

No historical research would get far without the heroic efforts of the keepers of our fragile archival heritage. Much gratitude goes to these skilled public servants: Dr Ian McClymont, Eldon Frost, Danny Moore, John Smart, David Walden, and a multitude of others from the National Archives; George Brandak from the University of British Columbia Archives; Ian Wilson, Doug Bocking and Ed Morgan from the

Saskatchewan Archives Board; Nancy Stundon and Peter Bower from the Manitoba Archives; and Carmen Carroll from the Nova Scotia Archives.

Among the academic and professional colleagues who have helped me most in this study of the CCF-NDP, I particularly want to acknowledge Keith Archer, Sharleen Bannon, Helmut Binhammer, Bill Brennan, Jim Cairns, Kelly Deonandan, Yvan Gagnon, Larry Leduc, Simon McInnes, Tony Miller, Allen Mills, Gillian Minifie, Jon Pammett, Norman Penner, George Perlin, Hugh Thorburn, Linda Trimble, and Walter Young. Gerda Pennock, Betty McIntyre, and Ursula Butz, secretaries in the Department of Political and Economic Science at the Royal Military College, provided great assistance over the years in typing early drafts of several of the chapters. Over the years, I have been the grateful recipient of grants for a number of modest projects that indirectly assisted my work on this current volume. Accordingly, I wish to thank the Social Sciences and Humanities Research Council, the Douglas-Coldwell Foundation, and the Arts Research Programme of the Royal Military College.

At Oxford University Press, Richard Teleky had the sensitivity to listen to my proposal and the often-tested patience to nurture it to fruition. Sally Livingston's suggestions for stylistic changes invariably led to improvements in the text, and her steady barrage of questions and comments ensured an analytically sharper and more thorough manuscript. Phyllis Wilson guided it through the production process with a steady hand.

One other group knows all too well the work involved in writing a book. To my parents and sister in Toronto who provided steady encouragement, and my wife Suzanne and daughter Kate in Kingston, who had to live with an author and make all too many sacrifices, much overdue and deeply felt thanks.

In the end, however, the final responsibility for this volume is mine. I welcome comments.

ALAN WHITEHORN

PREFACE

The fox knows many little things,
but the hedgehog knows one big thing.
—Archilochus

Isaiah Berlin, in his book *The Hedgehog and the Fox* (1970), suggests that while some authors try to relate every aspect of a topic to a single dominant theme, others choose to pursue several themes, and to employ a variety of perspectives on their subject. This book takes the latter approach.

After more than fifteen years of research on the New Democratic Party (NDP) and its forerunner, the Co-operative Commonwealth Federation (CCF), I have concluded that the best way to analyse a party as diverse as the CCF-NDP is to study it from several different angles. Each perspective, it is hoped, will reveal some important features of the party, but no single one on its own will be sufficient for a full understanding of this complex and enduring political organization.

As readers may discern in Chapter 2, many authors writing about the CCF-NDP have tried to present one big story. My more modest goal is to offer a number of less sweeping accounts in a series of shorter essays. Chapters 1 and 2 provide a brief introductory overview, and would be the best place to start for the reader with little background on the party and its history. Later chapters endeavour to explore more specific details about selected aspects of the party. Chapter 3, for example, outlines the party's five key manifestos, Chapter 4 analyses election campaigns and outcomes, and Chapter 5 examines the growth in size and importance of the party's political conventions. Chapter 6 discusses Tommy Douglas and David Lewis, two heroic figures who sustained the CCF and were instrumental in building the NDP. Finally, chapters 7, 8, and 9 respectively consider Ed Broadbent, the contemporary era, and the NDP's prospects for the future. Those who desire more detail may wish to consult the bibliography.

To David and Tommy, two pioneers who showed the way

ONE

Introduction:
An Overview of the Party

The roots of the federal New Democratic Party lie in the Great Depression of the 1930s. In 1932, 131 delegates from a variety of organizations gathered together in Calgary and decided to form the 'Co-operative Commonwealth Federation (Farmer, Labour, Socialist)'. A year later, the CCF held its first annual convention in Regina and drafted the Regina Manifesto, a statement of principles that is for many the touchstone of Canadian socialism. In 1992 the New Democratic Party, the successor to the CCF, celebrates sixty years of CCF-NDP history. Without a doubt, the party can take much pride in its political accomplishments. But that pride is combined with serious reflection and critical self-appraisal regarding the past, and some concern about the future.

Is the federal NDP stalled as a third party? Has it largely failed in its efforts to be more successful than its predecessor, the CCF? Why, despite its image repackaging, does the NDP continue to make so little progress in Quebec? What are the long-term prospects in the industrial heartland of Ontario? Is the party's provincial base in the west still its main strength? Has the NDP ceased to provide a clear socialist alternative to the two old-line parties? Has the NDP become more a brokerage party and less an ideologically-based movement? Why, after almost sixty years, has the NDP not made greater gains? In providing an overview of the party, particularly during the 1980s, this chapter will suggest some preliminary answers to these questions, which will be considered in more detail in later chapters.

SUPPORT

After reaching its peak at 15.6% in 1945, the federal CCF vote dropped consistently in the four subsequent elections: to 13.4% in 1949, 11.3% in 1953, 10.7% in 1957, and 9.5% in 1958. Like the Socialist Party of the United States,[1] the CCF was clearly on the path to oblivion. But the birth of the NDP gave new electoral vitality to Canada's socialist movement. Winning 13.5% of the vote in its maiden election, in 1962, the NDP did better than had the CCF in all but one of the elections it contested. On average, from 1962 to 1988 the federal NDP has acquired 17.2% of the vote, as compared with 11.1% for the CCF—a clear gain of 6.1%, and a 55% increase over its forerunner's record. In seven of the ten federal elections since 1962 the NDP has gained a higher percentage of votes than the CCF did even in its best year, 1945.

Only once, however, has the CCF-NDP received more than 20% of the federal vote: this was in 1988, when the party exceeded its 26-year average (1962-88) in every province or region except Manitoba and Nova Scotia (see Appendix Table 1). Although it has increasingly surpassed the 20% barrier in Gallup polls,[2] it has not yet become a major party on the brink of power.

Nor, despite these overall gains, has the NDP's electoral support shown improvement over the CCF's in all regions equally. Regionalization between and within parties is a fact of life in Canadian politics, and the CCF-NDP is no exception. When data are compared regarding the average federal vote by province for the CCF and the NDP (see Table 1.1), we find that in Saskatchewan support has declined from 34.7% for the CCF to 32.4% for the NDP. The biggest drop was in the years 1962-65, when the province returned no NDP MPs—the only period in the combined history of the federal CCF-NDP that this has been so. Several factors offer explanations: (1) resentment over the transformation of the CCF into the NDP in the only province where the CCF had formed a government; (2) disappointment over T.C. Douglas's departure from Saskatchewan politics to return to Ottawa; and (3) growing disenchantment with the provincial CCF as it neared the end of its second decade of uninterrupted power.

In part the NDP was formed with urban, labour-oriented Ontario in mind, and it was in that province that its greatest increase in support occurred: from a 10.7% average for the CCF to a 20.0% average for the NDP. The party has seen a virtual doubling of its Ontario vote, a seven-fold increase in the average number of seats won per election (from just over one in the CCF era to eight), and an equally large increase in the percentage of its total seats coming from that province (from 7.1% to 31.1%).

Table 1.1 Average Percentage CCF-NDP Federal Vote By Province: 1935-1988

Province	CCF (1935-58) %	NDP (1962-88) %	Difference
British Columbia	28.0	32.4	4.4
Alberta	10.2	10.6	0.4
Saskatchewan	34.7	32.4	−2.3
Manitoba	23.3	25.0	1.7
Ontario	10.7	20.0	9.3
Quebec	1.5	8.1	6.6
New Brunswick	3.0[a]	9.3	6.3
Nova Scotia	8.1[a]	12.1	4.0
Prince Edward Island	1.7[a]	5.1	3.4
Newfoundland	0.3[a]	9.4	9.1
Yukon/NWT	22.3[a]	24.6[a]	2.3
Canada	11.1	17.2	6.1

[a] did not contest every federal election in the province/territory; average is based only on elections contested.

The old CCF was an electoral disaster in Quebec, where it averaged a mere 1.5% of the vote. Some problems were present right from the start. Few Francophones attended the founding convention, and the name Co-operative Commonwealth Federation did not translate well into French. Most of Quebec's Roman Catholic population, and particularly its leadership, regarded the party as atheistic, materialistic, and anti-clerical.[3] In policy, moreover, the CCF stressed the need for a strong federal government and central planning at the expense of provincial powers and jurisdiction — another point on which most Quebeckers were especially sensitive. Finally, the heavy Anglophone membership of the Quebec CCF reinforced the CCF's image as a party antithetical to French Canadian interests.

Another reason for the NDP's creation was to make a new and better start in Quebec. While no significant breakthrough has yet occurred in a general election, the NDP, with an average 8.1% of the vote, has fared much better than did the CCF. Overall, the province has given the NDP its third-largest increase in votes over the CCF, and the third-highest percentage of the party's total votes (12.5%); judging by the 1988 election, more than one in ten NDP voters are now located in Quebec. And if the province has yet to elect a single NDP MP in a general election, the party has on two separate occasions acquired a solitary Quebec MP; once by means of a defection from the Conservatives (Robert Toupin, from 1987 until 1988) and once, more significantly, through a by-election victory (Phil Edmonston in Chambly

Table 1.2 Party's Total Federal Seats By Region: 1935-1988

Region	CCF (1935-58) N	CCF (1935-58) %	NDP (1962-88) N	NDP (1962-88) %
MARITIMES	4	3.6	4	1.6
Newfoundland	0	0	1	0.4
Prince Edward Island	0	0	0	0
Nova Scotia	4	3.6	3	1.2
New Brunswick	0	0	0	0
QUEBEC	0	0	0	0
ONTARIO	8	7.1	80	31.1
PRAIRIES	71	63.4	73	28.4
Manitoba	19	17.0	33	12.8
Saskatchewan	52	46.4	39	15.2
Alberta	0	0	1	0.4
BRITISH COLUMBIA	29	25.9	95	37.0
NWT/YUKON	0	0	5	1.9
TOTAL	112	100.0	257	100.0
East		10.7		32.7
West		89.3		67.3

SOURCES: Gibbins (1980); Beck (1968); Penniman (1975, 1981); Report of the Chief Electoral Officer (various years).

in 1990). Whether these small steps are indicative of potentially greater future gains for the NDP in Quebec, particularly during a general election, remains to be seen.

That the NDP has been better able than the CCF to establish a presence in all parts of Canada can be seen both in the greater percentage of ridings in which it has run candidates (61.3% for the CCF vs. 96.0% for the NDP)[4] and in the fact that it has increased its vote in almost all regions of Canada (see Table 1.1). For example, the average percentage vote for the NDP in the province in which its record has been the worst—Prince Edward Island—is still higher than the CCF's average in several provinces.

The CCF has often been portrayed as a western protest movement (e.g., Lipset, 1968: 188). Certainly its leaders came from the west, as did the vast majority of its MPs (89.3%) (see Table 1.2).[5] However, there has been a tendency by many to overestimate western and 'farmer' input in the CCF vote while underestimating eastern and 'labour' support. The CCF's electoral support was greater in the west (59.3%),[6] but not to the degree often assumed (see Table 1.3): on average, 40.7% of its total votes came from the

Table 1.3 Percentage of CCF-NDP's Total Federal Vote By Region: 1935-1988

Region	CCF (1935-58) %		NDP (1962-88) %	
MARITIMES	4.3		5.8	
Newfoundland		0.0		1.0
Prince Edward Island		0.1		0.2
Nova Scotia		3.4		3.0
New Brunswick		0.8		1.6
QUEBEC	3.6		12.5	
ONTARIO	32.8		42.2	
PRAIRIES	38.5		19.9	
Manitoba		12.2		6.7
Saskatchewan		20.8		8.6
Alberta		5.5		4.6
BRITISH COLUMBIA	20.8		19.4	
NWT/YUKON	0.0		0.3	
TOTAL	100		100[a]	
East	40.7		60.5	
West	59.3		39.6	

SOURCES: Cairns (1968); Beck (1968); Penniman (1975, 1981); Report of the Chief Electoral Officer (various years)
[a] does not total 100% because of rounding

east. Indeed, as early as 1949, twelve years before the NDP's founding, Ontario provided more of the CCF's votes than did the Prairies.[7]

With respect to total votes cast for the NDP, the more populous east (i.e., Ontario and Quebec), not surprisingly, accounts for the larger proportion: 60.5%, as compared with 39.6% from the west. Total votes, however, are far from the only criterion. The NDP's representation in Parliament continues to have a western orientation, with 67.3% of its seats coming from the west. This is a lower rate than in the CCF days, but still somewhat at variance with the party's total votes.[8] The 1988 election continued this pattern of asymmetry between total number of votes and seats. Nevertheless, the imbalance in distribution of seats does reflect the higher average levels of support for the NDP in the west ($\bar{x} = 25.0\%$ of all votes cast, vs. $\bar{x} = 10.7\%$ for the east).[9] For example, the 1988 election saw record-high NDP votes in three western provinces: 44.2% in Saskatchewan, 37.0% in British Columbia, and 17.4% in Alberta.

In two other important ways the NDP retains a very strong western orientation. On the one hand, 1987 data on the 276,128 members of the party affiliated indirectly through unions[10] (see Table 1.4) indicate that the east

Table 1.4 Organizations Affiliated to the NDP: 1987

SUMMARY BY PROVINCE/TERRITORY

Province	Affiliated locals	Affiliated members
British Columbia	56	28,874
Alberta	21	4,221
Saskatchewan	34	10,516
Manitoba	37	12,951
Ontario	516	209,748
Quebec	12	3,983
New Brunswick	2	84
Nova Scotia	10	2,096
Prince Edward Island	2	635
Newfoundland	2	3,020
Yukon/NWT	—	—
TOTAL	692	276,128

Table 1.5 Membership in the NDP: 1987

Province	N	%	X[a]
British Columbia	34,225	23.4	1,222
Alberta	12,677	8.7	603
Saskatchewan	38,086	26.1	2,720
Manitoba	21,263	14.6	1,518
Ontario	33,036	22.6	347
Quebec	1,696	1.2	22
New Brunswick	1,136	0.8	113
Nova Scotia	2,456	1.7	223
Prince Edward Island	169	0.1	42
Newfoundland	920	0.6	131
Yukon	227	0.2	227
Northwest Territories	230	0.2	115
TOTAL	146,121	100 [b]	

SOURCE: Data provided by communication with NDP federal office
[a] average federal riding membership
[b] does not total 100% because of rounding

in general and Ontario in particular accounted for the overwhelming majority (79.5% and 76.0% respectively). In contrast, 1987 data on direct individual members[11] (see Table 1.5) reveal that 73.0% of these were found in the west. To a considerable degree this may reflect the NDP's strong provincial bases in this region, since federal-party members are also simultaneously provincial-party members (except in Quebec from 1989 onwards). Until the 1990 upset victory in Ontario, the only provinces in which the CCF-NDP had formed governments were in the west: from 1972 to 1975 in British Columbia, from 1944 to 1964 and 1971 to 1982 in Saskatchewan, from 1969 to 1977 and 1981 to 1988 in Manitoba, and from 1985 to the present in the Yukon. Any decline in the party's provincial fortunes in the west, therefore, is likely to have an effect upon the federal party's position in terms of both membership and finances.

In Saskatchewan the Blakeney NDP government had been dramatically defeated in 1982. The party received only 37.2% of the vote, its worst showing in forty-four years, and went from 44 seats to 8, the most precipitous drop ever for the provincial CCF-NDP in Saskatchewan (Fox, 1982: 682-4). Nevertheless, a considerable NDP base remained, and in the provincial election of 1986 the party received 45.2% of the vote, a sizeable increase from 1982. In fact, this was the highest vote for any of the parties —and higher than in 1975, when the NDP had formed the government. But because the electoral system was weighted more heavily to the less populated rural ridings, the NDP won only 25 legislative seats (Fox, 1987: 414-15); the Conservatives, with only 44.6% of the vote but 38 seats, formed the government and stalled Allan Blakeney's attempted comeback. It would remain for Roy Romanow, Blakeney's successor in the province that pioneered Canada's socialist programmes, to return the provincial NDP to power. Certainly the NDP's record-high 1988 federal vote in Saskatchewan gave renewed reason for optimism on the eve of the 1991 provincial election, which was fought on the issues of privatization, government decentralization (Pitsula and Rasmussen, 1990), and the economic plight of Prairie farmers. Romanow was elected Premier with over 50% of the vote and a massive 55 of 66 seats. Saskatchewan was clearly back in the NDP fold.

In British Columbia in the 1980s, the provincial NDP, which had formed the government under Dave Barrett from 1972 to 1975, failed twice to return to power. However, with 44.2% of the vote in 1983, and 42.6% in 1986, down slightly from its previous high of 45.2% in 1979, the party was still in good health organizationally, and the record-high vote and seats won in the province in the 1988 federal election were promising. The ongoing financial scandals of Bill Vander Zalm's Social Credit government and the lacklustre performance of his successor Rita Johnston contributed to the collapse of the Social Credit vote in the 1991 provincial election. While the NDP vote itself again fell slightly to 39.8%, it was still sufficient to thwart the resurgent Liberal Party. The NDP won 51 seats and provincial leader Mike Harcourt became Premier of British Columbia.

The NDP's greatest success stories in the 1980s were its two provincial victories in Manitoba. Returning to power in 1981, the Manitoba NDP not only won the most seats in its history (34), but also received its highest vote ever (47.4%). In 1986, despite a decline in its vote to 40.6% (second place to the Conservatives), the party retained a slim majority of seats (30, to the Conservatives' 26) and continued, albeit precariously, as the provincial government for another two years. By 1988, though, suffering from defections and dissent, the government lost a legislative vote and Premier Howard Pawley chose to resign amidst the provincial election. After seven uninterrupted years in power, the NDP was ripe for defeat, receiving only 23.6% of the vote and 12 seats. New leader Gary Doer had to commence rebuilding the party not only from the opposition side of the legislature, but also from the more difficult position of third place. It appears, though, that voter dissatisfaction with the NDP was specific to 1988, as the 1990 provincial election saw a partial resurgence of the NDP's vote to 29%. With 20 seats to the Liberals' 8, the NDP is now the official opposition. Nevertheless, since the revitalization of the provincial Liberal Party the NDP still has to contend with the more complex calculations involved in a three-party system. The decline in the NDP's federal vote in Manitoba in 1988 is also a reminder that the provincial party will continue to face obstacles.

Alberta, historically infertile NDP territory, has seen a significant change in the party's fortunes. In four of the five provincial elections since 1971, the NDP's percentage of votes has increased, and a year after the 1982 election it finally formed the official opposition. In 1986 the Alberta party set records in both vote (29.2%) and seats (16) (Fox, 1987: 414-15). Although in 1989 the NDP saw its vote dip slightly to 26.3%—less than the Liberals' 28.6%—it still retained its 16 seats, and that was sufficient to remain as the official opposition. Alberta now offers one of the NDP's better hopes for electoral success, despite the rise of the Reform Party. In the 1988 national election Alberta gave the party both its best federal vote ever and its first Member of Parliament. This was something the CCF, although it was founded in Calgary in 1932, was never able to achieve.

As the decades-long Conservative dynasty in Ontario drew to a close in the 1980s, the provincial NDP hoped that it might be seen as the vehicle for political change, rather than the relatively weak provincial Liberal Party. In 1943, 1948, and 1975 the Ontario CCF-NDP had displaced the Liberals as the official opposition; now party activists expected that they could do so once more and put the NDP in a good position to form the government when the Conservative balloon finally deflated. But when the end of the Conservative era came, the opposition Liberals were catapulted to power, first as a minority in 1985 and then as a majority in 1987. With the Liberals under Premier David Peterson commanding huge leads in the polls, the only consolations for the Ontario NDP seemed to be, first, the famous—for some, controversial—1985 accord with the minority Liberal government concerning the legislative agenda, and second, in 1987, the party's somewhat precarious displacement of the Conservatives as the official opposition. Although, like its federal cousin, the Ontario NDP was clearly one of three major players, the immediate prospects for moving from opposition to government seemed slight. However, the sudden election call in the summer of 1990 changed everything. Plagued by scandals, rising taxes, growing concerns about the environment, and discontent over the defunct Meech Lake Accord, the Peterson Liberals suffered a stunning defeat. The NDP under Bob Rae ran a strong campaign, gained a record-high 37.6% of the popular vote, and, with 74 seats, formed the first social-democratic government in the history of Ontario.[12]

As the 1980s ended, no provincial NDP government existed in the country. The only major outpost of socialist administration was the NDP territorial government in the Yukon, elected in 1985. However, the recent victories in Ontario, BC, and Saskatchewan suggest that a new dawn is emerging for social democrats. Given the federal party's failure in its 1988 bid for an electoral breakthough, NDP strategists may have to content themselves with hoping that these provincial successes will be the key stepping stones to improved federal prospects.

ELECTORAL BIAS AND DISTORTION

The distortions inherent in the single-member constituency system were ably analysed in a pioneering study by Cairns (1968). This is a particular problem for a third party that endeavours to draw votes from across all regions. It is thus not surprising that, federally, both the CCF and the NDP have suffered by our current electoral system. Whereas the CCF averaged 11.1% of the vote, it collected only 6.2% of the seats (a difference of 4.9%). The NDP, despite increasing its overall vote to 17.2%, has collected only 9.3% of the seats (a difference of 7.9) (see Figure 1.1). If one accepts as a fundamental premise that, in a democratic polity, each vote should count equally, it seems reasonable to conclude that in both cases the party should have received a percentage of seats closer to its percentage of the vote. This is not a problem that is likely to diminish in the foreseeable future. In fact, the bias in the electoral system seems to be operating at least as strongly against the NDP as it did against the CCF, even though the NDP has acquired a significantly higher percentage of the vote. On average, the CCF should have received 79% more seats and the NDP 85% more; in the case of the 1988 election, the NDP's percentage vote would have given it 60 seats instead of 43. Modifications in our electoral system that might bring it closer to proportional representation would clearly help the federal NDP. Curiously, however, under Ed Broadbent the federal party was not a proponent of this idea, although under Audrey McLaughlin it has shown greater interest.

A number of scholars (Cairns, 1968; Gibbins, 1980) have observed that in addition to reducing the representation of a party, electoral distortions

Figure 1.1 Percentage of Total Votes and Seats Received by the CCF-NDP

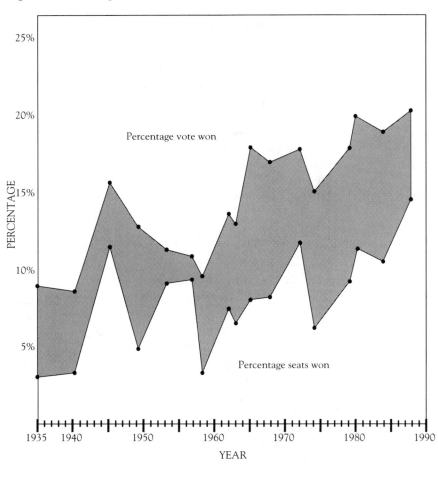

shaded area indicates amount
of electoral bias

can have a serious effect on its image. For example, while 40.7% of the CCF's vote came from the east, only 10.7% of its seats came from that region: this fostered the impression that the party was overwhelmingly based in the rural west—an image that did not always help the CCF in its efforts to present itself as a truly pan-Canadian party.

Although much has been made of the CCF-NDP's failure in Quebec and the reasons for it, one factor frequently overlooked is the bias in the electoral system. The CCF-NDP had from its birth contested federal elections in Quebec. From 1949 to 1965 the party consistently increased its vote—from

1.1% (1949) to 1.5% (1953), 1.8% (1957), 2.3% (1958), 4.4% (1962), 7.1% (1963), and 12.0% (1965)—yet no CCF-NDP MP was ever elected from any riding. Most recently, in the 1988 election, 487,971 Quebeckers, or one in seven (14%), supported the NDP, but not one of the province's 75 seats was awarded to the party. At the same time, some Quebec MPs won their seats with fewer than 16,000 votes. What might it mean if an electoral system was in place that could respond to the growing support for the party? Would the NDP have more articulate voices speaking on behalf of Quebec? Would it be encouraged to try harder in that province? Would the Canadian polity as a whole be better served if each party received adequate representation in each region of the country? If the federal NDP appeared less sympathetic to Quebec's concerns in 1989 than a few years earlier, part of the reason may have been the electoral system's failure to respond to the party's considerable efforts in the province the previous year.

In any event, in the 1988 election a party that won over 20% of the vote in Canada acquired no Members of Parliament east of the Ontario riding of Oshawa.[13] It is hard to imagine that Canada's regional tensions can be alleviated as long as such electoral imbalances persist. Rather, such a system seems likely to promote parochialism.

LEADERSHIP

In the history of the CCF-NDP there have been seven party leaders: J.S. Woodsworth, M.J. Coldwell, Hazen Argue,[14] T.C. Douglas, David Lewis, Ed Broadbent, and Audrey McLaughlin. The average tenure of McLaughlin's predecessors was 9.3 years, as compared with 11.2 years for the Liberals and 6.2 years for the Conservatives in the period 1932-88 (see Table 5.12b below). All three CCF leaders came from the west, as did the first NDP leader, Douglas, while his immediate successors, Lewis and Broadbent, came from Ontario in the east. The selection of McLaughlin returned the leadership to the west, although her Yukon riding is perhaps more properly described as northwestern.

Not surprisingly, under Broadbent the NDP acquired thirteen Ontario seats in 1984, the most ever. No matter what personalities might have been involved, a certain amount of tension was probably inevitable in a situation in which the party's leader was based in Ontario, while most of its MPs, 73.0% of its individual members, the most successful provincial New Democratic parties, and (at the time) the only NDP governments were all based in the west. To some westerners at the 1983 Regina convention (such as Saskatchewan MP Doug Anguish), frustrated over Broadbent's constitutional stand and the party's then-low standing in national polls, it seemed time for the leadership to revert to a westerner. Nevertheless, Broadbent was re-elected by acclamation, although not without a brief moment of doubt.[15]

Given that, on average, 60.5% of the party's vote and 79.5% of its affil-iated members have come from the east (see Tables 1.3 and 1.4), the case for a western leader is not as one-sided as many have assumed. Following the nadir of 1983, Broadbent saw both his personal popularity and that of the NDP soar to the top of the national polls. Like earlier CCF-NDP leaders, he became one of the most respected politicians in the country, and in 1988 he led the party to its highest percentage vote (20.4%) and number of seats (43). Despite these gains, however, the NDP emerged still very much in third place. The 1988 election, echoing that of 1945, demonstrated the vulnerability of a social-democratic party to a hostile bourgeois press[16] and a media campaign financed by big business; confronted by an ascendant socialist party, the forces of capitalism responded swiftly and effectively to thwart the challenge (see Chapters 4 and 8, and Read and Whitehorn, 1991). Unable to guide the NDP to a new electoral plateau, Broadbent resigned as of December 1989, having been a member of Parliament for more than two decades, and having served for fourteen years and four cam-paigns as party leader.[17]

As the first female leader of a major Canadian federal party, Audrey McLaughlin has a difficult task ahead. She has promised that the NDP will reach out more effectively to women. Yet historically women have not been the strongest supporters of the NDP. It remains to be seen whether her elec-tion as leader and the rise in the number of women in the paid workforce will be sufficient to alter significantly the previous pattern of gender support. It is also not clear how well a leader based in the north-west will do in the federal party's efforts to build a stronger base in central Canada and establish a greater pan-Canadian presence, particularly if constitutional matters remain at the fore. Despite Bob Rae's unexpected victory in Ontario, most of the NDP governments and McLaughlin's caucus are still largely based in the west, and this pattern may reinforce the federal NDP's image as a western regional party. It may also enhance the party's tendency to concentrate more energy in the western provinces, particularly after the disappointing Quebec results in both the 1988 federal and 1989 provincial elections. Whether the NDP's 1990 by-election victory in Chambly, Quebec, and the Ontario election breakthrough will lessen this tendency remains to be seen. The issue of regionalism both within and outside the NDP will be a major test of the McLaughlin leadership.

IDEOLOGY AND POLICY

Much has been written about the CCF-NDP's alleged shifts in ideology and policy (e.g., Cross, 1974; Zakuta, 1964; Young, 1969). More often than not this theme has been addressed in terms of a 'protest movement becalmed', ideological decay in a third party, and the 'embourgeoisement' of a working-class organization. While this literature will be discussed in detail in Chapter 2, and the party's manifestos in Chapter 3, it may be useful to provide some background here.

In the history of the CCF-NDP five key statements of principles predominate. The page-long Calgary Programme of 1932 was a provisional outline of the general socialist and humanitarian goals of the CCF, and served as a prelude to the document that followed a year later. The Regina Manifesto of 1933, setting out the CCF's programme at its first full convention, in the midst of the Great Depression, will always have special significance to most party members. The Winnipeg Declaration of 1956, drafted at the height of the Cold War and during world-wide debates over the means to achieve socialism, continued the ideological rethinking that ultimately led to the creation of the NDP and the issuing of the New Party Declaration in 1961. Finally, in 1983, a new Regina Manifesto, fifty years after the first, was presented to guide the party in the 1980s. Together, these five documents provide considerable insight into the evolution of socialist thought in Canada.

A certain mythology has arisen about the 1933 Regina Manifesto. Because of a few provocative passages, it has acquired an image somewhat more radical than the text as a whole merits. In fact, content analysis (see Table 3.1 below) reveals that it does not dwell upon the terms 'socialism' or 'socialist'; the solitary usage suggests a somewhat cautious approach—not unlike that taken in the 1950s. Instead, the drafters of the 1933 document[18] chose terms such as 'socialization' or 'social ownership', hoping that these would be less intimidating to potential supporters. While the party's language became even more moderate in the 1950s and early 1960s, the 1983 document is emphatic in its use of the term 'socialism'—far more so than any other official NDP statement of principles.

This is not to suggest that the socialism of the 1980s is identical to that of the 1930s. Canadian socialists have realized that any ideology, to be meaningful, must be an evolving doctrine that endeavours to change the environment, but in turn is also changed. An ideology that fails to interact with the socio-economic base will ultimately recede into quixotic scholasticism and irrelevance, as a number of Marxist-Leninist regimes have discovered.

The NDP is now, as was the CCF, a blend of different colours of the political rainbow, composed of individuals whose attitudes range from Marxism to left reformism.[19] However, there has always been a 'ginger group' striving to push the party further left. Over the years the names of these groups have changed—the Socialist Party of Canada, the BC Socialist Fellowship, the Ontario Ginger Group, the Waffle, and most recently the Left Caucus—but the outcome is generally the same: the militant minority may be sufficiently strong at times to provoke lengthy and often intense debate, but it is rarely able to construct a winning majority. For example, at the 1983 convention, the final revised draft of the Manifesto put forward by the more moderate mainstream elements of the party was approved by a two-to-one ratio. The Left Caucus organizational and strategy meetings attracted between 75 and 100 people; and in the elections to the governing federal council of the party, the Left Caucus leaders who chose to run averaged about 200 votes (20% of the total). This is enough support to be felt, but not enough to achieve any real power within the party.

At the outset of the 1990s, several issues are the focus of NDP attention. With the disintegration of the Soviet Union and the end of its domination of Eastern Europe, the NDP's long-term, sometimes delayed, goal of Canada's withdrawal from NATO and NORAD re-emerges in discussion. Is Canada's continued participation in such military alliances necessary? Is it consistent with involvement in UN peacekeeping operations? The NDP's opposition to Canada's military action in the Persian Gulf is a reminder that the NDP often differs from the other two major parties on defence policy (Archer and Whitehorn, 1990, 1991).

The question of the party's position on free trade continues to fester: the backlash against Broadbent and his strategists for allegedly abrogating leadership of the opposition to free trade in the 1988 election has been partially deflected by the change in leader, but debate over how to reverse the free-trade agreement goes on. If the Liberal Party lessens its opposition to the treaty, this may enable the NDP to reassert a more forceful leadership role among free-trade opponents. Certainly earlier survey data on party activists (Archer and Whitehorn, 1990, 1991) suggest that free trade should be a better issue for the NDP than the Liberals, given that the latter have been far more divided on the issue.

During the transition period between Broadbent and McLaughlin, the NDP itself was divided over both the process and the content of the Meech Lake Accord, as was evident in the lengthy debates on the topic at the NDP's two federal council meetings in the fall of 1989 and later at its federal convention in Winnipeg. Not only was the country at large split on this subject, but the two leaders differed significantly in their views: Broadbent voted for the Accord, while McLaughlin was one of only two NDP MPs who did not. Another handicap for the NDP in this area was the fact that the public generally perceives the party as less relevant on constitutional issues than on social programmes or the environment.[20] The re-emergence of extensive debate upon the twin topics of constitutional matters and Quebec's status is not likely to bode well for the party, despite the presence of NDP MP Phil Edmonston in the House of Commons. In the past, it has been the Liberals who have benefitted when such issues have prevailed.

The 1980s was a decade in which neo-conservatives dominated much of the Canadian policy agenda. The NDP has not fared well on issues such as government spending and the deficit, and the 1991 Ontario NDP budget is a reminder of that fact. The task for New Democrats in the 1990s will be to present its preferred agenda more effectively. Bob Rae's stress, in the 1990 Ontario election, on the environment and the populist theme of fairer taxes was a successful strategy that other NDP leaders may seek to emulate.

THE FUTURE

After almost six decades, what does the future hold for the party? Curiously, it was not until the Great Depression had receded, in 1944, that the CCF formed its first government, in the province of Saskatchewan. Similarly, despite the high rates of unemployment at the beginning and end of the 1980s and into the 1990s, the federal NDP's progress to date seems slower than expected. Contrary to the assumption of many, an increase in economic deprivation does not necessarily lead to an increase in support for a socialist party (Erickson, 1988). This comes as a paradox to most socialists who expect exploitation and poverty to generate immediate demands for political change. Why have the gains been less than anticipated?

While the NDP was born amidst great fanfare concerning trade union financial support, organizational assistance, and votes, there is some evidence to suggest that this support may not be as strong or enduring as many hoped. Data on rates of union affiliation to the NDP suggest a fairly steady decline, from a peak of 14.6% of all unions in 1963 to a low of 7.3% in 1984 (Archer, 1987, 1990).[21]

At the same time, Gallup data for the past two decades reveal that Canadians as a whole fear 'Big Labour' (33% in 1968 and 30% in 1987) far more than 'Big Business' (17% in 1968 and 15% in 1987).[22] Further evidence of a class-biased culture can also be seen in data (Chi and Perlin, 1979) showing that more Canadians prefer a right-wing party (28.6%) than a left-wing one (9.4%). In addition, more Canadians have indicated that they would prefer to see Canada move away from the ideology of socialism (35%) than towards it (23%).[23]

Perhaps not surprisingly, the CCF-NDP's social-welfare policies have fostered an image of the party as encouraging the growth of government spending and employment. In recent years this perception has become a greater liability as more Canadians are concerned that 'Big Government' is a greater threat (23% in 1968 vs. 42% in 1987) than either 'Big Business' or 'Big Labour'.[24] Certainly the size and scope of governments have grown in recent decades: combined government expenditures for all levels amounted to 20.7% of Canada's GDP in 1951, but by 1987 had increased to 43.1% (Bakker, 1990: 431). It appears that in the decade of the infamous year 1984, 'big brother' rather than 'being my brother's keeper' did indeed become the most pressing concern for many. The NDP's greater stress in recent years on decentralization is perhaps a recognition of the difficult path ahead towards the co-operative commonwealth and the twenty-first century.

NOTES

Earlier versions of this chapter appeared in Hugh Thorburn, *Party Politics in Canada* (Toronto: Prentice-Hall, 1985 [5th ed.]; 1991 [6th ed.].

[1] The Socialist Party went from an all-time high of 919,799 votes in 1920 to 6,898 votes in 1980 (Smallwood, 1983).

[2] The famous CCF example occurred in September 1943, when the party polled 29% vs. 28% for the Liberals and 28% for the Conservatives. More recently, in July 1987 the NDP polled as high as 41% vs. 31% for the Liberals and 23% for the Conservatives. In both cases, the poll results were electrifying to party members and political opponents alike, and on each occasion, big business intervened with an unprecedented effort against the socialist hordes. David Lewis's memoirs (1981) document the earlier campaign. See also Read and Whitehorn (1991).

[3] Of course, a substantial number of party activists, including J.S. Woodsworth, T.C. Douglas, and Stanley Knowles, were Protestant clergymen (Allen, 1975; Allen, 1973; Baum, 1980).

[4] Sources: Beck (1968) and data from the Chief Electoral Officer.

[5] Sources: Gibbins (1980: 115) and the Chief Electoral Officer.

[6] Data derived from Beck (1968), Cairns (1968), Penniman (1975, 1981), and the Chief Electoral Officer (various years).

[7] Derived from Beck (1968). It is also worth noting that the League for Social Reconstruction, the CCF's 'brains-trust', was largely an eastern phenomenon as well (Horn, 1980).

[8] This is a theme ably discussed by Cairns (1968).

[9] Provincial votes were averaged without weighting for population size.

[10] The three trade unions with the largest numbers of members affiliated to the NDP are the Canadian Auto Workers (CAW), the United Steelworkers of America (USWA), and the United Food and Commercial Workers (UFCW).

[11] With regard to membership data, the Chief Electoral Officer reports that in 1988 more persons in Canada donated to the NDP (120,703) than either the Liberals (37,911) or the Conservatives (67,926). Nevertheless, given the mass nature of a party such as the NDP, the total income received was smaller than for the Liberals and Conservatives. The latter two, reflecting their elite and more affluent origins as cadre parties, received larger income from fewer donors (Report of the Chief Electoral Officer, 1989). See Duverger (1963) on the differences between mass and cadre/caucus parties.

[12] The Liberals, with 32.4% of the vote, received only 36 seats.

[13] For more detailed analysis of the 1988 federal election, see Chapter 8 of this book and Frizzell (1989).

[14] In party literature and many press accounts, one name is consistently omitted. Argue, CCF leader in 1960-61, defected to the Liberals after losing the NDP leadership contest to Douglas, and later became a Liberal Senator and Cabinet minister. While this neglect is understandable as far as the NDP is concerned, analysts should focus more attention on Argue since he was a significant example of co-optation and the calculation that it is more desirable to participate in power immediately than to wait for an NDP government. Former Prime Minister Pierre Trudeau was another example of this phenomenon.

[15] John Bacher, a young member of the Ontario Left-Caucus, initially chose to run

for the leadership. Upon reflection and counsel from colleagues and foes alike, he chose to withdraw his nomination.

[16] One is hard-pressed to locate a major urban daily newspaper that fully supported the NDP in the 1988 federal election. The pattern has been the same in most federal elections.

[17] There can be no doubt that Broadbent was the party's greatest asset in the 1988 campaign. He presented an image of decency and integrity speaking on behalf of ordinary Canadians (see *Toronto Star* editorial, 6 March 1989). In an age when alienation and cynicism seem to thrive, there are too few such voices.

[18] Frank Underhill and F.R. Scott of the League for Social Reconstruction; see Chapter 3.

[19] See Hackett (1979; 1980), Bullen (1983), and Brodie (1985); data from Hackett and Brodie are derived from 1971 and 1979 surveys of NDP convention delegates conducted by Perlin and his associates. My own 1983 survey of NDP delegates reveals a similar break-down: Marxist 3.0%, socialist 29.6%, social democrat 44.6%, ecologist 1.3%, social gospel 3.5%, populist 1.0%, reformer 4.3%, liberal 1.5%; other categories and multiple responses account for the remainder of the replies. For further analysis, see Chapter 5. Some caution should be taken in the interpretation of these data. For many in the NDP the terms 'socialist' and 'social democrat' are interchangeable (Lewis, 1981: 301); also, convention delegates need not be fully representative of the general party membership.

[20] Environics poll, *Globe and Mail*, 15 Oct. 1988.

[21] It should be noted that numbers of members affiliated have continued to increase, but at a slower rate than unionization of workers.

[22] CIPO, *Toronto Star*, 16 Aug. 1978, cited in Fletcher and Drummond (1979); and Gallup Report, 16 Feb. 1987.

[23] Gallup Report, 5 Dec. 1988. In light of such public-opinion data, it is puzzling that radical critiques should suggest weak socialist commitment as a reason for the NDP's lack of electoral success.

[24] CIPO, 16 Aug. 1978, and Gallup Report, 16 Feb. 1987.

TWO

Historical Writings on the CCF-NDP: The 'Protest Movement Becalmed' Tradition

Despite its position as a third party, the CCF-NDP has been the focus of considerable academic attention; indeed, proportional to its size, more has been written about the CCF alone than about either of the major parties.[1] Yet the main themes of much of this literature have tended to be strikingly similar, and in recent years some conceptual models and hypotheses that once were innovative and fruitful have become excessively inbred and less productive for future research. In examining the historiography on the CCF-NDP, this chapter will attempt to outline the reasons for this conclusion.

By far the most frequent, best researched, and most enduring theme in the literature on the CCF-NDP is that of the 'protest movement becalmed'. This chapter will focus on five representative works[2] from this tradition: Leo Zakuta's *A Protest Movement Becalmed* (1964), Walter Young's *Anatomy of a Party* (1969), John Smart's 'Populist and Socialist Movements in Canadian History' (1973), Michael Cross's *The Decline and Fall of a Good Idea* (1974), and Robert Hackett's 'The Waffle Conflict in the NDP' (1979).[3] Since Young's study of the national CCF is the most extensive and articulate source utilizing this approach, it will be the focus of much of the discussion in this chapter.

'Socialists belong to movements, capitalists support parties.'[4] With this bold assertion, Young (3) proceeds to outline his major theme: 'the party-movement distinction is a useful one. . . . It is the general distinction that is applied throughout this study' (11).[5] Here, then, is the first of the 'protest movement becalmed' tradition's two primary hypotheses: that a dichotomy exists between a social movement and a political party. Quoting King (1956: 27), Young (4) defines a movement as 'a group venture extending beyond a local community or a single event and involving a systematic effort to inaugurate changes in thought, behaviour, and social relationships'.[6] Although he does not specifically define a political party, he states its purpose as 'winning elections in order to control the government' (3).[7] This narrow description seems to ignore both parties that are not electorally oriented, which exist even in democracies, and ideological parties that may be strongly committed to articulating policy differences in addition to the obvious goal of acquiring political power;[8] many revolutionary communist parties, for instance, have been committed to both social change and acquisition of power. Any definition that cannot embrace both of these important dimensions provides only a partial picture, of communist and socialist parties alike.[9]

Young and others attempt to overcome problems of definition and dichotomization by suggesting that both the CCF and, to a lesser extent, the NDP combine aspects of the social movement and the political party (Young: 6, 9, 116, 302; Hackett: 188, 190). This is the basis for the second general assertion of the 'protest movement becalmed' tradition: that the movement eventually is displaced by the political party. In other words, there is a shift in behaviour, over time, from that of a group committed to social change to that of a political organization seeking simply power. As Zakuta (70; emphasis in original) summarizes this transition:

> Sweeping internal changes, many of which continued thereafter, originated during the CCF's momentous rise. Broadly, they were: in *ideology*, a diminishing hostility to the social order, modification in the proposals to change it, and a shift of time perspective towards the present; in *structure*, an enormous increase in size and prosperity, a more formal and uniform organization, a larger, more specialized and more professional leadership, a flow of power from the branches to the centre, the establishment of firmer roots in the community, and a less cohesive informal organization; in *motivation*, a change from sectarian to more worldly incentives, centring on a greater desire for immediate victory. Briefly, they add up to a shift from the character of a political movement towards that of a conventional party.

With these two primary themes in mind, let us now examine in more detail the series of related arguments put forward in the 'protest movement becalmed' literature. While none of these authors puts forward every single one of these propositions, the cluster of ideas can be outlined in a general theoretical model of historiography.

Echoing Young's distinction between socialist movements and capitalist parties, Smart (204) submits that 'the traditional party is the opposite of a socialist movement'. Situated between two polar entities—the social movement and the political party—in Manichaean fashion the CCF-NDP itself becomes a battleground. For example, Hackett (190; emphasis in original) states: 'Tension between the social democratic or *party* organization and the socialist or *movement* orientations has been endemic to the CCF-NDP.'[10] According to Young (6, 3), 'Where movement and party combine . . . the aims of one frequently frustrate the aims of the other . . .'; '[the CCF] struggled to prevent the demands of the party from overwhelming the ethic of the movement.' Smart (206) even goes so far as to state: 'The membership of the CCF allowed its organization to be taken away from it and killed.' While a substantial portion of the commentary is descriptive, much of it is also prescriptive. The manner in which these writers judge 'movement' and 'party' soon becomes apparent.

Smart (204-5) commences his discussion of the contrasts between movement and party by suggesting that 'a socialist movement is decentralized', while a 'party is always strong on unity and discipline'. As the CCF was gradually transformed from a movement into a party, so 'step by step, centralization . . . was achieved' and, increasingly, the party executive was able to 'monopolize communications'.

These authors often discuss the centralization of political power within the CCF in conjunction with a related hypothesis. Stated simply, it is that the CCF 'provided an example of the operation of Michels' Iron Law of Oligarchy' (Young: 140).[11] Drawing upon Gaetano Mosca's *The Ruling Class* (1939) and Robert Michels's *Political Parties* (1962), these authors suggest a somewhat idyllic picture[12] of a movement as a collective of committed amateurs and volunteers who form a relatively egalitarian and polycentric organizational structure, characterized by a minimal amount of intervention from senior figures. In the words of Smart (204): 'A movement turns people on to the idea of their own power and responsibility as individual members of the collective.'

Examples of 'New Harmony', it is argued, rarely last for long. 'The executive officers quickly became a separate body in the party' (Smart: 205). 'The leaders of the CCF gradually centralized control', according to Young (67, 156), with the result that 'the party was ruled by [an] . . . oligarchy'[13] —what Hackett (189, 191) calls the 'party establishment'. These 'party leaders . . . use their power in such a way as to ensure their continuance in office, even if this means ignoring or perverting their [movement's] goals' (Young: 4).[14] Young, the author who has done the most detailed and original archival research on the CCF, states that 'the ruling élite in the CCF consisted of no more than 12 people: Woodsworth, Coldwell, Lewis, Scott, Grace and Angus MacInnis, Knowles, Andrew Brewin, George Grube, Lorne Ingle, Carl Hamilton, and Thérèse Casgrain'; even within this stratum, however, power was not shared equally, for 'Lewis dominated the socialist elite, as he did the whole party' (Young: 168, 163).

Much of the 'protest movement becalmed' literature dwells upon the enormous amount of power accumulated by such figures: 'The influence of this small group cannot be exaggerated' (Young: 169). Considerable attention is given to confrontations between the elite and the mass membership of the party;[15] the evidence cited usually takes the form of resolutions passed or party rebels purged. Young's assertion (238) that 'the CCF executive had always emerged triumphant from struggles with the rank and file' is echoed by Cross's conclusion (14) that 'party bureaucrats and their labour supporters were able to steamroller any opposition. . . .'[16] Young, an analyst more to the centre, and Cross, a 'left-wing' author, seem to agree on what ails the party. They do not, needless to say, agree on the cure.

The difference between the movement and the party is not simply a question of a decentralized social system versus a centralized one. It is also a question of size and intimacy. Members of the movement came together in the local club—a relatively small, highly intimate form of association. According to Zakuta (53), 'Many . . . found the movement so close to the centre of their lives that no clear distinction existed between politics, sociability, entertainment and even work.'[17] The party establishment, in contrast, 'tended to believe that better organization was the answer to all problems' (Cross: 13); better meant bigger. Thus the party emphasized the larger and inevitably more impersonal riding association. 'Unlike the clubs', Zakuta (62) notes, 'the larger and more formal riding associations met monthly instead of weekly and relegated discussion of socialist theory and international affairs to the background, concentrating instead on organizational matters.' Instead of feeling the sense of personal integration provided by membership in a supportive community (i.e., the movement's club), individuals within the more bureaucratic organization came to feel increasingly alienated. The movement/party dichotomy becomes in effect a microcosm of the *Gemeinschaft/Gesellschaft* dualism[18] of Toennies (1963) and others. Curiously, Zakuta fails to draw the parallel to the more general theoretical literature on the subject of community vs. society.

Along with the changes in size and intimacy, a corresponding shift occurred in rewards and motivational structure: in Zakuta's words (70), 'a change from sectarian to more worldly incentives, centring on a greater desire for immediate victory.' The movement's emphasis was upon the faithful masses, led by a charismatic figure (see Weber, 1964: 358-72), undergoing immediate sacrifices for some future common good; the only short-term rewards were symbolic in nature. The party's stress, in contrast, was upon material benefits, paid party employees, and a 'leadership [that increasingly] grew larger [and] more professional' (Zakuta, 109). As the party secretary and, to a lesser degree, leader were more likely to be administrators and bureaucrats, they came to personify the shift in the CCF-NDP as a whole.

These authors generally agree that the movement stresses ideology, whereas the political party is geared more to the image manipulation of public-relations tactics and shifting electoral strategy. Indeed, Hackett (188) summarizes the CCF-NDP's history as follows: 'Most writers have viewed conflict within the CCF-NDP . . . as one between "purists" and "pragmatists", between those who view the CCF-NDP as a movement pursuing ultimate ideals and goals, and those who see it as a party concerned primarily with electoral success.'[19] Even Young (4) notes admiringly: 'One of the characteristics of a movement is the dogged determination with which it clings to its ideals.'[20] Inasmuch as the movement was committed to an ideology favouring social change (Young, 3-4), it was necessarily dedicated to the re-education (Cross, 10; Young, 4; Hackett, 201) of the population. In contrast, a political party is more committed to the status quo and seeks only political power (Young, 58, 3), not the transformation of society. The New Left authors Smart and Cross are particularly harsh in their criticisms of the party. According to the former (210), 'The party became more and more an electoral machine, which debated nothing fundamentally and became more and more irrelevant to the real problems of Canadian society.'[21] One is not likely to find comments more critical than this even from political opponents.

While there appears to be substantial consensus on the main traits of the 'protest movement becalmed' model, there is, as one might expect, less agreement on the specific application of the model. All of these authors appear to concur with Young's assertion (9) that 'at the beginning the CCF was more a movement than a party,' and Cross's suggestion (11) that 'pragmatism grew ever stronger in the party'. Not all, however, would agree with Young's and Zakuta's claim that the movement in the 1930s was socialist, while the party in the 1950s was more social-democratic in nature. For instance, Cross, with a more left-wing viewpoint, argues: 'The CCF had never been a socialist party in the orthodox sense but rather a moderately left-wing social democratic movement. The NDP was created as a liberal party' (14). Nevertheless, all would agree that over time a shift has occurred from the left of the political spectrum towards the right. The starting and ending points differ, but the direction of the shift is the same, and, for most of these authors, the change is for the worse.[22]

To a substantial degree, the becalming of the protest movement overlaps with another shift in the locus of power in the CCF-NDP—away from the western farmer towards the eastern labourer. Note, for example, Hackett's speculation (202; emphasis in original) that '"pragmatic" unionism coincides more closely with the social democratic *party* than the leftist *movement* orientation'. The protest movement becalmed is also the protest movement 'easternized', as Young (124) suggests: 'The new direction in policy . . . came from the leaders in the East.' To what degree these two shifts are interrelated and can be analytically separated is not clear; nor is it clear to what degree one is the cause of the other. Certainly, however, the shift in ideology from the populist 'social gospel' to 'unionism' is presented as an example of the more general evolution.

These authors often select two figures to personify the sociological manifestation of the movement/party dualism. Usually the two individuals chosen as contrasts are J.S. Woodsworth and David Lewis. Cross writes:

> The polarities of the social democratic party were amply illustrated at Ottawa. On the one hand was the revered leader, Woodsworth, who tended to the 'education-movement' side of the debate. On the other side was David Lewis. . . . [who] came to represent the practical, political pole of the party spectrum. Power, for him, was the name of the game (10).

[Lewis was] the supreme bureaucrat (16).

In contrast, according to Young (10), 'Woodsworth's emphasis was not on power, it was on change.' If Woodsworth was a prophet (McNaught, 1959), Lewis was a mere politician.

In any evaluation of this literature, four questions arise. Is the movement/party dichotomy valid? Did a change from movement to party in fact occur? If so, did it occur in the manner suggested by these authors? And, finally, what impact, if any, has the 'protest movement becalmed' model had?

Turning to the first question, whether the movement/party dichotomy is valid, one may observe that at least two authors, Young and Smart, attempt to qualify the model. For example, Young (11) notes: 'The distinction between norm-oriented parties and value-oriented movements, like all such typologies, suffers if pressed too hard.' Not surprisingly, Young attempts to broaden the definition of a political party beyond the narrow one of simply seeking power,[23] noting (39) that 'it is possible to argue that all parties are ideological. . . .' This enables him to narrow the distance between the two polar terms—movement and party. Now that some of the traits of a movement can be attributed to a political party, the two need not always be in opposition.[24] Hence he can assert: 'The relationship between the CCF *qua* movement and the CCF *qua* party was close and interdependent. . . . As the argument is pursued it is increasingly difficult to disentangle one from the other, because, of course, the CCF was a *party-movement*' (301-2; emphasis in original). The result is a more complex pattern of relationships than that offered by the movement/party dichotomy. Young, with his extensive archival research on the CCF, in part acknowledges this failing in the model when he states (301-2): 'The movement and party aspects intermeshed, one aiding the development and aims of the other while at the same time hindering its development and distorting its aim.'[25]

Simplicity is a virtue in any theoretical framework; any model that necessitates extensive qualifications might best be dropped altogether. If it is not clear that the historical evidence on the CCF fits satisfactorily into the movement/party dualism, one might do better to start with a more comprehensive definition of a mass political party (see Duverger, 1963) as one that has a mass following, that engages in extraparliamentary activity (such as education) and that possesses an ideology (such as socialism).[26] Using such a definition means that one does not need to juggle two terms, 'movement' and 'party', to explain events in the CCF. A comprehensive definition of a mass party—that is, one variable—will suffice.

The questions 'Did the change from movement to party occur?' and 'Did it occur in the manner suggested by the "protest movement becalmed" literature?' are pivotal. If there is nothing from which to change (i.e., if the CCF began largely as a party, not a movement), then much of the 'protest movement becalmed' model falters. It is therefore essential to determine to what degree, if at all, the early CCF was primarily a political party and not a movement.

The archival evidence, I believe, indicates that the CCF in the 1930s was very much a political party.[27] Indeed, it was founded as a party precisely to overcome the pitfalls of the protest movements and quasi-parties of the 1920s (Morton, 1967). Among the groups that attended the 1932 founding Calgary Conference were numerous political parties: the United Farmers of Alberta, the Canadian Labour Party, the Dominion Labour Party, the Independent Labour Party, and the Cooperative Labour Party. In the main, then, the CCF was a federation of political parties.[28] During those early years, its founders were very clear in their desire to create a political party, and archival documents show that members frequently referred to the CCF as a party.[29] Such references during this period are usually ignored or downplayed by the 'protest movement becalmed' authors.

One interesting aspect of this literature is that in reference to the 1930s it pays great attention to manifestos and policy statements (i.e., the movement aspect), but very little to the constitution (i.e., the party attribute). Of the three authors who provide full reprints of primary documents, only one includes a copy of any CCF constitution. This suggests that the model has led researchers away from important facts about party political structure, and instead persuaded them to focus on a single aspect of the CCF: its ideology. For example, the 1933 CCF constitution has an entire section (no. 10) devoted to discipline of deviant members;[30] yet this feature, highly characteristic of a political party, is largely ignored.

While the 'iron law of oligarchy' theme is repeatedly emphasized for the later, 'party' period, stress on the 1930s as a 'movement' period has tended to obscure authoritarian elements within the CCF in the early days. The prime example dates to 1934, when J.S. Woodsworth, the 'prophet in politics', purged the entire Ontario CCF provincial council (Caplan, 1973). It is not clear that he had the legal right to take such draconian action,[31] and certainly no equivalent move was made by later CCF leaders. Yet the 'protest movement becalmed' literature dwells on the theme of centralized oligarchic rule only in the later period. Here is another case in which the model appears to have led authors away from important evidence.

In the attempt to identify personifications of the movement/party dualism, another weakness arises. Woodsworth is repeatedly portrayed as one who encouraged a pluralist and diverse anti-capitalist movement. CCF documents, however, reveal that in 1935 Woodsworth remarked: 'I'm not strong on discipline but I think no cause can serve two masters. . . .'[32] The record of a joint meeting between the CCF and the League for Social Reconstruction (LSR) in 1936 reveals that Woodsworth 'contended that loyalty to the decisions of the CCF must be disciplined', and 'stressed the need for greater discipline, and, if necessary, expulsion of disloyal members'.[33] Having observed at close hand the demise of the Progressives, Woodsworth was firm in his insistence upon building a strong party with some semblance of ideological unity. Communists need not apply for membership in the CCF. In contrast, at this same 1936 meeting David Lewis 'thought that the present policy of the C.P. [Communist Party] had a definite appeal, and that if it proved to be genuine, there should be a reconsideration of CCF policy'. In response to Woodsworth's call for greater discipline, Lewis 'pointed out the difficulties of such discipline, and its undesirability'.[34] In effect, at times the 'protest movement becalmed' model distracts these authors from the roles actually played by Woodsworth and Lewis. Only Young (116), the most meticulous of the researchers on the CCF, is perceptive enough to caution that 'both elements [radical movement and moderate party] were mixed in varying proportions in all the CCF leaders'.

The 1930s, the so-called movement era, also saw discussion of the need for ideological moderation and compromise for electoral reasons.[35] For example, after the 1934 election the Saskatchewan branch of the CCF dropped its radical doctrine of 'use-lease'[36] for farm land. The 1936 joint meeting of the CCF parliamentary caucus and the LSR national executive also discussed the question of altering the wording of the Regina Manifesto. They chose to avoid further action on this thorny issue and instead sought to draw up a completely new 'Immediate Programme'.[37]

In summary, there is substantial evidence that the CCF was quite clearly more a political party than a movement even in the 1930s. This provides a basis for noting a considerable degree of continuity in the CCF from the 1930s through to the 1950s—a continuity that is often missed by the 'protest movement becalmed' literature. This is not to suggest there was no change. Politics is very closely tied in with the process of social change, and the CCF is no different from any other political entity in this regard. However, to use a model that highlights certain types of change may cloud aspects of genuine continuity. In this sense, a broader definition of a political party might aid in providing new empirical insights into the CCF.

In addition to the problems of the archival evidence that the proponents of 'protest movement becalmed' model ignore, a question arises as to whether the developments they do cite can be explained only by their hypotheses. Data may not disconfirm the movement/party dualism, but neither do they necessarily confirm it. Other explanatory hypotheses may be available.

Hypotheses such as the 'iron law of oligarchy' can lead researchers to infer from the available data conclusions that are not necessarily justified. This so-called 'law', for instance, suggests in a classic zero-sum game that as power is centralized, so the power of the local rank and file diminishes: what the party leadership gains, the general membership loses. But is this assumption always valid? Is the central party office always parasitic? A CCF report by Harold Winch may provide a partial answer:

> [I] draw to the attention of the National Office the positive necessity of early action in Nova Scotia to set up proper organizational machinery. As the situation now exists there is actually no *real* C.C.F. Party. There are only units all over the Province with no central office; no Provincial Organization, no hook-up to other units, or a central body; no one to whom they can turn for advice or encouragement; no body to contact all units; to assist where necessary; no speakers, no organizers . . . . A proper form of organization must immediately be established so as to link the various units into a cohesive whole.[38]

The National Office of the CCF frequently acted as a catalyst for local CCF organizations, particularly in the weaker east, by providing literature, organizational advice, and financial assistance. In this sense a strong central office acted as a positive, not a negative, force. In helping to create new local CCF units, it was adding to the power of local members, not diminishing it, since to be scattered and disorganized is to have no power at all. One may, therefore, suggest that in a number of circumstances a plus-sum game seems a more reasonable scenario than does a sinister portrayal of Machiavellian national officers usurping power away from rank-and-file members.

Another way of interpreting this centralization of power is to place it in the context of the general environment in which the party operated. It may have been very difficult for the CCF to remain decentralized while society at large was tending towards centralization. The net effect of world-wide economic depression and the Second World War was to increase dramatically the role of the central government. Under such circumstances it is perhaps unrealistic not to expect a corresponding centralization in the subsystem (i.e., the political party).[39]

Environmental influence upon ideology is another area in which one may question the ubiquity of the effects of the 'iron law of oligarchy'. In the 'protest movement becalmed' literature it is frequently suggested that the party leadership was the major force behind the toning-down of the social-ist tenets of the Regina Manifesto; the underlying assumption appears to be that in a protest movement the ideology should remain as permanent as granite. An ideology, however, is a dynamic entity: as the socio-economic environment changes, surely it is not unreasonable for the ideology to follow suit.[40] Here one wonders about the Marxists who accept the 'protest movement becalmed' hypothesis and appear to ignore the socio-economic factors that are normally the foundation of their analysis (i.e., the socio-economic base and the political superstructure nexus). The alleged 'erosion of ideology' that is noted by all five authors, and that seems to alarm Smart and Cross particularly, is presented by all of them as permanent. Here the dualism of the movement/party model may have caused some conceptual over-generalization. While not stating so directly, they seem to assume a unilinear transition from movement to party, as irreversible as the change from *Gemeinschaft* to *Gesellschaft*. Without the burden of this cumbersome dualism, however, it is possible to perceive that the shift in ideology need not be a matter of permanent strategy, but rather one of shorter-term tactics—which can be equally important to survival.[41] Whether the trans-formations in party doctrine are short- or long-term is not as easy to discern as some suggest.[42]

In a culture and polity that are predominantly pro-capitalist, imperialist and anti-socialist, there are times during the long march to power when left-wing parties such as the CCF-NDP may have to respond with defensive tactics and strategy.[43] As Larry Zolf (1973: 63) so aptly states: 'Despite the Hartzian "fragment" theories of Gad Horowitz, there was no historical inevitability about the continued existence of socialism on Canadian soil; no more historical inevitability than, say, the continued existence of liber-alism on British soil'—to which one might add the example of the minus-cule Socialist Party of the United States.

After leading, albeit briefly, in the national public-opinion polls in 1943, in 1945 the federal CCF stalled as a third party and began a steady decline over the next decade and a half. While the shift to welfare liber-alism by Mackenzie King's Liberal Party has frequently been cited as the key reason for the decline in the CCF's electoral fortunes, archival evi-dence increasingly suggests that a much underemphasized factor was a massive barrage of anti-socialist (i.e., anti-CCF) propaganda.[44] Led by authors such as B.A. Trestrail and Gladstone Murray, this scurrilous pro-paganda was successful in part because of its ability to draw on the 'fright-ening language' of a few polemical CCF figures such as Harold Winch.[45] Given the anti-left bias of the press, it is not surprising that inflammatory statements by a few prominent CCF members were quickly distorted as being representative of the party as a whole and possessing a sinister intent that made the party an easy target for negative editorials.[46]

Badly bruised by this and other anti-socialist campaigns, CCF members approached the 1950s with some caution. The post-war depression had not materialized. The 1950s were clearly a boom period for North American capitalism. Unemployment in Canada had gone from a record high of 19.3% in 1933 to 3.4% in 1956 (Sterling and Kouri, 1979: 174). It would have been extremely difficult, if not impossible, for the CCF to survive in any meaningful sense as a political organization without moving to a position less harsh, less pessimistic, and less sweeping in its denunciations of capitalism. This was, after all, the age of Cold War hysteria and bipolar confrontations. This shift can be perceived as either a strategic retreat or a tactical withdrawal. If there is no resurgence of more radical, uncompromising doctrine later under more positive circumstances, policy change can be seen as a strategic shift. If, however, radical doctrines resurface within the party in less difficult times, the shift should be labelled tactical.[47] The emergence of the Waffle during the less restrictive 1960s and 1970s suggests that the party's alteration of its ideology need not be irreversible,[48] and could therefore in the long run be considered tactical.

Some of the effects of the 'protest movement becalmed' model have already been noted. It should also be evident by now that this literature has implications that go beyond a simple descriptive account of the CCF-NDP. Much of it contains an implicit, if not explicit, value judgement that the movement is morally superior to the party.[49] Strong evaluations frequently emerge from the movement/party dichotomy. Cross, for example, outlines the 'decline and fall of a good idea' (i.e., social democracy) as a kind of morality play, complete with quislings, class collaborators, and malevolent Machiavellian figures.[50] We all enjoy morality plays; indeed, our taste for them appears universal.[51] Canadian history and politics, however, are not so simple. We need fewer caricatures, shibboleths, and would-be theologians!

Part of the reason for their heavy reliance on a good/bad dichotomization of the movement/party phenomenon is the insufficient attention devoted by these authors to the general theoretical literature on political parties. It is interesting to note, for example, that they do not cite the relevant literature on party development in modernizing societies, much of which suggests that the formation or institutionalization[52] of political parties is essential for political development. The alternative is mal-integration (LaPalombara and Weiner, 1966: 405), instability, and the long-term decline of democratic political structures (Huntington, 1968). Political parties, in short, need not be, as these authors seem to suggest, the antithesis of democracy.

No study of the 'protest movement becalmed' literature would be complete without some speculation on the effect, if any, that it has had upon the CCF-NDP itself. Historians and political scientists, whether by intent or not, are activists inasmuch as their writings do influence people's thoughts and behaviour. This is particularly important when a party has been in existence long enough that most people must rely on academics to provide them with its history.

The 'protest movement becalmed' literature has dwelt extensively on the theme of oligarchy. While difficult to estimate, it seems likely that use of this anti-'party establishment' theme has had an effect upon the NDP. Many rank-and-file members exhibit attitudes of cynicism, fatalism, and even despair on organizational matters. How much of this is induced by 'us versus them' models in intra-party affairs? To the degree that their writings accentuate the separation of party leadership from members and infuse a sense of mistrust into party affairs,[53] academics are influencing the political process. Social scientists, for the most part middle-class in lifestyle and thought, may be too quick to raise the spectre of authoritarianism within a working-class party such as the CCF-NDP. A party of the 'have-nots' may lack the organizational finesse and public-relations techniques of more affluent, high-status organizations; underfunding and lack of sufficient full-time, paid professional staff may create communications difficulties. But academics should not value style over substance; the onus on the scholar is to go beyond mere appearances. Less simplistic, repetitive, and one-sided party histories might help to foster, albeit in a small way, a further step in the path towards the diversification and democratization of Canadian political culture.

The purpose of this chapter has been to present a case for better balance in the historiography on the CCF-NDP.[54] Although the 'protest movement becalmed' framework can be useful, it should not be belaboured.[55] The 'iron law of oligarchy' should not become a fetish. More frequent use of alternative hypotheses would foster more dynamic research. Now that the NDP papers are available for scrutiny,[56] the historiography on the CCF-NDP is at a watershed. A definitive work on the NDP, as meticulous in archival research as Walter Young's work on the CCF era, is yet to be written. It is to be hoped that the theoretical frameworks used in any future writings will match the excellence of the data collection that we have sometimes seen in the past.

NOTES

This chapter is a slightly expanded and revised version of an article previously published in William Brennan, ed., *Building the Co-operative Commonwealth: Essays on the Democratic Socialist Tradition in Canada* (Regina, Canadian Plains Research Center, 1985).

[1] Among the key works written on either the CCF or NDP are these: Archer, 1990; Avakumovic, 1978; Baum, 1980; Brennan, 1985; Bradley, 1985; Caplan, 1973; 1975; Cross, 1974; Heaps, 1991; Horn, 1980; Horowitz, 1968; Kavic and

Nixon, 1978; Kerr, 1981; Knowles, 1961; Lamoureux, 1985; Lipset, 1950, 1968; McAllister, 1984; McDonald, 1987; MacEwan, 1976; McHenry, 1950; Morley, 1984; Morton, 1974; 1977; 1986; Penner, 1977; Pratt, 1986; Sangster, 1989; Webster, n.d.; Wiseman, 1983; Young, 1969; Zakuta, 1964). To this list one can add biographies and autobiographies on the following party figures: Akerman (MacEwan, 1980); Blakeney (Gruending, 1990); Broadbent (Steed, 1988); Brown's autobiography (1989); Casgrain's memoirs (1972); volumes on Douglas by Shackleton (1975); Lovick (1979); Thomas (1982); McLeod and McLeod (1987); Whelan and Whelan (1990); Forsey's memoirs (1990); on Gillis (Harrop, 1987); Good's autobiography (1958); on Heaps (by his son Leo Heaps, 1970); on Herridge (Hodgson, 1976); on Irvine (Mardiros, 1979); on Jewett (Anderson, 1987); on Knowles (Trofimenkoff, 1982; Harrop, 1984); Lewis's memoirs (1981); a volume on the Lewis family, particularly David and his son Stephen (Smith, 1989); on Lloyd (by his daughter Diane Lloyd, 1979); on Lucas (Wright, 1965); MacDonald's autobiography (1988); several volumes on Canada's first female MP, Agnes Macphail (Stewart and French, 1959; Pennington, 1989; Crowley, 1990); on Nicholson (Dyck 1988); on Schreyer (Beaulieu; 1977); on Scott (Djwa, 1987); Stinson's memoirs (1975); on Underhill (Francis, 1986); on Ernie Winch (Steeves, 1960); and a number of volumes on the party's first federal leader, J.S. Woodsworth (Ziegler, 1934; Underhill, 1944; MacInnis, 1953; McNaught, 1959, 1980; Mills, 1991). In addition, there are several volumes with collections of mini-biographies of a number of party officials or activists: Heaps (1991); Lazarus (1977); Mather (n.d.); Melnyk (1989); Webster (n.d.). Puzzlingly, there are no book-length biographies of former CCF federal leaders M.J. Coldwell and Hazen Argue.

[2] Unless otherwise indicated, references to these five authors will be to the works specified in this text; years of publication will not be repeated in citations. Other publications that employ or refer to the same framework but are not discussed at length here include Chi and Perlin (1979); Landes (1983: 263-4); Surich (1975: 132); Black (1983: 14, 16); and Melnyk (1989: 6-7).

[3] A far longer publication by Hackett on the NDP is his monograph which appeared as a special edition of *Canadian Dimension* (1980). Unless otherwise indicated, however, references are to his 1979 article.

[4] One wonders where the communists fit in such a sharp dichotomization.

[5] See also Hackett (1979: 188).

[6] For a more recent general theoretical analysis of social movements, see Wilkinson (1971: 27), who outlines three 'quintessential characteristics of social movements': (1) they involve a deliberate collective endeavour to promote change; (2) they are based on a conscious volition and active participation of members, and (3) they show a certain degree of organization. The latter trait is important, for without it there is a tendency to ignore the organizational aspects of movements and thereby permit an easier contrast to the political party.

[7] This definition resembles the more general and satisfactory one by Joseph LaPalombara: 'a formal organization whose self-conscious, primary purpose is to place and maintain in public office persons who will control . . . the machinery of government' (1974: 509).

[8] The policy emphasis in the definition of political parties can be seen in Alfred de Grazia's description: 'a *party* is a group framing general issues and putting forward

candidates in elections' (1964: 509; emphasis in original).

[9] A more appropriate definition for a party such as the CCF-NDP is the following: 'A group of individuals acting collectively within some *organizational* framework for the purpose of winning political offices with a view toward changing public *policy*' (Blevins, 1974: 129; emphasis in original).

[10] See also Hackett's remark that 'key points of contention include whether the CCF-NDP should be primarily a socialist movement or an electoral party' (1980: 14).

[11] 'He who says organization says oligarchy.'

[12] The 'movement' period that supposedly characterizes early socialist attempts at self-help seems to be the socialist equivalent of Rousseau's state of nature in which harmony and justice prevail—at least within the confines of the movement.

[13] Young differs from the four other authors discussed in this chapter in that at times he qualifies his criticism of this 'oligarchy' by suggesting it is benevolent; the others suggest it is malevolent.

[14] As early as 1956, Fred Englemann suggested this theme: 'In addition to their dominant role in the initiation of policy, C.C.F. leaders show a tendency to perpetuate themselves' (1956: 168).

[15] In the case of Hackett's detailed case-study, the old establishment party élite is challenged by the youthful Waffle.

[16] It should be noted that their time frames differ; Young refers to the CCF and Cross to the NDP.

[17] Here the literature on the close bonds created in communist party cells is germane. See, for example, Duverger (1963) and Townsend (1969).

[18] *Gemeinschaft* designates a small-scale, intimate traditional community; *Gesellschaft*, a large, impersonal modern society.

[19] For Hackett (192), of course, 'in contrast to the Waffle's insistence on a "movement" orientation, other New Democrats tended to be more concerned with the party's [sic] electoral fortunes'.

[20] Note that he chooses the evaluative term 'ideals', not the more neutral 'ideas'.

[21] See Cross (17) for a similar comment.

[22] This is clearly the conclusion of Hackett, Cross, Smart, and Zakuta. Young's attitude is less clear-cut. He seems generally to favour the change but occasionally looks upon the early CCF years with a somewhat nostalgic perspective. For example: 'the New Democratic Party, successor to the CCF, is less democratic than the CCF because it is much less a movement than the CCF' (175).

[23] This is one of Lorne Brown's criticisms of *The Anatomy of a Party* in his lengthy review in *Canadian Dimension* 6, 8: 40.

[24] This is the essence of Smart's (204) comment that 'Young insists on posing the two aspects as necessarily opposite and at war by definition whereas the two are complementary in a parliamentary system.' Smart, in fact, is inaccurate in his characterization of Young.

[25] Elsewhere he comments: 'The party-movement both gains and loses because of the combination. . . . The relationship between the two is both beneficial and corrosive' (7); 'The *movement* may hinder the *party*; it may also keep it alive' (6); emphasis in original.

[26] For two innovative case studies on such parties see Crossman (1965) and Lifton (1963).

[27] On this I agree with P. Sinclair's comment (1973: 419): 'The history of the CCF [Saskatchewan] is best understood by emphasizing that it was more a political party than a social movement.'

[28] Actually, at first it was closer to being a confederation of parties.

[29] For example, note the following resolution passed at the 1933 Convention: 'Therefore be it resolved that all C.C.F. representatives . . . in no way enter into collusion with the other [sic] political parties. . .'(CCF Papers, National Archives of Canada, vol. 1/1). A letter from Woodsworth to Coldwell, dated 28 September 1935, stated 'I am not strong on discipline but I think no cause can serve two masters . . . . Otherwise our Party [sic] at Ottawa will be seriously encumbered . . .' (CCF Papers, NAC, vol. 107/1). See also Underhill's 'Mr Good's Political Philosophy', Canadian Forum, August 1933, reprinted in W.C. Good (1958: 186-8).

[30] 'Constitution of the Co-operative Commonwealth Federation', (Regina, 1933): 3 (CCF Papers, NAC, vol. 1/10).

[31] David Lewis notes: 'It was done, of course, in consultation with the National Executive, but the decision was made without express constitutional authority' (1981: 125). Even Woodsworth, in a letter to Norman Priestley, 6 March 1934, described the decision as being taken by 'available members of the C.C.F. Executive here in Ottawa . . .' (CCF Papers, NAC, vol. 107).

[32] Woodsworth to Coldwell, 28 Sept. 1935 (CCF Papers, NAC, vol. 107/1).

[33] 'Confidential Report. Summary of Discussions Between CCF Parliamentary Group and the L.S.R. National Executive' (28 March 1936) 11-12 (CCF Papers, NAC, vol. 168/7). Emphasis in original.

[34] Ibid.

[35] George Hoffman (1975; 1977) makes a similar point regarding the Saskatchewan CCF.

[36] The use-lease proposal favoured the transfer of the formal title of the farmer's land to the government, while permitting the farmer and his family the right to use the land and farmhouse indefinitely. Unfortunately, this plan was easily portrayed by political opponents as the bureaucratic and impersonal nationalization of all farm lands. See Hoffman (1975, 1983); Lipset (1968); McLeod and McLeod (1987).

[37] 'Confidential Report': 2 (CCF Papers, NAC).

[38] H. Winch [untitled report; n.d., c. 1938] (CCF Papers, NAC, vol. 106/5). Emphasis in original.

[39] Joseph Levitt has made a similar point with regard to the CCF's success in the 1940s as contrasted to its failures in the 1930s. He suggested that the cause need not lie in internal changes in the CCF, but rather in a shift in the environment: i.e., the war clearly demonstrated that central government planning and deficit financing were feasible (interview with author, 1978).

[40] Even Woodsworth, in his presidential address at the Regina Convention in 1933, advised the newly created CCF: 'We do not believe in unchanging social dogma. Society is not static. Knowledge grows, and each age must work out a new and higher synthesis. Such growing knowledge is dependent upon experience and action. Each new development, each new member of our organization should mean a fuller content in our body of Socialist doctrine' (Fowke, 1948: 39).

[41] In this regard, the Greek notion of cyclical change rather than the Judeo-Christian one of linear change may be useful to keep in mind.

[42] For example, one can well imagine party doctrine taking a more radical slant should the Canadian economy continue to falter. In this sense there is nothing inevitable about consensus politics or the 'end of ideology'. See Taylor (1970: chap. 1).

[43] The reference to Mao Zedong is deliberate, to underline how important it is for a progressive party to analyse objective conditions correctly. At some points tactical retreat may be the only alternative to annihilation. This is no less true for a democratic socialist party than it is for a guerrilla army.

[44] See, for example, 'Anti-CCF Propaganda File', CCF *Papers*, NAC, vol. 361; *George Drew Papers*, NAC, vol. 96/928 and vol. 130/1317. See also Chapters 12 and 14 of the Lewis memoirs (1981), Walden (1980), and Read and Whitehorn (1991).

[45] Lewis (1981: 252) offers several examples of the press reports of the following remarks by Winch: 'the power of the police and military would be used to force those opposed to obey the law', and 'those who defied the government's will would be treated as criminals' ('Crush Opposition By Force "Like Any Other Criminal" If Will of Party Resisted', Toronto *Telegram*, 10 Nov. 1943).

[46] Whenever a socialist party appears on the brink of power, extensive anti-socialist campaigns, employing a variety of legal and illegal means, seem to emerge. The campaign during the Ontario provincial election of 1977 in many ways was reminiscent of 1945 in terms of its rationale, the means employed, and its apparent success in thwarting socialism.

[47] Of course, what may be labelled tactical for the history of a party as a whole may appear to individual party members at the time as a shift in strategy.

[48] According to one party member, 'A protest movement cannot be becalmed. It may lose direction and focus, but the protest, the alienation, and the sense of injustice about the structural inequality and violence of capitalism cannot be destroyed. It simply forms into smaller pockets of discontent. The protest, to continue the analogy, is simply redirected into local squalls that will at a later date, during a future crisis of capitalism, re-emerge reunited with greater force.'

[49] Zakuta (142) notes that Michels's *Political Parties* has 'an excessive flavour of disenchantment and of exposé', but paradoxically fails to observe a similar flavour in his own work.

[50] Presumably the dedicated rank-and-file socialist members of the movement reflect the good, while the corrupt party officialdom eager to compromise with capitalism, private property, and imperialism in order to gain power, reflect the evil. Note, for example, the cover of Cross's book, in which Lewis is portrayed as smiling mischievously as the prospect of achieving socialism diminishes.

[51] Osgood (1957) outlines the very strong human tendency towards good/bad dichotomies. The 'protest movement becalmed' is just one specific example of this general phenomenon. See also Osgood (1979).

[52] Zakuta does occasionally refer to this process, as, for example, on p. 141: '"It [the CCF] simply went the way of all organizations". In technical language, it became institutionalized.'

[53] For a similar comment, see Epstein on Michels: 'he belongs to that substantial and once apparently dominant scholarly tradition that approached parties in an adversely critical if not destructive spirit' (1975: 238).

[54] This is a plea echoed by Hoffman (1975; 1977) and Thomas (1981) in their writings on Saskatchewan history. Already there are signs that this may be

occurring. Penner (1977), Horn (1980) Lewis (1981), McDonald (1987), and McLeod and McLeod (1987) have employed more varied themes, and generate optimism for a new generation of scholarship.

[55] Of particular concern are works on the CCF-NDP that, instead of conducting original archival research, rely too heavily on secondary sources. The result is that these authors' writings are less tempered by historical reality. With time, works in the 'protest movement becalmed' tradition have become somewhat inbred, and, not surprisingly, have increased their polemical tone.

[56] The would-be researcher is advised to consult Scotton (1977) and Weinrich (1982).

THREE

Party Blueprints

INTRODUCTION

A political party that advocates change must articulate in a systematic fashion its vision of a better world. The more sweeping the changes it seeks, the more elaborate its image of an alternative society will be. A party may present a clarion call for the construction of a 'new Jerusalem' based upon a different ethic and an alternative philosophy, or it may seek more modest reforms and limited improvements.

How much change the CCF, from 1932 to 1961, and the NDP, from 1961 onwards, have demanded remains an issue for debate between the party and its political opponents and even among party members themselves. Opponents have often portrayed the party as revolutionary in its ultimate goal and methods. Most CCF-NDP activists, on the other hand, would describe their party as committed to peaceful change while pursuing a significant redistribution of power and benefits in our society—although these social democrats and socialists are less likely to agree upon the institutional mechanisms required to accomplish these goals.

Over the six decades since the party's birth in Calgary in 1932, the scope and intensity of the changes it has sought have shifted with the changing conditions of Canadian society and the world. Indeed, as Lynn McDonald suggests in the title of her book *The Party That Changed Canada*, the CCF-NDP itself may be credited with a number of positive domestic changes. From the perspective of the 1990s it may be difficult to imagine the context of Canadian politics during the Great Depression. Almost half (46.3%) the population lived in rural areas; about a third (32.5%) of the workforce was engaged in primary industries such as agriculture, fishing, mining, and logging; only 33.7% of young people (15- to 19-year-olds) were in school; only 19.6% of adult women were in the paid workforce; a mere 15.3% of workers were unionized (Porter, 1967); and, most important, about one adult Canadian in five (17.6%) was unemployed (Fry, 1979: 174).

In the intervening years a significant welfare system has been pieced together (Cassidy, 1943; Guest, 1980; Lazarus, 1980; Struthers, 1983). Unemployment has been lowered, welfare measures such as unemployment insurance have been introduced, the work week is shorter, the workforce is more skilled, more women participate in the paid workforce, and more, better supplied schools and hospitals are available.

Given these changes, it should not be surprising that, over the years, the blueprints the CCF-NDP has presented in the form of manifestos have become less impatient with the prevailing social conditions. All socialist parties in the Western world have adjusted the specifics of their doctrine to fit the changes that have taken place. No society is unchanging, and any relevant doctrine must take into account such social changes.

Manifestos serve as beacons, indicating the direction in which a political party wishes to travel and the distance it strives to go. In the six-decade history of the CCF-NDP, five key documents emerge as major outlines of the party's vision of what Canada and the world were, still are, and should become. This chapter will examine them in detail,[1] beginning with the Calgary Programme of 1932.

1932: THE CALGARY PROGRAMME

The first party document to be discussed here is the Calgary Programme. Passed only as a provisional document at a conference of western labour parties—not all of whom would join the CCF—the document was soon eclipsed by the Regina Manifesto of 1933. The Calgary Programme's two paragraphs go into little detail, and some topics, such as international relations and federal-provincial relations, are not covered at all. Nevertheless, for a concise, albeit preliminary, summary of the CCF's aims and philosophy and the means selected to accomplish these, it is a useful document.

The first observation to be made about the Calgary Programme is what it doesn't contain. The classical Marxist language of revolution, violence, and class conflict is completely absent.[2] Amidst the desperate circumstances of the 'dirty thirties' (Horn, 1972), when so many people succumbed to more authoritarian methods, the document called for evolutionary and peaceful means to guide society towards an emphasis upon 'human needs instead of the making of profits' and to limit the action of speculators. Reflecting a collectivist critique of an excessively individualistic society, it urged the establishment of a state-sponsored welfare programme to aid less affluent Canadians, proposing the extension of social legislation to provide public insurance against the hardships of unemployment, old age, accident, illness, and crop failures. It called for an active and interventionist state that would replace the current economic chaos with a 'planned system of social economy for the production, distribution and exchange of all goods and services'.

Although the CCF from the outset criticized the worst excesses of unrestrained individualism and stressed that private profit should not have unlimited free rein, it nevertheless retained an important commitment to selected features of individualism. This can be seen in the party's willingness to blend public and private ownership in a mixed economy. On the one hand, the Calgary Programme called for a 'socialization of economic life', including 'banking, credit and [the] financial system', advocated social ownership of 'utilities and natural resources' and proposed the 'encouragement of all co-operative enterprises'— a moderate and selective list of areas to be owned and operated in the public domain.[3] On the other hand, it stated a strong commitment to defence of the family farm ('useland')[4] and home. Implicitly, much of the economy was to be left to private ownership, although it would be subject to government supervision of the economy.

In addition, the Calgary Programme provided a brief outline of the proposed party structure. The CCF was to be a federation of provincial groups drawn from three groups—labour, farmers, and socialists. While its purpose was unequivocally stated as socialist, membership would not be confined to socialists; the CCF would reach out to other groups and include progressive workers who were not necessarily committed to the socialist creed.

Although drafted during the Depression, this document lacked some of the sweeping rhetoric that would appear in other documents of this era, and even in portions of the Regina Manifesto. Analysis of the language employed (see Table 3.1) shows that while the conference delegates did not hesitate to use the word 'socialist' (three references, to only one in the longer Regina Manifesto), they did not use terms such as 'class', 'capitalism', and 'imperialism', all of which would appear in the 1933 document. On the whole, though, it is similar to the latter in temperament and thrust. Both were expressions of a moderate form of socialism with emphasis upon greater use of government planning, increasing social ownership within the confines of a mixed economy balancing public and private ownership, and, above all, willingness to pursue a peaceful and evolutionary path.

Table 3.1 Key Term Usage in Manifestos

	LSR	CP	RM	WD	NPD	NRM
NUMBER OF PARAGRAPHS	5	2	38	30	168	35
KEY TERMS:						
socialism, socialist	0	3	1	4	0	13
class	1	0	3	0	0	2
capitalism, capitalist	1	0	17	1	0	1
imperialism, imperialist	0	0	1	1	0	0
nationalization	0	0	0	0	0	0
socialization	3	3	15	0	0	0
public ownership	1	0	2	3	2	0
social democracy/democratic	0	0	0	1	1	0
social ownership	0	1	2	0	1	1
exploitation	0	0	3	0	2	1
co-operatives[a]	1	3	14	7	18	3
nation, national, etc.[b]	3	2	20	9	31	8
Quebec, Québécois	0	0	1	0	0	4
French Canada, etc.[c]	0	0	0	1	5	5

[a] Count does not include 'co-operate', 'co-operation', or 'co-operative federalism' and excludes use of the term in the party's full name or acronym.

[b] Count includes 'nationalism' and 'nationalist', but excludes 'nation' in League of Nations or United Nations.

[c] Count includes 'French Canadians', 'French speaking', and references to French Canadian traditions.

1933: THE REGINA MANIFESTO

Unlike the Calgary Programme, the Regina Manifesto was a lengthy and polished document. The initial draft was written by two outstanding eastern academics, Frank Underhill from the University of Toronto and Frank Scott from McGill University, assisted by several members of the League for Social Reconstruction (LSR), the CCF's informal think-tank and research arm (Horn, 1973, 1980). With minor modifications, the manifesto was ratified by the party delegates at the first full national CCF convention in 1933.

The Regina Manifesto eclipsed all other CCF statements for more than two decades, and even after the passage of the Winnipeg Declaration in 1956 it continued to dominate discussions. To this day, the Regina Manifesto is probably better known and more frequently cited than any other CCF-NDP manifesto, and for many Canadians it is the touchstone of Canadian socialism. For these reasons, the document is worth analysing at length.

The drafters of the 1933 manifesto were able to draw upon two important documents, the CCF's Calgary Programme and the LSR's Manifesto, both published a year earlier. Several scholars (Horn, 1973; 1980: 44;

Table 3.2 Comparison of LSR and CCF Manifestos

LSR (1932)	CCF (1933)
5 paragraphs	38 paragraphs
10-point programme	14-point programme
Introduction	Introduction
1 planning	1 planning
2 socialization of finance	2 socialization of finance
3 public ownership	3 social ownership
	4 agriculture and co-ops
5 import and export boards	5 external trade
4 co-operative institutions	6 co-operative institutions
6 social legislation and	7 labour code and social
freedom	insurance
7 public health services	8 socialized health services
9 constitutional amendments	9 BNA Act (constitution)
10 disarmament and	10 external relations and
international co-operation	disarmament
8 taxation and funding	11 taxation and public finance
	12 freedom and civil rights
	13 social justice and law reform
	14 emergency programme
conclusion	closing statement

Francis, 1986: 89; McNaught, 1959: 264) have drawn attention to the parallels between the five paragraphs of the LSR Manifesto and the 38 paragraphs of the CCF's Regina Manifesto. Given that Scott and Underhill were the chief authors of both documents, and that they were inspired by one man, J.S. Woodsworth, these similarities should not be surprising. In the Regina Manifesto, each of the LSR document's ten points is expanded into a paragraph-long analysis with an occasional section (e.g., agriculture[5]) added (see Table 3.2). Ideologically, the two are compatible statements of a moderate socialist blueprint for a better Canada.

In its opening section, the Regina Manifesto noted that 'catastrophic depression' was inherent in the capitalist system, and that 'glaring inequalities' were fostered by the 'domination and exploitation of one class by another'. Deploring the increasing concentration of power 'into the hands of a small irresponsible minority of financiers and industrialists', the CCF called for a stress upon 'the supplying of human needs and not the making of profits'. It favoured replacing 'chaotic' capitalism with a 'planned and socialized economy in which our natural resources and the principle means of production and distribution are owned, controlled and operated by the people'. 'Social reconstruction' towards 'economic equality' was feasible, but the Conservative and Liberal parties, as 'the instruments of capitalist interests', were incapable of leading the way there. By contrast, the CCF—a 'democratic . . . federation of farmer, labour and socialist organizations'—offered the possibility of 'social and economic transformation'. While positing the need for 'collective organization', the manifesto attempted to assuage fears by advising that the CCF would not 'interfere with cultural rights of racial [i.e., ethnic] or religious minorities' and promising a 'richer individual life for every citizen'. In addition, it clearly stated that the means to these ends would be non-violent: 'through the election of a government . . . supported by a majority of the people'. As J.S. Woodsworth, the party's first leader, often noted, goals and means are intertwined: achieving a more just and peaceful world by violent means is a contradiction.

Following this preamble, the manifesto proceeded to outline fourteen specific planks in the CCF's platform. The first addressed the need for a 'planned, socialized economic order' to 'replace the disintegrating capitalist system'. Planning was seen as the means to foster both the 'most efficient development' and the 'most equitable distribution'. A 'small body of economists, engineers and statisticians' would form a 'National Planning Commission' to oversee and co-ordinate the economy while working under the auspices of the Cabinet.

In the area of finance, the CCF urged the creation of a national 'Central Bank' and 'National Investment Board' to control credit, prices, and foreign exchange, and called for the nationalization of banking and insurance companies.

Social (i.e., public) ownership, whether federal, provincial or municipal, was to be extended to 'transportation, communications, electric power and other industries and services [deemed] essential' (e.g., coal, gasoline, bread and milk). While firmly repudiating 'any policy of outright confiscation', the party refused to 'play the role of rescuing bankrupt private concerns'. It suggested that 'the community must take supremacy over the claims of wealth', and that if labour could be conscripted in wartime, then in the desperate economic emergency of the worldwide Depression, 'conscription of wealth' was quite appropriate. This section concluded by stressing the freedom of workers to 'organize in trade unions' and their 'right to participate in the management of industry'.

Pointing to agriculture as Canada's greatest industry, the fourth section denounced the 'monopolistic corporations' for their 'exploitation of both primary producers and consumers'. In response to the dramatic fall in world food prices, it proposed an increase in monies paid to farmers as a means to increase their purchasing power, as well as crop insurance and improved credit policies. Although the security of the family farm under a CCF government was reiterated, there was also the collectivist suggestion that production might be improved through greater use of co-operatives. And, although the document condemned the 'economic nationalism'[6] that had seen the growth of 'tariff barriers', it called for the use of state (i.e., national) 'import and export boards' to foster overseas trade.

The fifth section echoed this theme, condemning the 'strangling of our export trade by insane protectionist policies'. Suggesting that 'the old controversies between free traders and protectionists are now largely obsolete',[7] it stated that Canada must enter into 'trade agreements' with foreign countries to stabilize prices.

Section 6 called for state legislation and credit to encourage the growth of both producers' and consumers' co-operatives, a theme raised earlier in reference to agriculture.

As a party seeking to defend the working class, in section 7 the CCF favoured a labour code that would improve working conditions. Although labour matters fell largely under provincial jurisdiction, the CCF pleaded the case for a national labour code that would be 'uniform across the country', even if this required amendments to the 1867 British North America Act.[8] This national standard would include 'state regulation' of health and safety conditions, income, and holiday benefits, and provide 'social insurance' covering 'illness, accident, old age and unemployment'; it would also prevent any gender discrimination in pay and limit the work week (the norm in 1930 was 53 hours [Porter, 1967: 91]). In addition, the CCF called for the introduction of 'industrial democracy', in which employees would have the right to 'effective participation in the management of . . . industry' by means of elected 'works councils'.

The CCF has been strongly identified with the establishment of publicly financed medical care in Canada (Naylor, 1986). The 1933 manifesto called for 'socialized health services' that should be as 'freely available as are educational services'. As T.C. Douglas, the father of medicare, was often later to plead, no one should be denied adequate medical treatment simply because of inability to pay (McLeod and McLeod, 1987). All three levels of government were urged to co-operate in this important social venture, 'which would stress the prevention rather than the cure of illness'.

The ninth section, on the constitution, noted that the British North America (BNA) Act (now known as the Constitution Act, 1867) was designed for an agrarian society, not an industrialized one, and that, with the growing centralization of the economy, the political division of power between federal and provincial governments must be adjusted. In particular, the federal government must have the constitutional power to deal with the 'urgent [national] economic problems' proliferating in the Depression. Once again the CCF attempted to mollify fears that any constitutional amendments would infringe upon 'racial [i.e., ethnic] or religious minority rights or upon legitimate Provincial claims to autonomy'. Finally, the Senate, the second chamber of Parliament, originally designed to protect the different regions of Canada, was characterized as filled by 'aged members' who had 'developed into a bulwark of capitalist interests'. The CCF's remedy (the same as the NDP's) was simple: abolish the anachronism.

In external affairs, the party stressed the twin goals of disarmament and peace. Commencing a tradition of distrust of military entanglements that would continue with the NDP, the CCF asserted its defiant opposition to 'all participation in imperialist wars'. Seeing capitalism as 'incompatible' with 'genuine international co-operation', it proposed to 'rescue' the League of Nations[9] from domination by 'capitalist Great Powers' and, while noting Canada's newly acquired political autonomy from the British Empire, warned against 'attempts to build up a new economic British Empire'.

In Section 11, on tax reform, the CCF condemned Canada's 'parasitic interest receiving class' and suggested replacing inequitable general taxes on goods (e.g., sales tax) with 'steeply graduated' income, corporation, and inheritance taxes. Revenue sources for federal and provincial governments were seen as needing 'immediate revision'.

The following section was entitled 'Freedom'. Noting the 'alarming growth of Fascist tendencies among all governmental authorities', the CCF criticized the 'lawless and brutal' police actions that had prevented public meetings by social critics[10] and the Immigration Act that had deported immigrants involved in such activism (see Roberts, 1988). In the view of the CCF, such actions were the mark of a 'panic-striken capitalist government'.

In section 13, on social justice, the manifesto noted that although 'economic inequality' was at the root of many injustices in the legal system, that system itself still needed reform. To ensure that the new system would be based not 'upon vengeance and fear but upon an understanding of human behaviour', the document proposed establishing a national 'commission . . . of psychiatrists, psychologists, socially-minded jurists and social workers' to oversee such reform.

The final section, 'An Emergency Programme', spoke directly to the desperation of an era in which almost one in five adult Canadians was unemployed. Emphasizing the federal government's responsibility to address the 'critical unemployment situation', with which the provincial and municipal governments had 'long been unable to cope', the CCF proposed an immediate increase in relief payments, guaranteed tenure of homes for the unemployed, and a 'far reaching programme of public expenditure' on housing, slum clearance, hospitals, schools, parks, and reforestation. These projects would provide jobs and income for the multitude of unemployed. While conceding that in the transition period some private businesses might be assisted, it characterized the global Depression as 'a sign of the mortal sickness of the whole capitalist system, . . . [a] cancer . . . eating at the heart of our society.' The document closed with this clarion call: 'No CCF government will rest content until it has eradicated capitalism and put into operation the full programme of socialized planning which will lead to the establishment in Canada of the Co-operative Commonwealth.'

This was the most famous, even infamous, passage of the Regina Manifesto. To some of the more militant party members, it was inspiring; to many political opponents and the unconverted public, it was often unnecessarily alarming. M.J. Coldwell, the party's longest-serving leader, described it as a millstone around his neck. Certainly it would be used by political opponents to portray the CCF as pursuing sinister, revolutionary goals.

The language of the Regina Manifesto reflected how glaring the inadequacies of the capitalist system had become by 1933. This document contained dramatically more negative references to capitalism (17) than positive references to socialism (1) (see Table 3.1), and was as much an anti-capitalist statement as a pro-socialist one.[11] In this respect, as several authors have pointed out, the manifesto fitted into the populist tradition (see Richards and Pratt, 1979; Laycock, 1990). Used once in the Regina Manifesto, the term 'socialism' was not mentioned at all in the eastern-based LSR document, and appeared three times in the western labour parties' one-page Calgary declaration. Thus the 1933 manifesto appears to represent a balance between the cautious approach of the LSR and the greater militancy of the western labour parties. The manifesto's preferred terms are the less-threatening 'socialization'/'socialized' (15 references) and 'co-operatives' (14 mentions) (see Table 3.1).

Not only does the manifesto denounce capitalism, but it is the first of the CCF's major statements to address imperialism. Again, there is only one use of the term, suggesting a desire not to frighten off would-be sympathizers with language that might appear doctrinaire and dogmatic.[12] That the mood of militancy grew as the Depression continued can also be seen in the document's use—the CCF's first in a national manifesto—of the word 'exploitation', and the greater frequency with which the term 'class' appears.

In its themes the 1933 manifesto represented another stage in the development of a democratic socialist blueprint for Canada. While it called for important changes in the economy, social values, and the political structure, it stressed that these were to be achieved by peaceful methods, under the direction of a more active state willing to take greater responsibility in economic planning and to foster more extensive public ownership in selected areas of the economy. Reflecting a reasoned collectivist critique of the self-destructive path of unrestrained egoism and individualism in the capitalist market economy, the manifesto called for a better balance of collectivism and individualism (e.g., public ownership of the largest industries while retaining a commitment to the family farm) and invoked a co-operative spirit of brotherhood to replace the prevailing conflict and class exploitation.

In calling for a consolidation of political rights and a wholesale expansion of economic rights, the CCF demanded that at least minimal economic and social benefits be available for all (e.g., the right to medical care, decent wages, safe working conditions) and urged extension of the right to participate in decision-making from the national level down to the local factories.[13] To grant democracy at the level of the federal state while the workplace remained autocratic seemed illogical and unbecoming for a free people; clearly, democracy needed to expand to other realms (Dewey, 1939).

The imprint of the academics from the LSR is evident in the manifesto's assumption that planners, trained in modern social science, would be able to manage society in a more humane and efficient way. Paradoxically, in the name of greater equality for all Canadians, the CCF blueprint proposed to create a powerful, centralized national planning board that, at the very least, suggested elements of managerial elitism (Burnham, 1941). Despite its efforts to placate groups concerned about infringements upon provincial and minority rights, the document inevitably advocated strengthening the role of the federal government. Its lack of appeal in Quebec is therefore understandable, and was certainly accentuated by the absence of any direct reference to French Canada or the province of Quebec[14] (see Table 3.1).

The CCF manifesto tapped the theme of nationalism explicitly in its stress on Canadian political and economic independence from the British Empire and implicitly both in its call for import and export boards and in its denunciation of imperialism and the 'capitalist Great Powers'. In fact — and ironically, for such a famous socialist document — it made far more references to 'nation' and 'nationalism' than to 'socialism'. Overall, however, the manifesto tended to emphasize an internationalist variant of socialism, criticizing such nationalist economic policies as tariffs. Not until the 1950s and, particularly, the 1960s would a more effective link be made between socialist and nationalist collectivism.[15]

Both the LSR and the CCF believed in the possibility of a better, more rational world. They believed that advances in the social sciences would provide the intellectual skills with which to govern more effectively and humanely. They assumed the inevitable power of reason and persuasion. In a sense, of course, all reformers are optimists; if they were not, they would resort to revolutionary means (Huntington, 1968). The Regina Manifesto reflected the CCF's confidence that a better world could be created peacefully. There was little recognition that the rich and powerful might prove difficult to dislodge, or that old parties could be slickly repackaged to sound more socially concerned — as when the Conservatives renamed themselves 'Progressive Conservatives'. The CCF was woefully unprepared for the anti-socialist propaganda campaigns to follow, particularly in 1943-45, when corporate-sponsored public-relations firms would portray the CCF as revolutionary and dictatorial (Lewis, 1981) — in utter contradiction to the goals and means stated in the Regina Manifesto. Finally, in its assumption that inequality and wars were largely caused by capitalism and imperialism, the manifesto reflected a certain naïvety, which later party statements would need to correct.

Despite all those criticisms, however, what strikes a modern reader is how accurate, in general, this 1933 document proved to be regarding the social, economic, and political changes that were to unfold over the next half century. Its major themes still seem timely—a sign that further progress is still to be made.

Why has the Regina Manifesto so dominated the history of the CCF-NDP? Part of the reason is its identification with the birth of the party. Another is that its conclusion is the most memorable and controversial passage of the party's many declarations. Lastly, to those who feel that the CCF-NDP has succumbed too much to the influence of pollsters, media advertising consultants and non-socialists, the Regina Manifesto recalls what seems now to have been a more heroic and clear-cut era.[16]

The party's first successful effort at reformulation of its principles was to be the Winnipeg Declaration of 1956.

1956: THE WINNIPEG DECLARATION

The decade following the Second World War did not see the expected return to world-wide economic depression. In Canada unemployment hovered at a respectable 3.4% in 1956 (Fry, 1979: 174). Western governments, both socialist and non-socialist, continued the interventionist policies initiated in earnest and followed so successfully in the war years. In response to the need for post-war reconstruction, welfare measures were often extended. In addition, important changes were unfolding in society at large. As the migration from rural communities to urban centres continued, Canada's rural population declined to 30.4% of the total by the end of the 1950s (Porter, 1967: 54). There was also a decline in the numbers employed in primary industry, to 13.1%; an increase in white-collar employees, to 38.6%; an increase in the numbers of young people (15 to 19 years) attending school, to 58.5%; an increase in the percentage of women in the paid workforce, to 29.5%; and an increase in unionized workers, to 34.2% (Porter, 1967: 89, 93, 98, 113).

Internationally, the early 1950s saw the dawn of the nuclear age and the era of bipolar confrontation between the two super-powers, the United States and the Soviet Union. While the Korean War had ended, new regional military alliances such as NATO, NORAD, CENTO, SEATO, and the Warsaw Pact had been created. The 1950s was the decade of Cold War hysteria, the 'better dead than red' mindset, and the McCarthyite witch hunts in which socialists were often falsely accused of being communists. It was also a time for socialists to summarize their collective experience of governing in countries such as Sweden and Great Britain, and to assess how well their platforms and programmes worked in practice.

In Canada it was evident that significant structural changes had occurred: in the type of work people did, in the industrial level of society, in the social and welfare measures available, and to some degree, in the distribution of wealth.[17] In short, the past two decades had brought important gains in the quality of life.[18] Canada in the 1950s was still not an egalitarian and just society, but it had moved a step closer in that direction. It was time for the CCF, along with socialist parties elsewhere, to update its manifesto to match the new era.

Whereas the drafting of 1933 manifesto was left primarily to two sympathetic academics, the 1956 Winnipeg Declaration was the result of a far longer and more complex democratic process. As Young (1969)[19] outlines it, the first major step towards a new declaration of principles was taken at the 1950 federal convention, when the venture was proposed by party chairman Frank Scott. In January 1951, the CCF executive appointed a committee composed of David Lewis, Lorne Ingle, Andrew Brewin, and Donald MacDonald to submit proposals. In March the national council meeting created an *ad hoc* committee (Lewis, Scott, Brewin, Ingle, T.C. Douglas, Hazen Argue, Grace MacInnis, Joe Noseworthy, François Laroche, and Clarie Gillis) to draft the new party statement. By June, the executive had approved a draft, and at the October council meeting Ingle and MacInnis were instructed to edit the document further. The draft statement was then published and opened to discussion from the party's general membership. Discontent surfaced quickly, particularly from British Columbia and Saskatchewan. Accordingly, the March 1952 council meeting decided not to present the document to convention later that year, planning instead to offer it at the next federal convention, in 1954; Brewin was to chair a small committee with this goal. The committee, however, did not submit a new draft to the 1954 convention. In January 1955 the issue was again raised at a council meeting, and a year later it was decided to proceed yet again with a new statement. In February the executive assigned Lewis, Morden Lazarus, Omar Chartrand, and Ingle to the task. Finally, following substantial debate, and without the consensus seen in 1933, the 1956 federal convention passed the Winnipeg Declaration. It had taken six years to complete.

At 30 paragraphs, the Winnipeg Declaration was slightly shorter than the Regina Manifesto. In including the French name of the CCF (Parti Social Démocratique), even the title of the 1956 document gave Quebec a recognition that had been lacking in previous manifestos. The introduction reminded the Canadian public of the CCF's long-standing commitment to 'democratic means' while reiterating the socialist assertion that 'private profit and corporate power must be subordinated to social planning' and the 'supplying [of] human needs and [the] enrichment of life'. It proudly noted that the CCF's Regina Manifesto had 'had a profound influence on Canada's social system', and that its supporters could take credit for helping to make Canada 'a better place than it was a generation ago'.

The first section pointed out that despite economic expansion, 'Canada is still characterized by glaring inequalities'; in fact, the 'gap between those at the bottom and those at the top of the economic scale has widened'. Among the social ills mentioned were slums, inadequate pensions, lack of income to cover medical costs, and insufficient funding for education. Observing that 'wealth and economic power continue to be concentrated in the hands of a relatively few private corporations', it concluded that the result was 'the domination of one group over another'[20] and 'a virtual economic dictatorship' that threatened 'our political democracy'.

In the next section the CCF decried the way the 'scramble for profits' had wasted both human and natural resources. To foster greater employment, education, and 'human growth', social planning was essential.

The need for planning was reiterated in the following section, which focused on the danger that 'unprecedented scientific and technical advances' could 'produce even greater concentrations of wealth and power'; 'the evils of the past [could] be multiplied in the future.' 'Intelligent planning' and 'conservation' were required to promote social justice and 'maximum opportunities for individual development'.

The section entitled 'Capitalism Basically Immoral' warned that 'economic expansion accompanied by widespread suffering and injustice is not desirable social progress', and that society must be motivated by a 'moral purpose'. Accordingly, the declaration stressed the need to 'build a new relationship among men . . . based on mutual respect and on equality of opportunity' so that everyone might 'develop his capacities to the full'.

In a key section entitled 'Social Planning for a Just Society' the CCF called for 'full employment', free from the twin extremes of 'inflation and deflation', and suggested that in building a co-operative commonwealth there would be 'an important role for public, private and co-operative enterprise'. Nevertheless, seeing public ownership as 'the most effective means of breaking the stranglehold of private monopolies', the party proposed to 'extend public ownership wherever it is necessary', and favoured strengthening co-operatives as the 'best means of ensuring justice'. At the same time, however, to alleviate the concerns of a sceptical public, the CCF once more expressed its willingness to protect family farms, homes, and 'all personal possessions'.

The next section, 'Building a Living Democracy', began by acknowledging as a positive step 'the growth of labour unions, farm, and other organizations of the people' and urging support for such groups. In addition, noting that in 'the present world struggle for men's minds and loyalties, democratic nations have a greater responsibility than ever' to lessen forms of discrimination and foster the greatest degree of democracy, the Winnipeg Declaration called for the enactment of a bill of rights.

The next two sections focused on the international scene. Facing the new atomic age, the CCF urged the 'prohibition of nuclear weapons' and removal of 'the international dangers which threaten the future of all mankind'. Like the NDP in later years, it advised that 'there has been too much reliance on defence expenditures to meet the threat of communist aggression', and suggested instead more aid to underdeveloped countries. Reaffirming its support for the newly created United Nations, the CCF stressed the need for greater 'international co-operation' and 'genuine universal brotherhood' in the quest for a 'world society based on the rule of law'. For these to be possible, however, 'imperialism, whether of the old style or the new totalitarian brand, must disappear'.

Returning to domestic matters, the CCF expressed its 'confidence in Canada and its people who have come from many lands'. It also acknowledged the role that 'British and French traditions' have played in 'our present parliamentary and judicial systems'. 'Properly applied in a spirit of national unity', the federal system was perceived to be capable both of equalizing opportunities and of 'protect[ing] the traditions and constitutional rights of the provinces'.

The 1956 document closed by drawing attention to the role of democratic socialism at a time in which the 'great issue' was 'whether mankind shall move toward totalitarian oppression or toward a wider democracy'. Under the heading 'Socialism on the March', it pointed out that 'many labour and socialist parties have administered or participated in the governments of their countries', and concluded: 'the CCF will not rest content until every person in this land and in all other lands is able to enjoy equality and freedom, a sense of human dignity, and an opportunity to live a rich and meaningful life as a citizen of a free and peaceful world.'

Even though the Winnipeg Declaration had taken six years to write, its restatement of party principles was still timely. As David Lewis noted in his memoirs (1981: 444), political opponents had used portions of the Regina Manifesto from the outset to misrepresent the CCF's position. A newer, more carefully phrased statement of principles would make such attacks more difficult—although, as subsequent events would reveal, not impossible. As Lewis also pointed out, by the 1950s the Regina Manifesto was somewhat less relevant than it had been two decades earlier. Although, as the Winnipeg Declaration itself observed, the Regina Manifesto had helped to bring about important improvements in Canadian society, that very success had, ironically, lessened its contemporary significance. Certainly the smaller percentage of unemployed and the higher levels of income and welfare benefits available meant that while economic and social inequality had not been eradicated, for many the situation was less desperate. But if the pressure on domestic issues had eased, international affairs had acquired a new urgency. Now, in the jet age, the horrific destructive power that the world had witnessed in Hiroshima and Nagasaki was coupled with a strategy of massive retaliation. Any relevant social document needed to address the political implications of such technological changes in the weaponry of war.

The merger of the two major Canadian labour congresses in 1956 also made this new statement timely. The electorally faltering CCF needed to make itself more attractive, particularly to the growing labour movement and urban population. A new and potentially less controversial statement of principles might offer some appeal to both groups.

Finally, with the passage of time the world had seen the formation of a number of socialist governments. These experiences with expanded roles for public administration provided an opportunity for overall evaluation and, where necessary, reappraisal of socialist theory. The mid-1950s saw many socialist parties rethinking the appropriate means to achieve their continuing goals (Lewis, 1981: 443-4). In Britain, Anthony Crosland's book *The Future of Socialism* offered an important contribution to this international debate. Nor was the intellectual questioning of methods confined to the Western socialist parties. In 1956 Nikita Khrushchev's famous 'secret' speech to the Soviet Union's Twentieth Communist Party Congress offered a riveting denunciation of Stalin's despotic rule.[21] Domestic and international factors were leading parties of all ideological shades throughout the world to re-evaluation, and the CCF was no exception.[22]

If means and ends are intertwined, did the re-examination of means imply an alteration in ends (Young, 1971: 137)? A number of authors have suggested that the replacement of the Regina Manifesto with the Winnipeg Declaration was part of a larger shift from a socialist movement to a liberal reformist party.[23] However, this emphasis on change has tended to obscure some important elements of continuity between the two documents. For instance, both proposed that in place of the one-sided individualism and preoccupation with private profit found in capitalism, there should be a more balanced mix in society of collectivism and individualism and also of public and private property. In addition, both strongly rejected violent and authoritarian means. In both cases, the overall vision remained the building of a more co-operative, peaceful, and just society and the pursuit of a 'common wealth' available to all.

Certain changes, of course, are obvious. As the product of the nuclear age and Cold War, the Winnipeg Declaration naturally paid significant attention to international developments. While the Soviet Union was not named, phrases like 'threat of communist expansion' and 'imperialism . . . the new totalitarian brand' were unmistakable references to the USSR. There was also a more conscious effort to clarify the different streams of socialism (Marxist vs. social-democratic) through the use of the adjective 'democratic' in half the references to socialism. Implicitly, the non-democratic forms of socialism were to be found in the Communist Party regimes that workers in both Hungary and Poland had tried, unsuccessfully, to challenge in 1956.

As many authors have pointed out, the Winnipeg Declaration did not offer as lengthy a list of industries to be socialized as the Regina Manifesto had. While still supportive of public ownership (3 references, versus only 2 in 1933), the 1956 document conveyed less confidence about its scope and effectiveness, adding the conditional phrase 'wherever it is necessary' in one reference. The language generally seems more guarded (see Table 3.1). In contrast to the Regina Manifesto, the Winnipeg Declaration made no use of the terms 'socialization', 'social ownership', 'exploitation', or 'class', and the number of negative references to capitalism diminished from 17 to 1. While there were more positive references to socialism, half were modified with the word 'democratic' and all were located in the last paragraph, almost as an afterthought—as if they were not essential to the rest of the document.

Doctrinaire phrasing had not won sufficient votes in the past, and the declining fortunes of the CCF were a stark reminder of that political fact. Whether the CCF would have fallen further and faster without the passage of the more moderate-sounding Winnipeg Declaration is impossible to tell. Certainly this is a question rarely posed by supposedly radical critics of the document. However, it is conceivable that, coming as late as it did, the new statement made little difference. The party's percentage of the national vote had been consistently declining since 1945, and by 1956 its fate was probably already determined. In the Diefenbaker Conservative landslide of 1958, the CCF was to make its worst showing since 1940, winning only 8 seats and 9.5% of the vote. A drastic change was necessary. The NDP could not come soon enough.

1961: THE NEW PARTY DECLARATION

Many of the trends evident in the 1950s continued into the 1960s. Increasing urbanization, school enrolment, and participation by women in the paid workforce were among the changes still occurring. Also on the rise was nationalism—both pan-Canadian and French Canadian. The 'quiet revolution' in Quebec did much to transform the political scene. As Knowles (1961: 83) observed: 'it is a new world. It calls for new ideas . . . [and a] New Party.' The CCF was in the process of a phoenix-like transformation; from the ashes of defeat, it was hoped, would emerge victory.

The reasons for abandoning the CCF as a vehicle for social reconstruction were many and complex. One of the more important goals was to make meaningful inroads into the French Canadian community in Quebec. The old CCF possessed a poor image among Francophones (Lewis, 1981: 454-68), and historically, the Quebec Catholic hierarchy had denounced the party for its allegedly atheistic, materialistic, and radical orientation (Baum, 1980). In addition, the party's firm commitment to strong federal powers in order to regulate and plan the economy had little appeal for a population concerned about provincial (i.e., Quebec) government rights as a means to protect its minority status from the English Canadian majority. For decades, the small Quebec wing of the CCF had relied heavily on English-speaking members to direct party affairs, and this reinforced the image of the party as an alien force in the close-knit Quebec community. To make matters worse, the party's full title, Co-operative Commonwealth Federation (not the most elegant phrase in English) did not translate well into French. For the CCF, there were just too many negative items in the ledger. A new bilingual party, it was hoped, could start afresh and reach out more effectively to the one in three Canadians resident in Quebec.

A second reason for creating a new party was that relatively few unions had affiliated with the CCF (Horowitz, 1968; Abella, 1973; Miller and Isbester, 1971). As the rural population diminished, the importance of new and stronger ties to the urban-based labour movement grew. A new party without the negative images identified with the CCF might prove more successful in appealing to workers—especially if the labour movement participated in its design, founding, and formal membership. The merger of the two leading trade-union congresses in 1956 offered a glorious opportunity to explore a stronger link between CCFers and labour (Lewis, 1981: 488).

The growing urbanization of Canada meant that the western and rural base could not be counted on to remain the CCF fortress it had been in the past. In Saskatchewan, for example, 21 federal seats were potentially available to win in 1935 (8.6% of the parliamentary total), but by 1958 this number had declined to 17 (6.4%) in an even larger House of Commons, and was likely to drop even further in the future (by 1988 the number would have fallen to 14, and the percentage to 4.7%). For a party wishing to retain a strong voice in national politics, a more urban emphasis was essential.[24]

The last reason for creating a new party was the growing realization that, even with support from farmers, labourers, and socialists, the CCF had not been able to find a sufficiently large audience, let alone a growing one. In terms of votes, members, and income, the federal CCF had consistently declined since 1945. In order to be more successful, it would have to reach out to additional groups. More effective linkages to French Canadians and labour would help, but it was still felt that a successful party would also have to tap the concerns of the middle-class and the 'liberally-minded'.[25] The CCF had always proposed a united front of what it saw as the two largest socio-economic classes: farmers and labour. The new party proposal simply added the middle-income group to the coalition.[26]

The Diefenbaker Conservative juggernaut of 1958 had not only devastated the socialist CCF but had also thrust the Liberal Party into disarray. Although the proposals for a new party pre-dated the Conservative landslide (Lewis, 1981: 486), the collapse of the parties of both liberalism and socialism suggested a potential opening for a new, progressive left-wing party that might include both socialists and reform-minded liberals; to some, the Liberal Party seemed vulnerable (MacDonald, 1988; Lewis, 1981: 483, 494). The recent election of the Democratic Party's John F. Kennedy as President of the United States was a reminder that an idealistic and progressive government need not be exclusively socialist.[27] In addition, a seemingly less doctrinaire party might prove more attractive to the growing numbers of non-aligned voters.[28] Finally, despite the Winnipeg Declaration, the CCF was still burdened with the albatross of the Regina Manifesto, and it was believed that a new party could at last put that association behind it.[29]

Thus there was a great deal of logic in presenting a new statement of principles to mark the birth of the new party. It nevertheless seemed ironic that, after taking six years to produce the Winnipeg Declaration, the party should begin drafting yet another statement so soon. Among the members of the National Committee for a New Party (NCNP) who were involved in the creation of both documents were David Lewis, Frank Scott, Andrew Brewin, and T.C. Douglas. Not surprisingly, the two documents would show philosophical similarities.

Forming the new party and drafting its manifesto was another time-consuming and complex process (MacDonald, 1988; Knowles, 1961; Young, 1969; Horowitz, 1968; Lewis, 1981). As early as December 1955, there had been discussions between individuals in the CCF and the Canadian Congress of Labour (CCL) about the possibility of replacing the CCF with a new organization capable of tapping wider support. While the newly formed Ontario Federation of Labour had passed a convention resolution endorsing the CCF in 1957, the two-year-old CLC voted in April 1958 in support of a political realignment and the formation of a new political movement. The New Party would encompass the CCF, labour, farmers, professionals, and other liberally-minded people committed to social reform and reconstruction (Knowles, 1961: 127-8). In May the National Committee for a New Party was created with equal representation from the CCF and the CLC,[30] in July the CCF voted unanimously in favour of a joint venture with the CLC, and by November 1958 the NCNP had issued its first pamphlet. In August 1959 the NCNP sponsored a large seminar on the new party's proposed organization and philosophy, and by January 1960 a study paper on the New Party programme was published and distributed. Later that same year the CLC convention (in April) and the last CCF convention (in August) gave their final blessings to the launching of the new political vessel. In April 1961 Stanley Knowles outlined the history leading up to the formation of the party, as well as its proposed organization and programme, in his book *The New Party*.[31] In content, the 9-page programme outline published in the Knowles book was very close to that passed later at the NDP's founding convention in August 1961.

Although the NDP was to present another official manifesto in 1983,[32] the 1961 declaration remains by far the more important, outlining as it does the party's initial aspirations and proposed blueprint for Canada and the world. Like the 1956 Winnipeg Declaration, it was based on extensive consultation with different groups, and the process of feedback and commentary was far more rigorous than would be the case for the 1983 manifesto. This makes the 1961 document a more representative statement through which to analyse at length NDP goals and policies.

At 168 paragraphs, the New Party Declaration is by far the longest of the CCF-NDP's manifestos. Indeed, for many it was too lengthy and detailed; this is no doubt one reason why it has been less widely read than the Regina Manifesto. The 1961 document was divided into four sections: Planning for Abundance, Security and Freedom, A More Complete Democracy, and Co-operation For Peace. These in turn were broken into 31 subsections, which together provided a comprehensive outline of the NDP's overall philosophy and programme.

The document commenced with a preamble pointing out that although Canada was 'a land of abundant resources', 'unemployment, waste, political corruption and commercialization of . . . values . . . have increased'; economic development was 'still unplanned, unstable and operated chiefly for the benefit of the few owners of great corporations'. In the face of 'new challenges everywhere', defence policies had to be 're-assessed' and English-French relations in Canada 'made more meaningful'. The statement called for 'a new spirit of social purpose' in which 'human rights and human dignity [would be placed] above the mere pursuit of wealth, and public welfare before corporate power'. Such goals would be achieved by 'new methods of social and economic planning'. Expressing the 'idealism' and 'progressive' aspirations of 'farmer . . . labour, co-operative and social democratic movements', the NDP invited all Canadians to join the new party.

In the first major section, 'Planning For Abundance', the NDP characterized itself as 'the party of full employment'—a condition achievable only through 'economic planning'. While proposing a guaranteed employment act to ensure everyone a job as a 'social right', as well as public funds for houses, schools, hospitals, and roads, the document also called for efforts to 'conserve our natural resources' and end 'senseless waste'.

An NDP government would plan not only for 'continuous [economic] growth' but also with a 'social purpose'.[33] While some increase in state intervention in the economy was acknowledged, the 'old' parties were portrayed as 'reluctant' actors; their talk of 'free enterprise' distorted the 'truth . . . that the economy is effectively in the hands of corporate giants' that had stifled 'true freedom of enterprise'. The means to 'curbing corporate control' and asserting 'direct public accountability' was through expansion of 'public and co-operative ownership' over utilities, resources, monopolies and 'major enterprises . . . affecting the entire nation'.

Promising to present its 'objectives' and 'means' in a 'detailed and explicit' fashion, the NDP evidently hoped to ensure there would be little opportunity for misunderstanding the goals and scope of its policies. A newly created economic advisory council would engage in planning, but would report to the Cabinet. Canadians were assured that 'all major economic groups' would be consulted and that 'planning would be democratic', despite 'radically new uses of traditional instruments' such as the budget, the national bank, and a newly created investment board. Concerned about past accusations that the CCF was unnecessarily centralist, the new party declared that it favoured 'co-operative planning' between the federal and provincial governments. To avoid 'unbalanced centralization' and ensure a 'guarantee of provincial rights', one proposal suggested was a 'permanent Federal-Provincial Planning and Development Council' to foster 'joint programs'.

Given that 'under corporation control of investment' Canada had experienced the 'humps and hollows' of inflation and unemployment, the party cautioned that investment must recognize 'social as well as economic considerations'. Accordingly, it recommended the establishment of a federal investment board to 'balance . . . public and private needs' and foster full employment. A 'Canada Development Fund' would also be set up to encourage Canadian investment, and new taxation measures would be implemented.

In addition to its concern regarding greater 'monopoly control over Canadian industry and resources', the NDP noted that 'most large corporations in Canada are themselves controlled from other countries, chiefly from the United States'. If 'unchecked', this trend would 'endanger Canada's political independence'.[34] Dismissing the so-called remedies of the 'old parties' as inadequate, the NDP called for legislation setting the 'minimum percentage' permissible for Canadian 'capital and membership' on corporate boards in the hope that these measures would commence the 'selective repatriation of Canada's resources and industries'. It also proposed encouragement of the 'processing of Canadian natural resources on Canadian territory'. In the interim, foreign corporations were expected at the very least to comply with Canadian laws—something that they had not always done.

Among the NDP's recommendations for more progressive taxes were an increased corporate tax rate, reductions in depreciation allowances, taxes on capital gains, and removal of federal sales taxes on the necessities of life. Overall, the goal was to ensure that more funds from private companies would 'flow into the public treasury'.

To protect consumers, the NDP called for government action to discourage 'misleading advertising, poor quality and overpriced goods', and favoured the increased use of generic drugs to reduce costs. In addition, it advised that an NDP government would 'fix limits on interest rates' and foster 'credit unions and co-operative organizations'. Consumer research and education would also be encouraged.

To plan 'rational and balanced energy and transportation programmes', it proposed the establishment of a federal energy commission in 'cooperation [with] the provinces'. Interestingly, in contrast to the party's later position, the 1961 statement also urged growth in nuclear-generated power.

In international trade the NDP recommended expansion. 'Tariffs are out-moded, patchwork attempts to protect domestic industry', the product of an economic system that 'tolerates unemployment'. While noting that many industries would need more specialization to operate in world markets, the party proposed to seek 'active association' with West European states, to 'foster trade' with Latin America, and to provide low-interest, long-term credits to the 'new nations of Africa and Asia'. It also called for the creation of an international trade organization.

On the topic of regional development, the NDP indicated that it would offer 'tax concessions and other assistance to private industry, as well as public investment' to locate industry in certain regions. In particular, it urged the creation of more public works in Atlantic Canada and a capital projects commission to oversee such programmes.

The 1961 document cautioned that without adequate planning, automation could result in 'misery and waste . . . on a stupendous scale'. Unspecified 'vigorous measures' were promised 'to protect the public against monopoly control' of automation. In the interim, retraining and relocation programmes were recommended for those displaced.

While suggesting that more citizens were 'needed' in Canada, the NDP cautioned that new immigrants must be 'protected against unscrupulous exploitation by employers and others'. New Canadians, the party promised, would be instructed in both official languages.

As one of the key groups composing the New Party, farmers received substantial attention in the 1961 statement of principles. The family farm was reaffirmed as 'the basic unit of agricultural production and a desirable institution'. Urging increases in both farm production and incomes, the NDP favoured lowering farm production costs by 'ending monopoly control over farm machinery, fertilizers, chemicals and other supplies'. Co-operatives were to be encouraged, and 'where necessary, public ownership . . . developed'. The NDP proposed low long-term interest loans to encourage young farmers, guaranteed prices and crop insurance, and federal marketing boards to co-ordinate the various provincial marketing boards; the value of the Canadian Wheat Board was reaffirmed. 'In co-operation with the provinces', the NDP urged that improved services be made available to farm communities. Internationally, a world food bank to facilitate the distribution of surplus food to the needy nations was recommended.

'Democratically controlled' co-operatives and credit unions were described as 'important forms of social ownership' that benefitted both producers and consumers in rural and urban areas alike; such organizations provided 'efficient service and competitive prices with leverage against exploitation by privately-owned monopolies'. The NDP proposed to create a Department of Co-operatives, which would liaise with any existing provincial counterparts.

Showing an increased sensitivity for the concerns of small business and its limited resources, the party suggested that government planning would provide 'real economic security'. It proposed creating a new division within the Department of Trade and Commerce to serve small business, and promised to secure capital at low interest rates to 'help small business'.

To assist the fishing industry, the NDP indicated its support for co-operatives, government marketing boards, guaranteed prices, and government aid and loans. It was also willing to provide more technical training 'in co-operation with the provinces'.

The preamble to the second major section, 'Security and Freedom', reminded readers of the CCF-NDP's long-standing commitment to a 'comprehensive, far-reaching and systematic program of social security'. Present Canadian standards were seen as 'inadequate'—a 'patchwork' that left 'entire groups of needy people' with 'little or no security'. Again deferring to provincial rights, the NDP indicated that Canadian standards would be established 'in accordance with the principles . . . [of] Co-operative Federalism'.

The demand for a national medical care plan available to all persons 'without regard to . . . ability to pay' was a major plank in the new party's social-welfare platform, as it had been in the CCF's. Such a health plan was expected to incorporate coverage for all medical treatment and prescribed drugs. Repeatedly emphasizing its intention not to encroach upon provincial jurisdiction, the NDP also expressed its wish to consult at 'all stages' and to 'co-operate' with the medical profession as well as the provinces.[35] To counteract the shortage of health-care personnel, it promised to expand medical teaching and research.

To extend similar welfare measures to the elderly, the New Party Declaration called for a 'new and realistic' retirement plan. Pensions should be transferrable from one location and job to another, and available to all over 65 years of age, without any means test; they should also be raised to provide half the income level attained during the best earning years.

Other services to be improved upon or extended were maternity benefits, family allowance payments, dependent survivors' benefits, and veterans' funding. Unemployment insurance was also targeted for an overhaul. All of these plans were to have built-in automatic cost-of-living adjustments (COLA clauses).

In the era of the 'conquest of space' the NDP issued another challenge: the 'conquest of disease'. Envisioning Canada as a 'vanguard of the world-wide offensive against disease', it recommended the establishment of a Canadian medical research centre that would work with foreign and international organizations.

Addressing the important concerns of labour, the New Party statement reiterated the CCF's call for a national labour code involving a minimum wage, a 40-hour work week, two weeks of guaranteed annual vacation, eight statutory holidays, health and safety codes, trade-union security, equal pay for both sexes for comparable work, and encouragement of nation-wide and interprovincial labour-management bargaining. The NDP also urged that the federal government be given the authority to ratify all International Labour Organization (ILO) conventions (i.e., resolutions). Here, yet again, the NDP indicated the necessity of seeking the 'co-operation of the provinces' for all such measures.

Expressing its disappointment that 'many thousands' were without proper housing, the NDP suggested the establishment of a federal housing authority that would work 'in close co-operation and consultation with provincial and municipal governments' to provide increased financial assistance for low-rental accommodation. It also promised that an NDP government would construct housing, limit mortgages to a maximum level of 3%, and eliminate land speculation and profiteering.

In their ideological goal of building a new and better society, socialists have tended to put great emphasis upon education. According to the 1961 NDP document, not only is education a basic human right enabling each person 'to develop his talents to the full', but it is also 'sound economics'. Conceding that 'provinces have an inalienable constitutional right to control all phases of educational policy', the NDP nevertheless noted that the provinces needed adequate financial means to do so. Accordingly, it proposed that the federal government negotiate 'financial arrangements with the provinces' to foster free education at all levels, scholarships, and expansion of schools and universities. It also urged encouragement of adult education programmes.

The publicly-owned CBC, the creation of which was rooted in the pioneering efforts of socialists,[36] was cited as facing attacks on its 'integrity and independence'. Stressing a nationalist cultural message, the NDP recommended an increase in the CBC's budget to expand the production of Canadian programmes. It also called for strengthening of the state-operated National Film Board and development of a film industry 'under both public and private auspices'.

The major theme in the third section of the New Party Declaration, 'A More Complete Democracy', was co-operative federalism. The new party wanted to make it quite clear at the outset that it was 'vitally concerned with relations between the federal and provincial governments.' Here the NDP 'strongly' affirmed 'its belief in the federal system' and 'the united development of the two nations'. Endeavouring to compensate for the CCF's lack of attention to French Canada and Quebec, the NDP promised that it would 'fully maintain and respect' the constitutional guarantees of 'the national identity of French Canadians and the development of their culture', that it was committed to the protection of cultural and religious rights, and that it would 'assure provincial autonomy'. To promote 'close collaboration' and co-ordination among all levels of government,[37] the NDP proposed the creation of a department of federal-provincial relations. Believing in the need for 'consultation at the highest level', it suggested the establishment of a 'regular Prime Ministers' Conference', and noted

that constitutional powers meant little if a province did not have sufficient funds to operate programmes. Accordingly, the party called for
increased federal grants to the provinces and anticipated greater 'joint
participation' of the two levels of government in financing programmes
for the 'general welfare'. Instead of 'unilateral federal decision[s]', 'free
negotiations and consultation' would be stressed. In addition the NDP
made it clear that one province's opting out of a programme need not
prevent the rest of the country from proceeding; however, it conceded
that in the areas of education and language a province that opted out
should not be financially penalized. Reminding Canadians of the unacceptable anomaly of Britain's retaining the amending power in Canada's
constitution, the NDP recommended constitutional change, to include
entrenchment of language and other rights and recognition of the role of
the Supreme Court.

The controversial sub-section 'Canada as a nation' endeavoured to
address the question of whether Canada was one nation or two.[38] In it the
NDP asserted that Canada was indeed 'a nation', but with 'two national cul-
tures'. It conceded that the 'French-speaking community frequently and
legitimately use[s] the word "nation" to describe . . . itself'. 'True Canadian
unity', the document suggested, would involve 'respect for both main cul-
tures'. Building on this duality, the NDP proceeded to recognize multiculturalism as well, promising to 'protect . . . all ethnic backgrounds', and
identifying Indians and 'Eskimos' for special assistance. It also reminded
Canadians that almost a century after its founding, the country still needed
a distinctive national flag and anthem; by 1961, apparently, even socialists
were not indifferent to nationalist symbols.

The section on democracy closed with yet another call for abolition of
the Senate. It also recommended upgrading the democratically elected
House of Commons by strengthening the committee system, improving
research facilities, requiring full disclosure of political contributions, and
imposing limits on campaign expenditures.[39]

The final section, 'Co-operation For Peace', opened with a preamble
noting drastic changes in the world. In view of the contemporary 'struggle
between democracy and totalitarianism', it pointed out that 'Canada
cannot evade its responsibility' and must stand for 'freedom', while recognizing that 'the nature of this struggle is constantly changing'. Warning
that 'revolutionary developments in weapons have underlined the danger
and absurdity of relying on military strength as the chief means of settling
international disputes', the NDP reiterated that 'Canada's foreign and
defence policies must be reappraised and reshaped'.

In the NDP's view, the 'best hope of progress towards a durable peace' lay
in the United Nations. To achieve global rule of law, each state must yield
some of its sovereignty. The party urged Canadian leadership in strengthening the UN; for example, 'in concert with other middle and smaller

powers', Canada could help to 'create a permanent international police force', and in the interim it should establish a 'mobile force' ready for UN service. The document also stressed the UN as the body to co-ordinate increased foreign aid from Canada. Finally, it urged that Canada cease voting as part of a bloc in the world assembly and support admittance of the People's Republic of China.

Characterizing the Commonwealth as a unique multiracial and geographically dispersed association of peoples that offered a positive alternative for international co-operation in place of the 'cold war', the NDP noted that Canada's bilingual makeup enabled it to provide expertise to a greater number of states.

While stressing Canada's ties to the North Atlantic community and welcoming the formation of the Common Market, the document expressed concern that while NATO 'has played its part in the maintenance of West European security. . . . it has concentrated on a military role and has failed to adapt its policies to the growing importance of the economic and social front in the present world struggle.' Accordingly, the NDP called for a 'reappraisal and change of NATO's policies and objectives'. Given that extension of nuclear weapons threatened 'disaster to the world', the party opposed 'Canada's troops being supplied with such weapons at home or abroad', and warned that in the event of an increase in NATO's nuclear orientation, Canada 'cannot remain in the alliance'. To relieve tensions in Europe there should be a demilitarization of central Europe and the 'simultaneous disbandment of the Warsaw and NATO pacts'. The document also questioned 'whether NORAD ever made any significant contribution to the defence of Canada' and, asserting that the agreement had 'outlived its usefulness', called for its termination.

The 1961 statement urged 'an immediate ban on nuclear tests . . . as a first step toward nuclear disarmament' and proposed the establishment of 'a non-nuclear club of nations pledged not to manufacture, store or permit nuclear weapons on their soil nor to use such weapons at any time'; this, of course, ruled out nuclear warheads for the Canadian-based Bomarc missiles. Since the NDP believed that 'disarmament has become a condition of survival', it favoured Canada's playing 'a much more dynamic role in the promotion of universal disarmament' and proposed an independent peace research institute to further such a venture.

The last sub-section addressed the topic of economic aid. Calculating that Canada had spent billions of dollars on defence but 'less than 5% of that amount per year on economic aid to underdeveloped nations', the NDP advocated 'drastically' altering this ratio and raising foreign aid to 2% of Canada's national income. To mobilize 'Canada's agricultural and industrial potential' to relieve global famine, government planning along with funds from 'both public and private sources' would be needed. The NDP envisioned expansion of world trade, extension of credits to developing states, and subsidies in selected exports. It also proposed expanding training for foreign students in Canada and mobilizing Canadian youth to work in an overseas volunteer service corps. Finally, instead of sounding a clarion call for eradication of the old order of capitalism,[40] its closing paragraph promised a review of Canada's domestic policies, particularly regarding 'immigration and racial discrimination, to ensure that they conform to the spirit of equality among peoples and nations'—a proposal with which few Canadians, socialist or otherwise, would disagree.

A lengthy, detailed, at times almost technocratic blueprint for social reconstruction, the 1961 New Party Declaration conveyed little sense of messianic vision of a new Jerusalem. It seemed well-adapted to wooing the liberally-minded. The question was, to what degree could such a document rally the socialists?

The Declaration did continue many of the important themes raised in earlier manifestos. It expressed concern regarding the enormous power of corporate monopolies[41] and the plight of the poor and unemployed, and criticized the persistence of 'exploitation' and excessive inequality. It called for a social net to guarantee that no one would fall below a minimum standard, and pointed to health care and jobs as important social rights that would expand political democracy into economic democracy.

The NDP outlined, as the CCF had, an increasingly interventionist role for the federal government. The state would be much more active in social planning[42] and in regulating conditions in industry in order to establish a more stable economy and redistribute wealth. Government-sponsored programmes would range from housing to health care and energy. Greater government expenditures,[43] it was optimistically assumed, would be made possible by increases in public revenues. To the oft-raised questions concerning the cost of such programmes and whether the country could afford them, the NDP replied that if Canada could raise the sums required to fight a war, it should be able to commit an equal effort to peace and social reconstruction for a better world.

The new party showed far greater sensitivity than had the CCF to the balance needed in a federal state, repeatedly endeavouring to assuage fears that a more active central government would both encroach upon provincial jurisdiction and operate at the expense of the French Canadian minority.[44] A substantial portion of the statement stressed the theme of 'co-operative federalism'. Canadian socialist theory had finally been adjusted to the realities of an ethnically diverse and regionally fragmented state.

Echoing the CCF's outline for a mixed economy,[45] the Declaration urged public ownership and co-operatives where necessary, but at the same time expressed strong support for the privately owned family farm. It also specifically addressed the plight of small business and affirmed that an NDP government would provide assistance to small private commercial ventures. In its desire to broaden the CCF's coalition of socio-economic groups, it endeavoured to appeal to the potentially progressive[46] strata caught between the working class and big business. Accordingly, the 1961 statement avoided such terms as 'socialism',[47] 'capitalism', 'imperialism', and 'class', in the hope that less strident language could address the issues of poverty and inequality without necessarily alienating the large middle class.[48]

In addition to calling for changes in domestic society, social democrats have often spoken out strongly for a new international order. At a time when so-called realists were positing the need for more and deadlier weapons at increasingly stupendous costs, the 1961 NDP statement offered idealism and hope in place of technological despair, calling for a less militaristic and conflict-oriented path, increased aid for the Third World, and greater power for the United Nations.[49] While reaffirming its opposition to 'totalitarianism', the NDP expressed its dismay over the emergence of the Cold War and questioned the long-term utility of the military alliances (such as the US-led NATO and NORAD and the USSR-led Warsaw Pact) born in the aftermath of the Second World War.

Finally, while the references to socialism were fewer than in the CCF's statements, the 1961 document showed an increase in references to another collectivist doctrine—nationalism—particularly with regard to the growing foreign ownership of Canadian industry and resources. In sum, the document was a sensible blend of universalism (stressing the UN) and parochialism (promoting Canadian nationalism).[50]

With hindsight, analysis of the new party's founding statement suggests two observations. The first is how closely the direction of Canadian society in subsequent decades has appeared to follow its recommendations. Medicare, expanded social services, more government planning, an entrenched charter of human rights, constitutional change, greater joint federal-provincial decision-making, the need for a national energy programme, greater concern for conservation, support for bilingualism, heightened recognition of French Canadian aspirations, and limits on foreign ownership were all issues raised in this document and all have been achieved to some degree. At the same time, the Declaration serves as a reminder of how much is still to be done. Among the more pressing concerns are spiralling housing costs, the urgent requirements of the Third World, and the necessity of stronger UN actions to limit the continuing threat of war and nuclear annihilation. The need for full implementation of a social-democratic programme seems as compelling today as in 1961.

How successful the New Party Declaration has been in winning over the liberally-minded, French Canadians, and voters in Atlantic Canada is another question. Still, there is no doubt that the 1961 statement helped to launch the NDP in a more successful direction than that of the faltering, oblivion-bound CCF.

1983: THE NEW REGINA MANIFESTO

By 1983, social changes including increased urbanization, education, and participation by women in the paid workforce, a shorter work week, and faster rates of automation and technological innovation (microchips, computers, satellites, lasers, robots, etc.) had left a dramatic imprint upon Canadian society. The world too had seen significant changes. At least six nuclear states were now in existence, and the number of nuclear weapons (approximately 55,000 globally) had grown tremendously.[51] There was also increasing global concern about the environment and big government. As the fiftieth anniversary of the Regina Manifesto approached, suggestions for a restatement of party principles for the 1980s were inevitable.[52]

At 35 paragraphs, the new Regina Manifesto was a composite of a draft by the federal policy review committee and the work of Jim Laxer, Peter Warrian, and Ed Broadbent, on the one hand, and, on the other, features of a western draft inspired by John Richards, Allan Blakeney, and Grant Notley (see Richards and Kerr, 1986). The new manifesto came at a time when east-west divisions within the NDP were raging over the party's constitutional stand and Broadbent's leadership was being tested by the party's poor showing in the polls (15% in June 1983).[53] Despite these obstacles, the NDP wanted to make the 1983 convention a celebration of a half century of Canadian socialism, and a new Regina Manifesto was to be the centrepiece.

The document's preamble began with the proposition that the 'pursuit of peace and democratic socialism' were the 'two imperatives of a more secure and just modern world'. It called for a new emphasis on 'peace', 'co-operation' and 'equality' as the means of replacing 'oppression and privilege' with 'a compassionate and caring society'.

Outlining its goals for the 1980s, the NDP sought to eliminate 'exploitation' by class, ethnicity, or gender and hoped to see an egalitarian society emerge in which each person could 'develop his or her talents to the full'; 'differences of origin, or religion and of opinion' in the 'human mosaic' would be not only 'tolerated but valued'.

Cautioning that human development could not occur 'when economic needs remain unsatisfied', it suggested that 'ecological priorities' should 'guide technological and economic decisions' to ensure the conservation of 'valuable common resources'. The NDP reaffirmed both its commitment to the 'family farm' and 'small business', and its belief in the right of aboriginal peoples to 'shape their own future . . . and to possess the institutions necessary to survive and flourish'. The two following paragraphs were designed to appeal to two important groups: women and labour. For the first, the party stressed the need to address gender discrimination and inequality, violence against women, and 'changes in the family', while for the second it emphasized workers' rights to 'participate in the trade union movement, . . . to engage in collective bargaining and . . . to withdraw their services if necessary'. Finally, the NDP noted the heightened dangers of war in the nuclear era and posed the challenge of a 'lasting peace' based on 'freedom, equality and social justice among nations and within nations'.

The means to achieve these goals were the subject of the next section. Reminding readers that democracy was 'at the heart of the socialist philosophy', the party indicated its wish to 'broaden and extend democracy into all aspects of human endeavour and to create real opportunities for people to participate in making the decisions which affect their lives'; it 'reject[ed] the capitalist theory that the unregulated law of supply and demand should control the destiny of society and its members'. Reflecting the 1980s' concern with excessive centralization and bureaucracy,[54] it also counselled that 'this planning must be an expression of the will of the people, not imposed on them from above'.

Stressing a strong commitment to the public sector, the new manifesto asserted that 'social ownership is an essential means to achieve our goals'. However, this did not mean 'simply the transfer of title of large enterprises to the state'; rather, it called for 'decentralized ownership and control'. Co-operatives and credit unions were cited as examples of ways to foster the 'progressive democratization of the workplace'.

Noting that 1983 was the fiftieth anniversary of the Regina Manifesto, the section entitled 'Our Historic Task' pointed out that the earlier document was an 'agenda of reform' for the 'common good' forged by 'ordinary people— despite major differences of region, ethnic origin and social class . . . [acting] together . . . independently of powerful "vested interests"'. Observing that in fifty years 'much has been achieved', and that 'Canada is a better place' than in 1933, it pointed to unemployment insurance and medicare as two legislative items that had 'changed the lives of millions'. Many other changes were also observed; for example, 'stronger provincial and local governments capable of realizing important tasks of economic and social development have emerged. The public domain has been expanded on a scale unimaginable in the 1930s.' Nevertheless, 'much . . . remains to be done. Poverty, mass unemployment, and unacceptable concentration of power and wealth persist', and environmental damage must be 'checked by strong measures'. Finally, noting the loss of a 'sense of community' in Canada's 'large, impersonal' and 'alienating' cities, and the prospect of nuclear warfare culminating in the 'annihilation of our species', the section closed by stressing the 'urgency' of these issues and the NDP's 'commitment to fundamental change'.

The last section was entitled 'Our Commitment to Canada', and, as in the case of the 1961 New Party Declaration, it addressed in detail federal-provincial relations and the subject of Quebec. Observing that any change in the Canadian federation must be based on 'respect for its regionalism, and for its duality', it acknowledged demands 'to decentralize, where feasible, political authority', but balanced this claim with the assertion that 'Canadians . . . also want a strong Canadian government. . . to guarantee our national independence' and to ensure each region an equal share in the country's prosperity. Reminding Canadians, as had the CCF before it, of the 'enduring problem' of the 'American corporate ownership of the Canadian economy', the NDP proposed that the federal government must serve 'as our collective instrument' to foster a 'more independent Canadian economy'. On the subject of Quebec the 1983 document noted that 'few French Canadians attended the 1933 convention'[55] and that, as a result, the party had 'underestimate[d] the importance Quebecois attached . . . to . . . their national assembly as the guardian of their culture.' While acknowledging that the people of Quebec should be able to 'determine freely their own future', it expressed the party's hope that they would 'not choose independence', but rather participate in a 'new Canadian union'.

Urging that 'we, in the NDP, join with those on the left in Quebec and French Canadians elsewhere', the manifesto closed with the declaration that the party would 'not rest content until we have achieved a democratic socialist Canada' in a 'more just, democratic and peaceful world.'

Despite the NDP's temporary decline in the polls in 1983, the new Regina Manifesto reflected a return to a more confident self-image as a socialist party. After the McCarthyite 1950s, the 1960s had seen a resurgence of radical and left-wing views; the Cold War was ending, and in North America 'socialism' was a term more openly and safely used. Accordingly, the new Regina Manifesto employed the word more often than any of the party's previous statements of principles, although it was still sufficiently cautious to add the adjective 'democratic' from time to time. As in all CCF-NDP statements, the goal was not to restrict democracy, as opponents often accused, but rather to expand democracy's reach from the political realm into the social and economic spheres. As in 1933, the party sought to democratize the workplace.[56]

While reasserting the party's commitment to public ownership, the 1983 manifesto again balanced this claim with endorsements of the family farm and small business. As in all four earlier manifestos, the vision was of a mixed economy. Government planning was endorsed, but there seemed less confidence that central planning could accomplish the enormous hopes expressed in the 1933 Regina Manifesto. The NDP in the 1980s seemed much more willing to embrace a decentralist variant of socialism (Whitehorn, 1974).

The product of a compromise between western provincial-rights advocates and federal party officials, the 1983 statement achieved a delicate balance in outlining federal and provincial powers. Again the concerns of French-Canadians received special attention.

The recent rise to prominence of the women's movement has left no political party, left or right, free of charges of gender bias and inequality. Despite their commitment to cultural change, socialist parties world-wide have in the past not shown themselves immune to elements of male chauvinism. For example, it was not until 1989 that the NDP elected a woman as federal leader.[57] In the 1980s, the party acknowledged this gender imbalance both in its new manifesto and in its embracing of gender parity for many key party posts. Reflecting this new concern, the last four party presidents—Marion Dewar, Johanna den Hertog, Sandra Mitchell, and Nancy Riche—have all been women.

In international affairs, the 1983 statement reiterated the NDP's long-standing nationalist message by pointing out the disadvantages of excessive foreign ownership and control of our economy. Notably absent, however, was any reference to the NATO and NORAD military alliances; by opting for brevity in 1983, the party avoided one of the more contentious aspects of its policy.[58] Still, on one issue there could be no doubt. Over the six-decade history of the CCF-NDP, every one of the party's statements has stressed the danger of war and the need for Canadians to work more energetically for peace. In the 1930s, the CCF's warnings were largely ignored, and Canada was plunged into the bloodshed of another world war. The public's response in the last decades of the twentieth century, when a new global war would be far more catastrophic, remains to be seen.

CONCLUSION

An overview of the five CCF-NDP manifestos suggests a considerable degree of continuity. In each document, the goal was a less stratified and more just society that would be more fully democratic and would help to lead the way towards a less conflict-prone world. The means to be employed were always peaceful and evolutionary. The principle of a mixed economy remained constant, although the mix varied depending on the desperation of the era. The party was also consistent in its call for greater government planning, although in recent years it showed signs of becoming less centralist and more sensitive to the balance of federal-provincial power. Overall, the party's vision throughout its half-century was for a socialist Canada.

The continuing socialist theme in the manifestos, however, is only part of the picture. An aspect of CCF-NDP manifestos too often ignored is that they have also advocated Canadian nationalism. Evidence for this suggestion includes the far greater frequency with which they have used the term 'nation' (73) than 'socialism' (21) (see Table 3.1). As both the NDP and the Parti Québécois have sought to show, the two collectivist doctrines of nationalism and socialism can co-exist, particularly when they both stress the theme of collective liberation. Nevertheless, a question arises as to which of the two doctrines is the stronger and more likely to endure. At the very least, an increase in nationalist sentiments can be at the expense of internationalism—an important feature of early socialist thought. In a world already too fragmented along parochial lines, any accentuation of this tendency can be catastrophic.

If the aspirations and content of CCF-NDP manifestos have been relatively consistent, so too has been the party's record of success. While its influence has been significant in improving the quality of life for the majority of Canadians, only a minority of those same Canadians ever supported the federal party. A breakthrough in Quebec continues to be elusive. Canadians seem to want the party and its ideas around, but they seem less willing to elect the federal NDP to power.

No conclusion would be complete without some speculation on the salience of written manifestos in the 1990s.[59] Just as educators in the 1990s ask whether Johnny still reads, one may question whether anyone, apart from a few academics, still reads party manifestos. There can be little doubt that half a century ago, the Regina Manifesto was circulated and read extensively. Copies of such pamphlets proliferated (see Weinrich, 1982). In contrast, the new Regina Manifesto was at first not widely distributed and does not appear to have been widely discussed by party activists in recent years, let alone cited at length by academics.

Part of the explanation for the declining interest in party manifestos has been the rise in importance of convention resolutions on specific policy topics. As the size of conventions has grown, so has the number of resolutions submitted, debated, and passed. By 1986 the federal NDP's collection of resolutions previously approved and still in force was reaching epic proportions, and almost defying accurate compilation.[60] Nevertheless, two advantages of these detailed resolutions are that they can focus on specific issues and that they can readily be updated. Manifestos, in contrast, are rigid statements almost etched in stone, and their policy relevance often declines with the passage of time.

Another major reason for the decline in importance of manifestos is the tremendous growth in the role and scope of radio and, particularly, television. Today's emphasis upon TV opportunities and photogenic leaders who can project a positive media image makes written party manifestos appear less significant. Ours is the age of the ten-second news clip and the cosmetic smile, not the construction of detailed blueprints[61] for a brave new world. In an earlier age one at least had a clearer idea of what parties stood for. The NDP has resisted this trend better than the two other major parties, but to a certain extent it too has succumbed to the new medium and style. Although it has passed far more resolutions and manifestos than its rivals, future party historians will no doubt have to compare televised political ads and leaders' debates. The age of manifestos in Canadian politics is in decline.[62]

NOTES

[1] Chapter 8 in McAllister (1984) offers a shorter and at times skewed textual analysis of several party documents.

[2] For Teeple (1972) this is tantamount to not being socialist.

[3] For an analysis of public enterprises and Crown corporations in Canada, see Laux and Molot (1988), Stewart (1987), and Ashley and Smails (1965).

[4] This should not be confused with the term 'use-lease' employed later by the Saskatchewan section of the CCF.

[5] The eastern intellectuals who had created the LSR had not dwelt upon this important topic, which would need to be addressed by any party that sought to tap western farm populism. By far the most comprehensive account of the LSR is offered by Horn (1980).

[6] It was not until later in the 1950s, and particularly from the 1960s onwards, that the party embraced economic nationalism. See, for example, discussions of the Waffle (Cross, 1974; Hackett, 1979, 1980; Bullen, 1983; Brodie, 1985) and the 1988 free-trade election (Chapter 8).

[7] Obviously this is one prediction that did not prove accurate. It is interesting how, over fifty years, the party shifted from a more internationalist socialist position on economic matters to one stressing the fusion of nationalism and socialism. Of course, in other areas such as foreign policy the CCF stressed Canadian autonomy and nationalism from the outset.

[8] Now referred to as Constitution Act, 1867.

[9] The precursor of the United Nations.

[10] The Communist Party of Canada had been banned since 1931 and many of its key leaders jailed (Penner, 1988). This harassment of the revolutionary Communist Party is often overlooked as a factor in the rise of the evolutionary, social-democratic CCF.

[11] The same pattern is evident in Marx's writings. Far more attention is devoted to criticizing capitalism than to outlining his vision of socialist or communist society.

[12] As it was, the United Farmers of Ontario felt that the CCF was too radical and eventually withdrew their support, despite Agnes MacPhail's efforts to maintain the links; this greatly weakened the CCF's immediate chances in Ontario.

[13] This theme would re-emerge in importance in the 1960s and become a rallying cry of the New Left (Pateman, 1970; Broadbent, 1970; Hunnius, 1971; Garson, 1977; Whitehorn, 1974, 1978, 1979a).

[14] A contemporary reader is struck by how little attention was devoted to linguistic and cultural factors.

[15] Among the Canadian student New Left (Sargent, 1972; Roussopoulos, 1970; Roussopoulos, 1973), the Waffle faction in the NDP was probably the most famous example (Hackett, 1979, 1980; Bullen, 1983).

[16] This document that the so-called radicals of 1933 felt was too tame would later be hailed as a radical statement.

[17] The data on percentage of income held by the top quintile vs. the bottom quintile in Canadian society do not reflect the dramatic changes hoped for by reformers. For example, the data reveal the following distribution of income for the bottom 20% of Canadian society: 6.1% (1951) vs. 6.6% (1961) (Forcese, 1975: 53); see also Hunter (1981: 56, 70); Ross (1980: 12). Of course, these data focus on income and ignore social services, which many believe have meant substantial improvements for the poorest strata in Canadian society.

[18] For more recent accounts on the Quality of Life measures, see Michalos (1980).

[19] See particularly pages 126-30 and 172-4.

[20] It should be noted that although the term 'class' does not appear anywhere in the

document, this passage is clearly an instance in which it could have been used.

[21] This early attempt at *glasnost* did not remain secret long.

[22] Students of Canadian history sometimes seem to focus excessively on Canadian factors alone to explain events, and too often ignore the important international context.

[23] See Chapter 2 on the 'protest movement becalmed' hypothesis and the question of ideological transformation.

[24] The fate of the rural-based Social Credit is a stark reminder of the soundness of this conclusion. In recent federal elections, no members of the Social Credit party have been elected. Yet Social Credit began the 1960s with more parliamentary seats than the NDP.

[25] In CLC resolutions regarding the formation of a 'New Party' (CLC conventions, April 1958 and April 1960). Even J.S. Woodsworth, at the founding of the CCF, sought to reach out to the professional strata; note, for example, his reliance on academics from the LSR. In 1984 party leader Ed Broadbent expressed a similar notion in his slogan 'ordinary Canadians'.

[26] It should be noted that in China even the revolutionary Mao proposed a united front of different classes, including members of the bourgeoisie. See, for example, his 1926 'Analysis of the Classes in Chinese Society'.

[27] As Cross notes (1974: 5), the NDP was inspired by both the British Labour Party and the American Democratic Party.

[28] By the 1990s the independent voter, presumably less ideologically inclined, has become an increasingly important part of the political landscape in Canada and other Western democracies.

[29] Actually, since most of the leading figures of the CCF stayed at the helm of the NDP, many members of the new party continued to feel a strong bond with the Regina Manifesto.

[30] Representation from New Party Clubs was added in 1959.

[31] A collection of essays on social democracy, the book *Social Purpose For Canada*, (ed. M. Oliver, 1961) was published on the eve of the founding convention, and went into greater detail regarding the issues and the agenda that the new party would need to tackle. Interestingly, this book included separate chapters on socialism and class—terms conspicuously avoided in the 1961 declaration itself. These linguistic omissions at the founding convention were rectified at subsequent NDP conventions; in 1963 for example, the term 'socialism' was again employed.

[32] The Waffle's 1969 Manifesto is excluded from analysis, as is the so-called Marshmallow statement of the same year: the former because it was never formally approved by the majority of delegates at a federal NDP convention; and the latter because, while it was an official resolution passed at an NDP convention, it dealt primarily with the single issue of foreign ownership and was not really a full statement of party principles over a wide range of issues. Cross (1974) reprints these two documents; the introductory essay is, however, somewhat polemical.

[33] As editor Michael Oliver noted, the book *Social Purpose For Canada* was intended to serve the same inspirational role for the NDP that the LSR's 1935 volume *Social Planning for Canada* had for the CCF. In 1985 another volume entitled *Democratic Socialism* (ed. Wilson) would appear with the same purpose.

[34] In this respect the 1961 document anticipated the Waffle manifesto by almost a

decade. Clearly the party had already staked out a stand on this issue before the formation of the Waffle.

[35] Given the doctors' strike in Saskatchewan the following year, this reference seems somewhat ironic.

[36] As co-founder of the Canadian Radio League, CCF pioneer Graham Spry played an important role in the formation of the CBC.

[37] How this would be possible if various governments had different ideological perspectives was not clarified.

[38] The decision to endorse the 'two nations' view led former LSR and CCF co-founder and ex-CCL official Eugene Forsey (1990) to depart from the NDP. It was also a factor in Pierre Trudeau's coolness to the party.

[39] The 1974 election finance reform law accomplished many of the goals of this proposal. See Seidle and Paltiel (1981).

[40] Indeed, the document did not even mention the competing systems of socialism and capitalism directly, although the entire statement involved a contrast between private corporate power and public worker-oriented power.

[41] Richards has suggested that this theme fits the populist tradition as well as the socialist one (see, for example, Richards and Kerr, 1986).

[42] It has sometimes been suggested that the CCF-NDP has shown greater consistency in stressing state planning than public ownership.

[43] Critics have sometimes accused the party of simply throwing money at social ills in the hope that some funds will achieve their purpose. This is part of the neo-conservative critique of both social democracy and reform liberalism.

[44] The influence of Frank Scott and Pierre Trudeau can be seen in their chapters on federalism in *Social Purpose For Canada*. Interestingly, Trudeau's chapter, despite its references to socialism and CCF manifestos, is reprinted in his book *Federalism and the French Canadians* (1968), which was published just prior to his successful run for the leadership of the Liberal Party.

[45] Horowitz (1968: 206) suggests that the new party statement was no less socialist than the Winnipeg Declaration.

[46] There was not a lot in this manifesto with which a member of the reform wing of the Liberal Party would disagree. In part, this reflected the New Party's efforts to attract progressive elements away from the Liberal Party. Although to many this attitude reflected a significant change in the party, it should be noted that even Mao strove to build an alliance of progressive strata during his attempts at revolutionary social reconstruction. The fact that such a document could be acceptable to a greater number of Canadians also shows how much the country had changed. Critics positing an ideological transformation of the CCF-NDP tend to ignore that the Canada of the 1960s was not identical to that of the 1930s. In many ways, the contrasts between the party and society had lessened, for reasons related to both internal party factors and external factors in society.

[47] One common interpretation suggests that the New Party Declaration was a major retreat from the idea of a socialist society. However, another explanation is at least as plausible. It may be that the choice of language was a tactical decision in order not to frighten away potential supporters. First, the word 'socialism' was employed in the two key books associated with the NDP's founding (Knowles, 1961: 93-4; Oliver, 1961). Second, the NDP, like the CCF, sought admission to the Socialist International (Horowitz, 1968: 206). Lastly, the NDP at

subsequent conventions freely embraced the concept of socialism. The cumulative evidence for the tactical interpretation seems persuasive.

[48] It should be noted that a great many Canadians subjectively identify themselves as belonging to the middle class (see, e.g., Pammet, 1991). In a sense, they see themselves as 'ordinary Canadians'.

[49] In the areas of defence and foreign policy, the technique of content analysis of policy manifestos is reinforced by findings from surveys of NDP convention delegates. See Chapter 5.

[50] This nationalism, however, recognized bilingualism and multiculturalism.

[51] Sivard (1987) reports that in 1986 the United States and the Soviet Union alone accounted for 22,000 strategic nuclear weapons, compared with 2,200 in 1956— a ten-fold increase in three decades.

[52] There is archival evidence that as early as the mid-1970s federal secretary Robin Sears approached several individuals about drafting a new statement of principles; however, the drafts did not appear to go beyond the federal secretary and a few readers.

[53] Gallup Report, 13 Oct. 1983

[54] One can note here the influence of the ideas of the New Left; see Sargent (1972). Both Jim Laxer and Ed Broadbent had been advocates of decentralized workers' self-management in the 1960s.

[55] More Francophones attended the 1983 convention than that of 1933 but they were still relatively few. See Chapter 5 for a report on the findings of the 1983 survey of convention delegates.

[56] Little was achieved in this direction for several reasons. Not only have the Liberal and Conservative parties been generally unsympathetic to industrial democracy but, even more important, the trade-union movement has remained sceptical about abandoning the adversarial labour vs. management pattern of industrial relations. Unions have been cool to the proposals for a more co-operative pursuit of the 'common wealth' by means of works councils and workers' self-management (Whitehorn, 1974, 1979; Nightingale, 1982).

[57] Thérèse Casgrain was the first provincial female CCF leader in Quebec; see Casgrain (1972); Trofimenkoff (1989). Alexa McDonough was the first female leader of the Nova Scotia NDP.

[58] See Chapter 5 for the 1983 survey of NDP convention delegates' attitudes to NATO and NORAD.

[59] Similarly, the declining importance of the newspaper medium has been noted by many.

[60] For an earlier compendium of resolutions passed see Scotton (1977). A more recent party effort at synthesizing policy positions based on convention resolutions is the 269-page 'Resolutions Reference' (New Democrats, 1986).

[61] Book-length outlines of the social-democratic vision are available. Among those inspired and associated with the CCF-NDP are the following group efforts: LSR, *Social Planning For Canada* (1935), Oliver, ed., *Social Purpose For Canada* (1961) and, more recently, Wilson, ed., *Democratic Socialism* (1985). Together this trilogy provides a comprehensive overview of social-democratic thought spanning a half century.

[62] One should not necessarily infer from this that our era is witnessing the end of ideology (see Bell, 1962).

FOUR

The Party in Elections

INTRODUCTION

While most of this book endeavours to offer an analytical overview of the CCF-NDP, it may also be useful to present a chronological account for the general reader who is not thoroughly versed in the party's history.[1] This chapter will do so by discussing each of the election campaigns that the CCF-NDP has contested. The party has been involved in seventeen federal elections (seven as the CCF and, to date, ten as the NDP). In each case, five aspects will be considered: the background to the campaign, the key issues, the party's main election pamphlet (where appropriate),[2] the total CCF-NDP vote and seat count, and the regional nature of party support and electoral success. In this fashion a capsule summary of each contest will be provided in a consistent format.[3]

THE CCF ERA
1935

The Co-operative Commonwealth Federation was one of several political parties that arose in the 1930s out of the agonizing economic crisis of the Great Depression and the devastating drought on the Prairies. The

CCF would, however, prove to be the most enduring of the new parties. The 1935 election was the first federal election contested by the CCF.

The party was led by a veteran member of Parliament, J.S. Woodsworth (McNaught, 1959, 1980; MacInnis, 1953; Mills, 1991: Ziegler, 1934), who had first been elected for the Independent Labour Party of Manitoba in 1921, in the aftermath of the Winnipeg General Strike. Not surprisingly, in the three short years since its creation the CCF had not completed the job of building a truly national organization by the time of the election; it did not run a full slate of candidates, and contested only 48% of the ridings. As befitted its largely western origins, all but three of the 118 CCF candidates ran in ridings west of the Ottawa River (Beck, 1968). In terms of votes (see Appendix Table 1) the party came third, with 8.8% of the national vote, barely edging out H.H. Stevens's Reconstruction party. Yet in terms of seats (Appendix Table 1) the CCF came fourth, with 7, substantially behind the largely Alberta-based Social Credit party, which had 17. As throughout the CCF-NDP's history, the party received a lower percentage of seats than of votes, and its success was somewhat skewed towards the west. British Columbia at 33.6%, Saskatchewan at 20.1%, and Manitoba at 19.4% provided the highest levels of voter support. All of the CCF's seats came from three western provinces, even though the largest number of its votes came from the more populous Ontario—a fact usually ignored in accounts stressing the party's western base in the early days. Those Ontario votes did not translate into seats, however, and in Francophone Quebec, Canada's second most populous province, where the CCF's operation was largely non-existent, it received a minuscule 0.6% of the vote. But, as David Lewis (1981) points out, if the party elected few MPs, its small caucus included a number of notable figures in Canadian politics. Accompanying the legendary Woodsworth was a young Saskatchewan clergyman, T.C. Douglas, who would soon become one of Canada's most successful premiers. Another Saskatchewan MP was M.J. Coldwell, the man who would succeed Woodsworth and serve as CCF leader for the longest term in the history of the party.

The key challenge for all parties in the 1935 election was to design a blueprint for ending the chaos and suffering of the Depression. The CCF publicized its newly penned Regina Manifesto, along with a two-page outline of an immediate programme offering a vision of an alternative economic and social order. Condemning monopoly capitalism with its unemployment, financial insecurity, and widespread suffering, and proposing socialization of banks and finance as a remedy, the party appealed for a national system of social insurance, public works and an end to farm and home foreclosures.[4] It called for revisions to Canada's constitution to ensure that the federal government possessed 'adequate powers to deal effectively with urgent economic problems'. In international affairs, the CCF favoured Canada's neutrality in any future war. But the CCF was not alone in offering reform; other voices presented the electorate with a distracting array of choices. For example, another western-based protest group, the Social Credit party (MacPherson, 1953; Irving, 1959; Thomas, 1977; Laycock, 1990), also endeavoured to speak for the farmers in the west and their frustrations with the corporate and business leanings of the government in Ottawa.

While the Liberals won the 1935 election, one-quarter of the electorate voted for parties other than the Liberals and Conservatives. Most significantly, the Conservatives, in large part blamed for government inaction in the Depression, emerged with a mere 40 seats. What remained to be seen was whether this discontent with at least one of the two old-line parties would coalesce around a new organization such as the CCF.

1940

The CCF fought its second national election in the midst of the catastrophic conflict of the Second World War. As in any wartime election, restrictions on material, personnel, and civil liberties complicated political campaigning. The revolutionary Communist Party had been declared illegal not so much for its communist doctrine as for its opposition to Canada's involvement in the war. Augmenting the CCF's controversial image as a socialist party, therefore, was the complication of its stand on the war. In the previous election, the party had sweepingly denounced all imperialist wars and expressed its support for neutralism in the abstract. When war finally came in 1939, members of the CCF were divided. Although the divisions between pacifists (e.g., federal leader J.S. Woodsworth) and those who volunteered for military service (e.g., Saskatchewan CCF leader George Williams) existed across the country, and at all levels, the increasingly ailing, 66-year-old Woodsworth had been out-voted in 1939 at an emergency meeting of the party's national council on the issue of Canada's war policy.[5] Ideologically, the CCF's position was midway between the Conservatives' full support of the war effort and the Communists' opposition to it. While the CCF opposed both military conscription of manpower and the compulsory conscription of labour introduced by the Liberal government, it did call 'for greater equality of sacrifice'. To achieve this, it urged better direction in the war effort through greater state economic planning. It favoured the nationalization of wartime industries as a means to prevent profiteering by capitalist monopolies.

Again the party failed to field a full slate of candidates, nominating only 96 (22 fewer than in 1935) for a possible 245 seats; there was clearly no hope of forming the government. Most of the CCF candidates (88.5%) ran west of the Ottawa River, and only in the western provinces did the party contest a majority of federal ridings. While in absolute votes the party's tally increased slightly, its percentage of the vote, not surprisingly, slipped to 8.5%. With 50% fewer candidates in Ontario than in 1935, the Ontario vote too was halved. In contrast, Saskatchewan provided the party with its largest total number of votes, highest percentage of the vote, and most MPs, with 5; the Saskatchewan results were a harbinger of things to come four years later, when the CCF came to power provincially. Overall, the federal CCF acquired 8 seats, one more than in the previous election, and, while third in terms of total vote, it remained fourth in parliamentary seats, behind W.D. Herridge's short-lived New Democracy party. (The Conservatives again came a distant second behind the victorious Liberals.) What was most striking about the new CCF caucus was the preponderance of Saskatchewan MPs elected, led by Coldwell and Douglas. The 1940 election also saw the victory in Nova Scotia of ex-miner Clarie Gillis (Harrop, 1987; MacEwan, 1976), the first CCF MP ever elected from the east. Once again, however, the more populous provinces of Ontario and Quebec failed to provide any CCF seats, and thus contributed to the CCF's remaining a minor party (Zakuta, 1964).

Although in the 1940 campaign Woodsworth was still listed officially as leader, increasingly the younger and healthier Coldwell was taking over as *de facto* leader of the party. It was Woodsworth's last election. His death in 1942 was to bring about a by-election in his Winnipeg riding that would see the emergence of another clergyman turned politician: the indefatigable Stanley Knowles (Trofimenkoff, 1982; Harrop, 1984). A socialist prophet in the capitalist wilderness, Woodsworth never saw the party achieve its first major electoral success, when in 1944 it formed the government of Saskatchewan. It would remain for others such as Tommy Douglas (McLeod and McLeod, 1987) to commence the construction of the new Jerusalem.

1945

The 1945 election took place in the waning days of the Second World War. Germany had surrendered, and Japan would follow suit a few months later. In many respects, the 1945 federal election was the pivotal contest for the CCF (Lewis, 1981: 261). The Soviet Red Army's victory in Stalingrad in 1943 had fostered a more positive image of the left in general. More important, both the CCF's ideas and its organization had begun to take hold. For example, large government expenditures and central state planning, ideas that had been routinely dismissed as unworkable socialist dogma by the capitalist press a decade earlier, became the policy norm during the war years. As the Canadian public prepared for the post-war era and rebuilding, the citizens who had left a collapsing old society with massive unemployment and poverty to take part in the war came to be seen as soldiers fighting for a new and better world; at the very least, these people should be assured of jobs, homes, and material abundance after such heroic sacrifices.

Organizationally, CCF membership had grown and the party had made significant provincial election gains, becoming the official opposition in the provincial legislatures of British Columbia (1941) and Ontario (1943), and establishing a toehold in Nova Scotia with its first seats in 1941. In 1942 the federal CCF acquired its first-ever Ontario seat with Joe Noseworthy's by-election victory over Conservative leader Arthur Meighen. The party even won a seat in the Quebec provincial legislature in 1944. None of these gains, however, equalled the stunning success of the Douglas-led[6] Saskatchewan CCF, which formed the first socialist government in North America. The party's provincial successes were also matched by improving federal prospects. In September 1943, a Gallup poll reported that the CCF was leading both the Liberals and the Conservatives in public support, although the race was tight (29% vs. 28% and 28%).[7]

The period just prior to the 1945 campaign saw a proliferation of CCF-related publications. Among the more important were *Make This Your Canada*, by CCF national secretary David Lewis and national chairman Frank Scott; the Ontario CCF's *Planning For Freedom*; and *Left Turn Canada*, by the new CCF leader, M.J. Coldwell. On the eve of the 1945 campaign the CCF national convention passed a series of resolutions outlining the proposed first-term programme of a CCF government. Later reprinted as a pamphlet entitled 'Security With Victory' (see Carrigan, 1968), the document outlined the CCF's emphasis upon extension of social ownership and social services.[8] The response to the upsurge in socialist materials and support was not long in coming. Large corporate interests became alarmed and, starting two years before the election contest, unleashed a counter-barrage of free-enterprise and capitalist propaganda.[9] As Lewis (1981) points out, the scale of this campaign was mammoth, and, combined with the slight shift to the left by the Liberals under Mackenzie King, the effect was devastating. The first consequences of this two-pronged attack could be seen in the highly charged Ontario provincial election,[10] which took place one week before the national vote. In Ontario, the number of people voting for the CCF declined despite the fact that almost half a million more people voted. Accordingly, the CCF's percentage of the provincial vote was cut by almost 10%. Even more significant, however, was the fact that the number of CCF seats plummeted from 34 to 8. These losses foreshadowed the results of the federal election.

Reflecting the party's improved prospects and higher aspirations in the pre-election period, the federal CCF ran 205 candidates (83.6% of all ridings), more than twice as many as in 1940, and at last offered an approximation of a fully national campaign. Only in Quebec was the slate of CCF candidates nowhere near full. As one would expect, given the doubling in numbers of candidates, the CCF showed significant gains, garnering 15.6% of the vote (an increase of 7.1% over the 8.5% received in 1940). As before, the west (most notably Saskatchewan with 44.4%, Manitoba with 31.6%, and British Columbia with 29.4%) provided the highest levels of CCF support. In contrast to 1940, however, Ontario now provided the largest number of CCF votes (almost a third of the party's total). Already there were hints that the party's base was beginning to shift eastwards in at least one important respect.

For the third time in a row, Mackenzie King led the Liberals to election victory. Despite the anti-socialist campaign, a record 28 CCF MPs were elected —good enough to give the federal party its first-ever third-place finish. The CCF elected 18 out of a possible 21 MPs from Saskatchewan; no doubt the provincial victory a year earlier and federal government cuts of financial grants to the province in 1945 (McLeod and McLeod, 1987: 136) were factors in their success. Again Ontario and Quebec candidates were shut out in a general election. The party's parliamentary caucus continued to have a decidedly western look; indeed, the CCF had more western MPs than either the Conservatives or Liberals. The greatly enlarged caucus saw the re-election of Coldwell, Angus MacInnis, and Stanley Knowles from the west and Clarie Gillis from the east. Among those elected from Saskatchewan were Ross Thatcher and Hazen Argue, both later to defect from the party and become prominent Liberals. (The former would become Premier of Saskatchewan and the latter a federal cabinet minister and Senator).

Despite the appearance of success, however, CCF expectations had been unrealistically high, and in many ways the 1945 federal election was a disappointment. It wasn't readily apparent at first, but 1945 was the beginning of the end for the CCF. From that point on, the finances and membership of the federal organization began to slide. Despite a partial reprieve in seats won in 1953 and 1957, the CCF consistently declined in its percentage of votes in all federal elections subsequent to 1945. It would take more than a decade for the final pages of the CCF's history to be closed, but 1945 was the beginning of the last chapter. It was not the bright new start for which so many of the party faithful had hoped.

1949

International events dominated much of the political scene in the late 1940s as the wartime alliance of Britain, the United States, and the Soviet Union was shattered, and the hopes for the newly created United Nations were dashed. The 1945 defection in Ottawa of Soviet cipher clerk Igor Gouzenko, subsequent espionage revelations (Bothwell and Granatstein, n.d.) and the Berlin blockade of 1948-49 were among the opening moves in the Cold War. The hardening of the divisions of Europe into Western and Eastern blocs was accentuated by the Communist takeovers in Eastern Europe (Hammond, 1975), the Marshall Plan (1948), and the formation of NATO (1949).[11] The global division was accelerated by the military victory of Mao Zedong and the rise of Communist China (1949).

While the CCF continued to be led by Coldwell, the two larger parties opted for new leaders: Louis St Laurent for the Liberals and George Drew for the Conservatives. Post-war reconstruction, along with the menacing international developments, dominated political discourse. The most memorable phrase of the 1949 campaign was St Laurent's portrayal of the CCF as merely 'Liberals in a hurry'—to which Drew replied that the Liberals were simply 'Socialists in low gear'.

The pamphlet 'Security For All' (see Carrigan, 1968) reflected the CCF's call for a well-integrated and planned social-security programme. It proposed a comprehensive health-care system, combined with a national labour code and re-establishment of price controls, and opposed any sales tax on necessities. The party urged the socialization of several major industries including rail, steel, and power, but cautioned that 'large areas can best be left to private enterprise' (e.g., agricultural land). Reminding the public that socialization was 'only a means . . . not an end', the pamphlet refuted suggestions that the party was 'doctrinaire'. It also tapped nationalist concerns by warning of the 'wanton alienation of vital Canadian resources to powerful private interests—interests controlled outside Canada.'[12] Addressing the growing concern about the Cold War, the pamphlet counselled that the 'developing Western European Union [i.e., NATO] is not and should not be a mere military alliance.' Despite reluctance among some in the party, criticism was also directed at the USSR: the CCF would 'fight against totalitarian dictatorship of every kind', and no co-operation with the Stalinist LPP (Communist Party) was to occur.

The fourth federal election contested by the CCF saw the party run 180 candidates in 69% of 262 ridings. Although in the west and Ontario the CCF slates were almost full, in Quebec the party ran in only 20 of 73 ridings (Beck, 1968).

In the end, a Liberal plurality of 49.5% of the vote translated into a massive victory, with 73.7% of the seats. The Conservatives, in contrast, continuing their electoral drought since the Depression, received only 41 seats. The CCF vote, at 13.4%, was down from the record high in 1945 of 15.6%, with the highest levels of support coming from Saskatchewan (40.9%), British Columbia (31.5%), and Manitoba (25.9%). While in Ontario the party received a more modest 15.2% of the vote, in Quebec, the result was an abysmal 1.1%.

The total number of seats won by the CCF fell by more than half, from 28 to 13—less than the number won in Saskatchewan alone in 1945. Yet the party still managed to retain its third-place status by edging out Social Credit, which won 10 seats. Most of the CCF losses occurred in Saskatchewan, where the number of CCF MPs was reduced from 18 to 5. Nevertheless, the CCF continued to hold more seats in the west than did the Conservatives. Another small positive note was the improvement in the regional balance of the CCF caucus: MPs now came from five different provinces, and included the first CCF member ever from Ontario.[13] Among the 13 CCF MPs elected, Coldwell was again joined by MacInnis, Knowles, and Gillis, as well as Thatcher and Argue.

All in all, the election of 1949 was a disappointment for the CCF. The situation would become far worse, however, in the 1950s, as the Cold War peaked and the CCF's electoral fortunes declined still further.

1953

The election held in August 1953 took place against a backdrop of optimism. The Korean war, begun in 1950, had in effect ended with a truce in July. The depression expected to follow the Second World War had not materialized; indeed, the decade promised relative prosperity, with an unemployment rate of 3.0% in 1953 compared to 20.0% two decades earlier (Archer, 1975). The prevailing mood of hope and enthusiasm was captured by the coronation of the young Queen Elizabeth in June 1953.

In its election pamphlet, entitled 'Humanity First' (see Carrigan, 1968), the CCF called for a national health insurance plan, government-financed low-cost housing, greater federal government aid to education, and nationalization of the important steel industry; it also proposed government ownership and control over the farm-equipment industry. While acknowledging that the post-war economy had grown, it speculated that such growth was fostered by a war economy. In international affairs, the party gave support to NATO in principle but criticized the military emphasis of the treaty and urged greater stress on joint economic objectives. Endeavouring to stake out a middle path in the bipolar world, the CCF condemned the 'ruthlessness' of both 'world communism' and 'world capitalism'. Finally the pamphlet expressed the party's internationalist hopes by calling for Canadians to play more a dynamic role in the United Nations.

Even after two decades of existence, the CCF still did not run a full slate of candidates. Nominating 170 persons to run in the 265 ridings (a rate of 64%), it offered candidates in only about 75% of the ridings in Ontario and 40% of those in Quebec (Beck, 1968), although in the west the roster was virtually complete.

The results were largely the same as in 1949. The Liberals won handily, and the Conservatives placed a distant second. Although the CCF, with 11.3% of the vote, placed third, well ahead of the western-based Social Credit party (at 5.4%), this percentage represented yet another drop. Continuing the well-established pattern, the highest levels of CCF support came from Saskatchewan (44.2%), British Columbia (26.6%), and Manitoba (23.6%). The more populous Ontario, however, continued to provide the largest absolute number of CCF votes. With the exception of Cape Breton (MacEwan, 1976), regions east of the Ottawa River gave the CCF less than 5% of their support.

Reflecting the sometimes quirky nature of the Canadian electoral system, the number of seats won by the CCF rose even though the national vote declined. With 23 seats, the party managed to retain its third-place standing ahead of Social Credit, which had 15.[14] All but two of the 23 CCF victories were in the west, and almost half (11) were in Saskatchewan. Among the western CCF members elected was Harold Winch, the son of long-serving British Columbia CCF MLA Ernie Winch (Steeves, 1960). The younger Winch, who had been the former provincial leader of the BC CCF (1938-53) and leader of the opposition in the legislature (1941-53) continued his pattern of electoral success federally. Another western MP, returning to the caucus after an absence of eight years, was a former social-gospel minister, Sandy Nicholson (Dyck, 1988). As was the case in the two previous elections, the CCF continued to have more MPs from the west than did the Conservatives. But the large central Canadian provinces of Ontario and Quebec provided scant CCF representation (1 and 0 respectively) in Parliament—a state of affairs that did not help the CCF in its efforts to become a pan-Canadian party. Despite its Saskatchewan successes in 1953, therefore, federally the CCF continued in its minor-party status.

1957

Internationally, the year preceding the 1957 election had seen several electrifying events: Khrushchev's secret speech denouncing Stalin, the Hungarian revolution, and the Anglo-French invasion of Egypt. No less important was the Treaty of Rome, signalling the beginning of the European common market. Domestically, 1956 had produced the controversial and bitter pipeline debate in Parliament, and the merger of the Trades and Labour Congress with the Canadian Congress of Labour into the Canadian Labour Congress (CLC), which was to have long-term significance for the CCF and social democracy in Canada. The Progressive Conservatives had selected the 61-year-old Prairie populist John Diefenbaker to lead their party back to power after more than two decades in opposition. In contrast, the Liberals remained with the 75-year-old St Laurent, and the CCF stayed with the ailing M.J. Coldwell, now 68. It was the dawn of the television era in politics.

In this federal election the CCF presented its new statement of principles, the Winnipeg Declaration of 1956. It represented the party's long-overdue attempt to recast the social democratic vision for the post-Depression postwar era (see Chapter 3). The CCF also issued approximately a million copies of an election pamphlet entitled 'Share Canada's Wealth'[15] (Meisel, 1962; see also Carrigan, 1968). While noting 'great economic expansion' in the 1950s, the latter nevertheless expressed the CCF's concerns about the unequal sharing of the benefits, and continued to call for increased taxes upon the rich and corporations. The party favoured lowering of interest rates, abolition of sales tax on necessities, and extension and improvement of pensions and other welfare benefits. To assist farmers it called for guaranteed prices and cash advances for stored grain, while for city dwellers it urged immediate action to end excessive land speculation. The party continued to warn that American corporations 'threaten our economic, and even our political independence'. It also urged a national energy policy that would see public ownership of all trans-Canada pipelines.

As in previous campaigns, the CCF ran in slightly more than half (162) of the 265 ridings (Beck, 1968), fielding candidates in virtually all ridings in the west (68 of 70), a majority of those in Ontario (60 of 85), and only about a third of those in Quebec (22 of 75) and Atlantic Canada (12 of 33). Among the more noteworthy riding battles was the contest between Hazen Argue, who for the moment was still with the CCF, and Ross Thatcher, who had already abandoned the party.

In terms of votes, the Liberals received a larger total than the Conservatives; however, the anomalies of our electoral system produced a Conservative victory. The CCF received 10.7% of the vote, its third consecutive decline. Of the 162 ridings that the party contested, its candidates lost their deposits in 112 (69%) (Meisel, 1962: 256). Although the highest levels of support came from Saskatchewan (36.0%), Manitoba (23.7%), and British Columbia (22.3%), Ontario provided the bulk of CCF votes with 274,069 —almost double the total of any other province (see Appendix Table 1).

After twenty-two years in opposition, the Conservative Party was finally victorious. Adding to the historic quality of the election was the fact that for the first time since 1926, more than three decades earlier, a rare minority Parliament had been elected.

Despite the continuing decline in its percentage of the vote, the CCF retained third place, winning 25 seats to Social Credit's 19. This was the federal party's second-highest number of seats to date, and gave some reason for optimism (Lewis 1981: 494). Continuing a long-standing pattern, most of the CCF's seats (22) were from the west, with 10 from Saskatchewan, 7 from BC (including the former logger Frank Howard), 5 from Manitoba, and only 3 from the east (all in Ontario). The party's success in the west was sufficient to outnumber both the Conservatives and the Liberals in terms of total western seats and reinforced its image as a voice for western Canada; this would, however, be a difficult feat to duplicate in the future, given the growing importance of the Prairie-based Diefenbaker. Ontario saw its CCF seats increase from 1 to 3. Of these gains —exclusively in the have-not northern periphery of the province—the most notable was the victory of Douglas Fisher, a schoolteacher, over the Liberal cabinet minister C.D. Howe. The death of Joe Noseworthy in 1956 had left the CCF's single Toronto seat vulnerable, and it was lost, as was the solitary outpost in Cape Breton. The result was that the CCF had no Members of Parliament from densely populated southern Ontario, nor from east of the Ottawa River. Clearly the federal CCF had a long way to go to achieve major-party status.

The minority Conservative victory of 1957 was the Tories' first step towards breaking the federal Liberals' stranglehold upon power. It also provided the potential for a smaller third party such as the CCF to play a highly visible role as balancer in a minority Parliament. It was, however, a dangerous game—as the CCF was to learn in the latter half of 1957-58.

1958

Late in the fall of 1957 the space age commenced with the Soviet Union's launching of sputnik, the world's first satellite. After the Liberals' disappointing performance in the election of that year, they selected Nobel peace-prize winner Lester Pearson to lead their party. The CCF was to fight one more campaign with Coldwell, but he seemed tired and the party worn out. Domestically, the election of 1958 focused on Diefenbaker's quest for a majority government. The CCF, on the other hand, as a third party, endeavoured to persuade voters that a vote for it was not wasted, and that minority government could be positive.

The party's election statement, entitled 'Let's Go Forward' (see Carrigan, 1968), was issued as both a pamphlet and a cartoon brochure. Given that the previous election had taken place only a year earlier, it is not surprising that there was little difference between the CCF's 1957 and 1958 platforms. The main new emphasis was the party's assertion that the Liberals had let the 'Canadian economy fall increasingly under the control of American corporations' and that the Conservatives, once in power, were no better. The CCF called for 'Canadian resources for Canadians', 'fair taxes', and extension of public ownership 'where necessary'. Despite its continued failure to make a breakthrough among Quebec Francophones, it urged that Canada become officially bilingual.

In what was to be the CCF's last federal campaign, several patterns established at the party's outset were still in evidence. The slate of candidates was less than full (63.7%; 169 of 265), and yet again, whereas CCF candidates were nominated in virtually every riding in the west, and a significant number in Ontario (63 of 85), only a minority of ridings in Quebec (29 of 75) and Atlantic Canada (9 of 33) were represented.

Once more the CCF's percentage of the vote dropped, this time to 9.5% —one of the worst showings in the seven elections fought by the CCF. The west again provided the highest level of support (28.4% in Saskatchewan, 24.5% in BC, and 19.6% in Manitoba), while Ontario again supplied the largest absolute number of CCF votes, with just over a quarter of a million. In contrast, the party's candidates in Quebec received a combined total of less than 50,000 votes.

Diefenbaker's charismatic oratory propelled the Conservatives to historic numbers of both votes and seats (208 of a possible 265). In the wake of this Conservative landslide, Social Credit did not win a single seat, and the CCF caucus was reduced from 25 seats to a paltry 8, its worst showing since 1940. Today, a party with so few seats would not qualify for official status in the House of Commons. The western base of the CCF crumbled under the onslaught of the Saskatchewan populist Diefenbaker. No CCF candidate was elected from Manitoba; even party stalwart Stanley Knowles went down to a rare defeat. In Saskatchewan, long the stronghold of Canadian socialism, only one CCF MP, Hazen Argue, survived. Even Coldwell, the Saskatchewan-based party leader, went down to his first defeat in two decades. In British Columbia only four CCF candidates were victorious (Harold Winch, Bert Herridge [see Hodgson, 1976], Ernie Regier, and Frank Howard). The re-election of three Ontario CCF members (Doug Fisher, Murdo Martin, and Arnold Peters) meant that, for the first time, caucus representation was almost evenly balanced between the west and the east. The group was, however, very small.

The 1958 campaign was to be the last for Coldwell and the CCF alike. The end came perhaps none too soon. The Canadian socialist movement appeared to be in disarray. For several years there had been discussions and preliminary work towards building a new political vehicle for the socialist cause (Lewis, 1981: 486), in which the newly formed Canadian Labour Congress was seen as an important potential ally. These initiatives would now accelerate.

Despite the electoral setback, another factor raising the possibility of future success existed. The Liberals too had been crushed by the Diefenbaker surge, reduced to a mere 49 seats and representation in only four provinces. Social democrats hoped that Canada's party system was in the midst of a transition. Perhaps social democracy would be reborn in the form of a new party that could displace the Liberals, as had been the case in the United Kingdom earlier in the century.

THE NDP ERA[16]

1962

The early 1960s ushered in a new age. In the United States, the election of the young and progressive John F. Kennedy was seen as promising a 'new' style of Democratic party politics. The revitalized American brand of reform liberalism acted as an inspiration in Canada. The Liberal Party held the famous policy conference in Kingston, Ontario, that helped to push it to the left, and in Quebec the formal beginning of the 'quiet revolution' was marked by the election of the change-oriented provincial Liberal party under Jean Lesage. Most significantly for the social-democratic movement, 1961 saw the birth of the New Democratic Party, formed through the alliance of the old CCF, unions affiliated with the CLC, and New Party clubs. The NDP drafted a program and selected as its first leader Tommy Douglas, a man who possessed a remarkable record of success both as an MP and as Premier of Saskatchewan. His provincial administration had pioneered in many areas of social legislation. However, Douglas's departure from Saskatchewan was not without controversy, as the province was racked by debate over the full implementation of state-run medical care, culminating in the infamous doctors' strike of 1962 (Badgley and Wolfe, 1967; Tollefson, 1963). Another dark cloud on the NDP's horizon was the dramatic departure, in early 1962, of Hazen Argue, the former CCF federal leader and NDP leadership candidate of 1961. Argue's defection came as an unpleasant surprise to party officials and members alike, and was accompanied by accusations that the new party was dominated by labour. Only months earlier Argue had wooed the labour vote.

Many publications relating to the NDP were issued in this period by the CCF, the CLC, and the National Committee for the New Party (NCNP). The formal statement of the party's philosophical stance, however, was the New Party Declaration (see Chapter 3), which was augmented by the publication of the party-inspired book *Social Purpose For Canada*. One commentator described the new party's statement of principles as 'more radical than socialist, emphasizing planning instead of nationalization' (Carrigan, 1968: 334). Indeed, there was no mention of socialism in the party's programme, although later NDP conventions would rectify this tactical omission.

In addition to these materials, the NDP issued an election programme that was reprinted in condensed form as 'A New Dimension' (see also Carrigan, 1968). A major campaign plank was a call to expand key welfare measures. Accordingly, the NDP demanded an immediate increase in pensions and abolition of all means tests; it also urged that any pension benefits be portable and transferable from job to job and province to province. Declaring decent medical care to be a core human right, the NDP argued that each individual should be provided for according to need, with funding from each according to ability to pay.[17] The proposed public medicare system was to be funded largely by the federal government, but would be administered provincially and would ensure free choice as to doctors for all patients. In the constitutional realm, the NDP called for the creation of a Department of Federal-Provincial relations and a royal commission on bilingualism and biculturalism. In international affairs, the party sought to 'reduce foreign control of Canadian industries'; somewhat paradoxically, however, it also called for new, freer trading arrangements.[18] Finally, on defence matters, it urged 'universal disarmament' and advocated no nuclear weapons for Canada; it also encouraged efforts to 'seek reappraisal and change of NATO's policies and objectives'.

As befitted a party endeavouring to make greater inroads than the old CCF had, the NDP ran more candidates, with a total of 218 for the 265 ridings. In the west and, somewhat remarkably, Quebec, the slates were full, and virtually so in Ontario (81 of 85) and Atlantic Canada.

More than a million Canadians voted for the new party in its first election—a record-high total to that date for the CCF-NDP. With 13.5% of the national vote, the party received its best share since 1945 but, even so, just barely edged out Social Credit, which received 11.7%. In general, the old pattern of receiving the greatest level of support from the west continued. This time, though, British Columbia (30.9%) displaced Saskatchewan (22.1%) as the top province. Manitoba again came third at 19.7%, and urban Ontario provided almost a half million of the NDP's total votes, while Quebec once more lagged behind at 91,000.

The Conservatives were re-elected, but with only a minority government. Most dramatic of all was the re-emergence of Social Credit in Parliament; fuelled by its breakthrough in Quebec, the party went from no seats in 1958 to 30 in 1962. Thus while the NDP acquired 19 seats, an increase from 1958, that was still only enough for a fourth-place finish. Saskatchewan, the bedrock of socialist representation, was shut out. Even party leader Tommy Douglas lost, to the shock and dismay of both the party faithful and the Canadian public. Hazen Argue, the lone Saskatchewan CCF survivor in the 1958 election, ran for the Liberals in 1962 and won. In contrast to the bleak Saskatchewan results, 10 of British Columbia's seats (almost half of all available) were won by the NDP. Amounting to more than half of the federal NDP caucus, the BC delegation included the young lawyer Tom Berger, who would later gain fame as head of the Royal Commission on the Mackenzie Valley pipeline. The second largest number of NDP seats (6) came from Ontario—the most the party had won there. Among those elected from Ontario were the architect of the new party, David Lewis (winning his first seat in the House of Commons), Andrew Brewin, and Reid Scott. In Manitoba former MLA David Orlikow achieved his first election to Parliament, starting a career in the Commons that would last until 1988.

Since the new party had been designed in part to win over more of Canada's urban population, the 1962 gains in BC and Ontario were gratifying. In another of the NDP's founding goals, however—to reach out for Quebec support—it clearly failed. Like the CCF before it, the NDP elected not one MP from that province. On balance, then, the NDP's first election, like the CCF's in 1935, was a disappointment. The road to social democracy was longer and more difficult than the party pioneers had anticipated.

1963

The minority Conservative government elected in 1962 stumbled into the 1963 election. En route, some cabinet members resigned, some refused to run again, and some even considered ousting party leader John Diefenbaker. As a result of having scrapped the Avro Arrow airplane in 1959 in favour of Bomarc missiles, the Conservative government was forced to address the issue of whether to arm the Bomarc missiles with nuclear weapons.

Thus the issues of defence and American interference in Canadian domestic affairs received unusual prominence in the 1963 election. The NDP's position on nuclear weapons, in contrast to that of the Liberals and Conservatives, was clear-cut: it strongly opposed any nuclear weapons for

Canadian forces either in Canada or in Europe. The party continued to stress its internationalist view that a permanent mobile force of Canadian troops should be available to the United Nations for peacekeeping operations throughout the world. It also urged that a country as affluent as Canada should increase its foreign aid to 2% of its GNP. In general, the NDP's platform resembled that of the year before.

Maintaining the trend established in 1962, the party again increased the number of its candidates, fielding 232 out of a possible 265 (Beck, 1968). As usual, a virtually full slate was offered in the west, while a high number ran in Ontario (80 out of 85), and a reasonable number in Quebec (60 of 75) and Atlantic Canada (23 of 33).

In contrast to 1962, the Liberals, not the Conservatives, gained the largest percentage of the vote. The NDP's percentage slipped 0.4% to 13.1%, but was still ahead of Social Credit's 11.9%. For the second time in a row, British Columbia provided the highest level of support for the NDP at 30.3%, and Saskatchewan again came second, but at a record low of 18.2% — a disappointing drop from the average of 34.7% during the CCF years. Manitoba provided the next highest level of support, at 16.7%. In Quebec, for the fifth consecutive time, the NDP's vote inched upwards, to a more respectable 7.1% and 151,061 votes: however, the bias in the electoral system ensured that even this increase did not give the NDP a single Quebec seat.

Not only was Diefenbaker's quest for a majority government denied, but the Liberals formed a new government — the third minority Parliament in four elections. The NDP saw a slight decline in both votes and seats. The party was third in percentage of the vote but received only 17 seats, two fewer than the previous year, and was again relegated to fourth place behind Social Credit, which had 24 seats. British Columbia provided 9 — more than half the NDP caucus — among them Colin Cameron, Harold Winch, and Bert Herridge. This time, despite his long tenure as Premier of Saskatchewan, federal leader Tommy Douglas had chosen to run in BC; this proved a wise decision, since the Saskatchewan-based Diefenbaker continued to be a formidable opponent in his home province, which once again failed to elect a single NDP member.[19] Ontario, with 6 seats, provided the second highest number of NDP Members of Parliament. David Lewis, however, having finally won an election in 1962 after five tries since 1940, was not among them. Three of the Ontario NDP MPs (Doug Fisher, Arnold Peters, Murdo Martin) were based in the northern part of the province, where unionized workers often proved to be a decisive factor (Archer, 1990). The NDP was able to retain only two seats in Manitoba, those of Stanley Knowles and David Orlikow, both of whom would have unusually strong records of electoral success for CCF-NDP politicians. And the party's only seat east of Ontario (Cape Breton) was lost.

While the public's lack of confidence in both Pearson and Diefenbaker[20]

was reflected in the fact that neither was able to form a majority government, the NDP nevertheless declined in both percentage of vote and seats
from the previous year. It was another disappointing result for the new party.

1965

By the mid-1960s the death of US President Kennedy was two years past,
but the dark shadow of violence continued to spread. In Quebec the FLQ
was pursuing the bombing campaign begun in 1963. The conflict in south-
east Asia escalated with the growing US involvement in the Vietnam War,
while in North America race riots shattered the liberal optimism of the
decade's early years.

In 1965 Canadians were to go to the polls for the third time in four years.
Many were tiring of elections—not to mention the ongoing personal
battles between Pearson and Diefenbaker. The minority Liberal government was plagued by a series of scandals, and the Conservative Party was
racked by challenges to Diefenbaker's leadership. The Social Credit Party
had increasingly been divided into the Thompson-led western wing, based
in Alberta, and the Caouette-led Quebec wing.

The provincial Saskatchewan CCF-NDP government, having survived a
bitter doctors' strike over medicare in 1962, had gone down to defeat in
1964 after two decades in power. The one provincial fortress for the party
had finally been breached. The NDP in Ontario was buoyed, however, by
two recent by-election victories (one provincial and one federal) by Jim
Renwick in Riverdale and Max Saltsman in Waterloo South. The party
therefore entered the 1965 campaign with some reason for optimism:
perhaps an urban breakthrough in central Canada was possible now. A slate
of 255 candidates (out of a possible 265) was an important step towards
major-party status. Nevertheless, there was disappointment in NDP circles
that the Liberals, not the NDP, had attracted the three so-called 'wise men'
of Quebec—Pierre Trudeau, Jean Marchand, and Gérard Pelletier—into
their ranks (Sherwood, 1966).

Among the campaign materials issued by the NDP was a pamphlet entitled 'The Way Ahead For Canada', which outlined the programme passed
by the 1965 federal convention (Fox, 1966). In it the party stressed the
need for more dynamic political leadership than that offered by the 'bick-
ering' of Diefenbaker and Pearson. The NDP continued to envision a more
activist government that would oversee an 'immense programme' of social
development. Among the NDP proposals were the creation of new depart-
ments of consumer affairs, science, and technology, a federal secretariat of
education, and expanded jurisdiction for the wheat board. The top priority,
however, was to implement immediately the findings of the Hall Royal
Commission and establish a Canada-wide comprehensive and universal
insurance programme (medicare). The NDP also called for increases in old-
age payments. Noting that Canada was facing the 'gravest crisis' of its

history and that even the survival of Confederation was in question, the party (prophetically) rejected the élitist proclivity towards 'closed doors [at] federal-provincial conference[s]'. Instead it called for close and permanent co-operation between the federal and provincial governments; one mechanism suggested to achieve this was the establishment of a permanent Federal-Provincial Planning and Development Council. The pamphlet reiterated the NDP's long-standing call for a Canadian constitution[21] and bill of rights. In keeping with the party's reformist populist image, it favoured electoral reform through lowering the voting age to 18 and requiring greater public accounting for all parties' finances. In foreign affairs, it called for an end to the Vietnam War, admission of Communist China into the United Nations, and a reappraisal of NATO's role; relatedly, the NDP proposed greater mobility for Canada's armed forces and greater involvement in UN peacekeeping operations. Finally, the NDP also raised the nationalist fear that the problems of foreign ownership were becoming 'more serious'.

When the count was tallied, the NDP had increased its percentage of the vote to 17.9%, surpassing even the previous peak of 15.6% won by the CCF in 1945. Perhaps more significantly, the NDP vote was dramatically greater than that of the fourth-place Social Credit, which received a mere 3.7%. British Columbia gave the NDP 32.9% of the vote, Saskatchewan 26.0%, Manitoba 24.0%, and Ontario 21.7%. This was the first time in the history of the federal CCF-NDP that it had received over 20% of the vote in Ontario. Even in Quebec, under the able tutelage of Robert Cliche, the NDP won 12.0% of the vote—its best showing yet,[22] and almost double the previous best. The Quebec NDP vote had increased for six consecutive elections; only Ontario gave the NDP more votes than Quebec's 244,339. Yet the unresponsiveness of our electoral system meant that the party still emerged with no seats in the province. Lack of electoral success was not confined to Quebec. One scholar estimated that nationally 72.9% (186 of 255) of the NDP's candidates lost their deposits (Beck, 1968: 394).

Pearson's Liberals were re-elected, but with yet another minority—the third in a row. Minority government, which had once been a rare political phenomenon, now appeared to be the norm. In both 1962 and 1963 Social Credit, despite receiving a smaller percentage of the vote, had displaced the NDP as the third-ranking party in terms of seats. In 1965, however, the NDP reasserted its ascendancy over the now splintered Social Credit and Créditiste parties and, in so doing, achieved another important step towards major-party status. Although it elected members from only three provinces, the NDP increased its seats to 21. For the first time in the history of the CCF-NDP, Ontario provided as many MPs in the Parliamentary caucus as any other province, matching British Columbia's 9. Joining David Lewis from Toronto were Andrew Brewin and John Gilbert, while Max Saltsman was re-elected in Waterloo. Doug Fisher had retired and his former seat was lost, but other northern Ontario MPs were re-elected. In British Columbia, party leader Douglas was joined by 8 members, including first-time MP Grace MacInnis, the daughter of J.S. Woodsworth and wife of the pioneering CCF MP Angus MacInnis. Manitoba's elected MPs included Stanley Knowles and the seemingly unbeatable David Orlikow, along with a young new member, Ed Schreyer, who would go on to become Premier of Manitoba from 1969 to 1977 and Governor General of Canada from 1979 to 1983.

The 1965 election, the last for Pearson and Diefenbaker, was to mark the end of an era in Canadian politics. A question lingering was to what degree the NDP's relative success could be attributed to the endless feuding between the Liberal and Conservative leaders and the resulting Parliamentary deadlock. Had the NDP benefitted from a vote against the two other parties rather than for itself? Soon both the Liberals and the Conservatives would select new leaders, while the New Democratic Party would delay leadership change for one more election. Time would tell if this decision was wise.

1968

As the 1960s closed, conflict and violence continued at an accelerated pace. The TV screens projected images of the turmoil of the cultural revolution in China, the intense battles raging in Vietnam, the race riots in US ghettos, and the mass demonstrations by radical students and peace activists. In Canada, too, change was in the air. Robert Stanfield had replaced Diefenbaker as leader of the severely fractured Conservative Party,[23] while the charismatic Quebecker Pierre Trudeau had been chosen to head the Liberals. The passion and violence unleashed by Quebec nationalism continued to grow with De Gaulle's 'Vive le Québec libre!' speech in 1967, and the St-Jean Baptiste day riot on the eve of the 1968 federal election. The commencement of Canada's second century also witnessed the resurgence of Canadian nationalism fuelled in part by the Watkins Report on foreign investment and the rise of the Marxist New Left.

The NDP, continuing its progress towards major-party status, ran virtually a full slate of candidates (263/264) in the 1968 election. Among the more prominent individuals running were TV personality Laurier Lapierre and McGill university professor Charles Taylor. Both were fluently bilingual and cited as possible future leadership candidates.

One of the major innovations of the 1968 campaign was the first televised leaders' debate in Canadian politics. The NDP campaigned on the theme 'You win with the NDP'. In response to increases in both inflation and the cost of living, it called for a prices-review board and more public funds for housing as a basic right for all citizens (Beck, 1968),[24] a guaranteed annual income for all, and (drawing upon the report of the Carter Royal Commission on taxation) tax reform. Citing the newly released

Watkins Report, the NDP continued to warn of the risks of excessive foreign ownership and economic domination of Canada. In foreign policy, the party criticized the escalation of the Vietnam War and called for cessation of US bombing of North Vietnam, as well as dismantling of the NATO and Warsaw Pact military alliances in favour of a common European security system. With regard to Quebec, the NDP continued to stress special status—a policy in sharp contrast to Trudeau's vision of Quebec's role in Canada.

In the end, the image of the dashing Trudeau standing against a torrent of stones hurled by militant Quebec nationalists at St-Jean Baptiste day demonstrations helped propel him to electoral victory with his promises of a 'just society' and a stronger federal system.[25] The NDP vote slipped to 17.0%, a slight drop from the then record high of 1965. For the first time since the new party's creation in 1961, Saskatchewan led in the federal NDP vote, with 35.7%; this was the first significant indication that Saskatchewan was returning to its CCF-era prominence in the federal socialist camp. The next highest level of support came from British Columbia at 32.7%, followed by Manitoba at 25.0% and Ontario at 20.6%. Party support in Quebec, however, fell under the Trudeau juggernaut and was almost halved, dropping from 12% to 7.5%, while in the other provinces, as usual, it remained below 10%.

For the first time in a decade, the Canadian electorate returned a majority government. Social Credit, however, failed to win any seats and the Créditistes were confined to 14 MPs, all in Quebec. The NDP acquired seats in four provinces for a total of 22—one more than in 1965, and the party's highest standing since its founding in 1961; nevertheless, it still fell short of the best CCF results in 1945, 1957, and 1953. British Columbia led the caucus with 7 MPs, a decline from previous elections in the 1960s. Saskatchewan elected 6, as did the more populous Ontario, while Manitoba completed the caucus with 3 NDP MPs. Yet again, Tommy Douglas was not re-elected and would have to await a by-election before returning to the House of Commons. But the oft-defeated David Lewis won his Toronto seat and acquired an even higher profile during Douglas's initial absence from the Commons. Not surprisingly, these developments, coupled with the decade's emphasis on youth, fuelled speculation about the party's leadership. While many of the younger would-be leadership figures failed to gain election, the caucus did include Grace MacInnis, Harold Winch and Frank Howard from BC. Among the Saskatchewan members were Lorne Nystrom, then the youngest MP ever elected, and newcomer Les Benjamin. And in Ontario, a young, radical political-science professor named Ed Broadbent had also won a seat for the first time. The 1968 election marked the official electoral start of the Trudeau years, but it was also the beginning of the end of the Douglas era in the NDP. Before the next election the party would select a new leader, albeit not yet from the new generation.

1972

The end of the 1960s and the beginning of the 1970s witnessed the Soviet invasion of Czechoslovakia, the Sino-Soviet border clashes, and the admission of Communist China into the United Nations. It also saw first the political victory of Richard Nixon and conservatism in the United States, and then the Watergate scandal. Culturally, by contrast, it was also the era of Woodstock. In Canada the Quebec cauldron continued to boil. In 1968 a number of separatist organizations came together to form the Parti Québécois, in the main a nationalist party but also to some degree a social-democratic one. Separatist bombings continued and became a prelude to the October Crisis of 1970, in which British diplomat James Cross and Quebec cabinet minister Pierre Laporte were kidnapped by FLQ terrorists. The death of Laporte and the invocation by the federal government of the War Measures Act shattered Canadians' assumptions about their peaceable kingdom and civil liberties (Berger, 1981). Of all political parties in the House of Commons, only the NDP voted against implementation of the draconian War Measures Act.[26] With little public support, it was a lonely stand by party leader Tommy Douglas, his colleagues, and his soon-to-be successor, David Lewis.

The beginning of the decade also saw great organizational changes for the NDP. Whereas in the CCF years only Saskatchewan had elected a social-democratic government, after a drought of several years without any provincial governments the NDP saw three western provinces turn its way. Ed Schreyer became Manitoba's first socialist Premier in 1969, and his victory was soon followed by those of Allan Blakeney in Saskatchewan, in 1971, and Dave Barrett in British Columbia, in 1972. These successes were tempered, however, by the ongoing intra-party turmoil between the more militant, nationalist, and youth-oriented Waffle (see Hackett, 1979, 1980; Bullen, 1983; Brodie, 1985) and older, more moderate party members. The highly charged 1971 federal leadership contest between veteran David Lewis and young Waffle academic James Laxer culminated in the selection of Lewis and reiteration of the NDP's stand as a moderate social-democratic party rather than a more militant, Marxist-inspired variant. The intra-party feuding largely came to a halt with the decision by the Ontario NDP to order the disbanding of the Waffle, in 1972.

In that year the NDP nominated candidates in 95% of the ridings (251/264), slightly fewer than in the two previous elections. The party's official campaign slogan was 'Canada needs more New Democrats in Ottawa', and its main election pamphlet was entitled 'Canadians working together to build a new Canada'. Calling for Canada to recover its 'economic independence' and cease being a mere adjunct to the US, this document demanded an end to the plundering of Canadian resources to fuel US industry, and opposed any continental energy deal (see Laxer, 1970);

one of the first steps it proposed was public ownership in the oil and gas industry. Full employment was stated as the primary economic goal, and the party repeated its call for a prices-review board. In addition to expressing concern about western alienation, it noted the growing gap between French and English Canada. To break the past pattern of preoccupation with inter-governmental negotiations, the party suggested instead a special constitutional convention that would include members of Parliament, provincial legislatures, and territorial councils, as well as spokespersons from the native peoples. Drawing upon the report of the Royal Commission on the status of women, the NDP endorsed equal pay for equal work, paid maternity leave, expanded day care, family planning, and dissemination of birth-control information. In international affairs, the NDP pamphlet called for a ban on all nuclear testing and the more radical position of withdrawal from both NATO and NORAD. Despite this comprehensive programme, however, in the end one theme dominated the 1972 campaign. In speech after speech Lewis hammered away at the 'corporate welfare bums', each time pointing out yet another glaring example of corporate tax avoidance and government handouts for the rich. Left populism (Richards and Pratt, 1979) at its oratorical best, it was a campaign backed up by a steady barrage of statistics and striking examples of corporate rip-offs.[27]

The electorate, no longer under the spell of Trudeaumania, gave no party a majority in the House of Commons; Trudeau's Liberals barely edged out Stanfield's Conservatives. The NDP received 17.7% of the vote—the second-best showing yet for the federal party. Saskatchewan led the way for the second time with 35.9% of the vote, and British Columbia came second with 35.0%, while the Yukon/Northwest Territories emerged in third place with 29.5%. Manitoba and Ontario, at 26.3% and 21.5% respectively, were the only other provinces in which the party received over 20% of the vote. While party support in Nova Scotia rose above 10% for the first time since 1945, the vote in all other provinces was below that level, and in elusive Quebec it continued to drop, this time to 6.4%.

The 31 New Democrats elected to Parliament set a record for the party in both number and percentage of seats (11.7%), even surpassing the CCF's best of 28 seats (11.4%) in 1945. The 1972 NDP caucus saw British Columbia and Ontario tied at 11 MPs apiece. Lewis, the party's first non-western leader, led a strong Ontario delegation that included, among others, Andrew Brewin, Ed Broadbent, Terry Grier, Derek Blackburn, and John Rodriguez. Among the 11 New Democrats elected from BC was Douglas, and among the 5 from Saskatchewan was Bill Knight, who would eventually become principal secretary to future leader Ed Broadbent and, later still, federal secretary of the NDP. Party stalwarts Stanley Knowles and David Orlikow provided two of the three Manitoba NDP seats. Finally, for the first time, the NDP had an elected representative from the Northwest Territories; the victory of native Wally Firth was the first in a series of electoral successes for the NDP in Canada's two territories—a tradition that continues into the 1990s under Yukon Premier Tony Penikett and NDP federal leader Audrey McLaughlin.

The result of the 1972 election was a Parliament in which Trudeau's minority government became dependent upon the support of the New Democratic Party—support that would be provided only if proposed Liberal legislation went some distance towards meeting the aspirations of the social-democratic NDP. It was, accordingly, a Parliament in which important social legislation would be introduced and approved, heightening the profile of David Lewis and his NDP caucus. But the arrangement was not without potential risks.

1974

In 1973 yet another war in the Middle East triggered an explosion in world oil prices, and in Canada spiralling costs for fuel contributed to the high inflation rate. As the price of its survival the Liberal minority government of Pierre Trudeau was forced to introduce measures consistent with the NDP's social-democratic agenda. Among the progressive measures that received attention were increases in pensions, a prices-review board, plans for a government-owned national oil company, a foreign-investment review agency (FIRA), election and party finance reforms, and the government's intention to purchase a major sector of the airplane manufacturing industry.[28] Who the public would credit for such reforms—whether a seemingly chastened minority government or a third-party balancer—remained to be seen.[29]

In 1974, the NDP nominated candidates in 99.2% (262/264) of the ridings; this was the last campaign in which the party did not run a full slate. In its official election pamphlet, entitled 'People matter more', the NDP focused on the cost of living as a key issue, and urged that the prices-review board have more powers; it also proposed a two-price system for key commodities and a ceiling on mortgage rates. With energy prices, a contributing cause of inflation, continuing to influence political discourse, the NDP reiterated its opposition to a continental energy deal, urging instead that Canada become self-sufficient in oil by the end of the decade. To achieve this, it proposed extending a major oil pipeline to Montreal and keeping Canadian oil prices below the world level. Reflecting its concern about the environment, the party called for an increase in research on renewable energy sources. Often a vanguard in recognizing aboriginal land claims and calls for native self-government, the NDP also favoured delay of the Mackenzie Valley pipeline to enable a proper assessment of the pipeline's impact upon native peoples.[30] Not surprisingly, however, Stanfield's proposal of 'wage and price controls' became the focus of the campaign, and NDP leader David Lewis spent considerable time attacking Stanfield even though he was only leader of the opposition, not the government.[31]

When the ballots were tabulated, the NDP vote dropped to 15.4%, its lowest rate in the last four election contests. In all of its key provincial strongholds (the four western provinces and Ontario), the party's vote declined. The strongest support for the NDP came in the Yukon/NWT, where the vote reached a historic high of 33.2%. Among the provinces, Saskatchewan led the way with 31.5% of the vote, and Manitoba was next with 23.5%. British Columbia, at 23.0%, dropped below 30% for the first time in the NDP era; this was even below the CCF average of 28%. Ontario at 19.1% fell below 20% for the first time in four elections, and of the remaining provinces, only Nova Scotia with 11.2% was over the 10% threshold. Curiously, though, New Brunswick, Newfoundland, and Quebec, while still below 10%, saw some increase in the NDP vote.

The NDP caucus had been virtually halved, falling from 31 seats to 16. Losses occurred in all four of the provinces where the party was usually strongest, but were most pronounced in BC, where the number of MPs plummeted from 11 to 2; only Tommy Douglas and Stu Leggatt remained. The decline in Ontario was less dramatic, going from 11 to 8, but among those defeated, to the shock of many, was party leader David Lewis. Nevertheless, for the first time in the history of the CCF-NDP, Ontario surpassed all the other provinces in caucus size; Ed Broadbent was re-elected, along with Andrew Brewin, Derek Blackburn, Arnold Peters, John Rodriguez, John Gilbert, Max Saltsman and Cyril Symes. In Saskatchewan, although the percentage of the vote going to the NDP was the highest of any province, the caucus was also cut, from 5 to 2; only Lorne Nystrom and Les Benjamin remained. The aging stalwarts Stanley Knowles and David Orlikow survived in Manitoba, as did Wally Firth in the Northwest Territories. Among the rare positive notes was the victory of clergyman Andy Hogan in Cape Breton, Nova Scotia—a mining area that historically had been a centre of party support dating back to the days of the CCF's Clarie Gillis. Overall, it was the smallest NDP caucus ever and a far cry from the glorious days of the preceding Parliament.

The defeat of David Lewis in York South marked the end of his all-too-brief career in the House of Commons. It also marked the final days of his short but dynamic tenure as federal NDP leader. Unlike Douglas, who had perhaps hung on too long to the leadership, Lewis bowed out swiftly. It was time for a new generation to lead Canada's social-democratic party. The stronger electoral showing in Ontario in 1974 would be a contributing factor in the choice of Ed Broadbent as the next federal NDP leader.

1979

In the five years from the time of the 1974 election, American president Richard Nixon had resigned, South Vietnam had fallen, and the Islamic fundamentalist revolution had triumphed in Iran. For social democrats in Western Europe there were important electoral losses in both Sweden and Britain, where Margaret Thatcher's election in 1979 marked the beginning of a decade of neo-conservatism. Despite the right-wing drift, the Three Mile Island nuclear accident was a catalyst to mounting concern about the environment. In Canada, the dramatic Quebec election of 1976 saw the separatist Parti Québécois come to power and proceed towards a referendum on sovereignty-association. Meanwhile, Trudeau had waited an uncommon five years to call an election, and both opposition parties had chosen new leaders: Joe Clark for the Conservatives, and Ed Broadbent for the NDP. The selection of Broadbent in 1975 marked the first time that the NDP had chosen a leader who was not from the older CCF generation. Organizationally, the NDP had experienced two key setbacks, with provincial election losses in British Columbia in 1975 and Manitoba in 1976. On the positive side, however, the Saskatchewan NDP had been re-elected in 1978, and in 1975 the Ontario NDP, under the leadership of Stephen Lewis, had formed the province's official opposition for only the third time since the birth of the CCF-NDP.

In the 1979 election the party ran a full slate of 282 candidates for the first time in the history of the federal CCF-NDP. This was an important milestone towards major-party status. Going into the campaign, the NDP benefitted from the election-finance reforms that it had helped to draft in the minority Parliament of 1972-74. Another boost was the *Toronto Star*'s endorsement of the NDP—a historic breakthrough in Canada's largest metropolis. In addition, the CLC launched a parallel canvass campaign among union members in the hope of improving upon labour's support for the NDP.[32] Also helpful was the free media exposure of the televised leaders' debate, the second in Canadian history. Whereas in the first, in 1968, the NDP had been relegated to minor-party status (the two major parties appeared first, then the two others joined them), this time all three parties were treated equally. It was yet another step forward for the NDP, and an especially important one in the TV era. To add to the good news, Broadbent was perceived to have done well in the debate. The campaign itself was more leader-oriented than usual for the NDP, with most of the party's ads showing Broadbent speaking directly to voters.[33]

The major election pamphlet was entitled 'New Democratic ideas for working on Canada's future'. Focusing on inflation and the cost of living, the NDP called for reinstatement of food subsidies, a roll-back on prices, and a ceiling on mortgage interest rates. To prevent the continued export of jobs, it proposed a national industrial strategy, and to ensure energy security, it advocated expanding the role of Petro Canada and cuts in exports of oil and gas. The NDP campaign literature also stressed the importance of tax reform, so that corporations would be required to return to paying their fair share of taxes. As a party closely identified with the birth of medicare, the NDP urged a halt in the decline in federal funds for the health-care system. In transportation, the NDP reiterated the western farmers' concern to maintain the Crow's Nest freight rates and called for cessation of all rail-line abandonments. Also expressing concern for less affluent groups such as natives and women, the election pamphlet concluded with a forceful condemnation of NATO and NORAD as 'costly' and 'worn out military alliances'.

The total NDP vote in 1979 went over 2 million for the first time, and at 17.9% equalled the highest previous percentage vote, received in 1965. Indeed, the party's vote rose in every province and territory except Quebec. Saskatchewan maintained the highest rate of support at 35.8%. Manitoba was next at 32.7%—the highest percentage yet for that province over the entire CCF-NDP era. The party's support in British Columbia, at 31.9%, was back to the normal range of over 30% (in 7 of 8 elections). Newfoundland, having witnessed several election increases for the party from a minuscule 1.2% in 1965 to 9.5% in 1974, now reached the astonishing level of 29.7%. The Yukon/NWT came next at 29.4%, followed by Ontario 21.1%. Nova Scotia at 18.7% and New Brunswick at 15.3% also represented record-high support, which raised speculation as to whether the party might finally achieve a breakthrough in the impoverished and alienated Atlantic region.[34] At the same time, the decline in the party's Quebec vote, to 5.1%, was a sobering reminder of the long road ahead in Canada's second most populous province.

For the first time in more than a decade and a half, a Conservative government was elected, albeit with a minority—and a smaller percentage of the vote than Trudeau's Liberals. Social Credit, dropping to 6 seats, was clearly on the road to oblivion federally, but temporarily retained its profile by propping up the shaky Clark government.

In terms of seats, the NDP rebounded from its near disastrous setback of 1974 to elect 26 MPs, the second largest number to date in the NDP era and third-best for the CCF-NDP. Although far from the 60 seats that Broadbent had aimed for, on the whole this was a solid start for his first campaign as federal leader. There were New Democrats from an unprecedented seven provinces/territories. British Columbia, recovering from the electoral disaster of 1972, led the way with 8 MPs, including newcomers Ian Waddell, Svend Robinson, Jim Fulton, Margaret Mitchell, Ray Skelly, and former Liberal Pauline Jewett. Ontario was next with 6—a decline for the second time in a row despite the leader's Ontario connections; joining the Broadbent-led Ontario caucus was Bob Rae, who would soon go on to provincial politics and eventually become Premier. Manitoba's 5 MPs included the usual duo of Knowles and Orlikow, along with newcomers Reverend Bill Blaikie (another minister in the social-gospel tradition), Rod Murphy, and Terry Sargeant. The four Saskatchewan MPs were Lorne Nystrom and Les Benjamin, and newcomers Father Bob Ogle and Simon de Jong. The three remaining MPs came from the periphery of the country: Andy Hogan from Nova Scotia, Peter Ittinuar from the NWT, and Fonse Faour, the first federal CCF-NDP member ever elected from Newfoundland.

The Conservative government of 1979 proved to be short-lived. Despite the fragility of his position, Clark falsely assumed that Canadians had given him a clear mandate. The government fell on an NDP non-confidence motion proposed by Rae, and in less than a year Canadians were in the midst of another federal election.

1980

In the short time between Canadian elections, the Sandinistas came to power in the Nicaraguan revolution, the US embassy in Tehran was overrun and its staff taken hostage by Islamic fundamentalists, and the Soviet Union invaded Afghanistan. In Canada, Trudeau announced his intention to step down as leader following his 1979 election loss. But after less than a year in power, the inexperienced and somewhat inept minority Conservative government was defeated on a non-confidence motion, and Trudeau was persuaded to lead the Liberals into the election.

Continuing the pattern established in 1979, the NDP ran a full slate of candidates, and once again it received a rare endorsement from a major daily newspaper—this time, surprisingly, Montreal's *Le Devoir*. The campaign was largely a rerun of 1979 (Morton, 1986: 198). Again the party leader was the focus, as exemplified in a pamphlet suggesting 'This time Ed Broadbent'. Broadbent's public approval rating as choice for Prime Minister had doubled from a year earlier, and among the leaders his ranking moved from third place to second, ahead of the apparently stumbling Clark (Gallup, 22 Sept. 1979 and 9 Jan. 1980). The 1980 election pamphlet was entitled 'A choice for Canadians', and once more inflation was the top issue. The NDP, like the public at large, was highly critical of the tough Conservative budget, favouring instead cuts in personal income taxes for lower- and middle-income Canadians. It accused corporations of not carrying their fair share of the tax burden and urged the introduction of a 'fair tax' system; this refrain would be heard through much of the Broadbent era. To deal with the ongoing economic crisis, the NDP proposed a mortgage assistance plan, called for a return to subsidies for bread and milk, and suggested the creation of a fair-prices commission. The second major issue of 1980 was energy. Critical of the 'artificial prices' set by multinational oil corporations and the OPEC cartel, and anxious to foster energy self-sufficiency for Canada, the NDP urged expansion of Petro-Canada and vehemently opposed the neo-conservative policy of privatization. Influenced by the example of Sweden, Broadbent called for a state-sponsored 'industrial strategy'. The pamphlet 'A choice for Canadians' also advocated a merger of CP Air and Air Canada and public ownership of the CPR. For the rural sector, the NDP promised legislation to prevent farm takeovers, while for the labour movement it suggested that unions should have the right to representation in Crown corporations. On the environmental front, it called for a moratorium on US oil tankers sailing down the Pacific coast and urged a review before constructing any more major airports such as the one at Mirabel. Reflecting the impending Quebec referendum on sovereignty-association, the party reiterated its support of the right of the people of Quebec to decide their future for themselves. On social matters, it promoted lowering pension eligibility to those 60 years of age, extending medicare to dental and optical services and drugs, and called upon the federal government to assume a greater share of health-care costs. Yet again, the NDP urged Canadian governments to recognize long-outstanding native land claims. Finally, in the controversial area of foreign affairs, the election pamphlet suggested the need to 'reconsider' Canada's commitment to NATO and NORAD.[35]

When the NDP vote was tallied, the total reached a new historic high of 19.8%—tantalizingly close to the elusive 20% landmark. Also encouraging was the fact that the NDP's percentage increased in all regions but Newfoundland. The highest level of support was in Saskatchewan, at 36.3% the best anywhere to that date in the NDP era. Almost as high were British Columbia at 35.3% and Manitoba at 33.5%, in both cases their highest percentages to that point. The Yukon/NWT, at 31.5%, also showed improvement over 1979, and marked the party's second-best performance north of the 60th parallel. Ontario, with 21.9%, achieved its highest level of support ever, and Nova Scotia at 20.9% also broke through the 20% barrier for the first time in the history of the federal party. Even in Newfoundland, the only province that saw a drop in the NDP vote, the rate of 16.7% was still the second-best ever, and a drop from the startling 1979 result was perhaps not surprising. New Brunswick, at 16.2%, saw a record federal social-democratic vote, and the three remaining provinces also managed to achieve increases over 1979: Alberta at 10.3%, Quebec at 9.1%, and Prince Edward Island at 6.1%.

In 1980 the Liberals achieved the majority of both votes and seats to produce a majority government, and in the process Trudeau's political career was resurrected. Social Credit, the NDP's chief rival as third party, finally slid into oblivion. Broadbent's second election campaign in two years saw the NDP again increase its seats, this time to a new high of 32 (11.3%). As has so often been the case, British Columbia led the way with a record 12 seats. Saskatchewan and Manitoba, tied with 7 apiece, both set provincial records for the NDP era. By contrast, Ontario's representation in caucus showed its third consecutive decline, from a peak of 11 in 1972 to 5 in 1980. The NDP's two outposts in Atlantic Canada (one in Nova Scotia and one in Newfoundland) were lost. In total, a whopping 84% (27/32) of the NDP's seats were now from the west. This situation—a largely western caucus under a leader from central Canada—was a recipe for tension in the caucus, particularly as regional strains buffeted both the party and Canada at large. Among the newcomers were Nelson Riis, Sid Parker, and Jim Manly from British Columbia, Doug Anguish, Vic Althouse, and Stan Hovdebo from Saskatchewan, Laverne Lewycky from Manitoba, and Ian Deans and Neil Young from Ontario.

As a result of Social Credit's failure to win any seats, the NDP became the sole 'new' party with representation in Parliament; this meant a higher profile for the NDP, and improved its chances of attaining major-party status. In hindsight, however, the 1980 Liberal election victory was only a temporary reprieve from the resurgent Conservatives. The Tories were to emerge with new vigour in 1984, when they would be led by a more polished, calculating, and ambitious leader.

1984

The first half of the 1980s brought electoral success to conservatives around the world, including Ronald Reagan in the United States and Helmut Kohl in West Germany. It also saw the Iran-Iraq war, the Falklands war, the Israeli invasion of Lebanon, the US invasion of Grenada, and Sikh-Hindu conflicts in India. In Canada, the federalist victory in the 1980 Quebec referendum had acted as the catalyst for Trudeau's attempt to reform the constitution by including a Canadian amending formula and an entrenched charter of rights.

By 1984 both the Conservatives and the Liberals had chosen new leaders. Thus the NDP's Broadbent would be the only veteran leader in the 1984 election. Nevertheless, the party went into the campaign with a sense of foreboding. The victory of Howard Pawley's NDP in Manitoba in 1981 was overshadowed by the crushing 1982 defeat of the NDP in the former socialist fortress of Saskatchewan. Organizationally, the NDP was still recovering from the intra-party frustrations, particularly on the part of western leaders Blakeney and Notley, over Broadbent's hasty endorsement of Trudeau's constitutional package earlier in the decade. The tensions climaxed at the 1983 federal NDP convention. What should have been a celebration of the fiftieth anniversary of the Regina Manifesto was a mixed affair. To add to the party's woes, James Laxer, former federal leadership candidate and now NDP research director, dropped a bombshell over the winter of 1983-84, when he first leaked to the press and then published a book characterizing the NDP's economic policies as seriously outdated (Laxer, 1984). Of even greater concern was the fact that national public-opinion polls in the spring preceding the fall election had found the federal NDP plummeting to a mere 11%. The party's own polling data had noted that the NDP was regarded as weak on managing economic issues, although it did much better on defending social programmes. Accordingly, the party's strategy emphasized the NDP's role in fostering social policies and defending 'ordinary Canadians', and in a number of ridings placed greater focus on its incumbent MPs than on the party label. Despite all the effort and energy spent on drafting the new Regina Manifesto of 1983 (see Chapter 3), this document was not given much publicity in the election campaign of 1984.[36]

Returning to a familiar theme from the early days of the CCF-NDP, Broadbent accused the old-line parties of being beholden to privileged corporate interests, calling their leaders, John Turner and Brian Mulroney, the 'Bobbsey twins of Bay Street'. The election pamphlet, entitled 'New opportunities for Canadians like you', suggested that the two former corporate lawyers were interchangeable, an image that Broadbent reinforced in his speeches by referring to the two as 'Brian Turner and John Mulroney'. In addition to the left populist message, the campaign emphasized the party's historic championing of the welfare state and its early and strong support for ending women's status as 'second-class citizens';[37] it also pointed out that only the NDP opposed Cruise missile testing and sought to turn Canada into a nuclear-free zone.[38]

By now TV debates had become the norm in Canadian politics. In 1984 there were three, one each in English and French and one special debate on women's issues. While Broadbent's performance in the debates was good—perhaps his best ever (Penniman, 1988: 175)—it was the exchange in English between Turner and Mulroney on the issue of patronage appointments that was the most memorable and, by the majority of accounts, the most influential. As a number of commentators have noted, it helped to produce the largest shift ever recorded in a federal campaign (Penniman, 1988: 161).

While running a full slate, the NDP saw its vote slip to 18.8%, down 1% from 1980; indeed, it dropped in every region of the country except Alberta and Saskatchewan. Nevertheless, 1984 still proved to be the party's second-best showing thus far in terms of votes. Saskatchewan, with 38.4%, saw its third straight increase. British Columbia, despite a slight dip in support, was next with 35.1%, and Manitoba came third with 27.2%, followed by the Yukon/NWT at 23.7%; Ontario, at 20.8%, was the only other province over 20%. Alberta, in its third straight increase, rose to 14.1%; this was a positive sign for the future in the province in which the CCF had been formed, but that had yet to yield a federal seat to the party. Nova Scotia and New Brunswick were the only other provinces over 10%, with 15.2% and 14.1% respectively. Quebec dropped to 8.8%, while PEI declined to 6.5% and Newfoundland to 5.8%.

The Conservatives led by Brian Mulroney won the most seats ever in Canadian history. The Liberal bastion in Quebec had been not only breached but vanquished. Amidst this Conservative onslaught, the NDP did far better than the CCF had in the 1958 Tory landslide. Instead of the mere 8 seats that the CCF claimed in 1958, the NDP won 30, a decline of only two from the previous election and far more than most had been predicting.[39] The third-highest total to date in the party's history, this alone would have been sufficient grounds for rejoicing. However, the collapse of the Liberals to their worst showing ever, in terms of both vote and seats, meant that the NDP's placement in the rankings had improved. Instead of running a distant third, the NDP was a mere 10 seats away from the decimated Liberal Party. Never before had the CCF-NDP been so close to second place.[40] Could this be the beginning of the end for the Liberals?

The composition of the 1984 NDP caucus was unusual in that Ontario led the pack, more than doubling its seats to 13 (the province's previous best was 11, in the historic 1972 election). British Columbia, while dropping 4 seats, was still a strong second with 8. Saskatchewan was next with 5, followed by Manitoba with 4. The west's combined total of NDP seats was still greater than that of the more populous centre and east, but was a far cry from the severe imbalance of 1980. Not surprisingly, the greatest number of changes in personnel occurred in Ontario. Broadbent, showing a better federal success rate than his predecessors Tommy Douglas and David Lewis, was re-elected. Former provincial NDP leader Mike Cassidy now joined former Ontario NDP leadership rival Ian Deans in the caucus, as did Steven Langdon and Howard McCurdy, both of whom would be future federal leadership candidates. The 1984 election also saw ardent feminist and non-smoking activist Lynn McDonald and radical clergyman Dan Heap build on their successes in earlier by-elections. By contrast, the western wing of the caucus consisted largely of veteran MPs such as Waddell, Riis, Robinson, Jewett, and Mitchell from BC, Nystrom and de Jong from Saskatchewan, and Orlikow, Blaikie, and Murphy from Manitoba.

Many party activists had felt that the 1984 election would be a key one for the NDP. Faced with declining support in the polls (as low as 11% prior to the election), on the eve of the election the party confronted the possibility of losing official status in the House of Commons. NDP federal secretary Gerry Caplan and pollster Vic Fingerhut were credited with major contributions to planning and directing the campaign strategy that saw the party's support in public opinion almost double to 19%. What made this particularly impressive was that it occurred in the face of a Tory victory of historic scale. Was this apparent turnaround a sign that support for the NDP would continue to grow? Or was it merely that traditional NDP-leaning voters were returning to the party after being temporarily mesmerized by media coverage of the Conservative and Liberal leadership conventions? As the contrasting interpretations had quite different implications, many in the party preferred the former, perhaps mistakenly.[41]

The 1984 election raised the hopes of many New Democrats that they might finally displace the dispirited Liberals. In 1988, at least, those hopes would be proved premature; that election will be explored in detail in Chapter 8 below.

NOTES

[1] Readers are advised to consult the following excellent reference books in this regard: Beck (1968); Carrigan (1968); Weinrich (1982). Unfortunately, none of these cover the post-1970 period. For both domestic and international background to the Canadian elections, see Myers (1986); Daniel (1987); Abbott (1990); and Grun (1975).

[2] In the majority of analyses of the CCF-NDP, the emphasis has been upon party manifestos (see Chapter 3). Unfortunately, coverage of election pamphlets has been far less common. While manifestos are extremely important in their attempt to formulate a comprehensive (i.e., ideological) world view, they are often directed at the more élite level of party activists who are riding members or convention delegates. Election pamphlets, however, are directed to the more sceptical, less sophisticated, mass public, and as such tend to be more eclectic, programme- and policy-oriented. Thus any comprehensive study of a political party should endeavour to analyse party manifestos and key election pamphlets. Whereas Chapter 3 focused on the former, this chapter will stress the latter.

[3] It should be noted that changes in the nature of Canadian society, the CCF-NDP, and election campaigns mean that this technique works better for some periods than others. For example, the emphasis on election pamphlets is more appropriate for the pre-television era of the 1930s than it is for the 1980s. On the importance of televised leaders' debates see Fletcher in Penniman (1988: 164) and Chapter 8 below.

[4] The 1933 party manifesto was expanded upon by the League For Social Reconstruction's epic *Social Planning For Canada*. See also the 1935 publication *Canada Through C.C.F. Glasses*.

[5] In Parliament, Woodsworth was the sole MP to vote against Canada's entry into the global conflict.

[6] Douglas had returned from Ottawa to become provincial CCF president in 1941; in 1942 he replaced George Williams as party leader, the latter having gone off to serve in the armed forces.

[7] By 1945, as in 1988, the party had already begun to slip in the polls by the time the federal campaign commenced. In both cases, the euphoria of initial high standings clouded strategists' perceptions of the party's more realistic prospects.

[8] The program included a national child-care system.

[9] The extensive involvement of big business in the anti-CCF campaign prefigured the corporate participation in the 1988 election. Even the language employed was remarkably similar: 'free enterprise' in 1945 and 'free trade' in 1988 (see also Chapter 8). In both cases, the corporate agenda proposed was a right-wing one, stressing less government involvement in the economy (Read and Whitehorn, 1991).

[10] In the midst of the Ontario election, CCF provincial leader Ted Jolliffe accused Conservative Premier George Drew of engaging in Gestapo-like spying activities upon his political opponents (Lewis, 1981; Caplan, 1973). Archival evidence proves that Jolliffe was correct in his charges (Lewis, 1981), but Drew's dishonest denials prevailed and the closing of the Premier's papers in the National Archives continues the cover-up to this day.

[11] The Warsaw Pact's creation in 1955 formalized the *de facto* division.

[12] This position indicates that the party was critical of foreign ownership twenty years before the Waffle Manifesto.

[13] Joe Noseworthy had won the seat earlier during the famous York South by-election of 1942, but it was a victory partially accomplished by the Liberals' decision not to run a candidate. Thus the CCF's success in the 1942 by-election was in reality a combined CCF/Liberal vote and not fully representative of actual CCF support.

14 Had the CCF repeated its 1949 seat count it would have been relegated to fourth place in 1953.

15 There were two versions of this document; one was a cartoon booklet and the other a more detailed pamphlet.

16 For a more detailed chronological account of the NDP era see Morton (1986); this volume is the latest update of his earlier books (1974, 1977).

17 This was a social-democratic equivalent of Marx's famous declaration.

18 This was in striking contrast to the NDP's 1988 election position of opposition to the US-Canada free-trade agreement.

19 Even the former CCF leader, would-be NDP leader, and now Liberal Hazen Argue went down to defeat.

20 One NDP pamphlet captured this theme by urging a vote for *Neither Diefenbaker nor Pearson.*

21 Interestingly, the NDP called for 'special status of Quebec as the guardian of French language, culture and tradition' and a 'guarantee to French-speaking minorities outside Quebec [of] the same linguistic rights that the English speaking minority enjoys in Quebec'. The parallel to some of the language employed in the Meech Lake Accord, more than two decades later, is striking.

22 This level was not surpassed until the 1988 federal election.

23 This change of leaders may have come none too soon. Prior to the PC leadership convention, the NDP had even managed to take second place from the Conservatives in one Gallup poll.

24 Other policy proposals by the NDP included expanding the medicare system, child care, national public auto insurance, increased availability of old age security payments, and the appointment of an ombudsman.

25 Ironically, one of the key chapters in Trudeau's book *Federalism and the French Canadians*, which helped propel him to success in the Liberal Party, was originally part of the NDP inspired-book *Social Purpose For Canada*, and depicts socialism and the CCF in relatively positive terms.

26 The vote was 190 for the measures and a mere 16 against. Public opinion was equally harsh, with polls suggesting that between 70% and 85% favoured the move (Saywell, 1970). The NDP decision, as had so often been the case, was based on philosophical principles rather than electoral considerations.

27 In addition, in 1972 Lewis and the NDP research staff published the book *Louder Voices: The Corporate Welfare Bums.*

28 NDP pamphlets from the period also claimed credit for income-tax cuts, subsidies on milk and bread, and delays in oil-price hikes.

29 The role of balancer is a tightrope act for the NDP. If a social-democratic party fails to achieve all of its agenda, it risks displeasing its own militants. If it concedes on too many issues, it becomes open to the 'Liberals in a hurry' charge. Among the electorate at large, there is often resentment that a smaller third party can set the agenda for larger parties; to many, this seems analogous to the tail wagging the dog, and is equally unacceptable.

30 Former BC NDP leader Tom Berger would distinguish himself in the role of Commissioner.

31 Some analysts believe that this focus on another opposition party merely drove some voters to the Liberals at the expense of the NDP. See, for example, Surich in Penniman (1981: 139) and Morton (1986: 187).

[32] In its union-oriented literature, the CLC employed the slogan 'The Perfect Union: Me and the NDP'.

[33] For an example, see Chapter 7.

[34] Curiously, the west, which also exhibits high levels of alienation, has shown a proclivity to vote for third parties while Atlantic Canada has generally retained traditional patterns of voting behaviour in its support for the Liberals and Conservatives.

[35] Broadbent's attempts at verbalizing a shift in the party's official position brought an angry rebuke from BC New Democrat Pauline Jewett.

[36] By contrast, in the 1935 federal campaign the 1933 manifesto was the centre-piece. The differences in emphases are no doubt in part due to the changed nature of the party (CCF vs. NDP), the contrast in style of party leaders (Woodsworth vs. Broadbent) and, perhaps most important, the shift in media (from print to television).

[37] The first woman elected to the House of Commons, in 1921, was Agnes MacPhail, a CCF pioneer.

[38] One 1984 NDP pamphlet referred to the party as the Nuclear *Disarmament Party*.

[39] The public-opinion polls in the spring of 1984 had placed the NDP at a precarious 11% and in danger of losing official status, which requires 12 seats in the House of Commons.

[40] In the two previous closest performances by the party, in 1949 and 1953, the CCF had come within 28 seats of the Conservatives. Note that neither of these two elections saw the highest number of CCF seats: that occurred in 1945.

[41] In an interview with the author conducted in Washington in 1988, Fingerhut continued to believe in the former interpretation.

FIVE

Party Conventions

INTRODUCTION

Beginning with a brief overview of the formal structure and responsibilities of NDP conventions and an outline of NDP leadership contests, this chapter uses survey data to focus on convention delegates themselves—their social backgrounds and attitudes towards various policy areas—and analyse how these findings relate to important areas of consensus and cleavage within the party. In addition, it offers an overall summary of the party's position on a number of key policy areas from 1971 to 1983;[1] while some differences between the NDP and the other two major parties will be noted, more on this topic can be found elsewhere.[2]

The systematic study of political conventions through the use of survey questionnaires is a relatively recent development.[3] Apart from the portion on leadership selection, the analysis here is based primarily on a survey questionnaire distributed by the author to all delegates at the 1983 federal NDP convention in Regina.[4] The survey sample is reasonably representative of the overall breakdown of convention delegates at large (see Table 5.1). Two other samples were used from earlier surveys conducted by George Perlin and associates among NDP convention delegates in 1979

Table 5.1 Convention and Survey Distribution of Delegates: 1983

	Full convention distribution %	Survey distribution %
From constituency associations	74.1	78.4
From affiliated union locals	12.4	7.2[a]
From Federal Council	7.1	5.0
From caucus	1.7	0.5
From central labour[b]	3.7	2.2
From Young New Democrats	1.0	2.0
Multiple response	—	3.7[a]

[a] Multiple responses almost always involved those delegates from affiliated union locals in Ontario. Apparently, many unionists have strong constituency orientations, as evidenced by their multiple responses to the question of how they became delegates at the convention. In part this is because they must be individual members of the party before they can be formal union delegates at NDP conventions.
[b] Head offices of specific affiliated unions and senior officials of the CLC.

and 1971. Together, these three surveys provide comprehensive data on the attitudes of party activists between 1971 and 1983.

THE NDP AS A 'MASS PARTY'

The New Democratic Party has its roots in the Depression of the 1930s, when a federation of farmers, labourers, and socialists came together to found the Co-operative Commonwealth Federation in Calgary on 1 August 1932. Twenty-nine years later, on 4 August 1961, the New Democratic Party, a fusion of CCFers, unionists and the 'liberally minded', was born in Ottawa.

In Maurice Duverger's classification (1963), the NDP is an example of the 'branch' type of mass party. It relies on a large dues-paying membership base to provide organizational clout in the political arena. In contrast to the Liberal and Conservative parties, it includes two types of members: those who have joined as individuals and those who belong to affiliated organizations. In the former category are members who have joined riding associations, campus clubs, and recognized socialist study groups, and who pay dues directly to the party. In the latter category are individuals who belong to trade unions affiliated to the NDP. Each person pays dues to the organization, which collectively has decided to affiliate with the NDP, and in turn this organization collectively forwards a certain monthly sum to the party. In 1987 there were 146,121 individual party members and 276,128 affiliated members (see Tables 1.4 and 1.5).

Its historic ties to the farm, labour, and socialist movements clearly mark the CCF-NDP as a newer type of party with strong extra-parliamentary roots and involvements. While conventional electoral politics is an important aspect of NDP activity, this is by no means the sole area of activity. For example, branch parties such as the CCF-NDP emphasize education—both of members and of the public at large—and various forms of agitation. As noted in Chapters 3 and 4, party manifestos and pamphlets abound.

As members of a mass party, NDP delegates also exhibit characteristics that differ dramatically from those evident in cadre-type parties (Duverger, 1963) such as the Liberals and Conservatives. For example, 98.0% of NDP delegates surveyed at the 1983 federal convention indicated that they had signed petitions, and 81.2% had participated in a protest march. Just under half (44.6%) had been involved in a strike,[5] and more than a fifth (21.1%) reported having engaged in a sit-in demonstration. Clearly, the NDP's extra-parliamentary involvement persists to this day.

NDP CONVENTIONS: FREQUENCY, SIZE, AND COMPOSITION

In the first few years of the CCF, despite the obstacles of slower travel and fewer funds, federal conventions were annual assemblies; since 1936 they have been held every other year.[6] The early conventions were small, intimate affairs; for example, the founding convention of 1932 attracted only 131 people, and even in the 1940s and early 1950s, delegate attendance remained in the 100 to 200 range (Engelmann, 1954). For the 1983 NDP policy convention, by contrast, 1,433 delegates gathered out of 3,000 eligible. Leadership conventions are usually even larger, involving over 1,600 voting delegates in 1971 and 1975 and over 2,400 in 1989. In half a century, CCF-NDP conventions have undergone a more than ten-fold increase.[7] What impact has the change in size had? More people, and perhaps a greater variety, now participate. However, it is also possible that decision-making has shifted away from conventions as they have become larger; certainly the type and amount of decision-making can be affected significantly by such changes (Dahl and Tufte, 1973). The increased media coverage, particularly via television, has also affected the way conventions operate, not to mention the cost of holding such meetings.

Convention delegates are selected by a number of means, of which the two most common are election by the constituency association (based on one delegate per 50-100 individual members) and selection by union local (based on one delegate per 1,000-1,500 affiliated union members).[8] While the majority of delegates are elected by their riding associations, a significant minority (ranging from a low of 16.1% in 1983 to a high of 31.2% in 1971) come from affiliated organizations (i.e., both union locals and central labour bodies).[9] A still smaller number are *ex-officio* delegates, such as members of Parliament or members of the federal council (the latter includes members of the party executive and table officers).

While most of the delegates indicated that they had previously attended either a federal or provincial NDP convention (80.3% in 1983), there was still a significant number who had not (19.7%).[10] The average number of federal or provincial conventions previously attended was six ($\bar{x} = 6.1$) (see Table 5.2); thus the delegates seem to have been relatively experienced.

Party membership data also suggest substantial continuity and background experience, with 53.2% of the delegates having been party members for 6 to 20 years ($\bar{x} = 14.4$) (see Table 5.3). Many delegates also held executive posts in party riding associations; for example, 38.3% were on federal riding executives, and 50.4% on provincial riding executives.[11]

Table 5.2 Conventions Previously Attended: 1983		Table 5.3 Years As a Member of the NDP: 1983	
Number	%	Number	%
0/no response	23.8	1	2.8
1	13.0	2	2.5
2	10.8	3	6.0
3	10.1	4	6.5
4	7.6	5	5.5
5	5.7	6-10	26.7
6-10	18.3	11-20	26.5
11-20	8.1	21-30	14.6
21+	3.3	31-40	6.9
		40+	2.9
N=407	$\bar{x}$=6.1		
		N=399	$\bar{x}$=14.4

While the most recent survey samples indicate that a growing proportion of delegates are women (see Table 5.4), men still predominate by about a two-to-one ratio (see also Bashevkin, 1985: 64, 163; Archer, 1991).

Conventions have usually attracted a disproportionate number of delegates in their thirties (see Table 5.5). What is perhaps most surprising about these data is how few people under 21 (e.g., only 4.9% in 1983) were in attendance, considering that the party prides itself on being 'new', 'progressive', and in tune with youth's problems.[12] More recent Conservative and Liberal leadership conventions have attracted a far larger percentage of young delegates.[13] How much of this can be explained by young people's enthusiasm for leadership campaigns, party encouragement and subsidization of youth involvement,[14] or the relevance of the agenda to today's youth is uncertain.

In terms of convention location, the CCF-NDP has had a decidedly western tilt, with 11 of 16 CCF federal conventions and, to 1991, 8 of 16 NDP conventions being held in the west. Reflecting the growth in importance

Table 5.4 Gender Distribution of Delegates: 1983, 1979, and 1971

	1983 %	1979 %	1971 %
Male	69.1	74.4	73.9
Female	30.9	25.6	26.1
N=	395	519	747

Table 5.5 Age Distribution of Delegates: 1983 and 1979[a]

Age	1983 %	1979 %
-21	4.9	3.3
22-29	12.5	18.5
30-39	31.7	29.2
40-49	14.7	18.3
50-59	16.7	16.7
60+	19.4	13.1
N=	407	520

[a] 1971 data not available to author.

of Ontario as a party base, 3 of the CCF and 6 of the NDP conventions have been held there. In contrast, Atlantic Canada had never been selected as a site for a federal CCF-NDP convention until 1991; this has perhaps been a factor in the party's poor electoral record in that region, and is certainly another example of the political alienation of the Maritimes. Similarly, Quebec, accounting for almost one-quarter of Canada's population, has been chosen only three times (twice in the CCF era and, remarkably, only once in the NDP period). This is hardly a pattern likely to entice Quebeckers to show more interest and involvement in the party; however, given the organizational weakness and, at times, disarray of the Quebec CCF-NDP (Sherwood, 1966), it is perhaps understandable.

As to delegate composition, NDP conventions, not surprisingly, are regionally skewed—in substantial contrast to Liberal and Conservative conventions. The largest percentage of NDP delegates came from Ontario[15] (see Table 5.6), the second highest from Saskatchewan, and the third highest from British Columbia; very few delegates came from Quebec and the Atlantic region. Clearly the NDP, like the CCF before it, still retains a distinctive western emphasis; territory east of the Ottawa River still remains largely untapped.[16]

Table 5.6 Regional Distribution of Delegates: 1983, 1979, and 1971

	1983 %	1979 %	1971 %
British Columbia	21.4	13.9	11.7
Alberta	10.4	2.7	2.8
Saskatchewan	24.1	14.3	13.3
Manitoba	9.5	5.2	7.8
Ontario	30.3	56.3	54.4
Quebec	0.7	2.5	5.1
New Brunswick	0.7	0.4	1.6
Nova Scotia	1.2	2.9	1.7
Newfoundland	0.2	0.4	1.5
Prince Edward Island	0	0	0
Yukon/Northwest Territories	1.2	1.4	0.1
N=	402	517	758
Location	Regina	Toronto	Ottawa

Table 5.7 Primary Language Spoken by Delegates: 1983 and 1971[a]

	1983 %	1971 %
English[b]	96.8	91.2
French	1.7	6.4
Both	0.9	—
Other	0.5	2.4
N=	403	764

[a] 1979 data not available to author.
[b] includes those who speak both English and another language, other than French.

It is clear from both election results (the federal CCF-NDP has never elected a member from Quebec in a general election) and the preponderance of Anglophone delegates (see Table 5.7) that the NDP has not drawn adequately from one of the two main linguistic groups in Canada.[17] Nevertheless, in the 1986-88 pre-election period, public-opinion polls showed the NDP to be competitive in voter preference among Quebeckers, and for a short period in 1987 the party even led in both the national and Quebec polls. In the same year the party gained its first Quebec MP ever, when Robert Toupin, elected in 1984 as a Tory, defected, albeit briefly, to the NDP; however, he soon departed from the NDP ranks, and by 1988 the party's popularity had dipped from the 1987 levels. The NDP once more landed in third place in the 1988 federal election and with no NDP Quebec MPs. Despite the 1990 by-election victory of Phil Edmonston in Chambly, the prospects for the NDP in Quebec once more seem dim.

Any discussion of the NDP will at some point require analysis of the class background of party members, delegates, and leaders (Michels, 1962). Relatively few delegates classified themselves as coming from either upper or upper-middle class backgrounds (see Table 5.8); by far the most common responses were working and middle class. What is worth noting is that over the three time periods surveyed, the working-class identifications declined, while middle-class numbers rose. Although the demographics in Canadian society at large are also shifting,[18] there is consistent evidence to suggest that the NDP's conventions now may have less of a working-class base than in the past. These data fuel allegations by left-wing critics that the party has forsaken its primary audience, the proletariat, and shifted allegiance to the middle class. While this allegation is not easily answered by one indicator, particularly a subjective one, it is also useful to contrast the NDP data with possible measures of the class profile of recent Conservative and Liberal conventions. Comparative measures of delegates' family income reveal that Liberal and Conservative conventions are more heavily skewed to the upper strata. For example, the percentages with family incomes over $50,000 in 1983 were 14.3% for the NDP, 26.1% for the Liberals, and 42.2% for the Conservatives.[19] Clearly, important socioeconomic differences still remain between the activists of the three parties.

Table 5.8 Subjective Social Class of Delegates: 1983, 1979, and 1971

Subjective Social Class	1983 %	1979 %	1971 %
Upper	0.5	1.6	1.2
Upper middle	11.1	13.5	12.8
Middle	45.1	38.3	29.7
Lower middle	14.2	13.7	18.8
Working	27.7	31.7	35.8
Lower	1.3	1.2	1.6
N=	386	496	734

The most common occupations listed by NDP delegates were skilled white-collar (14.6%), retired (11.4%), educator (10.6%), professional (10.6%), skilled blue-collar (10.1%), union administrator/official (7.9%), student (7.2%), homemaker (5.4%), and unskilled labour (3.9%) (see Table 5.9). The high cumulative percentage of the skilled white-collar, educator, professional, and union administrator/official categories (43.7%) reinforces the middle-class profile of NDP convention delegates.[20]

Table 5.9 Occupational Distribution of Delegates: 1983

Occupation	%
Professional	10.6
Owner or senior executive	0.5
Manager	3.5
Educator (teacher/librarian)	10.6
Small proprietor	3.0
Sales/clerical	3.5
Skilled white collar	14.6
Farmer	5.9
Skilled blue collar	10.1
Unskilled labour	4.0
Student	7.2
Homemaker	5.4
Retired	11.4
Unemployed	1.7
Union administrator/official	7.9
N=	404

It is clear from the survey data that a very high percentage (68.3% in 1983) of delegates have had at least some university or college education (see Table 5.10). This again suggests that more delegates are recruited from the articulate 'haves' in the country than from the least skilled and educated strata. No doubt convention registration fees of $175 in 1983 ($300 by 1991) are a contributing factor.

Table 5.10 Educational Level of Delegates: 1983

Education Level	%
Less than grade 12	17.1
Grade 12/13	14.4
Some or complete college/university	68.3
N=	401

Comparing data on the size of community in which delegates live is complicated by the fact that the conventions were held in different regions of the country, and that the 1971 survey employed two categories different from those used in 1979 and 1983. Nevertheless, some observations can be made (see Table 5.11). In general, the rural/urban profile seems reasonably consistent over time, with the majority of delegates coming from medium

Table 5.11 Size of Community in Which Delegates Live: 1983, 1979, and 1971

Size of Community	1983 %	1979 %	1971 %
Farm	8.4	6.3	4.9
Rural (under 1,000)	4.9	5.1	8.5
Town (1,0000-9,999)	12.8	7.4	7.6
Small city (10,000-99,999)	20.4	20.9	22.2
Medium city (100,000-499,999)	20.9	30.9	
			56.9[a]
Metropolis (500,000+)	32.7	29.5	
N=	407	512	740

[a] 100,000+ persons.

to large cities. The relatively low percentage of those from farms or rural locations indicates yet again that, unlike its predecessor, especially in the early years, the NDP today is to a very significant degree not a rural-based populist party.[21]

POWERS AND RESPONSIBILITIES OF NDP CONVENTIONS

In the history of the CCF-NDP, conventions have had a long and prominent role. As one would expect with a mass party, all the leaders (J.S. Woodsworth, M.J. Coldwell, Hazen Argue, T.C. Douglas, David Lewis, Ed Broadbent, and, most recently, Audrey McLaughlin) have been chosen at conventions.[22] All of the most important party manifestos (Calgary 1932, Regina 1933, Winnipeg 1956, New Party Declaration 1961, and New Regina 1983)[23] have also been ratified at conventions.

In addition, as an ideologically-based socialist party, the CCF-NDP puts great emphasis upon the passage of policy resolutions,[24] almost to the point of fetishism. In recent years these have been sufficient to fill entire books (Scotton, 1977; BC NDP, 1979; Manitoba NDP, 1979; Ontario NDP, 1983; New Democrats, 1986). No matter how many resolutions are passed, their numbers, and length,[25] continue to increase: at the 1983 convention 500 resolutions were submitted, though only 41 got to the convention floor.[26]

Over time, the role of the federal council has grown to include dealing with resolutions either not yet attended to or forwarded by the convention. The twice-yearly council meeting, composed in recent years of about 150 leading party representatives and now swelled to 200 with the inclusion of representatives from the councils of federal ridings, has become a mini-convention of its own. Indeed, NDP council meetings have come to resemble the first CCF conventions in the 1930s in size, intimacy, and scope for extended articulate debate.

LEADERSHIP SELECTION

The NDP has always invested its conventions with the powers of leadership review and selection.[27] In theory, each federal NDP convention tests the mandate of the leader, who in principle is elected for only two years and thus needs to renew her/his term at each subsequent convention, should she/he choose to run again. While the specific details for nomination have varied over the years, the general principle has remained unchanged. Any party member can run for the leadership of the party simply by gaining the required number of signatures of NDP convention delegates. As of 1989, a would-be candidate needs to acquire the signatures of 50 delegates from at least eight different ridings or affiliated organizations.[28] If two candidates are so nominated, a leadership contest ensues; if no rival is nominated, the incumbent leader wins by acclamation.

In practice, few meaningful leadership contests have emerged in the history of the federal CCF-NDP. Several explanations for this may be suggested. As the newest and smallest of the three major parties, representing the less affluent in Canadian society, the NDP has less money to spend on expensive leadership conventions. Adding to its financial woes by unnecessarily initiating a token leadership contest is not something sought by the membership.

Another reason for avoiding unnecessary challenges to the leader is simply that the NDP, like the CCF before it, is a socialist party operating in a society that is on the whole pro-capitalist: with so many external obstacles to overcome, it is felt that a socialist movement can ill afford to bicker with its leader,[29] and party unity is seen as necessary for the good of the socialist cause. Even self-described left-wing ginger groups within the NDP, though often disgruntled by the leadership's policies, may accept a number of the arguments against calling for leadership contests. In addition, it is often perceived that, as a sub-group in the party, the left fares better lobbying on policy resolutions or for less visible executive posts than seeking an all-out battle for the leadership—a contest that such forces are most likely to lose anyway.

Another plausible explanation is that, as an ideologically based party, the NDP is more concerned with policy debate and formulation than leadership selection, although the two processes need not be separate—as shown in the 1971 leadership contest in which David Lewis was selected.

Nor should Michels's iron law of oligarchy be overlooked as a possible explanation for the relative infrequency of NDP leadership contests. Michels suggested that despite democratic mechanisms, a leader still dominates the party structure. With greater access to party funds, staff, information, and media exposure, a leader is usually able to combine these resources into a strong base from which to challenge any would-be rivals. This is often enough to deter rivals from even entering the fray.

The very nature of the NDP's leadership review process tends to discourage challenges to the leadership. Delegates do not vote on their evaluation of the leader's performance in itself; they vote only if someone else is willing and able to run in a contest. Unless dissatisfaction is sufficiently high for a rival candidate to emerge, therefore, no real mechanism for measuring support for the leader exists. Without a two-step process of voting against a leader and then holding a leadership convention, there is little likelihood of mere negative voting against an incumbent without much thought as to the successor. The argument in support of the NDP's arrangement is that criticism without a viable alternative candidate is both unfruitful and susceptible to erratic shifts. In recent years, there has been growing discussion and speculation about the possibility and feasibility of shifting leadership selection from a convention of several thousand delegates to a direct ballot of all party members (Woolstencroft, 1991; Latouche, 1991; Carty et al., 1991). In the case of the NDP, which includes both individual and affiliated members, such a process could involve some 400,000 persons. Although the 1989 leadership convention passed a resolution to study the constitutional and procedural reforms necessary to alter the method of selection of the federal party leader (Hayward and Whitehorn, 1991),[30] the issue did not appear urgent two years later at the 1991 convention, when NDP delegates seemed more concerned with policy matters such as the constitution and free trade.

The CCF-NDP has had only seven leaders: Woodsworth (1932-42); Coldwell (1942-60); Argue (1960-61); Douglas (1961-71); Lewis (1971-75); Broadbent (1975-89), and McLaughlin (from 1989 to the present). In the same period, the Liberals have had six leaders and the Conservatives nine. The CCF-NDP has not shown a significantly greater penchant for changing its leaders (Courtney, 1973). Again, this appears to confirm Michels's observation at the turn of the century regarding the strong oligarchic tendencies in socialist parties.[31] Reflecting this tendency is the fact that the first three CCF leaders were elected unanimously by convention. Only in the NDP era has the leadership contest become in practice a significant phenomenon (see Table 5.12a and b).

Despite the party's working-class base, its leadership has come from a decidedly white-collar and professional background.[32] Of the seven leaders, two were originally clergymen, two were teachers, one was a lawyer, one was a social worker, and only one was a farmer (albeit a university graduate); it seems there was nary a proletarian in the lot. By the time each was chosen party leader, each was a successfully elected politician. Six were members of Parliament and one, T.C. Douglas, was a provincial premier.

Table 5.12a Ballot Results of NDP Leadership Contests[a]

1961	first ballot			
Tommy Douglas	1,391			
Hazen Argue	380			
TOTAL	1,771			

1971	first ballot	second	third	fourth
David Lewis	661	715	742	1,046
Jim Laxer	378	407	508	612
John Harney	299	347	431	—
Ed Broadbent	236	223	—	—
Frank Howard	124	—	—	—
TOTAL	1,698	1,692	1,681	1,658

1975	first ballot	second	third	fourth
Ed Broadbent	536	586	694	948
Rosemary Brown	413	397	494	658
Lorne Nystrom	345	342	413	—
John Harney	313	299	—	—
Douglas Campbell	11	—	—	—
TOTAL	1,618	1,624	1,601	1,606

1989	first ballot	second	third	fourth
Audrey McLaughlin	646	829	1,072	1,316
Dave Barrett	566	780	947	1,072
Steven Langdon	351	519	393	—
Simon de Jong	315	289	—	—
Howard McCurdy	256	—	—	—
Ian Waddell	213	—	—	—
Roger Lagasse	53	—	—	—
TOTAL	2,400	2,417	2,412	2,388

[a] No CCF convention had a contested leadership election.

Their average age on election as leader was 51.3. John Courtney's (1973: 178) remarks are equally applicable to more recent leaders:

> No political dilettanti these: each was the heir apparent. The social-ist party, the party most willing to experiment with leadership review and leadership accountability, the party claiming more openness and internal democracy than other parties, has been the one Canadian

Table 5.12b CCF-NDP Leadership Selection

Leader	Began as Leader	Age	Original profession	Region[a]	Number of candidates
J.S. Woodsworth[b]	1932	58	Minister	W	—
M.J. Coldwell[b]	1942	53	Teacher	W	—
Hazen Argue	1960	39	Farmer	W	—
T.C. Douglas[b]	1961	56	Minister	W	2
David Lewis	1971	61	Lawyer	E	4
Ed Broadbent	1975	39	Professor	E	4
Audrey McLaughlin	1989	53	Social worker	W(NW)	7

Leader	Number of ballots	Vote on first	Vote on final	Duration	Retirement age
J.S. Woodsworth[b]	—	—	—	10	68
M.J. Coldwell[b]	—	—	—	18	71
Hazen Argue	—	—	—	1	40
T.C. Douglas[b]	1	78.5	78.5	10	66
David Lewis	4	38.9	63.1	4	66
Ed Broadbent	4	33.1	59.0	14	53
Audrey McLaughlin	4	26.9	55.1	2+	—

[a] Indicates region (west, east, northwest).
[b] Experienced periods when House leader was not national party leader.

party since the introduction of leadership conventions to have selected as its leaders . . . [persons] who have followed the more traditional, the more hierarchical career pattern to the party's highest position. CCF and NDP leadership conventions have had the effect of altering only the way in which the . . . [persons] with extensive political experience are chosen as leaders, not the fact.

The average retirement age of the leaders is 60.7 years. Coldwell retired as leader in his 71st year,[33] Woodsworth in his 68th, Douglas in his 66th, Lewis in his 66th, and the deposed Argue in his 40th. Broadbent was 53 when he stepped down in 1989. Of the six leadership changes, at least two were health-related (Woodsworth and Coldwell) and two were due in part to age (Douglas and Lewis). In the three latter cases, the leader had also lost his seat in the House of Commons; given the paucity of safe CCF-NDP seats, such losses should not be underestimated as a factor in the leader's stepping down. Hazen Argue was the only leader who was, in a sense, challenged and subsequently defeated; technically, however, he was never challenged because he had been leader of another party — the CCF. Argue was one of the handful of caucus members who had survived in the 1958 election. Elected to lead the CCF only in its twilight year of 1960, during its transformation into the NDP, he was the youngest leader of the old party and was perhaps too young and politically immature to have been selected the first leader of the new party. The first-ballot landslide for T.C. Douglas at the NDP's founding convention suggests that the delegates felt as much.

All three federal CCF leaders were from the west, as was the NDP's first leader. In contrast, the next two leaders (Lewis and Broadbent) came from Ontario. This has helped to fuel accusations by some that the western farmer-based socialist CCF has been transformed over the years into a more eastern, labour-oriented and pragmatic party (Whitehorn, 1985a: 6; and Chapter 2 of this book). Certainly the more pragmatic emphasis can usually be seen in the outcome of the four leadership contests. The two final-ballot candidates have tended to be seen as representing the 'left' and 'right' of the party, and usually it has been the so-called 'right' candidate who has won (e.g., Douglas over Argue, Lewis over Laxer, Broadbent over Brown [R. Brown, 1989]).[34] In regional terms, the two final candidates in the 1961 contest were westerners; in 1971 they were easterners; and in 1975 an easterner and a westerner, with the easterner successful. The 1989 leadership contest pitted two westerners or, to be more precise, one westerner and one north-westerner, against each other, with the candidate from the sparsely populated Yukon victorious.

Although the number of leadership changes and contests form a very small base on which to generalize, several observations can nevertheless be made. The number of candidates (from one in 1933 to seven in 1989), and thus the competitiveness, has been increasing (Hayward and Whitehorn, 1991). Correspondingly, the percentage vote for the eventual winner on the first and final ballots has been declining. Some have speculated that this trend may also show increasing dissatisfaction with the final leadership choice. With more candidates in recent contests, the number of ballots required for victory has been four. Nevertheless, in all four NDP leadership contests, those individuals leading on the first ballot won and the final margin of victory was sufficient for a clear-cut decision.

In contrast to earlier NDP leadership conventions, which were largely dominated by white males, the past two contests (1975 and 1989) have included female and black candidates. In 1989, a woman finally won the federal leadership of a major national party in Canada. Audrey McLaughlin's victory made history and marked one further step in the long overdue shift in political power.

Having briefly analysed the leadership selection aspect of the convention decision-making process, we will now turn to another side of the democratic process: policy debate.

IDEOLOGICAL COMPOSITION OF NDP CONVENTIONS

Any large party is an aggregation of diverse interests. Often the differences within a party are as significant as those between parties.[35] Of the considerable attention that has been devoted to the CCF-NDP, much has focused upon ideological differences and policy debates within the party. The NDP is now, as was the CCF, a blend of different colours of the political rainbow (see Table 5.13). Whereas previously a plurality (45.7% in 1971) of party

Table 5.13 Ideological Self-Description: 1983, 1979, and 1971

Description	1983 %	1979 %	1971 %
Social democrat	44.6	52.9	40.6
Socialist	29.6	38.9	45.7
Reformer	4.3	2.4	3.4
Social gospel	3.5	—	—
Marxist	3.0	—	—
Liberal	1.5	0.6	0.9
Ecologist	1.3	—	—
Populist	1.0	—	—
Progressive	—	0.6	0.8
Multiple response[a]	8.9	—	—
Other	2.3	4.6	7.1
No response	—	—	1.5
	100.0	100.0	100.0
N=	395	501	776

— category not available
[a] employed more than one category

members saw themselves as 'socialists', in more recent years decreasing numbers have opted for this label (38.9% in 1979 and 29.6% in 1983). Instead, a plurality have selected the label 'social democrat' as their preferred self-description (44.6% in 1983, 52.9% in 1979 and 40.6% in 1971).[36] To some scholars, these data indicate a growing de-radicalization of the party and a significant shift away from socialist programmes (Brodie, 1985; Hackett, 1979; 1980) such as nationalization. While a case can be made for this position, there is also evidence to suggest the opposite. For example, an overwhelming majority (76%) of the 1983 delegates reported that they saw the NDP as a socialist party. Certainly opponents in the Conservative and Liberal parties, not to mention the National Citizens Coalition, reiterate this assertion. These findings, coupled with the fact that a third of the respondents indicated that they themselves are socialists or Marxists, suggest it would be premature to dismiss the party, as some have done, as merely 'liberals in a hurry'[37] or 'populists' (Richards, 1983, 1988).

The history of socialist parties is often filled with ideological schisms, purges, and defections. The CCF-NDP is no exception. From the CCF's founding in 1932 to the present day, there has always been a 'ginger group' endeavouring to guide the party into a more radical or even revolutionary path (e.g., the Socialist Party of Canada, the Waffle and the Left Caucus). Policy debates, votes on resolutions, and leadership contests are often interpreted in 'left vs. right' terms by participants and scholars alike. Convention delegates continued to believe that there was a 'significant'/'big' difference (68.3% in 1983) between the left and right factions within the NDP. To what degree such extensive and often prolonged disagreements have hampered the party's growth in the past is not easily determined. Certainly, many party members have asserted that the rhetoric of the minority at conventions has weakened efforts to woo potential new supporters into the party. Whatever the impact in the past, there seemed to be little support (only 11.8% in 1983) within the party rank and file for expelling 'ultra-left elements'.

It is conventional wisdom within the NDP that most members feel they are politically to the left of the party. Data from both the 1983 (see Tables 5.14 and 5.15) and 1979 surveys document such positioning. While the NDP was placed left of centre on the political spectrum ($\bar{x}$ = 3.4 on a 7-point left-right scale), NDP convention delegates placed themselves even further to the left ($\bar{x}$ = 2.8 on a 7-point scale). Does this suggest a widespread desire among delegates to see the party shift to the more left-wing position for which many radicals have called? Data from the 1983 survey indicate that a majority of delegates wished to see the party 'move more clearly to the left' (55.6%) and not 'present a more moderate image to the general public' (76.8%). The more recent 1983 data, however, show some variance from earlier related questions on this topic,[38] and suggest that there may have been a shift towards greater articulation of left-wing ideas in recent years.

CONVENTIONS AND INTRA-PARTY DEMOCRACY

Most NDP members pride themselves on belonging to a party quite different from the two older and more successful federal parties. These New Democrats believe that theirs is a more open and democratic party. Data from the 1983 survey found that a majority of delegates (55.7%) agreed with the statement that 'NDP conventions are extremely democratic'.In addition, 83.0% of the 1979 respondents indicated that they felt they were 'effective in influencing Party policy'. Yet in 1983 a significant minority

Table 5.14 Placement of NDP on Left-Right Scale: 1983

Left							Right
	1	2	3	4	5	6	7
	0.8%	15.5%	48.5%	21.4%	9.0%	4.1%	0.8%
N=388				$\bar{x}$=3.4			

Table 5.15 Placement of Self on Left-Right Scale: 1983

Left							Right
	1	2	3	4	5	6	7
	8.2%	38.7%	32.5%	13.1%	5.2%	1.5%	0.8%
N=388				$\bar{x}$=2.8			

(29.7%) did not believe that NDP conventions were 'extremely democratic', and even in 1979 nearly half (46.7%) of the delegates felt there was not enough 'rank and file participation in party decisions'.

Data are available from the 1983 and 1979 surveys on perception of the party leadership's responsiveness to 'ordinary members'; in both cases, Broadbent was the leader. In 1979 only a small percentage (17%) felt the leader was 'cut off too much from the opinions of ordinary party members'. Four years later, with the party at only 16% in the Gallup polls and still straining from both intra-party differences over the 1981 constitutional amendments and the proposed new Regina manifesto, almost half the delegates (48.7%) believed 'the NDP leadership does not pay sufficient attention to ordinary party members'.[39] On the other hand, although some have criticized the party leaders for relying too much on pollsters and technical advisers, almost three-quarters of the delegates in 1979 did not agree with this suggestion.

No discussion of intra-party decision-making, influence levels, and group lobbying within the NDP would be complete without some analysis of the role of labour in general and unions specifically. At the highly polarized Lewis versus Laxer leadership convention in 1971, almost two-thirds (63.3%) of the delegates responded that unions have too much influence within the NDP. By contrast, at the 1983 convention,[40] the overwhelming majority (67.0%) indicated that they did not believe trade unions have wielded too much power. Indeed, by an almost two-to-one ratio, convention delegates called for 'closer ties between trade unions and the NDP'.

Less systematic data are available for other groups within the NDP. Over the years, as farmers have declined as a percentage of the workforce, they have also declined in importance within the CCF-NDP. Indeed, the shift to a more urban-based labour party had begun even in the CCF years (Whitehorn, 1985b: 194-5, and Chapter 1 above),[41] and a driving force in the creation of the NDP was the desire to establish better links with the trade-union movement. Nevertheless, a majority of delegates (54.3%) at the 1971 convention called for farmers to have 'more say in determining the policy of the NDP'.

The attitudes of NDP members towards labour's influence in society can be contrasted with those of the Canadian public at large. Numerous studies have reported that the general public is more apprehensive about the power/influence of 'Big Labour' (e.g., 33% in 1968 and 30% in 1987) than of 'Big Business' (17% in 1968 and 15% in 1987).[42] Not surprisingly, NDP delegates do not echo the general public's view on this topic. More than three-quarters (78.5%) disagreed with the assertion that 'trade unions have too much power', and data from the 1979 and 1971 surveys reinforce these findings. Nevertheless, the 1983 delegates were evenly split (45.9%) on whether an NDP government should ever 'interfere with free collective bargaining'.

DELEGATE POSITIONS ON POLICY: 1971-1983

In addition to questions regarding general ideological orientation, delegates were asked about their positions on a number of specific policy areas.

The Welfare State

Socialists and social democrats have been instrumental in building the welfare state in Western societies. Historically, the CCF and the NDP have been at the forefront of the battle for such social-security measures as old-age pensions, family allowances, unemployment insurance, and medicare (Guest, 1980). Names such as J.S. Woodsworth, Stanley Knowles, and Tommy Douglas are closely identified with the founding of these programmes. As early pioneers for and current champions of the welfare state, not many New Democrats (5.1% in 1979) have agreed that there was a great deal of 'abuse of the social security and welfare programmes'. By 1987, however, the percentage agreeing—while still far lower than among Conservatives and Liberals—had more than doubled, to 11.4% (Archer and Whitehorn, 1990, 1991). While many of the gains in the welfare state were made in the years following the Second World War, the general public has recently shown a growing scepticism about the utility of such welfare measures and their cost. Support has increased for the imposition of means tests on those currently receiving universal income supplements. This debate has taken place even within the NDP. Data from the 1983 survey reveal that a majority (57.0%) of delegates opposed a 'means test in some social programmes', but a significant minority (36.1%) supported the idea (see Table 5.16 below). The pattern has been relatively consistent throughout the three time-periods sampled and is certainly in contrast to Conservative and Liberal responses to similar questions.[43] With the long-term demographic trend towards a declining percentage of the adult population in the workforce, the question of universality and its cost will become increasingly important even within social-democratic parties in the Western nations. Although, for the present, the NDP's belief in and support for the welfare state seems solidly in place, how popular such a platform will be to the electorate at large in the 1990s is another question.

The Role of Government

In the decade of the Orwellian prophecy, the public's fear of 'Big Labour' was superseded by fear of 'Big Government'.[44] Tapping this concern, neo-conservatism made gains in the United States, the United Kingdom, West Germany, and Canada. Historically, socialists have been identified with the establishment and expansion of many state services to meet pressing social needs. Thus they have been less inclined than the public at large to be critical of the growth of the government. Still, data from the 1983 survey suggest that even New Democratic opinion was divided as to whether 'big government increasingly is a major problem' (47.6% disagreed, but 42.9% agreed). Clearly, even socialists are concerned about the growth of state bureaucracy.

Public ownership and nationalization have been important, although not the sole, means employed by socialists to implement their vision of a better society. Data from the 1979 survey suggest a continued commitment to the public sector. For example, a massive 99.2% believed that 'in some cases government ownership is more desirable than private' and 97.6% disagreed with the suggestion that 'there is too much government ownership today'.

As Canada relies on the exports of staples, the resource industry is a key sector, and for the most part it remains heavily foreign-owned.[45] Throughout all three surveys, NDP delegates have shown a strong commitment to significant nationalization in this field. For example, 87.6% in 1983, 96.6% in 1979, and 70.2% in 1971 agreed that 'Canada should nationalize key/foreign owned resource industries'. This is a feature that distinguishes NDP members from both Liberals and Conservatives. Of course, specifics regarding the amount of nationalization are often the subject of intense debate among NDP members, even when they can agree on the general principle.

In recent years increasing attention has been paid to the size of government deficits, as Bob Rae's Ontario NDP government can attest. While a majority (56.7%) of NDP delegates in 1983 favoured 'reducing the deficit as much as possible', there seemed to be significant disagreement over how high a priority this should have, as indicated by the fact that a significant minority (31.3%) of the delegates disagreed with the statement.

Historically, most socialists have favoured central planning as a means to regulate the disruptive boom/bust cycles of market capitalism. The CCF stressed powers of the central government[46] even when it formed the provincial government in Saskatchewan. In the post-war era, however, there has been a significant shift in the federal-provincial distribution of powers in Canada, and the size and scope of provincial government activity have expanded substantially. This fact, coupled with the relatively greater success by the NDP at the provincial level in the west and a growing scepticism about the desirability of government centralization,[47] has resulted in increased commitment by the NDP to the powers of provincial governments. When the 1983 delegates were asked which level of government, if any, 'needs to be granted more power', only slightly more selected the federal government (20.9%) than the provincial government (18.7%).[48] By far the largest number, however, replied neither (39.8%).[49]

Data from the 1971 survey, while showing a desire among a majority of delegates to see more federal funds given to the provinces (51.9%), also suggest that a majority of delegates did not want to see provincial governments have more power. The 1979 respondents were given a choice between the following statements: (a) 'A policy of decentralization of federal powers to the provinces is the best way to keep this country together' or (b) 'More decentralization of federal powers to the provinces would weaken the federal government too much.' Delegates overwhelmingly selected the latter statement (72.8%). One can conclude that while the commitment to the power of the provincial government was greater in 1979 than in the early CCF years, a high level of support for a strong central government still existed.

Defence and Foreign Policy

Although the CCF-NDP has differed distinctly from the Liberals and Conservatives on defence policy, relatively little has been written about the party on this topic (Groome, 1967; Sims, 1977; Thorburn, 1986). Similarly, there have been very few questions on defence-related matters in previous NDP surveys. The sole statement posed in 1971 was that 'Canada should spend less on defence', to which the overwhelming majority (85.3%) of delegates replied in the affirmative. On a related topic, when delegates that same year were asked whether or not Canada should provide more effort and aid to underdeveloped countries, a large majority (74.1%) replied in the affirmative. This is clearly a party that sees itself as strongly committed to peace, not war, and foreign aid, not arms sales. It is very much in the tradition of socialist idealism as contrasted to the *realpolitik* that dominates so much of international politics.

The idea of the world carved into spheres of superpower influence and polarized in military alliances alarmed most New Democrats. Not surprisingly, party policy in general over the years has favoured Canada's withdrawal from both NATO and NORAD. Despite efforts in the past by some, including former leader Ed Broadbent, to reopen the issue of involvement in military alliances, no recent NDP convention has officially changed its position on the ultimate goal of withdrawal. The 1983 survey of convention delegates found that a majority (58.6%) disagreed with the suggestion that 'Canada should remain in NATO'. A similar majority (59.9%) disagreed with the idea of 'remaining in NORAD'. While a significant minority in each case (31.1% and 24.4% respectively) disagreed with the NDP's official policy on abandoning the two military alliances, the prospect for a successful fundamental shift of party policy seemed poor. Indeed, efforts in this regard appeared more likely to provoke lengthy and acrimonious debate and still leave a significant minority dissatisfied, whatever the outcome of any vote. Nevertheless, in the spring of 1988, on the eve of a national election, the NDP federal council—the policy-making body between party conventions—issued a report entitled *Canada's Stake in Common Security*. In general, the report was a much overdue in-depth analysis of plausible defence options. In one area, however, it opted for a compromise between the different positions in the party. The document formally retained the long-term goal of Canada's withdrawal from NATO, but it added the important qualification that the party would not actually withdraw from NATO during its first term of office. This was an ingenious attempt at a solution. How well it would sell to a public concerned about a party's faithfulness to principles was another matter.

From the days of J.S. Woodsworth, pacifism has been a significant force, although not always dominant, in CCF-NDP defence and foreign-policy positions. When asked in 1983 if 'Canada should disarm unilaterally', a surprisingly large percentage (59.2%) agreed. An even larger percentage (91.3%) opposed the placement of any nuclear weapons in Canada.[50] The NDP's recent opposition to Canada's involvement in the 1991 Persian Gulf War and preference for continued reliance on trade sanctions indicate that this pacifist tradition persists.

When delegates at the 1983 convention were asked 'which of the two superpowers is the greater threat to world peace,' almost two-thirds (65.1%) suggested that the US and the USSR were about equal in blame. Here again, the desire for Canada to pursue a path independent of the military alliances of the two superpowers appeared clear. Among those who selected one of the two superpowers as more of a threat, respondents in 1983 selected the United States far more often (by almost five to one) than the USSR. Clearly, in foreign policy the NDP is more critical of Canada's closest neighbour than of the USSR. This is perhaps understandable, given that critical information about the US is more accessible, but it is also puzzling, in view of the historic record of the Soviet Union in both domestic and foreign affairs.[51]

As early as 1971, most NDP delegates (66.8%) did not perceive the Soviet Union as a 'threat to Canada', and increasing numbers of delegates over the years (36.5% in 1979 and 57.8% in 1983) have called for 'closer ties with communist countries'. Despite a relapse in superpower relations during the Brezhnev/Reagan era (fostered on the one hand by the Soviet Union's invasion of Czechoslovakia and Afghanistan, and on the other by America's invasion of Grenada, and by increasingly bellicose statements in the mid-1980s by both superpowers about the militarization of space), most delegates in 1983 (47.5%) denied that 'détente is an illusion', although more than a third (35.4%) took a more pessimistic perspective. However, the arrival of the Gorbachev era and *perestroika*, followed by the breakup of the Soviet Union, has no doubt fostered even higher hopes among New Democrats that the Cold War can be superseded and a new age of international relations introduced.

Among the industrialized nations of the world, Canada has a disproportionate percentage of foreign-owned industry (see Levitt, 1970). The CCF was an early critic of this pattern of dependency and the NDP has continued this critique. Not surprisingly, an overwhelming majority of delegates at NDP conventions (96.3% in 1983 and 95.8% in 1979) believed that 'Canada's independence is threatened by the large percentage of foreign ownership in key sectors of our economy'. As to the proposed cost of remedies to this ill, more than three-quarters of delegates to all three surveyed conventions (81.0% in 1983, 76.7% in 1979, and 76.0% in 1971) felt that 'we should ensure an independent Canada even if a lower living standard was required'. The very strong support for these two positions among NDP delegates can be contrasted with the views of their counterparts in the other two major parties: 51.5% of Liberal and only 27.3% of Conservative delegates in 1984 and 1983 respectively agreed with the former statement, and 58.1% of Liberal and only 33.3% of Conservative delegates agreed with the latter (Blake, 1988; Archer and Whitehorn, 1990, 1991).

Inseparable from the question of foreign ownership in Canada is the preponderant influence of the United States on Canada generally (Godfrey and Watkins, 1970; Mathews and Steele, 1969; Laxer, 1973). To many Canadian nationalists, the US is the prime culprit. In addition, efforts to assert Canadian independence must occur not only in the economic realm but also in other spheres. Thus a very high percentage of NDP delegates (91.6% in 1983 and 92.5% in 1971) felt that 'Canada must reduce American influence on its culture and mass media'. In this regard, not even the trade unions—a key building-block in the NDP alliance—are immune to criticism. Surveyed delegates at all three conventions showed very high support (79.9% in 1983, 78.5% in 1979, and 79.0% in 1971) for the belief that 'Canadian affiliates of international unions should have full autonomy'.

In recent years there has been a ferocious debate over Canada's joining the US in a North American free-market zone; indeed, this was the key issue in the 1988 federal election (see Chapter 8). Data from the 1983 and 1979 surveys show that nearly three-quarters of NDP delegates disagreed with the statements that 'there should be no tariffs or duties between Canada and the United States' (74.7% disagreed in 1983) and that 'Canada should have freer trade with the United States' (72.5% in 1979). In contrast, a majority of Liberal and Conservative delegates (63.9% and 53.7% respectively) favoured free trade during this period (Blake, 1988; Archer and Whitehorn, 1990, 1991). Despite John Turner's emotional and dramatic opposition to free trade in the 1988 federal election, the attitude of Liberal delegates overall suggests less likelihood of long-term consistency and consensus in the Liberal Party on this issue. Clearly the NDP is the party most opposed to continentalism, and it is more likely to maintain its stance on the issue than are the Liberals under Jean Chrétien.

Quebec, French Canada, Bilingualism, and Regionalism

The issues involved in national unity have concerned the CCF-NDP as much as the other parties. Historically, the CCF arose with very little base in Quebec (Lewis, 1981: 454-68; Casgrain, 1972; Sherwood, 1966). The party was dominated by Anglophones unsympathetic to French Canadian demands for provincial rights, and in the CCF's haste to regulate the economy centrally, in order to reduce unemployment and augment social services, its members were insufficiently attentive to the concerns of the ethnic and linguistic minority—the French Canadians. Indeed, an important part of the NDP's mandate was to attract French Canadians to the new party.

In recent decades, French Canada's aspirations and the proper status of Quebec have received considerable attention at NDP conventions; indeed, they have frequently overlaid other debates and ideological cleavages within the party.[52] The question of whether or not Quebec is a 'distinct society' and should be granted 'special status', different from that of the other provinces, continues to be raised. While the question wording differed and thus any conclusions are uncertain, it did appear that NDP delegates in 1983 were less supportive of 'special status' for Quebec (46.2%)[53] than previously (63.9%).[54] Initially, of course, following the Quebec referendum of 1980, the urgency of the Quebec question, particularly outside Quebec, had declined. Nevertheless, earlier NDP survey questions suggested a willingness to provide some special recognition for Quebec 'within Confederation' (56.3% in 1979 and 66.6% in 1971) and a desire among a majority of delegates to grant French Canadians privileges in addition to those provided to other ethnic groups (58.7% in 1979 and 61.7% in 1971). How this differed from 'special status' in the minds of delegates is not entirely clear.

Over the years NDP delegates have shown strong support for the right of Quebec to self-determination. For example, 65.5% supported this principle in 1983 and 64.2% in 1971.[55] There has, however, been greater disagreement over whether or not the NDP should formally acknowledge such a right (in 1971, 48.5% agreed and 41.6% did not), lest it appear to support the separatist cause and invoke a backlash by western NDP supporters.

In the history of Canada, bilingualism has been a contentious issue. While in previous eras Canadian socialists have not been noted for staunch commitment to bilingualism, data from NDP surveys suggest strong support for bilingualism in more recent years (80.1% in both 1983 and 1979), although there was some drop-off in approval of the specific implementation of such policies. Nevertheless, NDP delegates showed more support than Liberal or Conservative delegates for a bilingual civil service.[56]

Western populist protest movements and regional alienation have a long tradition in Canadian politics, and both contributed to the rise of the CCF. To what degree is political alienation still a force among members of the NDP? While no direct measures of alienation were employed in the 1983 survey, the responses to one question may provide a clue. Almost two-thirds of the delegates (64.3%) agreed that 'central Canada has too much say in Canadian politics'. When the sample was broken down into regions, the percentage of high affirmative replies was 71.4% in BC, 76.2% on the Prairies, 75.0% in the Maritimes, and 80.0% in the NWT and Yukon. In contrast, only 39.8% in Ontario and 33.3% in Quebec agreed with the statement. Clearly, the delegates from the less populous periphery areas continue to exhibit attitudes of regional alienation.[57]

Women's Issues

The gender gap within the NDP is similar to that in other parties (Brodie, 1988; Bashevkin, 1985). In 1983 only 30.9% (25.6% in 1979 and 25.1% in 1971) of the delegates surveyed were women. While this is an increase over past years, women are still in general outnumbered by about two to one. Despite this discrepancy, most respondents (77.9%) did not believe that 'women are discriminated against within the NDP.'[58] All the same, an overwhelming majority (86.5%) of convention delegates thought that 'more women should be candidates for the NDP,' and when asked if they thought 'women are as effective as men as candidates,' most (92.3%) agreed. A large majority (72.1%) of delegates believed that 'the NDP should ensure that a significant percentage of its candidates and Party officers are women'. Delegates were less likely to support entrenchment of gender parity on the federal council (47.8% agreed vs. 36.7% opposed). Nevertheless, commencing at the 1983 convention, half of the council members and vice-presidents elected by the convention were required to be women. What impact, if any, did these changes produce both in the delegates' attitudes and in party priorities? They certainly helped to improve the rate of female participation at the executive levels of the party (Bashevkin, 1985: 213-21). The election of federal leader Audrey McLaughlin continued that process, as has the decision at the 1991 federal convention to strengthen the party's commitment to achieve gender parity in future candidate nominations for Parliament.

Several social issues are of great interest to women in particular. Although abortion, like the language issue, is a topic that arouses strong sentiments on both sides, the NDP has long supported the right to choice.[59] In 1983 an overwhelming number of NDP delegates (84.6%) agreed that 'abortion is a private matter which should be decided between the woman bearing the child and her doctor'. That this rate of support is dramatically higher than among either Liberal or Conservative activists (Blake, 1988; Archer and Whitehorn, 1990, 1991)[60] suggests yet another contrast between the NDP and the other two major parties.

Many people believe that pornography fosters sexist and violent attitudes and behaviour towards women and perpetuates gender inequalities. While no past survey data are available on NDP attitudes to censorship and pornography, it appears that in recent years many NDP members have shifted away from an earlier civil-libertarian viewpoint to one more compatible with a feminist position. In the 1983 survey, more than two-thirds (69.8%) of the delegates disagreed with the statement that 'there should be no censorship of any kind'. While most were willing to accept the principle of censorship, the number supporting a 'ban on pornography' was lower (49.0%), although this was still the dominant viewpoint.

With the increased participation and representation rates of women at NDP conventions and councils, and under McLaughlin's leadership, it seems likely that women's issues will continue to be more fully addressed within the party.

Ecological Issues

While much of the Western world's New Left has gone into socialist parties such as the NDP, in recent years some have formed Green parties, arguing that the traditional social-democratic parties such as the NDP pay insufficient attention to environmental issues (Gorz, 1980). Sparked by the relative success of their counterparts in Germany, Canadian Greens have now contested elections at both the provincial and federal levels. While to date none of these candidates has been elected, the Greens' potential for draining away both NDP votes and activists should not be lightly dismissed. Thus the question of how well the NDP addresses ecological issues can be important.

Among the attitudes to social issues that have consistently been shown by the Greens are opposition to nuclear weapons and nuclear reactors, recognition of the need for greater protection of the environment, scepticism about the benefits of industrialization and technology, and a preference for decentralization (Porritt, 1984; Milbrath, 1984). As already noted, a majority of NDP delegates in 1983[61] favoured unilateral disarmament and no nuclear weapons for Canada. A vast majority of delegates also called for a 'moratorium on building nuclear reactors' (83.0%), and for 'Canada to take a tougher stand on environmental polluters' (97.2%). While a majority (62.3%) of respondents accepted the proposition that 'industrial society is essentially a polluting society', almost half (48.7%) still believed that 'the good effects of technology outweigh its bad effects'. As noted earlier, NDP delegates seemed to be almost evenly split over whether or not big government is a major problem, with 42.9% agreeing and 47.6% disagreeing.

On five of seven key issues raised by the Greens, a majority of NDP delegates were in agreement with the Green position. On only two (the effects of technology and big government as a problem) was there a discordance of opinion. Whether this is sufficient to warrant the formation of an alternative party seems doubtful. Certainly the very small electoral support to date for the Green Party in Canada suggests that the NDP is, in the main, adequately covering ecological issues. In any case, the recent creation of a green caucus within the NDP would seem to ensure greater attention to green as well as socialist red issues. How well the green caucus will interact with trade unionists' concern about jobs remains to be seen.

Civil Liberties

Historically the CCF-NDP has been noted for its support of civil liberties. Indeed, a number of CCF members were active in the formation of the Canadian Civil Liberties Association, and many NDP members play prominent roles in the CCLA. As pointed out earlier, NDP delegates in 1983 favoured women's right to choose abortion (84.6%). Nevertheless, they were also found to favour censorship (69.8%) and banning pornographic materials (49.0%).

Capital punishment is an issue that has received renewed attention in recent years. While a clear majority of Canadians, most Conservative Party delegates, and almost half of Liberal Party delegates favour a return to capital punishment,[62] New Democrats for the most part remain steadfast abolitionists (77.8%). Clearly on this issue they are swimming against the public tide, and it is difficult to know how many votes, if any, such a position costs the NDP, particularly among rank-and-file blue-collar workers. Still, the NDP's position reinforces its image of humanitarianism and concern with individual rights.

On a more political aspect of civil rights, delegates at the 1979 and 1971 NDP conventions—echoing their leaders' position on the War Measures Act—strongly supported (76.2% in 1979 and 73.8% in 1971) the notion that 'legislation which interferes with the basic rights, like the special legislation in 1970 to deal with the FLQ [Front de Libération du Québec], should be adopted only in wartime'. By contrast, a lower rate of

Conservatives (59.7%) and Liberals (30.2%) agreed with this statement (Blake, 1988). Similarly, most NDP delegates in 1979 (78.1%) disagreed with the statement that 'certain restrictions on civil rights would be acceptable if it would help police reduce crime', only 16.3% agreed. A majority of Conservatives (53.7%) and a near-majority of Liberals (48.8%), however, did agree, and this suggests yet again that the NDP's position is quite different from that of the two other parties (Blake, 1988; Archer and Whitehorn, 1990, 1991).

By contrast, on the civil-rights issue of homosexuality, a plurality of delegates (49.4%) did not believe that 'the NDP should speak out more on the rights of homosexuals'. It is not known if this response pattern reflects philosophical reasons or tactical electoral considerations.

While many Canadians express concern over the number of non-European immigrants entering Canada, 92.2% of NDP delegates attending the Regina convention favoured a policy of 'admitting immigrants from all ethnic and racial groups'. This rate is higher than that for Liberal and Conservative delegates (79.1% and 67.3% respectively) and reinforces the NDP's image as a strongly internationalist and humanitarian party (Blake, 1988; Archer and Whitehorn, 1990, 1991).

In summary, on eight issues that could be rated on a civil-rights index, NDP delegates scored high on five (right to abortion; opposition to capital punishment; support for political liberties, civil liberties, and ethnic and racial equality) and lower on three (anti-censorship; tolerance of all publications, even pornographic materials; greater defence of homosexual rights). The record is less clear-cut than might be expected, and may suggest that a more conservative mood in the country is affecting even NDP delegates.

CLEAVAGES WITHIN NDP CONVENTIONS
Most Contentious Issues

No major political party, composed as it is of tens of thousands of members, can possibly represent all individuals' policy preferences and responses to specific issues. Consequently, any such party will experience internal tensions between those members favouring and those opposing particular policy options. While an individual party may find considerable consensus on some issues, on others there may be significant disagreement.[63] As can be seen from Table 5.16, the responses of delegates to 52 attitude statements reveal a very low level of consensus on 4 items, a low consensus on 16, a mid-level of agreement and disagreement on 12, a high level of consensus on 11 items, and a very high level on 9.[64] Overall, the spread indicates a reasonable balance of 20 fairly contentious items and 20 consensual ones.[65] While in most policy areas there are items on both sides of the consensus-cleavage continuum, some (e.g., women's concerns, defence, and foreign policy) seem to contain a greater number of

Table 5.16 Attitude Statements by Level of Disagreement: 1983

VERY LOW CONSENSUS ITEMS: DISSENT ABOVE 40%

	Agree %	Disagree %	Difference
Quebec should not be granted special status.	48.2	46.2*	2.0
An NDP government should never interfere with free collective bargaining.	45.9*	45.9*	0
Big government increasingly is a major problem.	42.9*	47.6	4.7
The central question of Canadian politics is the class struggle between labour and capital.	52.4	40.2*	12.2

LOW CONSENSUS ITEMS: DISSENT BETWEEN 30 AND 39.9%

Strikers should be able to collect unemployment insurance.	46.5	39.6*	6.9
Co-operation with Canadian communists is not possible on any issue.	39.5*	51.5	12.0
The NDP leadership does not pay sufficient attention to ordinary Party members.	48.7	38.4*	10.3
The NDP should move more clearly to the left.	55.6	37.4*	18.2
More Party funds should be under the jurisdiction of riding associations.	39.9	37.4*	2.5
Pornography should be banned.	49.0	37.0*	12.0
Canada should disarm unilaterally.	59.2	36.7*	22.5
Fifty per cent of the Federal Council should be composed of women.	47.8	36.7*	11.1
A means test may be necessary in some social programmes.	36.1*	57.0	20.9
Detente is an illusion.	35.4*	47.5	12.1
There should be closer ties between trade unions and the NDP.	58.8	33.2*	25.6
Industrial society is essentially a polluting society.	62.3	32.8*	29.5
An NDP government should seek to reduce the deficit as much as possible.	56.7	31.3*	25.4
The NDP should speak out more on the rights of homosexuals.	31.2*	49.4	18.2
The good effects of technology outweigh its bad effects.	48.7	31.2*	17.5
Canada should remain in NATO.	31.3*	58.6	27.5

MEDIUM CONSENSUS ITEMS: DISSENT BETWEEN 20% AND 29.9%

NDP conventions are extremely democratic.	55.7	29.7*	26.0
Quebec has a right to self-determination.	65.5	29.6*	35.9
Central Canada has too much to say in Canadian politics.	64.3	26.7*	37.6
There are significant differences between the left and right within the Party.	68.1	24.9*	43.2
Trade unions have too much influence in the NDP.	24.5*	67.0	42.5
Canada should remain in NORAD.	24.4*	59.9	35.5
There should be no censorship of any kind.	23.5*	69.8	46.3
Canada should seek closer relations with Communist countries.	57.8	23.4*	34.4
On occasion direct political action must be used in place of electoral politics.	63.8	23.3*	40.5
The NDP should become more of a social movement and less of a political party.	22.7*	70.4	47.7
The NDP should seek to present a more moderate image to the general public.	21.0*	76.8	55.8
The NDP should ensure that a significant percentage of its candidates and Party officers are women.	72.1	20.9*	51.2

HIGH CONSENSUS ITEMS: DISSENT BETWEEN 10% AND 19.9%

The NDP is a socialist party.	76.0	19.4*	56.6
Capital punishment should be re-introduced.	17.6*	77.8	60.2
There should be no tariffs or duties between Canada and the United States.	16.5*	74.7	58.2
Women are discriminated against within the NDP.	15.8*	77.9	62.1
A bilingual federal government is necessary.	80.1	14.9*	65.2
Abortion is a private matter which should be decided between the woman bearing the child and her doctor.	84.6	14.4*	70.2
There should be a moratorium on the building of nuclear reactors.	83.0	13.5*	69.5
We must ensure an independent Canada, even if that were to mean a lower standard of living for Canadians.	81.0	13.1*	67.9
Trade unions have too much power.	12.5*	78.5	66.0
Ultra-left elements within the Party should be expelled.	11.8*	78.6	66.8
Canadian affiliates of international unions should have full autonomy.	79.9	11.2*	68.7

VERY HIGH CONSENSUS ITEMS: DISSENT UNDER 10%

Canada should nationalize key resource industries.	87.6	9.9*	77.7
The NDP should be more active in municipal politics.	86.3	9.3*	77.0
No nuclear weapons should be permitted on Canadian territory.	91.3	7.9*	83.4
Canada must take steps to reduce American influence on its culture and mass media.	91.6	6.9*	84.7
On the whole, women are as effective as men as candidates for elected office.	92.3	5.5*	86.8
When Canada admits immigrants, it should take them from all ethnic and racial groups.	92.2	5.0*	87.2
More women should be candidates for the NDP.	86.5	3.5*	83.0
Canada's independence is threatened by the large percentage of foreign ownership in key sectors of our economy.	96.3	2.7*	93.6
Canada should take a tougher stand on environmental polluters.	97.2	2.5*	94.7

* indicates minority position.
NOTE: missing percentages are respondents indicating no opinion.

statements on the consensual side. In contrast, items dealing with internal party affairs, labour, government's role, and the welfare state were more likely to evoke divided opinions.[66]

Among the individual policy items that party members seemed most divided over were the growth and size of government, state-imposed limits on collective bargaining, special status for Quebec, and the nature of class relations in Canada.[67] Other intra-party differences, though on a slightly less divisive scale, were evident on the size of government deficits, universality of social programmes, Canada's involvement in NATO, and the global issue of disarmament. Whether the party should shift further to the left and co-operate more with other, more radical leftists were also contentious issues, as were banning pornography and speaking out in defence of homosexuals.

On the consensual side, the party stood united in its call for nationalization of key elements in the resource sector and reducing American influence over Canada's culture and economy. The NDP's strong opposition to nuclear weapons on Canadian territory and its demand for more resolute action on pollution were also evident from the response data. While a little less consistent in their levels of support, party members still indicated fairly strong opposition to free trade with the United States. This is further evidence that, of the three major parties, and despite the events of the 1988 election campaign, the NDP has been overall the most vocal in its criticism of US-Canadian economic integration.[68] NDP members, in contrast to many sectors of Canadian society, are strong defenders of women's right to abortion and are firmly opposed to capital punishment. Like the two other major parties, and in contrast to Preston Manning's Reform Party, the NDP is strongly committed to the constitutional principle of bilingualism.

Demographic Bases for Intra-Party Cleavages

As in all parties, a number of demographic variables seem to contribute to intra-party cleavages within the NDP.[69] Cross-tabulations of such variables[70] with the 52 attitude statements about society at large and the party itself suggest that education and community size had the greatest impact on delegates' tendencies to differ in policy positions,[71] while income and region had the least (see Table 5.17).

Table 5.17 Impact of Demographic Variables Upon Intra-Party Cleavages[a]

	Consistent response pattern with sizeable difference (over 10%)	Persistent response pattern with small difference (under 10%)
Education	22	11
Community size	21	10
Gender[b]	17	—
Age	16	18
Region	12	11
Income	8	13

[a] 52 possible cases.
[b] In contrast to other variables this is dichotomized, and it seems inappropriate to list where the difference is less than 10%.

Looking briefly at each demographic group, one may observe that the least educated showed a greater willingness to view social relations in terms of class conflict, and to favour government reduction of the deficit, free trade with the United States, staying in NATO, and banning pornography. In contrast, the most educated delegates were more likely to support women's entry into politics, bilingualism, and self-determination for Quebec, and more likely to oppose censorship and capital punishment. They were also more likely to welcome immigrants irrespective of background.

In terms of community size, the 1983 survey revealed that delegates from smaller communities were better disposed towards free trade, deficit reduction, staying in NORAD, and banning pornography, and less likely to favour special status for Quebec. Often NDP delegates from smaller communities can be characterized as tending to possess a more conservative perspective. Delegates from larger metropolitan areas were more likely to support bilingualism, Quebec's right to self-determination, and homosexual rights.

Gender differences can also be found in the data. Male delegates were more likely to wish to have the NDP present a moderate image, to oppose co-operation with communists, and to favour expelling ultra-leftists from the ranks of the party. Female delegates were more likely to support greater participation by women in politics, a ban on pornography, and the right to abortion. They also showed a stronger tendency to favour a shift to the left for the party, to embrace unilateral disarmament, to be concerned about pollution, and to support the rights of homosexuals. It may be that the trade-unionist influence contributes to the male pattern of responses. The data on women's attitudes and the 1989 leadership victory of Audrey McLaughlin give some justification to the argument that there may be a potential coalition of compatible interests within the party among feminists, radicals, gays, and ecologists.

Young socialists (e.g., members of the Waffle in the past) have often been identified with calls for the NDP to become a more activist party, willing to co-operate with other, often more radical groups, and to favour Quebec's national self-assertion. Older NDP members have tended to be less inclined to favour Quebec's demands for special status. They are also more willing to ban pornography and less inclined to speak out on behalf of homosexuals. The complexity of a mass of survey questions is demonstrated by the apparent breakdown of conventional wisdom on several items. Older delegates were more disposed to see class struggle as a central feature, while younger ones were more willing to impose a means test on some social programmes. Clearly, young NDP members are not as consistently radical as many have assumed. A new generation more critical of features of the welfare state may be emerging.

In any continent-wide polity, parties are bound to be influenced by regionalism (Gibbins, 1980; Whitehorn and Archer, 1989; Brodie, 1990). In 1983, NDP delegates from the west were more likely to oppose tariffs between Canada and the United States and to support unilateral disarmament. Delegates from the east (i.e., Ontario) were more in favour of women's participation in politics, pro-union positions, and Canada's involvement in NATO and NORAD. Clearly, defence and foreign policy matters were likely to reflect, and perhaps accentuate, significant regional differences.

Differences in income levels have a less pronounced effect than other variables but still can be discerned. Lower-income delegates were more inclined to view Canadian politics in the classic proletarian light of a struggle between labour and capital; these working-class radicals favoured seeing the NDP swing further left. Their financial concerns can perhaps be seen in their greater willingness to support Canada-US free trade. That low-income delegates were more critical of the NDP leadership's inattention to rank-

and-file members points to another instance of worker alienation (Schacht, 1971; Finifter, 1972; Geyer and Schweitzer, 1976; 1981; Schweitzer and Geyer, 1989), this time in the midst of the NDP itself. Low-income delegates were also more inclined to see big government as a major problem — a finding that should perhaps caution middle-class socialists against assuming that statist solutions would have widespread appeal. Finally, upper-income delegates showed a greater tolerance of women's entry into higher social ranks.

CONCLUSION

The data presented in this chapter suggest that the NDP is indeed a party with a difference, providing a significant contrast to both the Liberal and Conservative parties in terms of ideology and many policy attitudes (see also Archer and Whitehorn, 1990, 1991). At times, too, the NDP's voice of steadfast principle speaks in marked defiance of the public's mood, seemingly indifferent to the electoral consequences.

While differences between parties are often the most salient in politics, there are a number of intra-party cleavages with which all Canadian parties must deal. The NDP has shown itself to be no less susceptible than its rivals to urban/rural splits, regionalism, educational and generational differences, and gender inequalities. How it deals with these differences may well determine the party's success or failure at large. Certainly one pressing problem is the demographic fact that the NDP has strong representation in the west and in Ontario, but is woefully weak in Quebec and the Maritimes. To go from being a third party to a major one competing directly for power, the NDP will have to find new strategies and means for making inroads into these regions.

NOTES

This chapter is a revised version of an article published in George Perlin, ed., *Party Democracy in Canada* (Toronto, Prentice-Hall, 1988). Data collection was made possible by funding from the Social Sciences and Humanities Research Council (SSHRC). The encouragement provided by George Perlin and his generous access to earlier surveys of NDP delegates is much appreciated. Linda Trimble provided able technical advice and assisted in the coding of the data. Also providing extensive advice and assistance were Josette Arassus, Marie Thérèse Ferguson, and Jill Hodgson. Keith Archer, my colleague in research on the NDP, has provided insightful comments and supplemental information.

[1] For a partial analysis of a later 1987 survey of NDP convention delegates, see Archer and Whitehorn (1990, 1991) and Whitehorn and Archer (1989).
[2] Blake (1988) and Archer and Whitehorn (1990, 1991) endeavour to overcome this absence of comparative data.
[3] Beginning with Lipset (1968), who conducted two surveys of Saskatchewan

CCF provincial delegates in 1945 and 1946, John Courtney (1973), who studied all three major parties, and Walter Young (1971), who surveyed delegates at three provincial BC NDP conventions in 1963, 1965, and 1966, survey work on the NDP has mushroomed in recent years. George Perlin, Hugh Thorburn, Jayant Lele, and associates conducted two surveys of federal NDP delegates at the 1971 and 1979 conventions. Some of the earlier analysis of their data can be found in Lele, Perlin and Thorburn (1979), Brodie (1985), and Hackett (1979; 1980). More recently, Sylvia Bashevkin (1985) analysed the status of women at the 1982 Ontario NDP provincial convention, Blake, Carty and Erickson (1991) studied the provincial BC parties, Whitehorn surveyed the 1983 NDP convention in Regina, Archer and Whitehorn surveyed the 1987 federal policy convention, and most recently Archer (1991) analysed the Winnipeg leadership convention.

[4] Questionnaires were included in the delegates' convention kits and were returned to special boxes at the convention hall. Of 1,433 delegates, 407 filled out questionnaires, for a response rate of 28.4%. This rate is somewhat lower than that possible by means of a mailed questionnaire, but this method was the most practical one available.

The 1979 survey conducted by Perlin was based on a sample of 520 respondents to a mailed questionnaire.

The 1971 survey conducted by Perlin, Hugh Thorburn and Jayant Lele was also based on a mailed questionnaire, with a sample size of 776. As a leadership convention it had, of course, an unusually high number of delegates (1,739), and until 1989 was the only NDP leadership convention surveyed. Thus while some historical analysis of NDP and CCF leadership conventions will be offered, this study will focus more on policy attitudes.

Please note that while every effort has been made to include all the 1983 data where possible, space limitations have prevented reporting of many tables. In general, the sample size for attitude responses is 398, with a range from 403 to 379. Further details are available from the author.

[5] While this rate is certain to be significantly higher than for delegates at either Conservative or Liberal conventions, it is perhaps lower than might be expected for a labour-based party. The reason will become evident below, when the educational, income, and job profiles of NDP convention delegates are analysed.

[6] In the year when there is no federal convention, however, there is usually a provincial convention.

[7] Nevertheless, recent NDP policy conventions have not been even half the size of the latest Liberal and Conservative leadership conventions.

[8] The ratio of delegates to membership is skewed roughly 10 to 1 in favour of the constituency associations. See also Horowitz (1968: 74-5) for data covering the CCF years.

[9] Data provided through correspondence with the federal office of the NDP. It should be noted that these data do not include labour representatives already on the federal council. Given that very few union locals were affiliated to the CCF, data on labour representation at CCF conventions is either non-existent or sparse. Horowitz (1968: 81) estimates that the percentage was usually less than 5%; see also Engelmann (1954: 62). While much speculation has been offered about the role of labour unions within the NDP, on average only about one-quarter

of convention delegates are officially labour-sponsored. Of course, the percentage is usually higher when a serious leadership contest is anticipated. K. Archer (correspondance, 15 Aug. 1985) documents that the percentage of actual union delegates is significantly lower than the total possible (i.e., 21.5% in non-leadership contests and 47.9% in leadership struggles). It should also be noted that to be convention delegates from their affiliated organizations, trade unionists must also be individual members of the party, even though most of the persons they represent need not be. Thus the differences between riding delegates and union delegates should not be overstated. They are clearly both individual members of the party, albeit with different roles, clients, and methods of selection. See also Lele, Perlin, and Thorburn (1979: 84) on the election vs. selection aspects of union representation at conventions.

[10] It is worth noting that an NDP-sponsored survey found that while 56% of all delegates had previously attended a federal convention, 44% had not ('Women and Politics: The Survey of Delegates: 1983 Federal Convention: Basic Data Report' [n.d., NDP]).

[11] The substantial past and current experience of delegates stands in marked contrast to the phenomenon of 'instant party members' seen at Liberal and Conservative leadership conventions.

[12] The NDP's 'Women and Politics' survey found a comparable age break-down.

[13] Data provided by respective political parties from their convention reports. Perlin's surveys of the 1984 Liberal and 1983 Conservative conventions indicate that delegates 20 and under represented 6.6% and 19.2% of the delegates respectively.

[14] Certainly the NDP leadership has been cautious in fostering youth wings of the party since the Waffle episode. In the history of the CCF-NDP, it has not been uncommon for the youth section, when it existed, to take a more hard-line Marxist approach. See Lewis (1981: 385-7).

[15] The predominance of delegates from Ontario was a feature even during most of the CCF years. See Engelmann (1954: 62) for a regional profile of delegates from 1940 to 1952.

[16] As John Courtney points out, a selection mechanism based on rewarding larger ridings with more convention delegates is hardly likely to alleviate this problem. Certainly convention site also has a significant effect on regional distribution of delegates and creates some regional fluctuations in the numbers from one convention to the next. As of 1991, virtually all the federal CCF and NDP conventions (14 of 16 and 14 of 16 respectively) have been held in either the west or Ontario, accentuating the regional imbalance in distribution of delegates.

[17] Commencing in 1985, yet another attempt was made to enter NDP candidates in Quebec provincial politics in an effort to build a political beachhead. But the 1985 and 1989 campaign results suggest little basis for optimism. While some 1986 and 1987 polls suggested dramatic increases in support for the federal NDP, the 1988 federal election reminds us that polls can fall as rapidly as they rise. In addition, there is often a dramatic difference between percentage of votes and seats, particularly for a second- or third-place party (see Chapter 1).

[18] See for example Porter (1967), Kalbach and McVey (1971), Forcese (1975), and 'Social Class' in Marsh (1985). Goldthorpe and his colleagues (1968a; 1968b; 1969) endeavoured to explore the 'embourgeoisement' of the working class in Great Britain in their three-volume report on the affluent worker.

[19] Data from the 1984 Liberal and 1983 Conservative conventions are taken from Perlin's surveys; see Perlin (1988).

[20] This is actually a conservative estimate, for undoubtedly the student, retired, and homemaker categories would also include people from middle-class backgrounds; also, managers and executives account for 4.0% of delegates. See also Lele, Perlin and Thorburn (1979) on the income, education, and occupational background of NDP delegates. It should be noted that even so-called revolutionary parties such as the Communist Party of the Soviet Union and China had in their formative days a disproportionate percentage of leaders from middle-class backgrounds. Neither Lenin, Trotsky, nor Mao Zedong were from the poorest and least educated strata of their respective societies.

[21] Even the CCF in its latter years was increasingly an urban-based party; see Chapter 1. Of course, Canadian society itself has shifted from being 52.5% urban in 1931 to 75.7% by 1981 ('Urbanization', in Marsh [1985]).

[22] The six previous leaders served an average of 9.5 years. At 14 years, Ed Broadbent was the party leader with the second longest tenure. M.J. Coldwell served the longest.

[23] See Chapter 3 on the CCF-NDP's key statements of principles. Interestingly, four of the five conventions that have approved the party's major manifestos have been held in the west.

[24] The commitment to discussion of items in the resolution booklets can be seen in the determination of delegates to continue using writing tables in the already crammed convention halls.

[25] The Ontario NDP voted in the 1980s to impose a word limit on resolutions in order to keep printing costs down.

[26] Interview at NDP federal council meeting, 19-21 April 1985. For a comparison of numbers of resolutions and success rates for 1946-52, see Engelmann (1954: 62-3, 115-16). See also McHenry (1950: 37), who notes that even in 1946, 160 resolutions were submitted.

[27] For the first two CCF leaders, the procedure was actually a more complex hybrid two-step process involving first a vote within the caucus of MPs and then an election/ratification by convention of the leader as party president (Lewis, 1981: 499).

[28] As of 1989 a leadership candidate was limited to a campaign expenditure of $150,000, was required to list the sources of donations, and was allowed two free mailings to the convention delegates. In the past nominations were easier in that they required signatures from fewer ridings or affiliated organizations. The result was that from time to time fringe candidates (e.g., poet Douglas Campbell) appeared with no chance of posing a serious challenge. Tommy Douglas, David Lewis, and Ed Broadbent, as incumbents, all experienced such token contests, none of which was taken seriously.

[29] This may in part explain the unanimous choices for all of the CCF leaders.

[30] According to a draft report on a survey of the 1989 NDP leadership convention by Keith Archer, 'More than half of all respondents (52.4%) favoured the change to a "one member-one vote" system, slightly more than one-third (35.8%) were opposed and 11.9% were undecided or did not answer.'

[31] A critical review of this literature as applied to the Canadian case can be found in Chapter 2.

[32] Data on the vocational background, education, and income levels of NDP

delegates also reinforce this image. Perhaps socialist 'noblesse oblige' amongst the professional class accounts for the background of the leaders, or perhaps NDP delegates simply want the most educated and articulate leaders possible.

[33] One cannot help speculating as to whether the reliance on older leaders has helped or hurt the party. For example, Coldwell stayed on the longest and was the oldest at the termination of his tenure; he also oversaw the electoral decline of the CCF. While the leader's age is obviously not the only factor in the CCF's drop in popularity, it certainly seems to have contributed to it. In contrast, the provincial wings of the NDP seem to have opted for younger leaders.

[34] While in 1971 Broadbent was not among the final two leadership aspirants, it should be noted that he could be labelled at that time as centre-left, whereas as a candidate in 1975 his position was seen to be more to the right of Rosemary Brown. For a discussion of the Brown campaign see her memoirs (1989). The 1989 leadership convention was characterized by many as not being particularly strong on ideological differences. Nevertheless, in contrast to the pattern in past leadership contests, the so-called left-caucus supported the eventual winner.

[35] For example, the issues of bilingualism and abortion have divided all major Canadian parties. See also Blake (1988) and Whitehorn and Archer (1989). The NDP's fellow socialist party in Britain also exhibits such intra-party differences of opinion on policy issues (Whiteley, 1983).

[36] Some care should be taken in interpretation of these data. For a number of delegates several terms seemed equally apt, and certainly for many the terms 'socialist' and 'social democrat' are interchangeable (Lewis, 1981: 301).

[37] Coined by St Laurent in 1949, this phrase has been reiterated by scholars such as Teeple (1972). Laycock (1990) suggests that the terms 'populism' and 'socialism' need not be incompatible.

[38] As is so often the case in research over time involving different authors, the questionnaire wording differs, and this may explain some of the discrepancy in the findings.

[39] Indeed, for a brief period, there was even an effort by John Bacher, a young member of the Ontario Left Caucus, to challenge Broadbent for the leadership. Bacher subsequently withdrew his nomination.

[40] Of course, union influence is heightened in the midst of a leadership convention when union attendance rates increase, particularly if some of the candidates are seen as significantly more pro-union than others. Certainly David Lewis's candidacy at the 1971 convention saw a somewhat higher rate of union delegates. Lewis's long stewardship on behalf of the labour movement no doubt contributed to this phenomenon.

[41] As early as 1949, Ontario provided more CCF votes than did the Prairies. See Chapter 1.

[42] Canadian Institute of Public Opinion (CIPO), *Toronto Star*, 16 Aug. 1978 (Fletcher and Drummond, 1979) and Gallup Report, 16 Feb. 1987.

[43] A majority of Liberals (54.4%) and a large majority of Conservatives (74.1%) favoured means testing over universal provision of social benefits. See Blake (1988) and Archer and Whitehorn (1990, 1991).

[44] In 1968, only 23% cited Big Government as the greatest threat vs. 42% in 1987 (CIPO [1978] and Gallup [1987]).

[45] See, for example, 'Foreign Investment' in Marsh (1988, 1985), and Levitt (1970).

[46] This centralist stress (League for Social Reconstruction, 1975; Lewis, 1981: 461) in part explains the CCF's lack of appeal in the province of Quebec.

[47] This is part of the socialist debate that began in earnest in the 1950s and continued with the New Left in the 1960s (Crosland, 1963; Sargent, 1972).

[48] Of the sizeable sub-samples, only the Prairie region saw a majority of delegates select provincial government over the federal government for an increase in power. See also Whitehorn and Archer (1989) and Archer and Whitehorn (1990, 1991) for more recent observations of this same finding.

[49] This may be yet another example of concern with the growth in the size and powers of government. It should also be noted that a significant percentage wrote in the category 'municipal'. As a result, in the subsequent 1987 NDP survey conducted by Whitehorn and Archer, the municipal level of government was added to the questionnaire, and NDP respondents favoured the municipal level as the location for the greatest increase in power (Whitehorn and Archer, 1989).

[50] This is a position quite similar to that officially adopted by the British Labour Party.

[51] Comparative data on party supporters and members reveal that NDP voters take a more critical attitude towards the United States (CBC Research, 1985: 66; Whitehorn and Archer, 1989).

[52] This is a key theme in Hackett's analysis of survey data from the 1971 leadership contest between the Waffle's Jim Laxer and the so-called 'establishment's' David Lewis.

[53] Not surprisingly, a majority of westerners in 1983 opposed special status for Quebec, while a majority of easterners favoured it.

[54] Support for special status for Quebec was higher among NDPers than either Liberals (33.7%) or Conservatives (36.9%) (Blake, 1988). Results of the 1987 NDP survey on this question suggest that two-thirds of the delegates favoured 'special status' (Whitehorn and Archer, 1989; Archer and Whitehorn, 1990, 1991). Whether that finding will hold up following the Meech Lake backlash remains to be seen.

[55] With the exception of Quebec, there appear to be no significant regional differences among delegates on this issue. Among the few delegates who were from Quebec, not surprisingly, support for this principle is exceptionally high. See also Whitehorn and Archer (1989).

[56] Liberal support in 1984 for a bilingual federal civil service was 79.7%, while Conservative support in 1983 was 38.3% (Blake, 1988; Archer and Whitehorn, 1990, 1991).

[57] See also Whitehorn and Archer (1989).

[58] Unfortunately, no survey data on women's issues are available for the 1971 and 1979 conventions.

[59] As early as 1967 a resolution was passed by an NDP convention favouring the legalization of abortion (Scotton, 1977).

[60] Some caution is advised here, as the coding for the Liberal and Conservative surveys was different from that used for the NDP study.

[61] No related items are available for the 1971 and 1979 surveys.

[62] A 1982 Gallup poll reported that 70% of Canadians favoured the return of capital punishment (*Toronto Star*, 6 Nov. 1982). See Blake (1988) and Archer

and Whitehorn (1990, 1991) for Liberal and Conservative delegate attitudes on this question.

[63] Even though a party may exhibit consensus on an issue, this may not be the case for the public at large. In addition, as a smaller third party, the NDP is often at variance with the Canadian public's position on many important issues.

[64] For comparison, a similar analysis of areas of issue disagreement within the Conservative Party can be found in Perlin (1980: 154-5).

[65] There has been a deliberate effort to keep the statistical methods presented to a level intelligible to non-statisticians.

[66] Some caution is advised, since degree of controversy is also a function of the questions selected by researchers.

[67] This comment reflects only the level of disagreement, not the magnitude of the issues themselves or the intensity of respondents' beliefs.

[68] By contrast, the CBC reported that 74% of Canadians supported free trade on the eve of the 1984 election (CBC Research, 1985). See Frizzell (1989) for comparable data for the 1988 election.

[69] The existence of separate caucuses for women, youth, each of the provincial sections, and unionists accentuates these changes.

[70] With the exception of gender, each of the demographic variables was trichotomized into the following categories: education (1 to 8 years, 9 to 13 years, 14+), community size (farm to 9,999 persons; 10,000 to 499,999; 500,000+), age (under 29, 30 to 49, 50+), family income (under $20,000; $20,000 to $40,000; $40,000+), region (British Columbia, Prairies, Ontario). The delegate sample size for Quebec and the Atlantic region in the 1983 NDP survey was too small for meaningful statistical analysis. Thus regionalism in the NDP is often a somewhat truncated variable not quite reaching from sea to sea. The 1987 NDP convention held in Montreal, however, did provide a sufficient sample size to conduct analysis with a distinct Quebec sub-sample. (See Whitehorn and Archer, 1989.)

[71] Another variable also considered was that of delegate status (e.g., riding vs. affiliated union). Unfortunately, the 1983 sample size for unionists, particularly given the multiple-response problem in the question of delegate status, was far too small for meaningful statistical analysis. However, extremely tentative findings suggest that this variable may be salient in many cases.

SIX

Two Titans of the Party:
T.C. Douglas and David Lewis

This chapter will explore two legendary figures in the history of the CCF-NDP, T.C. Douglas (1904-86) and David Lewis (1909-81). Since, unlike so many other politicians, the former left no memoirs, Part I consists largely of a critical review of the literature on his career. Lewis, on the other hand, did complete the first volume of a projected two-part memoir, and this provides much of the basis for the more detailed examination in Part II.[1] The concluding section looks at some of the extensive literature comparing and, particularly, contrasting these two socialist pioneers.

PART I: T.C. DOUGLAS

Born in Falkirk, Scotland, in 1904, Thomas Clement Douglas first immigrated with his family to Canada in 1911. Returning to Scotland while his father fought in the First World War, the young Douglas came back to Canada just in time to witness the violent suppression of the 1919 Winnipeg General Strike. During this period he, like so many others in the city, was influenced by the radical social-gospel teachings of the Reverend J.S. Woodsworth. After working for several years as a printer's apprentice, in 1924 Douglas entered Brandon College to study for the Baptist ministry.

In 1930 the newly ordained minister took up a full-time position in a parish in Weyburn, Saskatchewan, where the bitter effects of drought, economic depression, and state repression of workers (including the Estevan coal strike of 1931) persuaded him of the necessity for social and political action. Active in the Independent Labour Party and present for part of the historic 1933 CCF convention in Regina (McLeod and McLeod, 1987: 48), Douglas ran unsuccessfully in 1934 as a provincial candidate for the Saskatchewan Farmer Labour Party, a CCF provincial affiliate. He won a federal seat for the CCF the following year. While serving for nine years in a small but able federal caucus led first by Woodsworth and later by M.J. Coldwell, Douglas began his return to Saskatchewan when he became provincial CCF president in 1941 and then undisputed provincial leader in 1942 (McLeod and McLeod, 1987: 103-5). In 1944 he was elected the first social-democratic premier in Canada.

The Douglas administration was noted for a number of significant innovations in government planning and social services. Of the programmes pioneered by his provincial government over the next two decades, no doubt the most important was government-funded and -operated universal medicare. Other goals pursued were northern development, economic diversification, improvements in rural services and education, expanded rights for trade unionists and civil servants, public auto insurance, and the fostering of Crown corporations and co-operatives. This expansion of government programmes took place under the sound economic management of provincial treasurer Clarence Fines.

Following the creation of the NDP and his election as federal leader in 1961, Douglas resigned as premier and went on to serve as NDP leader until 1971. During that time, Douglas saw the federal Parliament approve at the national level several of the measures that he had pioneered in Saskatchewan, including the right of federal civil servants to form unions (1966) and national medicare (1968). Under his leadership the NDP was increasingly critical of the escalating war in Vietnam and the growing foreign economic ownership of Canadian industry, and Douglas himself was a strong defender of civil liberties during the extraordinary events of October 1970, when the Trudeau government imposed the draconian War Measures Act. Although he stepped down as federal leader in 1971, he remained as MP and NDP energy critic until 1979, vigorously supporting the creation of Petro-Canada as a national institution in the mid-1970s. He died, however, in 1986 before he could lend his much-needed support to the nationalist crusade against free trade.

It is regrettable that a man who whose career of activism at the municipal,[2] provincial, and federal levels spanned half a century, and contributed so much to Canadian social and political life, did not write any memoirs. There are, however, two important edited collections of Douglas's speeches and comments that go a significant way towards providing systematic insights into his thoughts and experiences. *Till Power is Brought to Pooling: Tommy Douglas Speaks* (ed. Lovick, 1979) is an excellent compendium of speeches by Douglas from 1936 to 1978, each one is accompanied by a brief and useful introduction by the editor. *The Making of A Socialist: The Recollections of Tommy Douglas* (ed. Thomas, 1982) is somewhat closer to an autobiography. The edited transcript of a series of extensive private interviews conducted by journalist Chris Higginbotham in 1958, it offers some fascinating and frank insights into Douglas's thought. Unfortunately, though, while it provides an in-depth account of most of Douglas's Saskatchewan years, its coverage of his career in national politics is only partial, pre-dating the creation of the NDP.

For some time there was only one biography of Douglas, by Doris French Shackleton (1975). This work draws quite heavily on the 1958 Higginbotham interviews and, when doing so, presents a reasonable account. The post-1958 period, however, is covered with less historical depth and less balance, particularly in its rather one-sided and judgemental use of contrast between Douglas and his successor as federal NDP leader, David Lewis. Michael Bradley's account (1985) is in essence a co-biography of Douglas and Lewis with a conclusion drawn from Laxer's (1984) writings on the modern world economy. Drawing excessively upon Shackleton's biography and Lewis's memoirs, this volume is too often a weak paraphrase of other more analytical and original works. The most recent biography (1987) was written by Tommy McLeod, a long-time senior adviser to the Douglas government in Saskatchewan, and his son Ian. An impressive and balanced account, this work is an example of political biography at its best, and contributes significantly to our understanding of Douglas and his provincial administration, as well as his national career.

On a more general level, several edited collections have included commentary on Douglas or his Saskatchewan government. The first of these, by Lapierre et al. (1971), was published in Douglas's honour upon his retirement as federal NDP leader. In the main, it deals with issues confronting the federal NDP at the time, but it does include two articles, one by George Cadbury and another by Meyer Brownstone, on the Douglas-led Saskatchewan government. More recently, a special commemorative edition of the magazine *NeWest* (1987) published only a year after his death, offers insights from Ed Broadbent, Allan Blakeney, Des Morton, Carlyle King, Tony Mardiros, and Tommy McLeod, among others.[3] The most recent contribution is an edited collection by Ed and Pemrose Whelan (1990) that offers hundreds of personal accounts by local activists of how Tommy Douglas influenced them. To date, however, no overview on the political thought of T. C. Douglas exists.[4] Nor have his two periods in national politics, at the beginning and end of his career, received the attention one might expect.

For example, while much has been made of the importance of the social-gospel tradition in Canadian politics, Richard Allen's two volumes on the subject (1973, 1975) dwell on the pre-1930 period. They therefore ignore the young ministers such as Tommy Douglas, Stanley Knowles, and Sandy Nicholson[5] who, radicalized by the Great Depression, entered politics to serve a larger congregation and became prominent CCF MPs. Clearly the time is ripe for an overview of the social gospel after 1930—when, through the CCF, Douglas was among those who endeavoured to carry out its ideas.[6] Although biographies have been written of J.S. Woodsworth (McNaught, 1959, 1980; MacInnis, 1953; Mills, 1991; Ziegler, 1934), Knowles (Harrop, 1984; Trofimenkoff, 1982), and Nicholson (Dyck, 1988), their coverage of the social gospellers as a group and Douglas as a individual tends to be sparse.

Having earned two university degrees and started on a third—a PhD in sociology—Douglas was well on his way to a possible career as an academic when fate thrust him in a more political direction. Elected to Parliament from 1935 to 1944 and living in Ottawa for much of that time, he would have seemed a logical figure to be highly active in the late 1930s in the League for Social Reconstruction—Canada's equivalent of the Fabian Society. Curiously, though, while there is evidence that he was involved in some LSR meetings and activities, his role seems less than one might have expected, even taking into account that he was out west during part of the formative period of the LSR. Michiel Horn's superb account (1980) of the League for Social Reconstruction contains only two indexed references to Douglas. Was he too busy, as an MP, to get involved? Was the LSR too much an eastern-based organization, largely centred at the University of Toronto and McGill? Or was Douglas ultimately less inclined to scholarship and research? The irony is that in later life he wished academically trained people would become more active and create an LSR-like 'brains trust' for the NDP.

Of the books that have been published on the national CCF and NDP,[7] among the more famous are those by McHenry (1950), Young (1969), Penner (1977), Avakumovic (1978), Morton (1974, 1977, 1986),[8] and L. McDonald (1987). While all of these give positive portrayals of Douglas's skills and commitment, most provide little sustained analysis of the man himself, and few go beyond the best-known events of his career in the party. Only two, McHenry and Avakumovic, examine in detail the unique and pivotal role that Douglas's Saskatchewan government played in the survival and growth of the federal CCF-NDP.

David Lewis's posthumously published autobiography (1981) offers a number of references to Douglas.[9] In general, these are very favourable, although he does complain of Douglas's somewhat folksy style of storytelling (96). Lewis also devotes considerable attention to Douglas's Saskatchewan government, and while noting some initial lack of coherent direction, overall he suggests that the Douglas administration represented the 'proudest chapter of the CCF history' (480). Lewis also points out that even when he was Premier of Saskatchewan, Douglas's commitment to the national party's well-being was exemplary. As Lewis died before completing the second volume of his memoirs, however, his views on several important aspects of Douglas's career at the national level—including the founding of the NDP, Lewis's support for Douglas's leadership of the New Party, Lewis's later impatience at Douglas's postponement of his resignation, and Lewis's years as leader with Douglas in the new role of former leader and fellow MP —are not addressed.[10]

From 1944 to 1961, the focus of Douglas's career was the provincial government of Saskatchewan. Achieving five straight provincial election victories, Douglas was without a doubt the pivotal figure in Saskatchewan politics for almost two decades. Perhaps the most frequently discussed theme regarding the Douglas government is the nature of its ideology. Was it socialist? If so, how much and for how long? If not socialist, what type of regime was it? Needless to say, the answers to these questions vary.

By far the most famous and influential book on Douglas's Saskatchewan CCF government is the pioneering study of agrarian socialism by the American sociologist Seymour Lipset (1950, 1968). While this work, originally printed in 1950, is by no means a complete evaluation of that regime, it has nevertheless set the tone for much subsequent analysis. Focusing on organizational developments, Lipset (1968: 163-4, 188) suggests that the Saskatchewan CCF shifted from being a 'socialist party' to a 'populist', 'agrarian radical', and 'reform' movement: in short, that the CCF achieved popularity at the expense of ideological purity. He concludes that a socialist society is an elusive goal and expresses concern over the increasing bureaucratization and conservatism of a governing political party and its civil service.

Drawing upon Lipset's analysis several decades later, John Richards and Larry Pratt (1979) suggest that the CCF government was 'left populist', not socialist.[11] While noting some initial commitment to socialization and public ownership and some disagreement within the cabinet over this issue, they suggest that the Douglas government, in its increasing acceptance of external private property control, opted for a 'passive rentier ideology' (1979: 197). While they recognize the progressive nature of many of the Douglas government's reforms, Richards and Pratt's perspective is generally critical, favouring a more socialist path. Of course, in their definition of socialism they do not necessarily concur with others, including Douglas.

A number of Marxists and allegedly more militant socialists offer similar critiques of the Douglas government. For example, Sinclair (1973), Davis (1973), and Brown (1973), among others, argue that the CCF was not socialist. Most of these authors, as well as MacPherson (1985) and Rands (1981), also criticize what they believe to have been the bureaucratic, technocratic, and conservative orientation of the Douglas administration. Even Douglas acknowledged that his administration introduced fewer new programmes in later years and eventually became more tolerant of initiatives from private enterprise. This is a theme noted by Larmour (1985), Gruending (1990), McLeod and McLeod (1987), and Dianne Lloyd in her biography (1979) of her father, W.S. Lloyd, Douglas's successor as premier.

Towards the other end of the political spectrum is a harsher right-wing critique of the Douglas government. Tyre (1962: 9, 11, 83, 90) posits that the real goal of the CCF was to be found not in the more moderate 1944 election manifesto propounded by Douglas, but in passages of the supposedly 'doctrinaire' Regina Manifesto. Increasingly, in his view, the Saskatchewan CCF government resembled a Marxian socialist regime characterized by statism, regimentation, and bureaucracy; under the friendly Douglas image, the reality was lack of economic development, excessive state interference, and political patronage.

Several other authors have contributed to the debate, begun by Lipset, over the Douglas government's alleged lack of socialist commitment. Lewis Thomas (1981, 1982) and George Hoffman (1983) suggest that neither the Farmer-Labour Party (which became part of the CCF) nor the CCF itself was as radical as Lipset and others believe, and that the assertion that the Douglas regime moderated a previously radical programme rests on a faulty premise. Thomas notes that socialism does not consist solely of the input side of politics (i.e., public ownership and decision-making), but should also take into account the output side (i.e., a government's policies and distribution of benefits). He observes, for example, that over 60% of the 1948 Saskatchewan budget was spent on health, welfare, and education, and believes that many of these government programmes were of a socialist and redistributive nature. In an article (1971) in a commemorative volume (Lapierre, 1971) dedicated to Douglas, Brownstone suggested that the Saskatchewan civil service was less bureaucratic and more radical than commentators such as Lipset had so far suggested, citing the large number of dismissals and departures of civil servants following the 1964 Liberal victory. Lovick assumes that Douglas's commitment to socialism was sustained and genuine: it was simply phrased in the language of the Bible rather than that of the more strident Marxist class analysis.

Even though one-third of the McLeods' 1987 biography of Douglas (Chapters 11 to 20) covers the years when he was premier, a comprehensive scholarly volume on the Saskatchewan provincial government in that period has yet to be written. Nevertheless, it is clear that Douglas, with the assistance of treasurer Clarence Fines, took an indebted Saskatchewan and rebuilt its financial health. Not only did the Saskatchewan civil service under Premier Douglas pioneer in the expansion of provincial social services in the 1940s and 1950s, but many of its top officials would go on to become key administrative personnel (the so-called Saskatchewan mafia) in the expansion of the federal welfare state in the 1960s (McLeod and McLeod, 1987: 174; Steed, 1988: 129).

Douglas's passionate belief in universal hospital and medical care is a common theme in the literature. Many authors tell the story of Tommy's repeated childhood problems with osteomyelitis, from which he nearly lost a leg: Shackleton, McDonald, the McLeods, and Lloyd all suggest that his personal experience of the inadequacies of the health-care system fuelled his determination that no child ever again should go without medical care because of insufficient family income. It was no accident that the new Premier of Saskatchewan in 1944 was also the Minister of Health and would be largely identified as the father of medicare. Nor, as several also note, was it an accident that, having struggled against financial obstacles to achieve an education, Douglas oversaw a substantial improvement in the quality and funding of schooling in the province. The long list of other pioneering and progressive legislation implemented by the Douglas regime is well-documented in McHenry (1950), Lipset (1968), Richards and Pratt (1979), and Higginbotham (1968), among others.

Since the public at large often seems to prefer focusing upon individual political personalities rather than theoretical concerns, it is not surprising that an important aspect of the literature on the CCF-NDP treats Douglas as a personification of the party. In virtually every case the portrayal is positive. However, there are really two variants of these sorts of writings. The first draws favourable parallels between Douglas and other respected leaders in the party. For example, Trofimenkoff (1982) notes that both Douglas and Knowles had been printers, classmates, and social-gospel ministers radicalized by the Depression before running for public office on behalf of the CCF and NDP. A number of authors (Thomas, Bradley, Shackleton, McLeods) also note the close relationship between the parish minister Douglas and the ex-school principal M.J. Coldwell, who, as a provincial Farmer-Labour Party (i.e., CCF) leader in the 1930s and federal leader in the 1940s and 1950s, is often cited as Douglas's mentor; together, they formed a team of teacher and preacher.

The second variant of the personality theme in this literature endeavours to point out differences between Douglas and his colleagues. No political scenario would be complete without contrasts and alleged struggles between good and evil, or at least between different levels of goodness. The most striking examples of this theme, of course, can be seen in the literature on Douglas and Lewis, discussed in Part III below. But this is by no means the only pairing in which authors have emphasized differences. Thus even Trofimenkoff, while noting many similarities between Douglas and Knowles, suggests that in other ways they were quite different: 'Douglas was an organizer, Knowles an attender to detail. Douglas engaged in flights of rhetoric and sometimes of fancy; Knowles . . . is a plodder'. Even in their days together at Brandon College, Knowles, 'playing the number two role, was Tommy's cheer-leader in student elections. Douglas took honours in dramatics and debating; Knowles took them in academics' (1982: 186).

Naturally, these good friends— Knowles was best man at Douglas's wedding —are portrayed as complementary.

The relationship between Douglas and George Williams, Saskatchewan CCF leader from 1935 to 1941, was somewhat more conflictual and certainly less friendly. Thomas (1982), Shackleton (1975), the McLeods (1987), and Mrs Williams (see Kerr, 1981: 49-51) all suggest a certain amount of tension between the two men. Part of the reason was a residual effect of Williams's somewhat indelicate replacement of Douglas's friend Coldwell as provincial leader, when he won a seat in the 1934 election and Coldwell did not. Another reason was the controversial co-endorsement of Douglas by the Social Credit Party in his 1935 federal election campaign (see McLeod and McLeod, 1987: 56-68), which evoked a strong negative outburst from Williams as Saskatchewan provincial leader. Policy differences were also a factor. For example, as the Second World War approached, Williams advocated wholehearted military involvement; Mrs Williams's suggests he saw the CCF as too inclined towards pacifism. Promptly enlisting, Williams tried to keep the leadership in absentia, but Douglas was elected to replace him. Despite their earlier differences, Williams returned near the end of the war to serve, albeit briefly, in Douglas's historic first cabinet.

Far more acrimonious was the relationship between Douglas and Ross Thatcher, a CCF MP from 1945 to 1955 who then left the party and later became Saskatchewan Liberal leader and Premier from 1964 to 1971. Douglas himself suggests he 'despised' few men, but this defector who 'proceeded to malign his former colleagues, and criticized all the things that only a few years before he himself had been advocating' certainly qualified for contempt (Thomas, 1982: 354-5). The acrimonious 1957 debate at Mossbank, Saskatchewan, between the two men, in which Thatcher berated Douglas for the inefficiencies of Crown corporations (Tyre, 1962), did little to improve their personal relationship. It did, however, heighten Thatcher's image as a new opponent of socialism and helped to pave the way for his eventual victory over the two-decade-old socialist administration.

Douglas's relationship with Hazen Argue (1921-91) became similarly testy. A CCF MP from 1945 to 1962, after serving first as House Leader and then as the last CCF federal leader (1960-1961) Argue too defected, eventually becoming a Liberal cabinet minister and controversial Senator. At the NDP's founding convention in Ottawa in 1961, ex-Saskatchewan premier Douglas handily crushed Argue's leadership bid 1,391 votes to 380. A year later, echoing Thatcher's questionable style of departure, Argue abandoned the NDP. If, apart from press clippings and the biography by the McLeods, there is relatively little published coverage of Douglas's later federal career, there is even less academic analysis on Argue. Shackleton briefly summarizes Douglas's final attitude to Argue with the accusation of 'betrayal'. This is a charge very similar to the one Douglas levelled a few years earlier at Thatcher. A proposed biography of Argue, if it ever appears, might provide some further insights.

Douglas's relationship with his successor as Saskatchewan CCF premier, Woodrow Lloyd, was quite different. Douglas's preferred choice to guide the Saskatchewan party, Lloyd was left with a bombshell soon to explode — the medicare crisis. An account of this conflict and Douglas's role in it can be found in the books on the 1962 doctors' strike in Saskatchewan by Badgley and Wolfe (1967) and Tollefson (1963). That Dianne Lloyd, in her 1979 biography, is uncritical of her late father is not surprising; what is perhaps unexpected is that she makes relatively few references to Douglas. When she does, they are often by way of contrast and in a slightly critical vein. For example, along with others (e.g., Gruending, 1990), she notes that Douglas was a far more charismatic figure than Lloyd, and thus made it difficult for a less dynamic person to succeed him. Along with Gruending, Lloyd also hints that her father was perhaps more socialistically inclined than the key figures in the Douglas administration.[12]

Finally, every author agrees that Douglas was a superb debater and orator.[13] This is no minor factor when one considers that the ideas and doctrines he sponsored were not always the most popular ones among the public at large. Clearly Douglas's verbal skills enabled him to lead his party to greater success than might otherwise have been the case; many a farmer, one suspects, voted more for Tommy the man than for the CCF as a party or the cause of socialism. Even ideological opponents (e.g., Tyre, 1962: 41-2, 54) have conceded that he was an extremely effective campaigner, and was perhaps the key factor in a number of his party's victories. His attentiveness to others and his dedication to the cause of social improvement, from his days as a young radical clergyman to the end of his eminent political career, are acknowledged by virtually all authors. The commentary on his successor as federal leader, as we shall see in the next two sections, has been more divided and, at times, controversial.

PART II: DAVID LEWIS

The political career of David Lewis spans virtually his entire life (1909-81). He was a member of several radical labour parties in Montreal in the 1920s, a founding member of the League for Social Reconstruction in the 1930s, national secretary of the CCF from 1936 to 1950, a long-serving member of the CCF-NDP federal executive from the 1950s onwards, a key member of the National Committee for the New Party, which founded the NDP in 1961, one of the most dynamic Members of Parliament in the 1960s and 1970s, a pivotal player in the minority Parliament of 1972-74, and federal leader of the NDP from 1971 to 1975.

For many commentators and party activists alike, the stories of Lewis and the federal CCF-NDP are intertwined. Elsewhere in this book (particularly in

Chapter 2) some analysis has already been offered concerning the portrayal of Lewis's role within the party. The primary focus here will be a number of key themes raised in the Lewis memoirs, *The Good Fight* (1981); in Smith's volume on the Lewis family, *Unfinished Journey* (1989); and in two other books that Lewis wrote, *Make This Your Canada* (with F.R. Scott, 1943) and *Louder Voices: Corporate Welfare Bums* (1972).[14] These will be combined with some personal reflections by the author, who for three years served as research director for the Lewis memoirs.

To understand David Lewis's political ideas,[15] it may be useful to explore in chronological order some of the key events and people that influenced his life.

Few observers would dispute that David Lewis was a highly politicized and determined individual; indeed, some would add the adjective 'tough'. What is less well known is how early in his life Lewis's politicization began.[16] His was not a typically innocent and protected North American childhood.

David Lewis was born a member of the Losh family (Losz in Polish) in 1909 in the small Jewish village of Svisloch in tsarist Russia. A highly rural, poor, and largely illiterate peasant society,[17] politically Russia was an almost feudal autocracy on the abyss of revolutionary change (Trotsky, 1959). Tsar Nicolas II ruled over a multi-ethnic empire that included millions of Jews, and 'discrimination, persecution and pogroms' (5, 227) were widespread. Indeed, the Losh family's village was burned down in 1910, when David was only a year old (Smith: 93).

Any ethnic or religious minority located near the border of a state often experiences the dislocation of shifting political boundaries. So it was with Svisloch.[18] Lewis's memoirs recount vividly how, during the First World War, when he was just six, the German troops moved through the town like a tornado. After several nights of bombardment during which families huddled in cellars for protection, they came out to see the 'unnerving' sight of dead men lying in 'pools of blood' (7).[19] For the next three years the town was occupied by the German army.[20] The schools were officially forbidden to operate, but the young Lewis defied the ban to 'surreptitiously' attend a religious school in a cellar. Later he wrote that 'the experience of the war and the German occupation . . . matured a little boy beyond his years' (8).

Svisloch was soon to feel the effects of yet more violence. The eight-year-old Lewis and his family 'rejoiced' at the overthrow of the outmoded and repressive tsarist regime, and were optimistic about the new provisional government of Kerensky. But their hopes were soon dashed as the second and far more violent phase—the Bolshevik Revolution[21] led by Lenin's Communist Party—commenced.

The First World War and the intertwined Russian revolutions might well have been enough to politicize any youngster. However, the chain of devastating political events continued unbroken. As part of the 1919

Versailles Treaty, the state of Poland was recreated and Svisloch was placed under its jurisdiction. But the fragile peace was soon shattered by war between Poland and the Soviet Union, and, occupied now by the Red Army, Svisloch was thrust into the midst of the Soviet civil war.

Lewis's father, who was a local leader in the Marxist Jewish Labour Bund, had supported the Mensheviks and distrusted Lenin's Bolsheviks even before the revolution.[22] As Lewis notes, his father became 'outraged' by some of the repressive deeds of the Bolshevik government and publicly condemned such actions (8-10). The arrival of Soviet troops soon unleashed the wrath of Lenin's communists and the first steps in a reign of terror were taken. As Lewis recalls, 'the Bolsheviks arrested a number of the town's residents, among them my father. To our horror, they threatened to execute him because he was a leading Menshevik who had publicly condemned the Soviet regime' (10).[23] After members of the community petitioned on the elder Lewis's behalf, his life was spared. Six decades later, his son still vividly recalled his feelings: 'Now a mature eleven-year-old, I was angered by this Bolshevik cruelty. . . . It was an unforgettable experience which evoked a deep and lasting animosity toward all communists' (10). These memories would have a significant effect on Lewis's view of the various factions within the Canadian political left in later years.

The return of the Polish army to Svisloch brought more brutal torture and reprisals. With few prospects for a better future, the Losh family, like so many East European Jews, decided to emigrate to a safer land.

Renamed Lewis to appease immigration officials, the family arrived in Montreal in 1921. But if Canada provided a far less dangerous setting, for a poor Jewish family life in xenophobic Quebec could still be difficult (452). Even more disorienting than the change in the family name was the inability to speak English.[24] Lewis describes 'feeling dumb', 'growing more and more discouraged and downcast', and experiencing 'shame and humiliation' (15). However, armed with a copy of Dickens's *The Old Curiosity Shop* and characteristic determination, he 'spent hours reading' (16) and soon mastered the language.[25]

Even as a young adult, Lewis was not spared the effects of catastrophic events. While he was still a student at McGill University, the world-wide economic depression of 1929 wreaked its havoc. David's father, like millions of other workers and immigrants, struggled with layoffs, declining income, and eventually ill health. Global economic woes were soon compounded by the forces of political extremism with the rise in the 1930s of Hitler's virulent brand of anti-Semitism and fascist violence. Although Lewis and his immediate family were no longer in the direct path of Nazi atrocities, he did risk his life during brief trips to Germany and Austria in 1934 (70-3) when he met clandestinely with fellow socialists and Jews. His father Moishe became involved in efforts to rescue Jews from Nazi oppression and later post-war poverty. Moishe, with the help of his son, pleaded repeatedly with Canadian government officials to allow more such refugees to immigrate to Canada (343-4; Smith: 144-5, 213-4; Abella and Tropper [1982]).

The revelation of the genocide of millions of Jews had a profound impact upon many, including Lewis. Whereas previously, as a Jew in the tradition of the socialist Bund (27, 31; see also Smith: 395), he had opposed Zionism, henceforth he 'ceased being critical' of it (227). This was as far as he was prepared to go towards Jewish nationalism.

In the thirty-six years from his birth until the end of the Second World War, David Lewis had experienced unusual hardships and 'traumas' (452). This may be one of the reasons his political skills were so sharp and quick. Many of his colleagues in Canada, used to a more gentle and forgiving environment, often could not see dangers that Lewis knew first-hand. Some well-meaning leftists, for example, believed for far too long that Stalin and his fellow communists were simply misunderstood, or would somehow change. Lewis knew otherwise, and eventually they would too (Crossman, 1949; Penner, 1988).

A key force in the political education of the young Lewis was his father Moishe (sometimes known as Morris), a 'comrade of principle and wisdom' whom David 'loved . . . deeply' (366). As a very young child David had listened attentively to political discussions in his parents' home, and even as a schoolboy he had been taken by his father to polit-ical meetings (2, 18, 20; Smith: 145). A former yeshiva student who had turned from religion to radical politics,[26] Moishe was a 'thoughtful and contemplative', largely self-educated man who 'spent every spare minute reading' (3-4). Becoming a prominent and respected local leader in the Jewish Workers' Bund (3-4) in Svisloch, he was one of many calling for revolutionary changes in tsarist Russia.

The Bund, aligned with the Mensheviks, was critical of the élitism and excessive violence of the Bolsheviks, and instead advocated a less auto-cratic and more participatory form of Marxism (8, 27; Smith: 63-7, 107) with a radical trade-union base. As presented to David Lewis by his father, it was to prove an important political heritage. Emphasizing a 'sense of justice, . . . identification with workers . . . commitment to equality and democratic procedures, . . . fierce anti-communism, . . . secular humanism, . . . multi-culturalism, [a] sense of international community, [and] anger with exploitation' (Smith: 132-3), it provided the cornerstone of David Lewis's political world view.

The collective impact of the ideology of the Bund and of his father implanted in the young David Losh a core of beliefs that he would later describe as 'hard nosed, . . . Marxism of the revisionist kind' (27).[27] This continuing humanist Marxist heritage of the Bund is a key theme in Smith's volume on the three generations of Lewises.

While this is not the place for an in-depth analysis of Lewis's political thought, it may be worthwhile to note its key features and their similarity to the Bundist position. In the early part of his career, for instance, as was the case for so many activists in the early days of socialism and the CCF, Lewis took a rather internationalist perspective. As a survivor of the First World War, he looked upon nationalism with some scepticism,[28] although this perspective began to change from the 1950s onwards, when concerns increased about the degree of foreign ownership of Canadian industry and resources.[29]

Having experienced the injustices in the social systems of both Europe and Canada, Lewis tended to see political and social relations in terms of class inequality and Marxian categories,[30] and was far less inclined to eschew confrontational language than were those from the more idealistic social-gospel tradition who foresaw a co-operative path to the New Jerusalem. Relatedly, in international affairs Lewis rejected the utopianism of Woodsworth's pacifism in favour of a more realistic policy of collective security that nevertheless was still committed to the assistance of the wronged and the less powerful.

As Smith points out, the Jewish Workers' Bund was active not only in the formation of a socialist party but also in the politicization and organization of workers' trade unions; developing a strong nexus between the socialist and labour movements was seen as crucial to the collective liberation of the working class. In his long service as a party official in the CCF and a lawyer in the trade-union movement, Lewis drew upon this tradition, which came to fruition with these two groups' sponsorship of the NDP.

Another feature in Lewis's thought that seems compatible with the ideology of the Bund was his inclination towards a centralist variant of socialism (e.g., emphasizing the need for a centrally planned economy, the powers of the federal government on constitutional matters, and the need for a strong national office with regard to party organization).

One of the most important Canadian influences on David Lewis's early intellectual and political development was the small group of Montreal academics involved with the League for Social Reconstruction[31] (Horn, 1980) and largely centred at McGill University, which Lewis entered in 1927. These Fabian-style socialists included Frank Scott, Eugene Forsey,[32] and King Gordon.[33] In the words of Lewis himself, 'the emphasis which my professor friends gave to the need for positive programmes was . . . an invaluable addition to my philosophic kitbag' (27).

Nevertheless, the most influential of all was Frank Scott.[34] Starting in 1929, their friendship would continue for the next half century. A young professor of constitutional law, a decade older than Lewis, initially Scott performed the role of mentor and 'inspiration' (337). For example, he encouraged the impoverished undergraduate to apply for the prestigious Rhodes scholarship. Winning such an international award would prove a key step in the advancement of Lewis's career intellectually, politically, and even financially.

Lewis's interview for the Rhodes scholarship is now part of Canadian political folklore.[35] The examining committee included Sir Edward Beatty, the president of the CPR, one of Canada's largest and most powerful corporations. After 45 minutes of questioning by the committee, Sir Edward turned to Lewis and asked: 'Lewis, if you became the first socialist prime minister of Canada, what would be the first thing you would do?' With a 'defiant glint' in his eyes, Lewis shot back: 'Nationalize the CPR, sir.' 'Sir Edward smiled with amusement and the other [committee] members exchanged silent glances which I could not interpret' (34). In a rather unorthodox follow-up interview a day later, Lewis was grilled about his political views and attitude to the Russian Revolution. Although Lewis was 'not conciliatory', with the tolerance of Beatty he was approved as the first Jewish Rhodes scholar from Quebec (224). Lewis writes: 'I have never felt as grateful to anyone as I did to Beatty at that moment' (35). Usually cited as evidence of Lewis's brashness[36] and somewhat confrontational style, this episode to many conveys a happy story of a poor immigrant boy achieving career success and upward social mobility in part, at least, as a result of corporate largesse; Beatty is personified as the humane face of capitalism. However, the exchange between the young socialist and the CPR executive was in some ways only the preliminary round in a far more aggressive and serious struggle.[37]

While politically Lewis was experienced far ahead of most in his age group, the years at Oxford (1932-35) were still formative, particularly when combined with trips to continental Europe. They enabled Lewis to see first-hand the work of the influential British Labour Party and to establish close contacts with socialist authors and leading figures in the Labour party. Among the latter was Stafford Cripps, a lawyer, MP, and former cabinet minister who, according to Smith, was both a close friend and a mentor (184-5). Certainly Cripps offered Lewis a job in his law firm, and his colleagues in the Labour Party promised the articulate young man a safe seat in the British parliament. In declining both, Lewis chose Canada and a far more difficult political path.

One radical socialist professor at Oxford with whom Lewis came into contact was G.D.H. Cole, the leading proponent of guild socialism[38] and later the author of the monumental seven-volume *History of Socialist Thought*, published in the 1950s. While Lewis was already a seasoned veteran of left-wing politics,[39] Cole's erudition and sweeping knowledge of socialist theory were valuable influences. As Lewis notes in his memoirs:

> I have always felt grateful for the good fortune which brought me close to Cole. I attended a study group on socialist theory and practice, which he guided, and when I changed [from law] to P.P.E. [Philosophy, Politics and Economics], he agreed to be one of my tutors. During my last year I spent many hours in his study . . . and we became good friends. . . . While I did not always agree with his judgements, I learned a great deal from him (63).[40]

Nevertheless, Cole's decentralist guild socialism[41] (Cole, 1918) failed to influence Lewis, as did later advocates of workers' self-management in the 1970s (Broadbent, 1970; Whitehorn, 1974, 1978, 1979a).

While at Oxford, Lewis received several mailings from J.S. Woodsworth, federal leader of the newly created CCF, including, in 1933, a copy of the recently drafted Regina Manifesto (65). When, two years later, Lewis completed his studies and was tempted to stay in Britain, Woodsworth encouraged him to return to Canada:

> there [is] a wonderful field for your activities here in Canada. I had heard the rumour some time ago that you might enter public life in Great Britain, I can understand the openings that there would be there, but . . . we can assure you plenty of hard work and more or less uncertainty, but at the same time, a great opportunity to wake up and organize this young country of ours (quoted in Lewis: 75-6).

Although, as Lewis notes, the letter offered 'no glittering promise of ease' (76), he nevertheless 'felt the irresistible pull of Woodsworth's appeals' (84), and returned to Canada just as the country was preparing to go to the polls.

After a somewhat disappointing federal election for the CCF in 1935 (see Chapter 4), it was clear to many that the party needed vastly improved organizational operations, particularly at the centre (110-13). Fresh from his first-hand observations of the British Labour Party, Lewis commenced work as the part-time national secretary of the CCF[42] and opened the party's new and extremely modest headquarters; it lacked a washroom and had only a sand floor (117), but in the Depression such conditions were not unheard of. When, within two years, M.J. Coldwell, Lewis, and others suggested expanding the scope of the party's national office and employing a full-time national secretary, Woodsworth was not enthusiastic because the party lacked the funds and he was concerned about excessive centralization (125). Once more, however, F.R. Scott played a major role in advancing Lewis's career. One of the senior voices in the CCF and LSR, Scott recommended Lewis's becoming full-time national secretary of the CCF in 1938, and together with Coldwell helped to overcome Woodsworth's misgivings (127). This was not the last time Woodsworth would be outvoted on an important matter within senior party circles.[43]

Lewis was to serve as national secretary for fourteen years in all—longer than anyone since.[44] Even more impressive was the range of his activities. He was not only an essential administrative official[45] in an underfunded and understaffed office, but also a key party theorist, drafting manifestos and writing on ideological matters.[46] In this sense, he was a party secretary in the European tradition, not simply the bureaucrat that a number of commentators (e.g., Cross, 1974: 16) have suggested. During his tenure, publications such as *Across Canada* and *News Comment*, pamphlets, and study guides emerged with reasonable regularity from the national office.[47] Few, if any, of his successors, working with larger budgets and, usually, more staff have maintained such an extensive range of involvement,[48] and certainly the national party's publications programme in recent decades has often been almost non-existent except at election time. An enduring national party newspaper remains only a dream, while a national magazine has survived only intermittently (the latest incarnation being *Alternative*).[49]

As national secretary from 1936 onwards, Lewis came into contact with many party activists. The three with whom he worked most closely, and upon whom he came most to rely, were the inner circle of Coldwell, Angus MacInnis,[50] and Frank Scott (220, 337; Djwa and Macdonald, 1983: 87), although he often added the names of Stanley Knowles[51] and Tommy Douglas to the select list of those working in 'harmony' with him (326, 372).[52] Most of these men worked closely on the committee drafting a new statement of principles and the National Committee for the New Party (424, 497).

Particularly important to Lewis was Coldwell (1888-1974), a former teacher and alderman from Saskatchewan who served in Parliament for an uninterrupted 23 years—a remarkable success rate for any politician in Canada, and particularly so for a socialist one. As Woodsworth became increasingly ill, Coldwell took over for him on an acting basis in 1940 and, after Woodsworth's death in 1942, succeeded him as federal leader. His 18-year tenure as leader (1942-60), was the longest of any in the federal CCF-NDP.[53] Describing Coldwell as a 'magnificent' person with a 'natural charm and gentle sympathy' and 'unwavering generosity of spirit' (86, 87, 90), Lewis characterizes him as a leader with a high degree of 'credibility' (220) and even goes so far as to say he loved him (90, 499). This is high praise indeed from a man not known for public expressions of affection.

In many ways, Coldwell was a mentor for Lewis.[54] Nearly a generation younger than Woodsworth, Coldwell was also a less austere figure, more compatible in temperament and style with Lewis. Woodsworth was an uncompromising—some would say rigid—religious visionary and idealist who was willing to stand alone in Parliament and proclaim unilaterally the relevance and viability of pacifism while the world marched to war. Coldwell, like Lewis, was more secular, worldly and practical in recognizing the need for a realistic commitment to collective security to foster peace.[55] As Lewis notes, 'I felt that I worked with Coldwell but that I worked for Woodsworth' (90). Coldwell and Lewis were also closer both in their political views and in their organizational analyses. For example, Coldwell had pushed for the creation of a more professional, permanent and centralized national office (125-6)—a decision of which Lewis was the main beneficiary.

Among the qualities that Lewis, a distinguished speaker himself, admired in Coldwell was his 'trait of understatement. . . . he could speak with indignation without sounding shrill or strident . . . . He tended to deal more with program than with philosophy, more with bread-and-butter policies than with theory, but he seldom failed to build a frame of first principles on which to mount his attack on injustice' (87). This passage sounds very much like a description of its author in later years. Certainly Lewis himself eventually learned the power of understatement to win over sceptical audiences.[56] As he was wont to point out, the lesson for would-be radicals is that a speaker's language must to a reasonable degree suit the audience; effective public speaking and mass education require discipline, not self-indulgent rhetoric.

Another mentor was Scott, first as a faculty member at McGill University[57] and later as one of the two pivotal figures in the LSR.[58] Before long, however, Scott and Lewis became virtual equals as high-profile spokesmen for the national CCF (Scott as national chairman and Lewis as national secretary) and served together on party committees drafting numerous party documents. Both were on the 1939 committee that drafted a statement on the CCF's position at the outset of the Second World War, a statement that needed to satisfy the various ideological strains within the party (173). Both were also members of the historic National Committee for a New Party (NCNP) that oversaw the transformation of the CCF into the NDP. As national secretary, Lewis consulted with Scott 'almost daily', (222) and had 'great respect for [his] judgment' (32), 'quickness of mind', 'wide knowledge, intellectual curiosity, and flexibility' (220). He also admired Scott's ability to combine theory and practice (380). In 1943 their collaboration produced *Make This Your Canada*,[59] of which a remarkable 25,000 copies were sold in less than a year. Not surprisingly, the two shared many ideas over a wide range of political topics, and rarely disagreed.[60] Both men, echoing developments in socialist parties elsewhere in the world, recognized the need for a restatement of CCF principles in the 1950s, and played key roles in drafting the Winnipeg Declaration of 1956. Both fluent in French, the two were also among the very small band promoting the CCF in Quebec.[61] Scott, the son of an Anglican archdeacon, and Lewis, 'the son of a free-thinking Jew' (458) were like David challenging the Goliath of the reactionary Roman Catholic hierarchy in Quebec (Baum, 1980). In the rest of the country, they endeavoured to convince their colleagues that more effort was needed to transform the somewhat regionally-based CCF into a pan-Canadian party with a strong base in both French and English Canada. Needless to say, they shared a strong commitment to a bilingual Canada[62] and, within it, a bilingual social-democratic party, and they did so at a time when few Anglophone Canadians, socialist or otherwise, were so inclined (464-8).

Their political partnership was not the only area in which Scott benefitted Lewis. The older man exuded confidence and sociability, not to mention the financial affluence of a 'comfortable and established family' (221),[63] all traits with which a former immigrant like Lewis might wish to identify, at least on occasion. Most important, Scott possessed a wide range of intellectual interests. An 'academic, poet, philosopher, theorist, and satirist' (220), he provided the highly partisan Lewis with brief moments of respite from the political wars—an 'opportunity of pulling the curtain down on the political stage from time to time' that was 'like a release from mental bondage' (222-3). His importance to Lewis is perhaps best illustrated in the fact that Lewis selected Scott to address the funeral of his father—a service that he was to perform again, three decades later, at David's own funeral. Lewis, not normally noted for expressions of affection, offered the following evaluation of Scott: 'I loved the man because he exuded life and verve and a sense of humour and a sense of the absurd and because it was a joy working with him' (Djwa, 1987: 128-9).[64]

During the 1940s and 1950s, the CCF had closer relations with the Canadian Congress of Labour (CCL)[65] than the Trades and Labour Congress (TLC). Even so, the presence of a number of communists in the CCL hampered the latter's working relationship with the socialist CCF (303; Horowitz, 1968; Abella, 1973). To make matters worse, the communist leadership internationally had shifted from the authoritarian Lenin to the brutal Stalin.[66] Given Lewis's experience with communists as a boy in Svisloch, it is not surprising that he took a critical and uncompromising stance towards communist militants and emissaries from Moscow (Penner, 1988).

The only time when Lewis entertained illusions about the communists was for a couple of years in the mid-1930s (107); by 1938, however, he saw the ruthlessness of the Stalinist Communist International (298, 149). The language that he employs in this regard is consistent and uncompromising. The Soviet Union under Stalin was an 'intolerant and cruel dictatorship'; 'Stalin's incredible barbarism' showed the 'paranoia' of a 'medieval despot' (18, 481). Nor were 'there really [any] autonomous local communist parties outside the Soviet Union' (42, 150); the Communist Party of Canada was merely a 'puppet' of Stalin (150; see also Penner, 1988; Whitehorn, 1991) and as such reflected the dictator's own lack of ethical standards (107, 291, 42).[67]

Lewis realized that it might be difficult for many younger people to appreciate how serious the challenge posed by the communists was in earlier decades; today, he wrote, they seem like 'demons of the past' (152). However, during the world-wide depression of the 1930s, many people either had inadequate access to information or were disinclined to look for critical information on the Soviet Union and communism, and as a result these two forces had considerable influence. For Lewis, though, the Stalinist threat was real. Moreover, Communist militants caused substantial disruption in the labour movement. Lewis was at the forefront of the socialist response to the communist challenge (Horowitz, 1968; Abella, 1973; Smith, 1989: 307-9). Indeed, he fought it so strenuously that he was accused of letting it become an 'obsession' (301, 348-9). In his memoirs

Lewis wrote: 'I make no apology for it' (298). Today, some of the most damning indictments of past communist misdeeds come from former Leninists themselves. Lewis's analysis and prescriptions, while occasionally unpopular at the time, proved to be more viable in the long run than many of his contemporaries'.

In 1950, with CCF prospects dwindling, Lewis finally decided to step down as national secretary and instead practise law, in hopes of easing his family's financial burdens. Nevertheless, his extensive involvement with the CCF continued. Given his long tenure as federal secretary, Lewis was an obvious choice for a number of executive positions. He thus served as party vice-chairman in the early 1950s, and as chairman and then president in the late 1950s and early 1960s.

In partnership with Ted Jolliffe,[68] who was Ontario CCF leader from 1942 to 1953, Lewis specialized in labour law from the early 1950s to the late 1960s. As might have been expected, this work enabled him to widen his already extensive contacts with senior trade-union officials and, in so doing, to foster stronger links between the struggling CCF and the increasingly united labour movement. Such relations would prove crucial in the creation of the New Democratic Party.

The 1950s were difficult years for Canadian socialists as the post-war economic boom seemed to belie the socialists' pessimistic predictions about life under capitalism. The Cold War between the Soviet Union and the United States generated an East-West rigidity in international relations and polarized the ideological spectrum. North America had become a hostile environment for the left of any shade, and there was little room for social democrats to manoeuvre. CCF membership and income declined. During these difficult years, Lewis played a pivotal role not only among the party faithful[69] but also in the drafting of both the 1956 Winnipeg Declaration and the 1961 New Party statement (see Chapter 3), both attempts to update social-democratic principles and policies from the 1930s for the post-war era. Among the major factors that needed to be addressed in any socialist revisions were the relative affluence of the consumer society and the nuclear balance of terror.

An older generation of veteran socialists (see MacDonald, 1988: 112, 176-7; Forsey, 1990: 130; Djwa, 1987), who had lived through the 1930s Depression, the 1940s World War, and the 1950s Cold War, acknowledged with gratitude[70] the positive role that Lewis played in keeping alive a social-democratic party capable of articulating a vision of a more just society based on a mixed economy. In contrast, a younger generation of New Leftists (e.g., Cross, 1974), living in a more affluent age when the ideological left was more in vogue, accused Lewis of betraying socialism.[71] These latter-day radicals called for massive public ownership, greater criticism of the market mechanism, and heavier reliance on state central planning. Time would tell which interpretation would prove the more enduring.

With the defeat of the aging federal leader M.J. Coldwell in the 1958 Conservative landslide, the CCF caucus was reduced to a small rump (see Chapter 4). While Hazen Argue was chosen in a close vote as caucus leader, Lewis and a number of the party's executive officers made it quite clear that they did not want him to become the next federal leader (Young, 1969: 235-8). Despite their strenuous efforts, delegates at the 1960 CCF federal convention overruled the national council and unanimously elected Argue as the last CCF federal leader. A year later he lost in his bid to become the first leader of the New Democratic Party, and within a year after that he shocked his colleagues with his announcement that he was leaving the NDP. Later joining the Liberals, he was eventually rewarded for this cross-over with a Senate position.[72]

The Argue affair raises several questions. It has often been claimed that Lewis imposed his will upon the party's mass membership. However, in 1960 the rank and file, not to mention the more militant leftists, who wanted Argue as their champion, clearly overcame the objections of Lewis and others. The fact that today Argue is seen as an embarrassment, is never mentioned in official party literature, and certainly is not cited favourably by the radicals in the party, suggests that Lewis's judgement was correct. Still, there are some nagging questions. Were Lewis's actions in part a catalyst for Argue's dissatisfaction?[73] Would Argue have stayed a loyal member of the party if Lewis and other members of the executive had shown more willingness to recruit new MPs into the inner decision-making circles? Although it is clear that Lewis was not inclined to nurse his colleagues' egos, it is still hard to imagine that Argue would not eventually have bolted in any case.

The phoenix-like rebirth of the CCF as the NDP was a complex and lengthy process that, as Lewis notes (486), began well before the 1958 election, and continued with scores of meetings for the rest of that decade and into the next, in the CCF, the CLC, and New Party clubs and seminars.

While Tommy Douglas was to become the NDP federal leader, Lewis was the architect of the party (McLeod and McLeod, 1987: 206; MacDonald, 1988; J. McLeod, 1988; Smith: 387); to many, it was 'the party that David built'. In the words of Young, 'It was the culmination of some twenty-five years of effort on the part of David Lewis, above all, to make the CCF into a Canadian version of the British Labour party' (1969: 133).

The creation of the New Party (Knowles, 1961) involved three goals. One was to strengthen the bond between the labour movement and a social-democratic party. Increased union affiliation to the party was one way (Archer, 1990); another was co-sponsorship of a new joint party (i.e., the NDP) by the CCF and the CLC.

Lewis and his fellow members on the National Committee for the New Party (NCNP) were all too aware that the portion of the Canadian electorate devoted to the left side of the political spectrum in general and socialism in particular was insufficient for a federal election breakthrough. Thus they reasoned that some effort must be made to win over the centre-left portion of the spectrum—the liberally-minded.[74] This calculation would necessarily require an ideological shift, whether tactical or permanent. It also meant widening the class base of the party to include more middle-class elements—an unfulfilled goal of Woodsworth's at the founding of the CCF in the 1930s.

A third and crucial goal was to achieve a breakthrough in Quebec, a province that was in the midst of profound social transformation. With the 'quiet revolution' of the early 1960s, this traditionally insular, rural community, dominated by the Roman Catholic church, was becoming a more modern, secular, and urban society.[75] Party strategists hoped the new Quebec would be an environment more friendly to the social-democratic cause.[76]

Given the CCF's history of selecting as its leaders Anglophones from the west, the choice of a new leader, along with a new platform, for the New Party took on added symbolic importance. The most likely candidates were the current CCF leader, Hazen Argue; the highly successful Premier of Saskatchewan, Tommy Douglas; and the former CCF national secretary and key trade-union lawyer, David Lewis. Yet only Argue and Douglas chose to run. Lewis's decision was a complex one, with reasons both for and against. On the negative side was the stark fact that he had never won election to Parliament in the entire CCF era. Given the federal party's electoral record in recent years, a leader with no election victories was one risk the New Party could do without. Douglas, by contrast, had put together an impressive string of uninterrupted victories from 1944 to 1961 in Saskatchewan, and could foster a positive image of the party's ability to govern with fiscal restraint, administrative competence, and social justice. For the farmers and others in the west who were concerned that eastern trade unions and/or Quebec might take over the new party, a Douglas candidacy had the added advantage of assuaging some of those fears. Finally, a substantial number in the party believed that Douglas was better with people than Lewis was, and that a Lewis candidacy might produce a more divisive founding convention, particularly if he ran against Douglas.[77]

Perhaps the major reason for Lewis's reluctance to be a candidate, however, was his memory of the anti-Semitic attacks upon him and the CCF that were part of the big-business propaganda campaign in the 1945 federal election (Read and Whitehorn, 1991).[78] Certainly he did not wish to be the target of such attacks again. Nor did he wish to see his party become vulnerable once more to such an onslaught (McLeod and McLeod, 1987: 217). Was Lewis correct in his fears? Much of Canadian society in the 1950s was still pretty WASPish. Toronto, for example, had yet to become the cosmopolitan centre that it is now. Quebec was only just emerging from the authoritarian grip of the Roman Catholic clergy. For all his personal ambition, Lewis was detached enough to analyse the situation logically. Canada at that time was not likely to be receptive to a Jewish leader of a third party striving to make inroads into the political mainstream. Historically, Lewis probably made the correct decision. A decade later he would still make history as the first Jew to lead a major political party in Canada. Yet of all the sacrifices Lewis made for the CCF-NDP, the decision in 1961 may have been one of the most difficult, and it would weigh ever more heavily later in the decade, as the bilingual, urban-based Lewis watched the unilingual Douglas struggle in Quebec. If the 1961 founding of the NDP was not David Lewis's time to lead the party, it certainly should have come before 1971.

David Lewis achieved a reputation as one of Canada's finest parliamentarians. Yet in fact his tenure in Parliament was relatively short.[79] For example, he failed to gain entry to the House of Commons in every effort he made as a CCFer (1940, 1943 by-election, 1945, 1949). He won his first attempt for the NDP in 1962, but lost again a year later. It was not until the mid-1960s that he was able to achieve several consecutive victories (1965, 1968, 1972). His last attempt in 1974 led to his defeat as MP and subsequent resignation as federal NDP leader. Overall, Lewis was victorious in only four of ten attempts. What were the reasons for this low success rate?

In the three and half decades of election contests in which Lewis was a candidate, there was no one single reason for his relative lack of success. He lost for different reasons at different times and in different places (Montreal, Hamilton, and Toronto). One reason, of course, was that Lewis espoused ideas that were considered radical in the 1940s and were for the most part unpopular with the Canadian public. In the history of the federal CCF-NDP, the overwhelming majority of its candidates have not been successful. While antipathy towards socialism has diminished to some degree in recent years, a significant problem for left-wing politicians in Canada is still the fact that more Canadians identify with the ideological right than with the left.[80] To compound this problem, the privately-owned mass media often show a decided tendency to present a less than fair and balanced portrayal of social-democratic doctrines and candidates,[81] and the NDP, like the CCF before it, lacks the financial resources to purchase sufficient media time to overcome such hurdles.

A second reason is that as party national secretary, executive officer, and later federal leader, heavily involved in planning and administering the party's national election campaigns, Lewis was more at home discussing the grand strategy of socialist theory than attending to the details of local riding matters (266). One can imagine his good friend Stanley Knowles remembering the wedding anniversaries or birthdays of riding members. Lewis, by contrast, preferred the more analytical, less personal realm of ideological debate. Unfortunately, our electoral system does not always reward such proclivities.

Given the state of CCF and, to a lesser degree, NDP finances, it was perhaps understandable that senior activists such as Lewis would need to take on a great many tasks. With hindsight, perhaps he should have set a more modest agenda for himself (e.g., directing the national campaign but not running as a local candidate). But modesty was not Lewis's hallmark. Moreover, in the 1930s and 1940s especially, the issues were too pressing and the conditions too desperate. The party needed as many able candidates as possible, and Lewis's reputation was such that many CCF riding associations were more than willing to have such a distinguished figure as their candidate.

Nor did Lewis always make the best personal choice of riding in which to run. A foreign-born, Jewish, socialist candidate, even running in the Montreal Jewish ghetto, faced a strong communist presence on the left and the xenophobic Duplessis and rigidly anti-CCF Roman Catholic Church on the right. In the 1940s, the social-democratic CCF operated with an enormous handicap. Interestingly, in the mid-1940s Lewis declined the opportunity to run in a relatively safe seat in Winnipeg, a city with a strong radical labour tradition[82] in a region where the party had done much better historically. His decision not to run in the west was no doubt based in part on the fact that his roots were in central Canada. In addition, as national secretary he was particularly aware that, to be successful nationally, the party needed far greater and stronger representation in the two heartland provinces. In any case, his poor early electoral record in Quebec and Ontario was not unique. Robert Cliche, Charles Taylor, Laurier Lapierre, Eugene Forsey, and many others before and after were even less successful.

In October 1970, Canada's self-perception as a peaceable kingdom was shattered by the kidnapping of James Cross and Pierre Laporte in Montreal. These dramatic events occurred against the backdrop of continuing separatist violence (Morf, 1970; Gellner, 1974). The response of the Trudeau government was the imposition of the War Measures Act, an unprecedented use of such draconian powers in Canada during peacetime. As both the Liberal and Conservative parties and the Canadian public at large supported the government, the NDP[83] was the only party in Parliament to oppose this erosion of civil liberties and creation of arbitrary state power.[84] Even the offices of the NDP in Montreal were raided; all the files were searched and the staff questioned (Haggart and Golden, 1979; 103-6).

Both Tommy Douglas and David Lewis spoke passionately and eloquently against the implementation of the War Measures Act. Lewis, the bilingual deputy leader and former Quebec resident, was particularly important in addressing the French-speaking media. Quebec party activist Charles Taylor noted that Lewis, 'as the only caucus member with a real grasp of the Quebec scene, . . . carried a heavy responsibility.'[85] For their stand against the War Measures Act Douglas, Lewis, and the NDP suffered abuse and denunciations;[86] according to Shackleton, 95% of the mail received by the federal party was critical (1975: 302). NDP support plummeted by more than a third in public-opinion polls, from a respectable 20% to 13%—an alarming drop for a third-place party.[87] At the time it was a lonely battle; years later, many would safely agree that it was one of the NDP's most shining hours.

No doubt the pinnacle of any party career is to become national leader and elected spokesperson. For Lewis, who had laboured in the CCF since the mid-1930s and had been the key architect of the NDP, the lure of becoming federal leader was irresistible. In 1961 he had deferred to Douglas, but by the late 1960s he had become restless. When Douglas finally stepped aside, an unprecedented number of candidates came forward (see Chapter 5), of whom Lewis was by far the oldest; the other four were from a younger generation of socialists.

The 1971 leadership convention was an extremely polarized one, with radical Waffler Jim Laxer leading a strong challenge to the more orthodox social democrat Lewis.[88] In a party that had previously seen only unanimous (Woodsworth, Coldwell, Argue) or first-ballot (Douglas) elections of its leaders, Lewis suffered the ignominy of four long ballots. While he led on every one, he did not show much growth on either the second or third. It was only when the delegates were forced to choose between the young and largely inexperienced Marxist-leaning Waffler and the veteran party official that they finally gave Lewis the votes he needed and a mandate.

A disproportionate number of the accounts of this leadership contest have been written by younger leftists, often sympathetic to the Waffle (Hackett, 1979, 1980; Bullen, 1983; Brodie, 1985). In many of these there has been a tendency to see a vote for Laxer as a vote for the Waffle. This interpretation ignores an important maxim in politics: that a vote is not necessarily for someone, but may be against another. It is likely that a significant number of delegates voted not so much for Laxer or the Waffle (he got less than 23% of the vote on the first ballot) as against Lewis. In a youth-oriented era, at 61 he was for some delegates a person whose time had already passed. To others, his stance in certain policy areas was unacceptable (e.g., public ownership, defence and foreign policy, Israel). A few may have felt a Jewish leader was an inadvisable handicap for a third party. To some, perhaps, the 1971 convention was a chance to get even for past slights or perceived offences;[89] to others, the early ballots may have offered a chance to humble the front runner, a man whom many saw as immodest.[90] For Lewis, the pain of the long leadership contest lasted many years;[91] though never publicly expressed, it was no less deeply felt by this old and proud man.

The polarized leadership contest was only one round in an ideological and organizational battle that racked the NDP in the late 1960s[92] and early 1970s. Laxer and Mel Watkins were the key spokesmen for the Waffle, while the Lewises, particularly Stephen,[93] led the other. The CCF-NDP had always had a militant Marxist ginger group, from the affiliated Socialist Party of Canada in the 1930s, through the Socialist Fellowship in the 1950s to the Waffle in the 1970s. Thus for the senior Lewis there was a sense of déjà vu about the Waffle (385-7). While in general he had little patience for what he regarded as doctrinaire groups,[94] he somewhat uncharacteristically counselled his son to be more cautious when confronting the Waffle (see Smith: 440-2, 475). Perhaps this was the more protective father speaking, rather than the tough party veteran and federal leader;[95] perhaps too it was the wisdom that comes from many previous battles (387). In any case, the differences between father and son were not so much on fundamentals as on questions of timing and tactics.

The relationship between David Lewis and Pierre Trudeau was an important one that had begun in the 1950s, when each had dealings with key Quebec CCFers Frank Scott (Djwa, 1987) and Thérèse Casgrain (1972). Trudeau had been increasingly active in progressive social organizations and seemed a logical recruit for the CCF (PSD)[96] and the soon-to-be NDP (Smith: 387). Intellectual leftists from the ranks of millionaires are perhaps an erratic base from which to try to build a mass working-class party, but the social-democratic movement in Quebec was in a desperate condition, and Trudeau looked promising. He had helped in Casgrain's CCF campaign (Djwa, 1987: 335; Clarkson and McCall, 1990; Lewis, 455), attended some New Party meetings (Sherwood, 1966), and contributed an important chapter to *Social Purpose For Canada* (ed. Oliver, 1961), which appeared in conjunction with the birth of the NDP. However, Trudeau was far less willing to accommodate Quebec nationalists than were the NDP architects, and thus his relationship with the CCF-NDP was brief.[97] With Jean Marchand and Gérard Pelletier he abandoned the social-democratic cause for the immediate prospect of power with the Liberal Party. For some in the NDP, it was a sign that Trudeau was a dilettante (Casgrain, 1972: 139). For others, it was a clear indication that this would-be reformer was merely another power politician serving the well-to-do. The phrase 'just society'[98] would soon become yet another broken Liberal promise.

Despite major differences in social background and the social causes they served, Lewis and Trudeau did share several key personality traits. Both were strong-willed—some would say arrogant—men who placed great stress on logic and rationality. Trudeau's favourite motto was 'reason over passion'; similarly, Lewis's favourite phrase when criticizing opponents' ideas was 'that's not logical'.[99] That many colleagues were not always able to live up to the rigorous intellectual standards set by these two political leaders is not surprising.

While Trudeau and Lewis had sparred during the October crisis of 1970, the 1972 federal election campaign[100] was the latter's first as federal leader. Using the increasingly unpopular Trudeau as his foil to propel the NDP into new prominence, day after day Lewis hammered away at the penchant of Canada's 'corporate welfare bums'[101] for avoiding taxes and receiving government handouts. A dramatic theme backed up by a steady barrage of statistics and striking examples of corporate rip-offs, it was a powerful combination of socialist theory and evidence, and very much in the tradition of the best of British Fabian socialism. By the end of the campaign, Lewis and the NDP had won a record 31 seats in a minority Parliament,[102] and over the next two years they would achieve an unprecedented profile and level of influence.

When the new House of Commons assembled, there were several possible reasons for the NDP to support the Conservatives. Not only did Robert Stanfield appear a less autocratic and more likeable individual than Trudeau, but propping up the Conservatives could have improved the NDP's bargaining leverage in a minority Parliament. To many socialists, however, supporting the right-wing conservatives was anathema.[103]

Philosophically, the social-democratic NDP had more in common with the Liberals, particularly the left-of-centre reformers. In the early 1960s there had even been speculation about secret merger talks between the two parties.[104] Second, the Conservatives competed directly with the NDP in the west, and this made co-operation with that party far more dangerous politically for many sitting NDP MPs. Finally, the overriding fear after the 1972 election was that the Conservatives might be about to repeat the pattern of the 1957-58 two-step landslide. Thus the New Democrats' 1972 electoral gains were overshadowed by fear with regard to the next contest. Given the minority Parliament, another election was likely to come soon.

With hindsight,[105] many Canadians consider the 1972-74 minority Parliament to have been one of the most productive and progressive in recent Canadian history (see Chapter 4). For the NDP, however, there was always some uncertainty as to whom the public would credit: the seemingly more reform-minded government, or the third party that drew up a list of legislative demands and voted for the government on such measures. A related question was when to pull the plug on the government. The NDP caucus was divided. Some, like Lewis, wanted an earlier election,[106] while others, including a number of MPs from the west who feared losing their seats to the Conservatives, favoured a delay. Ironically, among the more timid on the question of the election timing were some of the younger and supposedly more radical MPs. Although Lewis, with no young family and mortgage to worry about, and nearing the end of a long political career, was far more audacious, given his poor electoral track record it was in some ways a puzzling position.[107]

The focus of the 1974 campaign was Stanfield's proposed wage and price controls,[108] a platform that Lewis, not surprisingly, spent considerable time attacking, even though the Conservatives were only the opposition, not the government. Stanfield's pessimistic analysis and frank proposals alarmed the electorate sufficiently to shift more votes to the Liberals at the expense of the NDP. In the end the public still got wage and price controls. Among the NDP MPs defeated was Lewis, in his home riding of York South. The 1974 federal election marked both the end of his all too brief career in Parliament and the final days of his tenure as NDP leader. Unlike Douglas,

Lewis bowed a swift exit. It was time for a new generation to lead Canada's social-democratic party.

Politics is not only based upon ideological discourse and debate; it is also very much a matter of personal relationships. In the case of David Lewis, one group of people is crucial: his family. Perhaps one of Lewis's greatest legacies is the life-long family commitment to socialism that he inherited from his father.[109] A remarkable political family, the Lewis clan may be Canada's social-democratic equivalent to the Kennedys.

In the list of key political advisers and colleagues cited by Lewis in his memoirs, almost every one named was a man. Politics in the days of the CCF particularly was very much a man's world. There was, however, one woman who played a key part in Lewis's political career: Sophie Carson, who later became his wife.

High-school sweethearts and daring lovers at Oxford, they travelled together in the dangerous continental Europe of the 1930s. For a brief period, Sophie served as a typist for the federal CCF; on at least one occasion she helped David when he solicited much-needed funds for the CCF from prominent Jewish unionists in New York; and she acted, in effect, as a single parent while David was away on frequent lengthy trips on behalf of the party (65, 74, 86, 136). David and Sophie made a remarkable team. Whereas he excelled in grand theory and strategy, her strength was in the social realm. Lewis himself acknowledged the power of her charm:

> Our children have often teased me that [Sophie] was the better politician because of her warmth and her instant interest in people she met. She proved it during our encounters with the union leaders in their sumptuous offices. The meetings were no longer stiff occasions, with me, the mendicant, pleading before the philanthropist union president; they became much friendlier and more informal conversations (136).

Cameron Smith devotes an entire chapter of his 1989 book on the Lewis family to the moving love letters between Sophie and David. In one passage (257-8), he writes:

> Sophie was vibrant, strong-willed, and demonstrative, and so was her love. But it was a love that needed to celebrate itself. In England it was possible. They went to plays and concerts and all kinds of functions. They took long walks. They went on trips and vacations together. They held hands. They discussed books they were reading. They talked sense and they talked nonsense.
> They rejoiced.
> In Ottawa it wasn't so easy.

While David revelled in the political spotlight and enjoyed national prestige, Sophie paid a disproportionate part of the cost. As the burden of

child-rearing increasingly rested on her shoulders, David's absences generated a profound loneliness (see Smith: 258, 268-72, 279). Nevertheless, she
took great pride in his career and contributed to it in ways that most did not
see, easing his doubts, providing advice about people, and ensuring the existence of a home to which he could return (see Smith: 180, 201, 259). In the
end, she silently shared the final painful secret of his impending death from
the same illness that had felled his father several decades earlier.

The love letters between David and Sophie Lewis included in Smith's
book (Chapter 16) reveal a romantic side in Lewis that few could have
imagined. Modifying the standard image of the tough labour negotiator and
party official to include the sensitive, loving—albeit far too often absent—
husband and father is perhaps not easy for some. In recent years, however,
the breadth of David Lewis's interests and the complexity of his personality have become more evident. Despite the primacy of politics in his life,
Lewis possessed considerable affection for the gentler pursuits of poetry and
art, and enjoyed close friendships with both Frank Scott and A.M. Klein.[110]
The arts were also something he shared with Sophie.

In the history of the CCF-NDP there have been several political families.
J.S. Woodsworth's daughter Grace Woodsworth MacInnis would later
become an MP. Ernie and Harold Winch sat in the British Columbia
provincial legislature as a father-and-son team for a record twenty years
(Steeves, 1960), the latter becoming BC CCF leader and still later a federal
MP. John, the son of long-serving MP Andrew Brewin, is now also an MP.
However, for numbers, staying power, political clout, and, in the eyes of
many, ambition, the other families pale beside the Lewises.

David Lewis's eldest son, Stephen, was elected to the Ontario legislature
in 1963 while in his mid-twenties and was Ontario provincial NDP leader
from 1970 to 1978. Stephen's younger brother Michael served as Ontario
NDP provincial secretary and is now an organizer with the United Steelworkers of America, responsible for political liaison; his work was pivotal in
the last provincial election. One of his younger twin sisters,[111] Janet
Solberg, is a prominent executive officer in the provincial party and has
served both as provincial party president and member of the crucial Strategy, Election and Planning Committee. All three played important roles[112]
in the NDP's historic 1990 electoral breakthrough in Ontario.[113] Stephen, as
former provincial leader, supervised the work of the transition team, and
recently Janet has begun work in the Premier's office.

The last few years of David Lewis's life were devoted to work on his
memoirs while he taught at the Institute of Canadian Studies at Carleton University.[114] A few months after his death in May 1981, the
volume entitled *The Good Fight* was published. Spanning the half-
century from 1909 to 1958, it covers most of the CCF era (1932-1961)
and offers Lewis's colourful commentaries on people and events, as
well as original research from archives across the country (including the

almost inaccessible papers of George Drew, the Ontario premier of the 1940s who was an arch-enemy of socialism).[115] The book was well reviewed when it first appeared,[116] and continues to be extensively cited.[117] *The Good Fight* was to have been the first of two volumes. Regrettably, the second, which would have been invaluable in its coverage of the NDP era—was not sufficiently advanced to be completed.[118] One can only hope that in time the gap will be partly fixed by a comprehensive biographical study of this extraordinary man.[119]

PART III: DOUGLAS AND LEWIS

The contrasts in style and complex relations between Tommy Douglas and David Lewis have been the subject of considerable comment. Starting at the level of personality, many authors—including Avakumovic (1978), Bradley (1985), Forsey (1990), McLeod and McLeod (1987), Shackleton (1975), Smith (1989), and Steed (1988)—have endeavoured to compare the two men. Summarizing their differences in background, Steed (1988: 129) writes: 'Scottish-born Tommy, prairie evangelist, business-minded socialist; [vs.] Polish-born David, urban intellectual, labour lawyer, backroom organizer.' According to Shackleton (1975: 224), 'Douglas was a different man from David Lewis—in personality, in approach to party management, and occasionally in his point of view on public policy.' A similar comment is offered by Steed (126)—'Tommy Douglas and David Lewis; two more intense and different personalities would be hard to imagine'—while Bradley (157) notes that 'Tommy Douglas and David Lewis were . . . two very different sorts of men'. Indeed, Bradley's book is for the most part an extended contrast between the two men. Note, for example, this passage (157-8):

> Tommy was always completely *there* as a person, but there was always something withheld or even anxious about David Lewis . . . . while David Lewis took himself very seriously, Tommy Douglas didn't take David Lewis very seriously at all . . . and didn't take himself too seriously either. Tommy rarely stood on any sort of ceremony or dignity, he was just confident and secure. . . . Lewis was always conscious about his image and dignity. He could be a stickler for what can only be called protocol. He was not informal. . . .
>
> Tommy Douglas had no façade . . . what you saw was the man. The 'essence' of Tommy Douglas was always right up front . . . which is why . . . thousands . . . felt perfectly free to refer to him as 'Tommy' when meeting him, and not 'Mr Douglas'. . . .
>
> Of the two, it was David Lewis who erected a barrier between himself and the outside world . . . . it was eastern academics and eastern media pundits who viewed David Lewis in [a] favourable way, not average men and women who voted.

Bradley characterizes the differences between the two men in the following fashion. On the one side, inspired by a humanist and moral Christianity
and drawing upon western CCF farm populism,[120] Douglas showed a compassionate, trusting, and tolerant bent. He offered a relevant vision of a
better world. On the other side, motivated by Marxist methodology and
relying upon an eastern NDP worker-focused intellectualism, Lewis revealed
a mechanistic, paternalistic, and dogmatically ideological perspective.[121]
According to Bradley, Lewis's path was a selfish dead end, and he concludes
that Douglas's direction is the correct course for the party to steer if it wants
electoral success. This prognosis, however, seems far too a convenient
blend of the ethical and the pragmatic.

Shackleton's 1975 account of these two personalities is less sweeping, but
the theme of contrast is still very much present in her biography of Douglas.
On the one hand, she describes her subject, with his rural and somewhat
old-fashioned roots,[122] as inspired by a social-gospel Christian morality, and
pursuing a more sensitive and co-operative style. Ideologically, according to
Shackleton, he was inclined to be more tolerant than Lewis of left-wing
ginger groups such as the Waffle[123] and placed greater stress on socialism.
With respect to policy, she observes Douglas to have been critical of military alliances such as NATO sooner than Lewis. On the other hand, Shackleton portrays the latter as urban and modern, influenced to some degree by
Marx and Lenin,[124] and possessing a more conflictual leadership style. She
suggests that Lewis was less willing to accept ideological diversity, and that
it was he who, along with his son Stephen, precipitated the so-called
'purge'[125] of the Waffle movement.

The McLeods (1987: 233) also employ contrasts between Douglas and
Lewis, suggesting that 'Douglas listened and Lewis talked. Douglas . . .
would hang back from debate. Lewis . . . spoke frequently and forcefully.'
They cite (234) Grace MacInnis's comments:

> I think Douglas always believed that two heads were better than one
> . . . . I think he always believed genuinely in co-operation, and I think
> he lived that way, and that's why people loved him.
>
> Lewis would listen while everybody talked and then he would sum
> up the discussion, and the summing up often didn't have any relation
> to what had been said. But it was so brilliant and so well done. I think
> it was his very brilliance that made us a little discouraged at times.

Eugene Forsey, a veteran of many left-wing causes over the decades, was
a close observer of the two socialist pioneers. His memoirs (1990: 130) offer
a comparison of their respective speaking styles:

> Tommy Douglas was a superb speaker of the homespun type. The
> speeches of his successor David Lewis were in the grand, classic style
> of English parliamentary oratory, with echoes of Gladstone, Rosebery,

Asquith. Tommy, with his wit and fund of pithy and apposite stories, perhaps got closer to his audiences; and he had what David never had, a chance to show what he could do when the electors had given him the power to do it.[126]

Several authors have suggested that Douglas and Lewis also performed different roles within the party. Steed, for example, offers this picture: 'Loveable Tommy, hard-nosed Lewis; they were a stereotyped couple, Lewis the tough cop who made the hard decisions that freed Tommy to fly on his charisma.' With his oratory, 'Tommy was [the party's] public face, David its organizational guts' the one who did the 'unremitting back-room slogging' (1988: 126, 130, 93).[127]

The leadership question is perhaps more complex. In the late fifties and early sixties, Lewis was suggesting Premier Douglas as federal party leader and Douglas was initially proposing the bilingual Lewis (McLeod and McLeod, 1987: 184, 218). At the 1961 convention, Lewis, the architect of the NDP, supported Douglas's national leadership. In turn, Douglas as new leader encouraged Lewis to run for Parliament in 1962 (Smith, 1989: 392). By the late 1960s, when the NDP appeared to some to be lacking a sustained momentum (see Chapter 4), Lewis and others were increasingly restless concerning Douglas's tenure as leader, particularly in view of the dramatic decline in the latter's ability to get elected. At first Douglas indicated that he would step down as leader by 1969; however, he reconsidered and delayed the transfer of power until 1971. Stephen Lewis had tried to hasten the process of leadership change in 1968 in a rather tactless trip to Vancouver to meet with Douglas.[128] No doubt the proud and spirited Scot resented attempts to push him out.[129] The elder Lewis, too, was frustrated by the delay in his opportunity to be leader after serving the party in so many roles for so many years. With hindsight, it seems that both Stephen Lewis and Douglas made mistakes in judgement: the former in posing such a request and the latter in not stepping down sooner. These errors merely illustrate that distinguished politicians are no less human than anyone else.

While many authors make extensive and, in some cases (e.g., Shackleton and Bradley) perhaps excessive use of the Douglas-Lewis dualism, several do at times concede that there were a number of similarities between the two. For example, both were born outside Canada in the first decade of the twentieth century. In a sense, they were outside agitators, perhaps carrying a sense of poverty and exploitation acquired first in the European setting.

Certainly both were exposed early to dramatic and violent political events, including world war, political strikes, and state repression of dissidents. While Douglas's father was fighting in Europe, Lewis and his entire family were living in the midst of the war's eastern European front. While the young Tommy Douglas was peering over the rooftops to watch

Canada's most famous labour revolt, the Winnipeg General Strike of 1919, Lewis, in a small village in the western part of Russia, was experiencing the sweeping turmoil of the Russian Revolution. In the midst of social unrest, both young men witnessed attempts by a coercive state to suppress legitimate dissent. Douglas watched the repressive actions by the forces of Conservative Prime Minister Robert Borden, while Lewis saw first-hand the beginnings of the reign of terror of the new communist regime of Lenin.

Another thing that Douglas and Lewis shared was the important influence of M.J. Coldwell on their respective careers.[130] Indeed, in a sense both were protégés of Coldwell. With encouragement from Coldwell, Douglas became Saskatchewan provincial CCF leader, a role in which the older man had previously served. Similarly, Lewis succeeded Coldwell, with his blessing, as national secretary of the CCF.

It has often been suggested that Douglas and Lewis stood in contrast as the idealist and the realist, the gentle preacher and the tough party bureaucrat. These stereotypes miss the richness and diversity in both Douglas and Lewis. Neither man was as simple as the caricatures some observers have drawn. People who worked closely with Douglas knew how tough and demanding he could be. As Steed reminds us, 'despite his nice-guy image, [Douglas was] a hard-driving politician'; under 'Tommy's amiable façade hid a very tough core' (1988: 127, 154; see also Morton in *NeWest*, 1987: 17-18). Two key party strategists have made similar comments. Bill Knight, originally from Saskatchewan, notes that 'Douglas was every bit as tenacious in his opposition to the Waffle as Lewis',[131] while Terry Grier from Ontario suggests that

> David was thin-skinned—I revered David . . . . most people didn't realize how sensitive David was. He wasn't as tough a guy as Tommy. Tommy could be a tough bugger to work for. He could be miserable, nag you to death. David was a nicer person (quoted in Steed, 130).

Clearly, both men had their sensitive and not-so-sensitive moments. Authors would do well to recognize both traits in each.[132]

Short men who more than compensated with their enormous will and determination, both were workaholics who possessed tremendous energy and endurance—traits that their colleagues and subordinates came to know all too well.[133] Part of the force fuelling their drive was an indefatigable dedication to human justice. Their steadfastness and zeal for reform cast a long and profound shadow among party activists and Canadians at large.[134] In the words of the Whelans (1990), people were emotionally 'touched by Tommy'; they genuinely loved the man. Lewis, largely through the power of his intellect, also inspired people and won respect.[135] Both leaders were able to attract legions of loyal followers.

Any personalities active in politics as long as Lewis and Douglas were bound to have some disagreements on policy. The efficiency of the early

Saskatchewan CCF government, the formation of NATO (Lewis, 1981: 348-9) and the most appropriate time to opt out of NATO were three important questions on which they disagreed. Yet on the whole the policy differences between the two seem relatively small.

Ideologically, both were committed social democrats who, like most in the NDP, were also ardent Canadian nationalists.[136] Their nationalism was reflected in their criticism of the Canadian government's acquiescence to American foreign policy, particularly during the Vietnam War. Although neither man lived to see the free-trade debate of the late 1980s, even in the days of the CCF both expressed profound concern about the loss of Canadian sovereignty caused by the exceptionally high levels of foreign ownership in the Canadian economy in the 1950s.[137] In one speech in the early 1960s, Douglas offered the following warning:

> I like Americans. I have relatives who are Americans. I like my relatives, but I don't want them moving into my house and taking over every room until I have to sleep in the basement.[138]

Tommy Douglas, like David Lewis, would have expressed strong misgivings about moving so extensively towards total free trade with the United States. These two social democrats argued passionately that Canada should pursue its own distinctive path, guided by a different set of values.

In the end, therefore, it would be unwise to overstress the differences between Douglas and Lewis. For all their disagreements, they both stayed in the same political party for their entire adult lives, and they both demonstrated an untiring devotion to the socialist cause until their deaths. Moreover, as Steed (1988: 126) reminds us, 'They couldn't have done what they did without each other.'[139]

Dwelling on somewhat contrived and judgemental contrasts between such important party figures is not always fruitful, nor is it historically warranted. However, human beings seem to need personifications—and someone to blame when things do not work out as hoped. In Chapter 2 it was suggested that perhaps it is time to exorcise the traces of demonology in the literature on the CCF-NDP and move on to other matters. The solidly researched, delightfully written biography of Douglas by the McLeods is an example of what can be achieved by rising above simplistic caricatures and hagiography.[140] Among future projects that might prove beneficial are a more in-depth analysis of Douglas's Saskatchewan government, and a volume of careful textual analysis on the political thought of Lewis, Douglas, and other leading CCFers.[141]

In an age too full of pettiness, patronage, private self-interest, and cynicism, Tommy Douglas and David Lewis stood as two pillars of principled politics and service to the community. In stature these two socialists tower over most contemporary politicians. Their passionate defence of civil liberties during the October Crisis of 1970 is a stark reminder of the sometimes lonely path they took. Neither reached the new Jerusalem, but each led us closer. Canada is a better country for their presence.

NOTES

[1] The disparity in length of the two sections should by no means be interpreted as a reflection on the relative importance of the two men.

[2] In Weyburn, Saskatchewan, Douglas served as minister of a parish active in a number of community endeavours.

[3] An earlier version of Parts I and III originally appeared in this collection (*NeWest*, May 1987) under the title 'Douglas and the Historians'.

[4] To a degree, this may reflect the suggestion by some, such as Lovick (1970: 41), that Douglas was less an original thinker than a populizer of ideas.

[5] Nicholson later became a CCF organizer, MP, and MLA.

[6] Baum (1980) covers the Roman Catholic tradition for the 1930s and 1940s but offers no indexed reference to the Protestant clergyman and socialist Douglas. Another problem with the literature overall is that it too rarely discusses the disadvantages of the social-gospel tradition. In one of my last discussions with Douglas, he indicated that he felt the social-gospel movement was not without weaknesses, and that more rigorous analysis was needed.

[7] For greater detail on the historiography of the CCF-NDP, see Chapter 2.

[8] Despite different titles, these are three editions of the same fine work.

[9] References to this work will omit the year of publication and cite page numbers only.

[10] In his biography of three generations of the Lewis clan, Smith (1989) does briefly touch on some of these topics.

[11] The McLeods suggest that 'Douglas came to symbolize a government that was activist, rather than overtly socialist' (1987: 181). Laycock (1990) suggests that populism and socialism need not be mutually exclusive categories.

[12] One should, however, be careful not to read too much negativity about Douglas in this, since the entire work is a somewhat pessimistic and sombre account.

[13] The Douglas-Coldwell Foundation released a commemorative kit that included the Lapierre volume (1971) and a record of some of Tommy's most famous speeches. According to Douglas aficionados, the cream-separator speech and the parable of mouseland are among the best.

[14] The fact that Lewis could write three books during his hectic life of political activism is a tribute to his stamina and his analytical, even scholarly, bent. In each case he worked extensively with others: Scott in 1943, Boris Celovsky and the NDP caucus research staff in 1972, and Whitehorn and the Lewis memoirs research staff (David Walden, Robert Sims, Shirley van Eyk, Marilyn McGregor and Joan Patterson) in the late 1970s. Reflecting Lewis's disposition to present sound and critical theoretical analysis that is solidly rooted in either socio-economic data or archival research, each volume is quintessential Lewis, a blend of theory and practice.

References to Smith (1989) will omit the year of publication and cite page numbers only.

[15] Some aspects of Lewis's personality and ideas have been discussed in Chapter 2.

[16] Lewis notes that 'even as a very young boy I preferred to stay in the house listening to the adult conversation' (2); 'All my experiences as a boy, combined

with the influence of my father, had committed my thoughts almost exclusively to the social struggle and the instruments needed for political victory. Doubtless I was in danger of becoming one-dimensional' (20). See also p. 55, and Smith (147-8, 162).

[17] It was 82% rural in 1913 (Mickiewicz, 1973: 54).

[18] In the twentieth century, Svisloch has been governed at various times by Moscow, Warsaw, and Berlin; see also Smith (103) regarding the various cultural ties of the town to different regions. After the anti-socialist attacks on the CCF in the 1940s and the Soviet-Polish border changes of the Second World War, Lewis tended to refer to his origins as Polish.

[19] Russia, ill-prepared for modern warfare, suffered horrific numbers of casualties (Urlanis, 1971).

[20] Not surprisingly, Lewis as an adult condemned foreign invading armies and was an early and consistent foe of imperialism, whether German, Russian, or American.

[21] The Russian Revolution actually began as a military coup.

[22] In 1903 the Russian Social Democratic Labour Party split into two Marxist factions. The Bolsheviks under Lenin favoured a party that would be organizationally more restrictive in its criteria for membership. Lenin's pronouncements on 'democratic centralism' sought to create a 'vanguard party of professional revolutionaries' that would guide the masses of workers. The Mensheviks under Martov favoured a more open basis for party membership. For some Marxists, such as Rosa Luxemburg, the Leninist variant was the first step towards dictatorship.

[23] According to Smith (114) Moishe Lewis went into hiding for ten days.

[24] His first language was Yiddish.

[25] Together with his new name, Lewis's mastery of English led many Canadians to believe he was Welsh. While he never hid his Jewish origins, given the anti-Semitism prevalent in earlier decades and the anti-Soviet feeling during the Cold War, being mistaken for a Welshman was not an error with which he was necessarily displeased.

[26] In this he was not dissimilar to many Canadian clergymen from the social-gospel tradition who went on to become political activists, including J.S. Woodsworth, T.C. Douglas, Stanley Knowles, and more recently Andy Hogan, Bob Ogle, Dan Heap, and Bill Blaikie. See L. McDonald (1987).

[27] See also Lewis (55, 458); Smith calls it 'parliamentary marxism' (169, 174, 186, 187, 231, 236, 239-40).

[28] Given the frequent linkage of nationalism with religion and emotionalism, Lewis not surprisingly opted for a secular orientation (458; Smith: 396-8) and a stress on logic (Smith: 454).

[29] It certainly occurred well prior to the emergence of the intensely nationalistic variant of socialism associated with the Waffle. As noted above, Lewis's attitude to Zionist nationalism also mellowed after 1945.

[30] He also possessed a more theoretical framework than many of his colleagues in the CCF-NDP. Stephen Lewis's comments on his own socialist ideas seem equally applicable to his father David; see Smith (446-7).

[31] Another cluster of LSR academics was centred at the University of Toronto. While Lewis was an early member of the LSR in Montreal, his departure for Oxford in 1932 seriously interrupted his involvement in the crucial period when

LSR members were drafting the 1933 Regina Manifesto. When in 1935 the LSR published the highly influential collaborative volume *Social Planning for Canada*, Lewis was still away in Oxford.

[32] Forsey would go on to become Director of Research at the Canadian Congress of Labour and later the Canadian Labour Congress. Among his influential works are his volume of essays on the Canadian constitution (1974), his epic on Canadian trade unions (1982), and his recently published memoirs (1990).

[33] Lewis writes that Gordon, a theology professor, LSR member, and co-author of *Social Planning for Canada*, was a 'friend on whose judgment and advice I relied a great deal. . . . We seemed to share a common approach to policy' (126-7).

[34] Lewis lists Scott as one of the four key persons 'whose advice and help were most valuable' during his early CCF years (Djwa and Macdonald, 1983: 87).

[35] For example, it is cited in J. McLeod's *Oxford Book of Canadian Political Anecdotes* (1988: 230-1).

[36] It is somewhat ironic that Lewis in 1932 would be noted for calling for more nationalization when later, during the debates about the Winnipeg Declaration and New Party Statement in the 1950s and 1960s, he would be accused by some of largely abandoning public ownership.

[37] As noted in Chapters 4 and 8, in both the 1945 and 1988 elections, when it appeared that the social-democratic CCF-NDP might achieve an electoral break-through, a number of powerful and affluent corporations advanced vast sums of money to stem the working-class tide (Read and Whitehorn, 1991). In both cases the CPR was a major donor to ensure the perpetuation of monopoly capitalism in Canada (Lewis, chapters 12 and 14; and financial data on political parties from the Chief Electoral Officer for 1988).

[38] See Smith (188). 'Guild socialism' is a decentralized system of workers' self-man-agement and industrial democracy; see Cole, 1967; Whitehorn, 1974, 1978, 1979.

[39] Smith (162) suggests that Lewis's presence there was a major reason why Oxford did not become the haven for communist agents that Cambridge did; however, one suspects that Cole's long tenure and powerful influence as a teacher, partic-ularly in presenting a radical decentralist and anti-Leninist vision of socialism, were more significant. See, for example, the commentaries on the British left by Wood (1959: 28) and Carpenter (1973: 120).

[40] See also Smith (173, 188). Lewis was not alone in this regard: both Ed Broadbent and Bob Rae have kept copies of Cole's *History of Socialist Thought* in their own inner offices. Cole also influenced other key CCFers such as Ted Jolliffe, who later became Ontario CCF leader in the 1940s and a labour lawyer in a high-profile legal practice with David Lewis.

[41] Lewis, like so many of his fellow members of the LSR, seems to have embraced the more technocratic aspect of Fabian socialism in this regard. Ironically, one of the earliest critics of the Fabians' centralism was Cole.

[42] This appointment was designed to ease the work-load of M.J. Coldwell, who had been serving as both national secretary and Member of Parliament.

[43] Woodsworth disagreed with the CCF's decision to vote for entry into the Second World War. Lewis felt that although Woodsworth's pacifism was 'courageous and beautiful', when confronted with the 'inhuman barbarism' of Hitler it was 'irrel-evant' and 'did not speak to the reality of the immediate crisis' (175).

44 The post is now called 'federal secretary', in deference to Quebec nationalists. See Forsey (1990) for a reaction to this linguistic revisionism.

45 In his capacity as national secretary, David Lewis hired Donald MacDonald to work in the federal office. MacDonald went on to become Ontario provincial leader from 1953 to 1970, when he was succeeded by Stephen Lewis.

46 Lewis himself notes: 'my own inclination [was] always to seek the theoretical basis' (380). Long-time friend and political colleague Kalmen Kaplansky suggests that Lewis believed that ideology and organization must be intertwined ('Notes for David Lewis Memorial Meeting', 14 Sept. 1981).

47 Here too Lewis's role seems more that of an educator in a social movement than of the bureaucratic party pragmatist that authors from the 'protest movement becalmed' tradition tend to portray; see Chapter 2.

48 Among the reasons for this are the rise in importance of the party's research staff on Parliament Hill (a group that was virtually non-existent for the entire CCF and early NDP period), and the increase in the number of NDP MPs and their staff. Subsequent federal secretaries have also lacked the flair that Lewis, the former Rhodes scholar and champion debater, possessed.

49 In conversations, both Douglas and Lewis, as retired federal leaders, regretted the lack of national party publications.

50 Angus MacInnis (1884-1964) was a unionist turned political activist who had served as an alderman in Vancouver before entering the federal scene. Commencing in 1930, MacInnis served uninterruptedly as an MP until 1957. Lewis describes him as possessing 'uncommon good sense' and 'realistic insight' (93). While they did 'not always agree' and he found MacInnis 'too rigid on occasion' (93), Lewis says that he had 'great affection' and 'respect' (384) for him. 'When parliament was in session, there was hardly a day that I did not consult MacInnis by telephone or in person' (Djwa and Macdonald, 1983: 87). It was MacInnis who accompanied Lewis to oversee the acceptance of the first union affiliation to the CCF in Cape Breton in 1938 (Lewis, 155; see also Earle and Gamberg, 1989). Perhaps one of MacInnis's most notable CCF activities was his defence of Japanese Canadians amidst the racist hysteria of wartime British Columbia.

51 Stanley Knowles (b. 1908), a social-gospel minister in the tradition of Woodsworth (see Trofimenkoff, 1982; Harrop, 1984), acted as a champion for Canadians in the long struggle for adequate pensions and became a widely respected expert on parliamentary procedure. After his defeat in the 1958 federal election, he became vice-president of the Canadian Labour Congress and was a key member of the NCNP. While Lewis notes his 'great affection' for Knowles, he nevertheless draws attention to the contrast in their styles: whereas Knowles never 'provoked antagonism', Lewis engaged in 'confrontation' (200). Another difference between the two was that Knowles exhibited great attention to—if not preoccupation with—detail (201). The far more flamboyant Lewis was more interested in theory. Despite these differences, the two made an effective team, whether in a Winnipeg by-election in 1942, in the NCNP in the 1950s and early 1960s, in Lewis's leadership race in 1971, or in Parliament over several decades (Trofimenkoff, 1982: 188).

52 Some commentators such as Young (1969: 162-3, 167-9, 237) have concluded that this small group of men constituted an inner élite within the party and thus confirmed Michels's iron law of oligarchy; see Chapter 2 for a critique.

53 Curiously, no book-length biography of Coldwell has yet been written, although at least three people have tried.

54 Coldwell performed the same role for Douglas. See McLeod and McLeod (1987) and earlier in this chapter.

55 Both Coldwell and Lewis seemed to have a better grasp of foreign affairs than many of their fellow CCFers. Examples of this were Coldwell's stand on German rearmament and the Korean War (174, 427-8) and Lewis's concerns about the ruthless nature of the world communist movement under Stalin.

56 Interview with author; see also the Lewis memoirs (55, 191). Relatedly, Smith (289) cites the following passage from an interview with Lewis by Richard Gwyn: 'I've been angry all my life. . . . But when I speak softly I'm uncomfortable because I know I sometimes do it for the image. When I speak in anger, that's how I really feel'(*Toronto Star*, 27 May 1981). Certainly understatement makes academic content analysis difficult, since the intention may well be far more radical than the deliberately muted language suggests. Having worked closely with Lewis, I can attest that while he favoured more temperate language in public, his personal analyses were often more rigorous and radical. This is a key theme in Smith's portrayal of Lewis's marxist parliamentarianism.

57 Years later, another McGill professor, Charles Taylor, would become a key confidant of Lewis in party affairs. He also wrote the introduction to the Lewis memoirs.

58 The other pivotal figure in the LSR was Frank Underhill, a man with whom Lewis was much more distant (Francis, 1986).

59 For an account from Scott's perspective, see Djwa, 1987, Chapter 13.

60 See also Djwa and Macdonald (1983: 82). One important exception was over the imposition of the War Measures Act in October 1970, which Lewis strongly opposed.

61 See Chapter 22 of the memoirs.

62 Later, Scott would serve on the Royal Commission on Bilingualism and Biculturalism.

63 Scott was a high-status WASP from Westmount in Montreal at a time when it was fashionable to be so.

64 Their friendship may also have been made closer by the fact that Scott had 'no political ambitions whatsoever' (222).

65 In 1943 the CCL declared the CCF to be the political arm of labour.

66 The recent shift by many contemporary communists to a more humanistic, pluralistic, and market-oriented approach significantly undercuts the credibility of earlier attacks by communists upon the CCF-NDP's social-democratic platform. Now even many former communists stress a mixed economy and human rights, and reject the dictatorship of the proletariat.

67 Interestingly, this is a theme also raised by a number of East European Marxist humanists (Kolakowski, 1968).

68 Jolliffe (b. 1909), a Rhodes Scholar and a member of Cole's study group at Oxford during the same period as Lewis, was a close friend (270) and a man of 'outstanding' intellectual capacities (204). As Ontario provincial leader of the CCF in the mid-1940s, when the anti-socialists launched their campaign to forestall any future CCF advances, Jolliffe made a controversial counter-attack, the so-called Gestapo speech of 1945 (in which Lewis was alleged to have had a hand) (see memoirs, Chapter 12). Many in the party believed that this dramatic speech

contributed to the CCF's disappointing third-place finishes in both the federal and provincial elections. See Chapter 4.

[69] While Lewis's role was undoubtedly central, some authors (see Chapter 2) have tended to overemphasize it. One reason for this may be that most researchers naturally focus on the extensive and easily accessible files of the CCF-NDP federal office (in the National Archives of Canada), which are not necessarily representative of the entire membership. This archival collection includes the correspondence between the national office and the provinces but little of that between one provincial section and another. In the former, there are many of Lewis's letters; in the latter, relatively few. (This was one of the reasons the archival research for the Lewis memoirs was not confined to the National Archives; see memoirs appendix, 'A note on sources'.) Other possible reasons for overemphasizing Lewis include his extensive use of the national office staff and resources, which heightened his profile, as well as his enormous staying power as national secretary and in other executive positions. In addition, his intellectual breadth and depth, combined with his oratorical skills and forceful personality, ensured that he could not be ignored. Finally, the 'iron law of oligarchy' theme employed by some researchers may have led them to focus excessively on administrative officials rather than rank-and-file members. (Of course, it is also easier to locate and study such officials.) One exception to this pattern is Melnyk's delightful collection (1989) of mini-biographies of rank-and-file activists.

[70] One partial exception was Frank Underhill, co-founder of the LSR and co-drafter of the Regina Manifesto. A number of accounts regarding the controversy over who would control Woodsworth House (left intellectuals or socialist party officials) exist, and range from pro-Underhill (Francis, 1986; Smith: 296-7), to relatively neutral (Morley, 1984: 85-6), to pro-Lewis (Lewis, 1981). Underhill went from being a prominent CCFer in the 1930s to supporting Lester Pearson's Liberals in the 1960s. While Underhill's estrangement from Lewis pre-dated his formal departure from the CCF-NDP, Underhill's increasing scepticism about socialism may have contributed to his negative perception of Lewis.

[71] Much of this literature (see Chapter 2) has suggested that Lewis had a deradicalizing impact. An alternative hypothesis raised by Smith (285-6) and others is that Lewis had a decidedly more rigorous and Marxian framework than many party members (e.g., social-gospel activists and agrarian populist reformers). For example, the Lewis and Scott volume *Make This Your Canada* did not hesitate to employ such words as 'class', 'capitalism', and, to a lesser degree, 'imperialism'. One should note, however, that Lewis's ideological perspective was not a doctrinaire or closed Marxism, but rather more open-ended.

[72] In recent years the Liberals were no more happy with Argue, who before his death in 1991 was accused of abusing Senate privileges.

[73] Young (1969: 236-7). Doug Fisher, Argue's former campaign manager, suggested so in a published response to Whitehorn (Kingston *Whig-Standard*, 9 March 1983).

[74] It should be recalled that until the last half of the 1980s the Liberal Party had, overall, a rather solid record of electoral success with such a strategy.

[75] See Toennies (1963) on the shift from *Gemeinschaft* (community) to *Gesellschaft* (society).

[76] In fact, this proved to be the case. Unfortunately for the NDP, this phenomenon

occurred mainly at the provincial level, and the recipient was the Parti Québécois. One of the figures that Lewis sought to steer into the federal NDP was Pierre Elliott Trudeau. While Trudeau had worked with the prominent Quebec CCFers Frank Scott (Djwa, 1987) and Thérèse Casgrain (1972), the three Quebec 'wise men' (Trudeau, Jean Marchand and Gérard Pelletier) opted instead for the reformist Liberal Party under Pearson.

[77] The polarized 1971 leadership convention lends credibility to this argument.

[78] One ironic aspect of these attacks was that Lewis was a secular Jew and not a Zionist (see Lewis, 5-7, 19, 31, 226-7, 329; Smith: 199).

[79] Unlike a number of successful CCF-NDP MPs, Lewis never ran for provincial or municipal office.

[80] See Chapter 1.

[81] The CCF had difficulty getting either press coverage for CCF events or opportunities to rebut blatantly inaccurate accounts; see Lewis (310). In the NDP era it has been extremely rare for the federal NDP to be endorsed by a major Canadian newspaper.

[82] Lewis (232); Smith (302). See also note 122 below.

[83] Not all NDP MPs agreed with the party's stance. The four who broke party ranks were Barry Mather, Max Saltsman, Frank Howard, and Mark Rose (Shackleton, 1975: 303). Other CCF-NDP notables who leaned towards the Trudeau government on this matter included Scott, Casgrain, and Schreyer (McLeod and McLeod, 1987: 266).

[84] See Berger (1981: Chapter 7). Among the books confiscated was a volume on Cubism—presumably the art book was mistaken for one on Castro's revolutionary Cuba. Far more disturbing were incidents such as the one in which both parents were taken away while the children were left to fend for themselves, an example cited in a speech (and later a pamphlet) by Lewis. In outlining the serious philosophical problems of such unrestrained state power while citing specific cases of abuse, the speech was quintessential Lewis, a blend of theory and practice in which moral outrage was reinforced by concrete examples.

[85] Taylor, in his introduction to Lewis's memoirs (xv). Charles Lynch, veteran national reporter, writes: 'At no time was I more captivated by [Lewis's] powers of argument and his courage than during the Quebec crisis of 1970, when more forcibly than his then leader Tommy Douglas, he stated the case against the application of the War Measures Act and braved the wrath of an aroused public. I myself was totally on the side of Pierre Trudeau and . . . could not have been more opposed to the things Lewis was saying. . . .' (1983: 165). For slightly different interpretations, see McLeod and McLeod (1987: 263); Shackleton (1975: 299, 303).

[86] A noted Quebec academic, Taylor writes: 'People have forgotten now how alone the NDP stood in those days, the butt of virulent hatred for its resistance to the general climate of panic and anger' (in Lewis, 1981: xv; see also Berger, 1981: 211; Harrop, 1984: 109-10).

[87] Gallup reported in December 1970 a remarkable 87% public approval rate for the government's actions. Among the party leaders, Douglas suffered the most, with 36% indicating a lower rating than before vs. only 8% a higher one (Gallup Report, 12, 16, 19 Dec. 1970).

[88] Ironically, in the 1980s Laxer was more favourable towards the Liberals. This apparent deradicalization of former members of the New Left may be due to the

fact that young radicals come from a transitory category—students—who initially have low status and income but soon become affluent professionals and are often co-opted into the socio-economic and political establishment.

89 Interview with Janet Solberg, December 1990. See also Smith (471).

90 This perception was reinforced at the convention bear-pit session, in which Lewis seemed perplexed when asked to list his flaws or weaknesses.

91 Interview with Janet Solberg, 1990. See also Zolf (1973); J. McLeod (1988: 232); Smith (471).

92 The first round had occurred at the 1969 federal convention in Winnipeg, where the Waffle Manifesto was debated and defeated. The so-called Marshmallow Resolution, co-written by Lewis and Charles Taylor, passed instead by 499 to 268. (Morton, 1986: 95). See Cross (1974) for transcripts of the two documents.

93 David's son Stephen had become leader of the Ontario NDP in 1970 and would remain so until 1978. As close political confidants, Stephen recalls, he and his father talked on the telephone every day (interview, January 1991).

94 Note, for example, Lewis's comments on the British Columbia Marxists in the party (93, 170, 376, 463) and a similar criticism of the British Independent Labour Party (45). Lewis also clashed at times with the pacifist Carlyle King (380-1, 345-6).

95 Interview with Stephen Lewis, 1991.

96 In the late 1950s the Quebec wing of the CCF was renamed the Parti social démocratique du Québec.

97 McCall (1982: 93); Djwa (1987: 336); Sherwood (1966). In this regard, he and Eugene Forsey (1990) were in agreement (correspondence, Michael Oliver to Whitehorn, 17 May 1991).

98 The phrase 'just society' had previously been employed in the CCF's Winnipeg Declaration of 1956 (see Chapter 3)—a plausible source of inspiration for Trudeau. Similarly, the CCF-NDP and F.R. Scott were early advocates of entrenching a Canadian charter of rights, and in all likelihood influenced Trudeau's thinking (Djwa, 1987: 333, 337; Lamoureux, 1985: 132-3).

99 Interview with Janet Solberg, 1990. It is also worth noting that, like Margaret Trudeau, Sophie Lewis protested against her husband's one-sided perspective—although she was a good deal more restrained in her reactions than her younger counterpart (see M. Trudeau, 1979). For a detailed account of the plaintive correspondence from Sophie Lewis to her husband, see Smith (Chapter 16).

100 For more detail see Chapter 4.

101 The campaign theme was later woven into a book entitled *Louder Voices: The Corporate Welfare Bums* (1972).

102 One disturbing though often ignored note was that the NDP percentage of the vote had only increased from 17.0% to 17.7% and was still lower than in 1965. Our electoral system, however, masked that fact.

103 Ironically, the NDP did so in Ontario under the leadership of Stephen Lewis in 1977.

104 See MacDonald (1988: 143-5). More recently there have been calls for greater co-operation between the two parties—for example, during the drafting of the 1985 Ontario Liberal-NDP accord and in the midst of the 1988 free-trade election.

105 At the time, many resented the idea that a relatively small third party could set so much of the legislative agenda.

[106]Personal discussion with David Lewis. See also Smith (473-4).

[107]Janet Solberg suggests that her father did not want to be accused of propping up the Liberals (see also Chrétien, 1985: 78). Since a number of left critics over the years had accused Lewis of betraying socialism, some even labelling him a liberal, one can imagine his reluctance to provide ammunition for such charge. Steed (1988: 183) also notes the Tory taunts that Trudeau and Lewis were in political bed together.

[108]For details see Chapter 4. During the 1974 campaign Lewis wore a common daisy to distinguish himself from Trudeau and his more aristocratic rose.

[109]For a detailed and well-crafted account of the three generations of the Lewis family, see Smith.

[110]In his memoirs Lewis notes: 'Fortunately for my development and my sanity, my interest in literature never waned.' Klein and Lewis co-founded the magazine the *McGilliard* during their days at McGill, and the topic of Lewis's essay for his Rhodes application was culture (20, 31, 33). See also U. Caplan's (1982) biography of Klein and Djwa's (1987) biography of Scott.

[111]The other, Nina, does not live in Canada at present.

[112]One criticism of Cameron Smith's otherwise fine account of the Lewis clan is its relative lack of attention to Michael Lewis and Janet Solberg.

[113]Any movement for social change seems to need both a prophet who can captivate the imagination and convey a vision of a better world and someone else who can build the organization and administration required to sustain such goals (Hoffer, 1951). The eloquent and charismatic Stephen excels in the first role, while Michael and Janet have been exceptional in the latter, less glamorous tasks. Their father, out of necessity, had to perform both roles.

[114]In the 1940s Lewis had served on a committee to help create Carleton University (233).

[115]It is inexcusable that the government papers of an Ontario premier should remain closed to public scrutiny a half-century after they were created at public expense. Such secrecy does not serve the public interest, but rather perpetuates the hiding of individual misdeeds.

[116]There is one very curious exception, and that is the case of the NDP's Saskatchewan *Commonwealth*, which initially refused to review the memoirs.

[117]In many ways, the Lewis memoirs have displaced Young's fine pioneering volume (1969) on the CCF in citations.

[118]Many continue to ask whether someone else could not have finished the work that Lewis started. Unfortunately, the CCF years were the easier to research. One of the problems with work on the NDP years was that few archival collections were accessible in the latter half of the 1970s. A second factor was that during the NDP era, important and controversial work was far less likely to be written down; the telephone age has made the historic record more difficult to piece together. In addition, research on the CCF era was far more interesting than on the later period, and, not surprisingly, Lewis and his research staff spent a disproportionate amount of time on the former. For these reasons, far too little research was completed on the NDP era; moreover, as in the case of the CCF volume, Lewis had written no detailed outline of the planned chapters for his staff. The NDP period was also so recent that a detached perspective was more difficult. Finally, a number of the key staffers had already left the Lewis

project and were employed elsewhere. It was a difficult decision not to go ahead with a second volume of the memoirs, but under the circumstances it seemed the correct choice.

[119]Even an edited collection of Lewis's speeches would be a valuable contribution. Lovick's volume (1979) on Douglas provides an admirable model.

[120]Douglas's roots were actually in the urban socialist tradition, first in Scotland, then in Winnipeg, and later in Weyburn, where he was president of the local Independent Labour Party.

[121]Smith (1989), while less critical of Lewis, also suggests a difference between the reformist social gospel of Douglas and the more radical Marxism of the Jewish Workers' Bund (222-3, 231-3).

[122]In terms of their careers in elected office, Douglas served longer in the earlier, more agrarian age of the CCF, while Lewis was successful electorally only in the more urban, union-oriented era of the NDP. In a sense, one represented the past, when large, populist rallies were the order of the day, while the other represented the television age.

[123]Steed (1988: 161) also suggests this theme.

[124]The irony and inaccuracy in such portrayals is evident when one considers that David's father, Moishe Losh, had been sentenced to death by the Leninist Bolsheviks; this made the younger Lewis highly suspicious and critical of communists thereafter (Lewis: 10; see also Smith and Part II of this chapter).

[125]Actually, the NDP called only for the disbandment of the Waffle as a group, not the expulsion of any individual members. See MacDonald (1988: 177). The largely self-congratulatory collection of essays published in 1990 (in *Studies in Political Economy* 32 and 33) to celebrate the twentieth anniversary of the Waffle offers a different portrayal.

[126]Douglas was famous for the humorous stories with which he would open his speeches. Lewis, by contrast, was noted for his inability to tell a joke. Douglas won in 8 of 10 general elections and by-elections he contested for Parliament between 1935-44 and 1962-79. He was also one of the longest-serving premiers ever (1944-61) in Canadian politics, winning five straight provincial elections and losing only his first provincial contest in 1934. In total, Douglas served more than four decades in the federal and provincial legislatures. By contrast, Lewis won only 4 of 10 federal contests he entered, none of them during the CCF era. In total, he served a little more than one decade as MP. One important reason for the difference in success rates is that Douglas ran in the west, where the CCF was stronger, and Lewis in the more difficult east. See Chapters 1 and 4.

[127]In a number of discussions I had with Lewis while working on his memoirs, he indicated that he felt the role of national secretary was to perform whatever difficult and unpleasant organizational tasks were required, and in so doing spare the elected leader from being seen as engaged in such actions. Clearly, his perception of his role influenced his behaviour.

[128]See also Smith (1989: 414-15) There is some evidence that Stephen made the trip without the prior knowledge of his father (Stephen Lewis interview, cited in McLeod and McLeod, 1987: 271, and author's discussions with David Lewis). Whether Douglas would have fully believed there was no prior consultation is another matter. The younger Lewis's impatience for leadership change also involved his own personal ambitions to displace the long-serving Donald

MacDonald as Ontario NDP provincial leader; see MacDonald (1988: 163-73). With the benefit of hindsight, one might suggest that Stephen became provincial leader too soon and departed prematurely (see also Smith, 1989: 422-3).

[129]As retiring leader in 1971, it would have been improper for Douglas to indicate any preference among the leadership candidates. However, the delay in stepping down can be interpreted as an implied criticism of Lewis, as can some of Douglas's comments prior to the convention. Note, for example, the following comment in 1970: 'There is such a thing as a generation gap. You need leadership that is closer to the young people of today' (Lovick, 1979: 219). There has also been some informal speculation that Douglas may not have cast a ballot for Lewis. The McLeod volume is curiously silent in this regard, although it does indicate Douglas's enthusiasm for Laxer's writings.

[130]Coldwell's influence on these two great men is an important reason for a biography of him. The fact that he served longer as federal leader of the CCF-NDP than anyone else is another strong argument.

[131]In Steed (1988: 154), citing McLeod and McLeod, pagination unspecified.

[132]See also Chapter 2 regarding Woodsworth and Lewis.

[133]Both Douglas and Lewis experienced illnesses related to overwork. See McLeod and McLeod (1987: 125, 182, 298), Lewis, (432-3); and Smith (257).

[134]They both were named to the Order of Canada.

[135]While Douglas appeared more popular than Lewis among the party rank and file, there seems to have been a quieter respect for Lewis at higher levels. In part, this was due to Lewis's greater analytical bent and the fact that Douglas in private could be far more demanding than his public persona suggested (Steed, 1988: 180; also interviews with author, 1990).

[136]See Whitehorn (1988: 290-1) and Chapter 5.

[137]See, for example, chapters 3 and 4 with regard to the CCF manifestos and election pamphlets from this earlier era.

[138]*Vancouver Sun*, 4 April 1963, cited in McLeod and McLeod (1987: 243). In addition, one social democrat noted: 'Good neighbours need to keep good fences. Can you imagine living next door to a neighbour with ten times the children that you have (10 children to your one) and who suggests the desirability of no fences between the two households? There is little doubt that what might once have been an orderly and peaceful backyard of the smaller household would soon become overrun' (interview with author, 1988).

[139]Even the McLeods (1987: 159, 168) note that Lewis's advice was helpful at times in recruiting outside experts such as George Cadbury and Ken Bryden to Saskatchewan and in formulating policy.

[140]While the Douglas record is overall an excellent one, the McLeods wisely chose to point out occasional errors of judgement and personal clashes. Though a very decent man, Douglas was not a saint in politics. The biography deals frankly with his flirtations with the Social Credit Party in the 1930s; his, at times, cool relationship with Lewis; and his delayed commitments to the defence of Japanese Canadians, the promotion of women, and bilingualism. But these lapses, while not insignificant, were few and rarely enduring.

[141]Laycock's volume (1990) on different types of populism is an example of extensive textual analysis.

SEVEN

Ed Broadbent

ED BROADBENT: A BIOGRAPHICAL SKETCH

Ed Broadbent led the New Democratic Party for half of the 1970s and virtually all of the 1980s. Curiously, for a man with such a long tenure and such a high profile as Canada's most popular party leader, at least in recent years, Broadbent has been the subject of relatively few books. Early in his career, on the eve of his first venture into an NDP leadership race, Broadbent himself drafted an 85-page booklet (1970). But no other volume about him appeared until the eve of the 1988 federal election, when two were published in anticipation of an NDP electoral breakthrough. Judy Steed's book (1988) at times resembles an authorized biography, but nevertheless provides the most comprehensive account to date of his life. An extensive set of interviews with Broadbent (1988) was edited for a volume published in French; no doubt this was intended as a public-relations vehicle for the party in the province where it has yet to make any significant inroads.[1] Unfortunately, no equivalent volume was produced in English for the part of Canada where Broadbent and the NDP have been far more popular and stood the best chance for electoral gains. Common to all three of these works is that they were composed in a spirit of optimism with regard to specific goals: in 1970, the leadership of the party, and in 1988, gains in Quebec and electoral victory in Canada. In each case, these hopes were disappointed.

In contrast to former NDP federal leaders Tommy Douglas and David Lewis, who both were born overseas (in Scotland and Russia respectively), Broadbent was born a Canadian in Oshawa, Ontario.[2] He was also the first federal leader of the party who had not been a CCFer. Whereas Douglas and Lewis had established their reputations in the 1930s and 1940s, Broadbent, born in 1936, was not even present at the NDP's founding convention (Steed: 200); in 1961 he was preoccupied with his first marriage (to city planner Yvonne Yamaoka [Steed: 79])[3] and his academic studies. Another difference was the relatively young age (39) at which Broadbent became leader; Douglas had been in his mid-fifties, and Lewis in his early sixties.

Broadbent also came from a slightly different class background than Douglas and Lewis. As a result of his father's alcoholism and gambling, by the time Ed Broadbent was in his teens the family had lost not only their house but their lower-middle-class socio-economic status (Steed; xvii, 32); initially a salesman, Percy Broadbent eventually became a clerk at the General Motors plant in the strongly unionist town of Oshawa. From these difficult beginnings the young Broadbent emerged determined to excel in his studies and to distrust the emotional excesses he had seen in his father.

From preachers such as Woodsworth and Douglas to teachers[4] such as Coldwell and Broadbent, the CCF-NDP, while speaking on behalf of the toiling masses, has had a tradition of choosing well-educated leaders. Although both Douglas and Lewis had more than one university degree (Lewis had three BAs, while Douglas had a BA and an MA, and had started on a PhD), Broadbent, the first federal NDP leader to have completed a PhD, was a former university professor.[5]

Broadbent's doctoral thesis (1966, University of Toronto), in political science, was an analysis of John Stuart Mill and the theme of 'co-operative individualism' as a contrast to 'possessive individualism' (Macpherson, 1962).[6] Mill (1806-73) was a pivotal figure in English political thought, bridging the chasm between individualist classical liberalism and collectivistic socialism.[7] A continuing subject of debate more than a century after Mill's death is whether he was a socialist or reform liberal. Perhaps not surprisingly, this is a question also posed by some left critics about Broadbent.

Broadbent was strongly influenced by the writings and teachings of Canadian political theorist C.B. Macpherson and British academic Michael Oakeshott.[8] Interestingly, while both thinkers were collectivists, neither was a social democrat: the former was a Marxist, the later a conservative. Among the lessons Broadbent took from Macpherson were the importance of class and the need to restructure society to foster the full growth of each individual. From Oakeshott he learned about people's reluctance to accept change, the fact that it takes time to persuade them to move to a new political position, and the need to respect different viewpoints.

Tommy Douglas, David Lewis, and, to a lesser degree, Stanley Knowles were three key politicians, spanning the CCF and the NDP eras, who had a significant impact on Broadbent.[9] As might be expected, Douglas, the legendary socialist leader, was a greater inspiration at first, but later David Lewis's influence grew, particularly as their relationship warmed. The monk-like Stanley Knowles and his constant presence in the House of Commons also provided Broadbent with a quiet source of strength and continuity, particularly on legislative procedural matters, during his years in Parliament.

Apart from David Lewis, CCF-NDP leaders have not been fluent in French, and Broadbent was no exception. Although he worked hard to overcome this linguistic handicap, he never mastered French to the level of his political rivals; the French-language TV debate in the 1988 election, especially, was a harsh reminder of this fact.[10] Whether a more fluent presentation would have significantly improved the party's performance in a province historically infertile for the CCF-NDP remains an open question.

More important, no doubt, than his facility in French were Broadbent's debating and speaking skills in English. Whereas Douglas and Lewis both excelled in oratory, Broadbent's speeches were more workmanlike; indeed, in the earlier years his public speaking was noted for its awkwardness. Although in time it improved significantly, two factors appear to have inhibited the development of his rhetorical style. One is his distrust of emotionalism, which, one suspects, he sees as a trait reminiscent of his father. The other factor is his scepticism, as a former professor of political theory, regarding the distortion and simplification of rhetoric.[11] Of course, following in the footsteps of such legendary orators as Douglas and Lewis, Broadbent was bound to seem less effective.[12] However, in the era of the ten-second TV clip, oratory before large crowds is no longer as important as it once was.

Broadbent's strength was his personal integrity. By the late 1980s the phrase 'Honest Ed' had come to signify not only Toronto's most famous department store but Canada's most popular political leader.[13] Indeed, Broadbent's image of trustworthiness became the basis of much of the NDP's 1988 federal election campaign (Whitehorn, 1989, and Chapter 8).

Among other important personality traits[14] that Broadbent developed while growing up in difficult family circumstances was a strong streak of determination. He was a hard worker who had learned to endure amidst adversity. His earnestness and resilience would make him a solid leadership figure for any political party. Although lacking the flash of a Pierre Trudeau, he also did not possess Trudeau's arrogance. For many voters the image Broadbent conveyed was one of likeable competence. Above all, in the age of television, he was someone with whom 'ordinary Canadians' could identify.

As has often been the case for CCF-NDP leaders, Broadbent proved to be more popular than his party among most Canadians. Despite this popularity—or perhaps in part because of it—veteran NDP activists were sometimes less enamoured of him (Steed: 197, 318; 'Goodby Ed', *Toronto Star*, 2 Dec. 1989). For some of these, Broadbent was not radical enough, pursued wrong or questionable policies (such as those on Canada's constitution) or was too élitist in his leadership style.[15]

Broadbent's electoral career commenced in 1968, at the height of Trudeaumania. While his fellow academic became Liberal Prime Minister with a majority government, Broadbent was elected with a plurality of a mere fifteen votes in his hometown of Oshawa. Hardly a convincing win, it was one of only half a dozen NDP victories outside western Canada.

As befitted a young academic who had studied under C.B. Macpherson and entered politics in the midst of the 1960s, Broadbent became involved with the New Left (Roussopoulos, 1970; Sargent, 1972; Reid and Reid, 1969) and showed a particular interest in the more radical concepts of workers' self-management and industrial democracy (Hunnius, 1970). He was present at the discussions that led to the creation of the Waffle in 1969 (Hackett, 1980: 7; Bullen, 1983: 193; Broadbent, 1988: 72; Morton, 1986: 92-3), Canada's version of the student New Left;[16] indeed, Broadbent has sometimes been credited with coining the phrase that gave the group its name.[17] In part inspired by a reinterpretation of Marxism, the Waffle sought to infuse Canadian socialism with a more confrontational style and more forceful language. This new ginger group placed greater emphasis on four key policy areas: (1) nationalist concerns with excessive levels of foreign (i.e., US) ownership of Canadian industry; (2) stating unequivocally the right of the nation of Quebec to self-determination; (3) the quest for greater workers' control through the mechanism of industrial democracy; and (4) strong endorsement of feminism.[18] Steed (142-4) notes that these areas were the specialities of, respectively, Mel Watkins, Jim Laxer, Broadbent, and Krista Maeots.

The 1969 NDP federal convention in Winnipeg provided the first major opportunity for the young activists spearheading the Waffle to test their mettle. In place of the increasingly pragmatic programmes that the CCF-NDP had issued in 1956, with the Winnipeg Declaration, and 1961, with the New Party Statement, the Waffle proposed a more Marxist-inspired manifesto (Cross, 1974). But while Broadbent had an early hand in the birth of the Waffle Manifesto, he was by nature more temperate in his language and needed to be more cautious if he was to succeed in re-election as a Member of Parliament. Accordingly, he tried to encourage key members of the Waffle to rewrite the document in a more moderate direction (Steed: 145-6). Failing in his mediating efforts, Broadbent helped to draft a counter-document, the so-called 'marshmallow' manifesto (Steed: 147; McLeod and McLeod, 1987: 278), which was approved by the convention (Morton, 1986: 95; Hackett, 1980: 26; Bullen, 1983: 197). Ironically, the victorious document is largely unread today, while the Waffle Manifesto continues to attract interest, particularly from young students.

The second round of the internal party feuding over the Waffle occurred at the 1971 NDP federal leadership contest. Broadbent, while one of the New Left generation, was also a Member of Parliament and thus in some ways a figure in the party establishment. He also disliked the increasing tendency within the party in general and the Waffle in particular to engage in personal attacks rather than ideological discourse. As a candidate, therefore, he endeavoured to straddle the growing gulf between the Waffle and the mainstream of the party. He failed miserably. In the acrimonious atmosphere of the 1971 convention, there was no sign of the elusive co-operative commonwealth in which brotherhood peacefully reigns. On the first ballot Broadbent placed fourth of five, with 13.9% of the vote. The result was a shock to him, and in retrospect he believes he shouldn't have run (Steed: 163, 159). Still, his candidacy provided him with valuable experience in running for the leadership, and gave him a higher profile in the party.

Broadbent's profile was heightened still further when he was selected to serve under newly elected NDP leader David Lewis as chair of the NDP parliamentary caucus in the minority Parliament of 1972-74. With the defeat of Lewis in the 1974 federal election, Broadbent was chosen by the caucus as interim leader. Unfortunately, a number of NDPers did not feel that he performed particularly well in this new role. At first Broadbent announced that he would not be a candidate in the 1975 leadership race. According to some commentators, he was unhappy with the lack of support in senior party circles. Others have suggested that this was a tactic to draw greater commitment for his candidacy from hesitant senior party figures. Another factor in his initial reluctance was Broadbent's concern for his young family; some have also hinted that Lucille was not keen. Nevertheless two months after pulling out of the race, Broadbent proclaimed that he had changed his mind. It was to prove a wise decision.

From second-last place in the polarized 1971 leadership race, Broadbent went on to win the 1975 contest. Why this turnaround? Part of the answer can be found in his potential competitors for the leadership. Lewis, of course, was about to retire and commence work on his memoirs. Jim Laxer, after finishing second in 1971, had, along with most other members of the Waffle, left the NDP and formed a somewhat fractured, electorally unsuccessful, rival party. The fluently bilingual John Harney, who had come third in 1971, had lost his seat in Parliament, like so many other NDP MPs in 1974, and thereby weakened his leadership candidacy; he was to come in a distant fourth in 1975, just behind Saskatchewan MP Lorne Nystrom.

Like a seasoned marathoner, Broadbent showed steadiness and staying power in the leadership quest. Nevertheless, his victory took four ballots, and with just under 60 per cent of the final vote, his margin of victory over Rosemary Brown was the smallest for any CCF-NDP leader to that time.

While the vote was in part a function of the greater number of candidates than in earlier contests, clearly Broadbent had not been the first choice of many delegates.[19]

The federal campaign of 1979 was the first for Broadbent as leader. Given the mounting dissatisfaction with Liberal Prime Minister Pierre Trudeau and the low public confidence in the young and inexperienced Conservative leader Joe Clark, it is perhaps not surprising that Broadbent became the focus of his party's election campaign.

One TV ad ran as a stark printed message moving up the screen: 'A lot of Liberals and Conservatives believe that Ed Broadbent would make the best Prime Minister. They say, if Ed Broadbent were the leader of their party, he'd win the biggest landslide in Canadian history. People don't have the same kind of nagging doubts about Ed Broadbent they have about Trudeau and Clark. Maybe it's time to put aside the old Liberal and Conservative myths and simply vote for the best man. If enough people did that, Ed Broadbent would be the next prime minister of Canada' (in Penniman, 1981: 290).[20]

Hoping to win at least 50 seats,[21] Broadbent ensured that for the first time ever the party ran a full slate of candidates. He was also aided by the free air time in the televised leaders' debates, where he performed well (Clarke et al., 1991: 103), and by a rare editorial endorsement from *The Toronto Star*. Instead of 50 seats, however, he had to settle for 26. (For more detail on this election, see Chapter 4.)

In several respects, the NDP and Broadbent provided stronger opposition than the Liberals to the newly elected minority government of Joe Clark. The Liberals were not used to being in opposition, and with Trudeau's announcement of his resignation, they were in some disarray. In less than a year the minority Conservative government of Joe Clark was toppled by an NDP non-confidence motion proposed by a young MP named Bob Rae, and Broadbent plunged into yet another election.[22] There was not enough time to fundamentally alter the NDP's strategy in the 1980 election (Morton, 1986: 198), and so once again the emphasis would be on Broad-bent himself—a decision reinforced by the fact that his public-approval rating as choice for prime minister had doubled from a year earlier and his ranking among the leaders moved from third place to second, ahead of the stumbling Clark (Gallup, 22 Sept. 1979 and 9 Jan. 1980). Underlying the campaign strategy was Broadbent's belief that the Canadian public simply needed to be awakened to the fact that it already embraced a number of social-democratic ideas and programmes and hence should logically support the NDP.[23] To highlight this point, one NDP ad took the form of a quiz listing a number of propositions and inviting readers to choose which ones came closest to their own views (Steed: 236-7). Not surprisingly, the quiz was constructed in such a way that a great many people would likely agree with the NDP's positions.

Although the NDP's total vote of 19.8% was the best yet, it was a long way from that of the victorious Liberals who, led by a resurrected Trudeau, formed a majority government. Social Credit, the NDP's chief rival over the years as third party, finally slid into oblivion, leaving the NDP the sole 'new' party with representation in Parliament. As a result, Ed Broadbent and the NDP would in future acquire an even higher profile.

Despite the Liberals' majority, they had only two seats west of the Ontario border (Penniman, 1981: 408-9; Feigert, 1989: 74-5). Wishing to move on major constitutional change (particularly in light of the upcoming Quebec referendum), Trudeau saw his need of a pan-Canadian base and boldly offered Broadbent and his NDP caucus (with 27 of 32 MPs from the west) a number of cabinet seats. It was a chance for social democrats to share in governing Canada (Steed: 239-41). Given Trudeau's earlier contacts with the CCF-NDP in the late 1950s and early 1960s, the offer was not without logic. Broadbent, however, turned it down. Coalition government is not a significant part of the Canadian parliamentary heritage, and NDP members generally were not enamoured of the Trudeau government's record.

Undeterred by Broadbent's rejection of his cabinet overtures, Trudeau proceeded with his mission to introduce historic alterations in Canada's constitutional structure. In early October 1980 he again approached Broadbent. This time the subject was possible constitutional changes, two of which—patriation of the constitution to Canada and entrenchment of a charter of rights—had been advocated by Canadian social democrats for several decades (Broadbent, 1988: 135), and had the support of Douglas, Lewis, and Knowles. To Broadbent such proposals seemed not only reasonable but particularly important to pursue in the wake of the 1980 Quebec referendum. Without widely consulting the younger generation of his NDP colleagues, he agreed in the main to Trudeau's proposals (Steed: 244-6; Gruending, 1990: 194-5). It was a serious error in judgement. In agreeing so swiftly, Broadbent failed to provide sufficient opportunity for the various members of his party (particularly the largely western caucus, powerful provincial NDP leaders, and the solitary NDP premier, Allan Blakeney of Saskatchewan) to have their full say (Richards and Kerr, 1986: 6)— a surprising omission, given the fiercely democratic culture of NDP politics. Broadbent's lack of consultation seemed particularly puzzling coming from a former theorist and advocate of participatory democracy; given the western skew of the caucus, some suggested, his action was unnecessarily provocative. The result was that, while the bulk of the caucus supported Broadbent, a number of Saskatchewan MPs (including former leadership rival Lorne Nystrom) broke with him on the constitution and took a stand closer to Blakeney's (Gruending, 1990: 202-3).

Blakeney was more sceptical than Broadbent about the benefits of a US-style charter of rights and its corresponding enhancement of the powers of the Supreme Court; he was also more inclined to strengthen provincial powers, particularly in relation to natural resources.[24] The policy disagreement between Broadbent and Blakeney festered as the constitutional debate continued. For many within the NDP this was a distressing time of conflict among friends.[25] Even a secret meeting in March 1981 overseen by two CCF-NDP patriarchs, Douglas and Lewis, did not succeed in mediating between Blakeney and Broadbent (Gruending, 1990: 203; Steed: 252).

The divisions were not confined to the top of the party pyramid. The 1981 federal NDP convention culminated in a long and emotional debate among delegates on the topic of the Canadian constitution. In the end, the federal party backed Broadbent (Gruending, 1990: 204; Morton, 1986: 206-7), but it was not a happy gathering. To compound the party's troubles in this period, in May 1982 the NDP government of Saskatchewan, long a socialist fortress, went down to a crushing defeat.

The nadir came in 1983, at a time when the party desperately wanted to celebrate the fiftieth anniversary of the Regina Manifesto. When the delegates convened at Regina they were presented with not one draft manifesto but several. Chief among these were the official draft approved for discussion by the party's policy review committee and federal council (reflecting the ideas of Broadbent, Jim Laxer, and Peter Warrian), and another, the so-called June 22nd Statement, of which the main architects were westerners John Richards, Allan Blakeney, and Grant Notley (Richards and Kerr, 1986). Unfortunately, the ill will over the constitution spilled over into the drafting of the new Regina Manifesto. The June 22nd document came very late and with virtually no warning.[26] The two draft documents represented different visions of social democracy in Canada, the first tending towards a stronger pro-federalist position and the second leaning more towards provincial rights. Eventually a compromise was reached and the final document was a collage of the two drafts, pieced together by Laxer and Warrian (see also Chapter 3). Despite the acrimonious process, this new Regina Manifesto is not without merit. Curiously, however, while it should be one of the four key ideological statements of social democracy in Canada (along with those of 1933, 1956, and 1961), the document was largely ignored immediately following the 1983 convention, and was not readily available in printed form until the late 1980s.[27]

The winter of 1983-84 continued the party's ebb. Caucus research director Jim Laxer's Christmas present to his colleagues was the so-called Laxer Report (later published as a book entitled *Rethinking the Economy* [1984]), in which he called for a reformulation of social-democratic thought in the 1980s. Few could disagree with such a premise.[28] The problem was that the press received a copy before Laxer's boss, party leader Broadbent, did. At the very least, this was seen as an act of disloyalty to a man who had endeavoured to bring Laxer back into the party. To many, it also seemed dishonest, since Laxer had been employed by the party to do the work and had published it without advance notice, let alone permission. There was some initial talk of a lawsuit, but the NDP never pursued the matter; such adverse publicity would not help the party, and would only increase sales of the book. The attempted rehabilitation of Jim Laxer in the NDP was over. The 1984 episode confirmed what some had felt more than a decade earlier, in 1971: that Laxer was a bright and provocative one-man show, but too often lacked the discipline and co-operative spirit necessary to be a team player in a major political party. Academia was where he belonged.

Finally, in the latter half of 1984, NDP fortunes began to take a turn for the better. First, at the convention to elect a successor to Pierre Elliott Trudeau, the Liberals chose John Turner instead of the then left-leaning and far more populist Jean Chrétien.

The second positive development for the NDP was its decision in the winter of 1983-84 to replace the departing Larry Ellis with Vic Fingerhut, a US-based pollster who had done work for trade unions in Canada. The NDP, like the CCF, had for decades been somewhat amateurish in its polling operations, and it called in Fingerhut to help revive flagging social-democratic spirits.

The 1984 campaign (see Chapter 4) was a crucial one for Broadbent and the NDP. Pre-election Gallup polls from March to July were reporting the party in danger of dropping below the 10% level; a number of journalists went so far as to predict the demise of the federal NDP.[29] Even some NDP staffers feared for their jobs. Armed with more systematic polling from the party's core regions, however, the NDP and federal secretary Gerry Caplan were able to discern that the public perception of the party's strength lay in the domain of social issues (i.e., issues of the heart), while its weakness lay in issues of economic management (i.e., issues of the head). The NDP strategists planned their campaign accordingly. They also decided to emphasize incumbent NDP MPs for whom public support was greater than for their party. To their relief, Broadbent performed well in the television debates and ran what was perhaps his best campaign.[30] Echoing David Lewis's successful left-populist[31] attack upon 'corporate welfare bums' in 1972, Broadbent depicted the Liberal and Conservative leaders, both former corporate lawyers, as the Bobbsey twins of Bay St, suggesting that only the NDP spoke on behalf of 'ordinary Canadians' and would protect important social programmes.

The election results were a tonic. The NDP's 18.8% of the vote and 30 seats, combined with the dramatic collapse of Liberal support, particularly in Quebec, gave the NDP a higher profile in the House of Commons, in the media,[32] and among the public at large. NDP fortunes were at last on the upswing.

In April[33] of 1987, most Canadians were surprised by the announcement that a first ministers' conference at the Prime Minister's summer residence at Meech Lake had produced a new constitutional accord. Broadbent was among the majority of people who initially saw the new document as a positive step towards including Quebec into the constitutional structure.

This time, though, he was more careful about the decision-making process within the party (Steed: 301), taking more time to listen to the opinions of his caucus and colleagues. Yet in the end Broadbent was no less determined to embrace the proposal.[34] His desire to accommodate Quebec was rooted not only in a sense of justice[35] but also in electoral considerations. Quebec would be a necessary jumping-off position if the NDP was ever to break out from third place. Generally, the impression in 1987 was that Broadbent handled the Meech Lake Accord reasonably well—certainly better than he had the constitutional negotiations of 1981. Seeming to confirm this perception, a Gallup poll in July 1987 showed the NDP's popularity at a record high, and the party enjoyed several by-election victories (most notably that of Audrey McLaughlin in the Yukon).

From the nadir in 1983, Broadbent and his party were now moving towards the zenith. How far would they go? Were the changes of historic proportions? Would Canadian social democrats equal their British counterparts and displace the Liberals? Broadbent felt he saw evidence in the polling data to confirm his belief that the Canadian public was now closer to the social-democratic policies of the NDP than ever before.[36] As he and the party rose in popularity, however, the NDP leadership started to become more cautious. The language employed, increasingly constrained by polling considerations, became decidedly duller. Some critics have charged that polls were displacing party principles. Others have suggested that it was more a matter of apprehension: like performers suddenly thrust onto a high wire, NDP strategists were afraid to make a deadly mistake. The gamble to win Quebec was a large one; such an opportunity might never come again. Yet part of the reason behind the high level of public approval for Broadbent and the NDP was their image of honesty, openness, and earnestness, combined with an appropriate dose of humility. Now that they had achieved first place in the polls, there appeared to be a slight backing away from these traits; a whiff of the arrogance of power was beginning to emerge. The shift was barely perceptible at first, but for careful observers a steady and disappointing pattern was beginning to emerge.

Scepticism, however, had no place amidst the party's plans for a breakthrough in Quebec and the march to power in Ottawa. To a capacity crowd attending the 1987 federal convention in Montreal, Terry Grier, chairperson of the election planning committee, announced that the NDP would be launching its most ambitious and costly campaign ever. It would be truly national in scope and would devote substantial funds to a French-language campaign in Quebec. History was in the making, the delegates were promised.

The 1988 federal election was one of the most polarized and important contests in Canadian history (see Chapter 8). Free trade was, overwhelmingly, the dominant issue (Frizzell et al., 1989; Clarke et al., 1991). Before the campaign, remembering the frustrating setbacks of the 1974 campaign on wage and price controls, NDP strategists were concerned about the dangers inherent in a single-issue campaign. Broadbent continues to believe that the predominance of the free-trade issue hurt the NDP's prospects in the pivotal provinces of Ontario and Quebec, which together account for 174 (59%) of the 295 seats in the House of Commons. Although, even with hindsight, he says he would not have altered the party's election strategy,[37] it seems likely that Broadbent's fervent desire to make a breakthrough in Quebec did lead him to underestimate English Canadian nationalism and opposition to free trade. Certainly the fact that Quebeckers were more inclined to support free trade than were voters in other provinces (Environics poll, 2-10 Oct. 1988) made the NDP more reluctant to pursue the issue vigorously, lest it alienate Quebec voters (see Chapter 8, and Whitehorn in Frizzell [1989]). Did NDP strategists misread the polling data on free trade and see it largely as a 'managing the economy' issue (an area in which, according to polls, the NDP historically does poorly)? Party members continue to agonize over this question (Mason, 1990) and even scholars, several years after the election, cannot agree.[38]

If mistakes were made in grand strategy, there were also errors in tactics. Two highly publicized comments that created problems for the NDP were, first, Broadbent's suggestion that the demise of the Liberal Party was both possible and desirable, and, second, his response to the question of minority English rights in Quebec (see Chapter 8). In the eyes of many, Broadbent's apparent unwillingness to take a clear stand in defence of Anglophone rights[39] not only tarnished his image of sterling integrity, but made him appear indecisive, as if he were trying to avoid difficult issues. It was a damaging image to project in the midst of an election. In their longing to believe that a historic breakthrough was imminent, most party activists chose not to question key assumptions that the Liberals were in total disarray and that John Turner would prove to be as hapless a campaigner in 1988 as he had in 1984. Neither proposition was accurate. Finally, if the NDP overestimated the durability of Broadbent's positive persona, they underestimated Brian Mulroney's magician-like campaign skills.

Whatever mistakes the party leadership may have made, however, it remains clear that these were not the only, or even the most important, reasons for the NDP's failure to achieve a breakthrough in 1988. Moreover, to attribute excessive blame to Broadbent and his staff does little to further our understanding. Commentators and current NDP strategists would be wise to go beyond scapegoating and instead explore the class base in politics. In one respect particularly there was an uncanny resemblance to the 1945 federal election (Read and Whitehorn, 1991): in both cases, the party's lack of success had less to do with the errors of overworked individual social democrats than with the intervention of big business. To protect their monopoly capitalist agenda, corporate interests launched a massive advertising campaign in 1988 that, as in 1945, thwarted the socialist challenge. Social democrats would be wise to heed this bitter lesson in class politics: corporate conspiracies do exist, and in an age of mass advertising, elections can be bought.

While the NDP came out of the election with its best-ever vote and number of seats, it slipped to a distant third place. The window of opportunity had closed and to make matters worse for a party that has usually been able to console itself with moral victories, in this case there was a depressing sense of moral defeat. The backlash of blame was not long in coming. There were indications of growing restlessness, if not outright discontent, with Broadbent's leadership. Several high-ranking union leaders (Gerard Docquier and Leo Gerard of the United Steelworkers of America and Bob White of the Canadian Auto Workers) wrote scathing letters. Even two veteran MPs, John Rodriguez and Howard McCurdy, were critical of their leader. But Broadbent refused to be pushed out. After a decade and a half as leader, his response was a mixture of justifiable pride and characteristic determination. He would pick his time and place of departure. In the end, as he had often done before, he made the correct decision for the well-being of his party. Despite protestations from those most loyal to him, Broadbent chose to depart gracefully. In so doing, he ensured peace in the party and an opportunity for orderly renewal.

Following Broadbent's resignation in 1989, he agreed to head the newly created International Centre for Human Rights and Democratic Development in Montreal. Time will tell if he and his staff can turn this centre into an innovative and dynamic organization and show that he did not merely accept a patronage position, as some Canadians initially assumed. Certainly most of the world is lacking in strong democratic traditions and institutions, though what a Canadian-based agency can achieve is an open question. Whether such a unit can avoid possible future government cut-backs, as called for at the 1991 Conservative convention, or survive the post-Broadbent era also remains to be seen. The prospects for success globally are daunting. Still, the task is important enough to be worth the effort. One suspects that John Stuart Mill would have approved of Broadbent's commitment to search for ways of extending democratic principles.

THE BROADBENT ERA: AN EVALUATION

While the Broadbent era is still quite recent, some preliminary observations can be offered. First, on the 1980 coalition-government offer, it appears that an important opportunity may have been too readily dismissed. Perhaps playing a role in government would have improved the NDP's image on economic matters and enhanced public perceptions of its readiness to govern. Canadians might even be better served with more broadly-based coalition governments. Did the lack of a liberal-social democratic centre-left alliance increase the prospects of a neo-conservative victory later in the 1980s? Will such an opportunity arise again? If so, what is the appropriate response?

On the matter of the constitution, it is clear that in 1980 Broadbent responded too quickly, and perhaps too warmly, to Trudeau's initiatives, and in so doing alienated several prominent New Democrats in the west.[40] Similarly, in 1987 he endorsed Mulroney's Meech Lake initiatives, and over time upset increasing numbers of party members in English Canada.[41] In both cases, discontent with Broadbent's actions was strongest in the west, but it was by no means confined to that region. Constitutional conflicts are among the most divisive, and no major party in Canada has been spared intra-organizational tensions over these issues. While Broadbent had some criticisms concerning both Trudeau's and Mulroney's proposals[42] (Broadbent, 1988: 135-6, 147-50), he felt in the main that both were worthy of support. What Broadbent did not seem to grasp sufficiently was that not everyone was prepared to agree so readily with the prime minister of the day. To many, Broadbent also appeared too eager to please Quebec, a province that was relatively late in coming to certain democratic principles[43] and that had never shown much support for a federal social-democratic party. Broadbent did not seem to appreciate the magnitude of the opposition to his position on the constitution. In the 1988 federal election, perhaps he went too far to accommodate Quebec (see also Broadbent, 1988: 153); certainly it cost him support both within the NDP[44] and in English Canada generally. He was, and still is, willing to pay that political cost for the sake of Canadian unity and keeping Quebec in the federation. In the end, however, political neophyte Audrey McLaughlin was much closer to most rank-and-file New Democrats in this thorny area. Ironically, almost two decades earlier Broadbent (1970: 15) had written:

> Since Confederation, there have been two main struggles taking place in Canadian history. The first concerns unity, the second equality . . . this focus on the theme of unity and its representation as a constitutional problem has had the effect of obscuring and even obliterating the class issue of equality.

No doubt many New Democrats today would agree with these comments.

A third area in which Broadbent's judgement can be questioned was on the topic of free trade. Data on activists in Canada's three major parties indicate that the NDP is the most critical of unrestricted free trade with the United States (Archer and Whitehorn, 1990, 1991; Blake, 1988). In view of this firm base of support for a nationalist critique of the Conservative government policy, many New Democrats saw Broadbent's inaction in the 1988 election as a betrayal. It remained for Liberal John Turner, himself the head of a party paradoxically quite divided on the issue (Archer and Whitehorn, 1990, 1991; Blake 1988), to lead the crusade against the deal. Many New Democrats continue to believe that Ed Broadbent and his closest staff faltered at a crucial juncture in Canadian history. These activists could accept losing an election, they say; they had laboured many years in the political wilderness. What they could not accept was losing without fighting the good fight for Canadian sovereignty. Broadbent's rebuttal remains that he and his closest colleagues feared the consequences of a single-issue campaign.

Among some members of the NDP, Broadbent's position on questions of participatory democracy was also disappointing. In the 1960s he was one of the key Canadian advocates of a radical variant of socialism in the form of industrial democracy and workers' self-management (Broadbent, 1970; Hunnius, 1970). Indeed, Broadbent boldly predicted that 'industrial democracy will probably develop as *the* question for the 1970's' (Hunnius, 1970: 63; emphasis in original). Given that the concept of workers' self-management has never been particularly popular with most Canadian trade-union officials, perhaps it is not surprising that Broadbent as NDP leader backed away from speaking extensively on the topic.[45] For those expecting greater leadership in this area, however, the lack of promotion from a high-profile politician was a let-down.

One of the puzzles about the NDP is that despite its left-populist tradition, it has not embraced one of the key concepts of the early twentieth-century populists—the public referendum. This is something that one would have expected from a party committed to new democratic forms of mass partici-pation. It is also something that one would have expected from Broadbent, in view of his early support for industrial democracy. Surely if workers ought to participate in complex technical matters involving factory invest-ments, Canadians at large should have the right to take part in the policy-making and constitution-making processes of their country. The 1980 ref-erendum in the province of Quebec worked well, as did those in Britain dealing with such major issues as constitutional devolution of powers for Scotland and Wales and a free-trade zone in the European Common Market. Moreover, as a measurement of public opinion on a single issue, a referendum is far more precise than any election. Yet Broadbent opposed the use of referenda in Canadian politics; drawing on the earlier Canadian history of plebiscites, he saw the mechanism as potentially too divisive.[46] By contrast, Audrey McLaughlin seems more receptive to the idea.

If as party leader Broadbent did not vigorously pursue all the theories of participatory democracy that he espoused as a young professor,[47] was it that the taste of power and the comfortable atmosphere of Parliament Hill had lessened some of his radical fervour? Some thought so. Others suggested that the radical young academic in the corduroy jacket had been displaced by a middle-aged party leader wearing a tailor-made suit. Another possible explanation is that other issues had simply assumed greater priority, both for Broadbent and for the public at large. The 1980s were not the 1960s.

The last critical observation that one might make regarding Broadbent's leadership is that it did not do more to foster the reformulation of socialist thought in Canada.[48] In 1970, Broadbent warned: 'If we New Democrats stay within the welfare state in terms of our policies and vocabulary, we will deserve the dismissal by Canadians which will inevitably follow' (Hunnius, 1970: 63). Yet although he was a very popular and effective professor of political theory at York University prior to his entry into politics, and the author of a political booklet in the 1970s, the Broadbent era produced few major works in Canadian social-democratic thought. During his tenure only two volumes significantly related to the federal NDP's philosophy and programme were published.[49] The first was an edited collection entitled *Democratic Socialism: The Challenge of the Eighties* (Wilson, 1985),[50] based on a Vancouver conference of party activists and theorists sponsored by the Boag Foundation. The second collection, *Canada: What's Left?* (Richards and Kerr, 1986) was the product of a conference in Edmonton that included among its participants some who had played key roles in drafting the rival western manifesto of 22 June 1983. Disappointingly, NDP leader Broadbent was not present at either of these conferences, and did not contribute to either book.[51] Since his departure as leader two new edited collections focusing on policies for social democrats—*Debating Canada's Future: Views From the Left* (Rosenblum and Findlay, 1991) and *Social Democracy Without Illusions: Renewal of the Canadian Left* (Richards et al., 1991)—have appeared, both of which had their origins in the waning days of the Broadbent era and were financed in part by the Douglas-Coldwell Foundation.

Ed Broadbent has said that Canadian socialist theory is not very sophisticated.[52] In preferring to look elsewhere for intellectual nourishment (Steed: 336)—for example, to the US magazine *Dissent*—Broadbent is not alone among left intellectuals. Still, there is an element of the colonial mind-set in this attitude. Broadbent's disdain for Canadian socialist intellectuals is in large degree reciprocated by the academic left (Richards and Kerr, 1986). It seems that the decades-old gulf between left academics and Canada's social-democratic party persists.[53]

Broadbent concurs with suggestions that the absence of an enduring Canadian equivalent of the British Fabian Society has been a 'hindrance' to fostering both social-democratic thought and political gains for the CCF-NDP.[54] It seems curious, therefore, that as federal leader he was not a catalyst for the formation and growth of such a group. It is still possible that in the future he may play a key role in the Douglas-Coldwell Foundation. Like former Ontario NDP leader Stephen Lewis, however, to date Broadbent has seemed to take more interest in the international arena than in domestic matters. Given the desperate plight of much of the rest of the world, this focus on international developments is perhaps understandable.

What are the hallmarks of the Broadbent era? No doubt the most obvious was the heightening of the federal NDP's profile under his leadership. From being one of two minor parties in a four-party system the NDP moved up to become one of the country's three major parties, and broke the 20% vote barrier for the first time.

One explanation of the Liberal Party's dominance for much of the twentieth century has been its ability to win a large block of Quebec seats and acquire substantial support from the Canadian middle class (Meisel, 1975). The New Democratic Party was created in 1961 with the goal of altering the pattern of Liberal predominance in Canadian politics. Yet despite the eloquence of the first two NDP leaders, Tommy Douglas and David Lewis, the NDP was not able to achieve a breakthrough and convert the centre-left liberally-minded.

In the late 1980s, Broadbent made yet another attempt to realign the voting pattern of Canadians. Hoping to take advantage of a breach in the weakened former strongholds of the Liberal Party, he geared much of the NDP's pre-1988 election activities towards wooing Quebec voters. Broadbent and his principal secretary, George Nakitsas, fervently believed that the NDP could accomplish a breakthrough in Quebec (Broadbent, 1988: 128, 143), particularly if special efforts were made.[55] But the strategy did involve some risks. Would the party need to shift policy emphases to be more attractive in Quebec? If so, at what cost elsewhere? For example, would the attempt to win in Quebec by downplaying the free-trade issue alienate English Canadian nationalists battling the treaty? Did the attempt to win the support of Quebec nationalists lessen the stress on minority English rights in that province? What was the cost, if any, of such a perception in the west and Ontario? Finally, given the bias in Canada's electoral system, would increased public support for the NDP in Quebec actually translate into any sizeable number of NDP seats from that province in the House of Commons? To Broadbent's credit, the NDP federal vote in Quebec reached the previously unheard-of level of 14%; only once before (in 1965) had it even passed 10%. Unfortunately, as noted elsewhere in this book, our electoral system does not easily recognize such efforts to broaden the regional base of support for a party (Cairns, 1968), and despite receiving close to a half million votes in Quebec, the NDP failed to win a single one of the province's 75 seats. Was Broadbent realistic in expecting so much from Quebec? The province remains a political quagmire for the NDP. No matter how much effort the party puts in, the results continue to seem largely fruitless, the Chambly by-election victory notwithstanding. In failing to achieve a breakthrough in Quebec, Ed Broadbent joined a long list of distinguished CCF-NDP leaders from J.S. Woodsworth to David Lewis. Unlike most of his predecessors, however, Broadbent had devoted considerable effort towards a Quebec breakthrough, committing extra personnel, funds and attention to the province. It was a gamble worth taking, and had Broadbent not attempted it, he would have been accused of timidity and blamed for lack of imagination in designing an electoral strategy.

The second key group that the New Party strove to convert to its cause in 1961 consisted of the liberally-minded from the middle class. Whereas the old-style socialists Douglas and Lewis were largely unsuccessful in this regard, Broadbent, perhaps more attuned to left populist concerns than his predecessors, made greater gains. Although Lewis had made good use of a populist theme in the 'corporate welfare bums' campaign of 1972, Broadbent's 1984 campaign phrase 'ordinary Canadians'[56] seemed to tap into a broader vein of middle-class discontent,[57] and in so doing raised the NDP to a higher plateau of support (19.2% of the vote in four contests under his leadership, vs. 15.4% in four elections under Douglas and 16.6% in two contests under Lewis).

One prime example of Broadbent's efforts to move the party closer to the political mainstream by making its policies more credible and realistic was his approach to the topic of NATO (Steed: 264, 334). Determined to convey to the Canadian public that the NDP was a responsible organization, ready to govern, he encouraged a review of the party's previous promise to withdraw from NATO. The culmination of this review came in the spring of 1988, when the party's international affairs committee and federal council issued a document entitled 'Canada's Stake in Common Security', announcing that if the NDP formed the federal government, it would not leave NATO during its first term of office.[58] While foreign affairs are not generally an area of great concern to most Canadians, Broadbent believed that such a policy shift[59] would help to broaden the party's appeal and enhance its credibility.

Surprisingly to many, in the 1988 election campaign Broadbent failed to captivate either the press or the public the way he had in 1984. Why? No doubt the polarization of the electorate on the free-trade issue was a major factor. In the heated and dramatic debates between Mulroney and Turner, Broadbent seemed to be on the sidelines. Clearly he had misjudged the magnitude of the free-trade issue, and felt disinclined and/or helpless to change matters. He was certainly less emotional in the language he used. In the end, though, the New Democrats were victims of their own excessive expectations. Too few cautioned that a breakthrough would not necessarily occur. The lessons from 1945, outlined in detail by Lewis (1981) and others (Caplan, 1973), seemed to be ignored.

Another hallmark of Broadbent's tenure was internal to the NDP. When Tommy Douglas departed as federal leader in 1971, the party was badly divided between the centre-left and the militant Waffle. When David Lewis stepped down in 1975, a dispirited party was recovering from a humbling electoral setback. Broadbent may have lacked the oratorical brilliance of his immediate predecessors, but under his leadership the party in the main experienced organizational stability. He endeavoured to heal the divisions between former Wafflers and those closer to the ideological centre.

The Broadbent era also saw the party introduce direct-mail fund-raising and systematic polling. At times, such as in 1984, lack of funds meant that polling methods were not as good as they could have been. At other times, a more democratic ethos and greater imagination could have fostered more effective sharing of the survey data with a wider circle of senior party members, particularly in the parliamentary caucus.[60] (Interestingly, the 1992/93 election planning committee, based on the successful Ontario 1990 provincial model, is structured in such a way as to alleviate some of the problems associated with the method of decision-making in the 1988 federal campaign.) Despite its lapses in consultation, the Broadbent team laid the groundwork for a more solid era of polling. In 1984 the NDP leadership felt obliged to look to the United States for a strong pollster with social-democratic leanings. In the 1990s, the McLaughlin team has selected the Winnipeg-based Dave Gotthilf, the architect of the 1990 Ontario and 1991 BC victories and once again hopes are high.

There are at least two other important organizational changes in the NDP that took hold under Broadbent. The first was the significant increase in the number of women participating at all levels of the party. By the 1980s gender parity had become the watchword. While this phenomenon is now a general tendency in all major Canadian parties and thus is not unique to the NDP, Broadbent nevertheless increasingly recognized and tapped the growing strength of the women's movement. The women's caucus is now the most powerful lobby group within the NDP and was a major force in the election of Audrey McLaughlin as Broadbent's successor.

Another major organizational change, and one that is directly attributable to Broadbent, was the introduction of the councils of federal ridings. As outgoing leader he was greatly concerned with the predominance of the provincial wings of the party in the intertwined constitutional structure of the NDP; indeed, the provincial leaders' role in the federal council was sometimes likened to that of powerful feudal barons. Membership lists were held by the provincial sections alone and jealously guarded for fund-raising purposes. In most parts of the country and on most occasions it was in the provincial riding associations, not the federal ones, that party members met, and as a result provincial concerns usually received a higher priority. Local activists interested in national politics were too often left with little opportunity to get involved at the federal level of the party. Broadbent envisioned a regional council of federal ridings as a way to foster greater activity in the federal wing, particularly between elections. The goal of a better mechanism for membership participation in the federal party is laudable, even if so far the outcome has been greater organizational complexity and rivalry for funds.

Although Broadbent did not leave under the circumstances that he and his colleagues might have wished, the party he handed on to Audrey McLaughlin was in relatively good shape. The majority of NDP members were initially disappointed at not moving out of third place in 1988, and a great many blamed Broadbent or his senior personal staff, but as time passed most could appreciate the fact that under Broadbent's leadership the party had finally broken the 20% threshold and was now solidly positioned to aim for new heights in the 1990s.

For a party accustomed to the leadership of such extraordinary individuals as Tommy Douglas and David Lewis, the choice of the more 'ordinary' Ed Broadbent was an important and historic change. As a more typical Canadian, in some ways he was a reassuring figure, particularly to the middle class. This in part explains the NDP's greater electoral support under Broadbent (19.2%) than under Douglas (15.4%) and Lewis (16.6%). Unlike his two immediate predecessors, Broadbent was able to win personal election in every one of the seven federal election contests he entered, serving in Parliament for over twenty uninterrupted years, fourteen of them as federal leader. This was an exceptionally strong track record for the NDP.

No doubt part of Broadbent's success can be attributed to his personality. Increasingly, political scientists recognize the part that the personalities of party leaders play in elections. In an age of growing alienation and voter cynicism (Dalton, 1988; Clarke et al., 1991; Gregg and Posner, 1990), the electorate's quest for honest political figures is not insignificant. Broadbent's unease with rhetoric prevented him from becoming a great orator. Nevertheless, his concern for accuracy was apparent, and in television interviews he projected an image of both warmth and thoughtfulness. Many Canadians felt that they could relate to Broadbent and valued his daily comments in the all-important TV scrum just outside the House of Commons. In person he seemed to take genuine pleasure in campaigning and meeting people. Despite his PhD, he came across as a populist, not a stuffy intellectual (Steed: 196). Accordingly, Ed Broadbent became the NDP's biggest asset throughout the 1980s.

All this stress on personality did, however, have a cost. Socialist ideology became less central to the party, and NDP policy seemed increasingly a blend—like J.S. Mill, the topic of Broadbent's PhD thesis—of reform liberalism and socialism (Christian and Campbell, 1990: 224-33). While organizationally, Broadbent left the party in solid shape, he offered little in the way of an inspired vision towards which social democrats should head. If divisiveness was the danger for the NDP when the Broadbent era began, the problem at the end of his tenure was blandness. What was 'new' about the New Democratic Party in the 1980s? Was the party committed to new democratic forms of political involvement such as referenda, proportional representation, MP recall, employee and consumer participation on the boards of Crown corporations, or even direct balloting by all party members in the selection of its leader? Did the public still see the NDP as a new party, or increasingly as part of the political establishment? Most Canadians cannot remember a time when the NDP did not exist. Newness is less and less likely to be an attribute most Canadians now associate with the NDP.[61]

Still more disturbing is the question of what is 'left' about the NDP today. Are Canadian social democrats, as Prime Minister St Laurent suggested in 1949, merely 'Liberals in a hurry'? The question arises irrespective of who leads Canada's social democratic party. Certainly New Democrats are not alone among socialists in looking for a restatement of political direction. What should the left agenda be for the 1990s? Are new democratic forms of collectivism possible? What mechanisms should be employed? Which, if any, should be abandoned? These and other questions will be explored in the concluding chapter of this book.

In any event, if a political party is to have a future, first it must survive. Ed Broadbent ensured that Canada's social-democratic party not only survived, but grew. At the same time, his leadership was noted for its decency and integrity. In contemporary politics, that is a significant accomplishment.

NOTES

[1] As a public-relations vehicle, this volume (Broadbent, 1988) ignores some controversial areas (e.g., NATO). It is also worth noting that the book includes some minor factual errors (e.g., the date of the birth of the CCF, and the suggestion that only in 1988 was there a close three-party fight).

[2] Contrary to the implication in Broadbent (1988: 74), he was not the first Canadian-born CCF-NDP federal leader. J.S. Woodsworth was born in Etobicoke, Ont. and Hazen Argue in Moose Jaw, Sask. M.J. Coldwell, however, the longest-serving CCF leader, was born in England.

[3] He married Lucille Munroe in 1971.

[4] The educational and vocational backgrounds of CCF-NDP leaders has led *Globe and Mail* columnist Jeffrey Simpson to describe such party figures as members of the 'chattering classes'.

[5] In this regard, Broadbent's level of academic training was comparable to that of Pierre Trudeau. One should also note the substantial influence of the many university professors active in the LSR during the first decade of the CCF (see Horn, 1980).

[6] Interview with Ed Broadbent, 1989; see also Steed (1988: 55). Further references to Steed in this chapter will omit the year of publication.

[7] On the relationship of the concepts of individualism and collectivism to the differing ideologies (conservatism, liberalism, socialism) see the highly influential work by Horowitz (1968), a revised excerpt from which can be found in Thorburn (1991).

[8] Interview with Ed Broadbent, 1989; see also Steed: 87, 98.

[9] Interview with Broadbent, 1989; see also Steed: 93, 125, 183, 192.

[10] Broadbent's lack of fluency is somewhat ironic given that his wife Lucille is thoroughly bilingual.

[11] Interview with Broadbent, 1989.

[12] Broadbent was not always the best judge of what to retain from his written texts, as indicated in the controversial 26 Oct. 1988 election speech in London, Ont., in which he failed to mention the layoffs at the Fleck plant owned by a prominent pro-free-trader (Fraser, 1989: 464).

[13] See Gallup 18 Aug. 1988. Clarke et al. (1991: 197; 1984: 115) found in their

surveys of all four election periods from 1979 to 1988 that the trait most frequently attributed to Broadbent was honesty.

[14] For Steed's comments on Broadbent's personality see pp. 101, 124, 134, 135, 170, 180-2, 209, and 347 of her book.

[15] If Trudeau and Broadbent are representative of politicians with advanced university degrees, one must wonder if the latter sometimes discourage a consultative style. One suspects that former professors think that they know much more than their advisers with less university training. In addition, such intellectuals are more likely to have worked out a formal world view and perhaps less likely to modify such a philosophical framework. Interestingly, however, Lester Pearson fits this pattern less well.

[16] A survey conducted by professors Thorburn, Perlin, and Lele of Queen's University found that students represented the largest category of Wafflers attending NDP conventions (Hackett, 1980: 20-1).

[17] He is reported by some to have said: 'If we are going to waffle, I'd rather waffle to the left' (Morton, 1986: 92; Bullen, 1983: 193; Hackett, 1980: 7; Steed: 144; McLeod and McLeod, 1987: 277; Penniman, 1981: 193).

[18] See back issues of *Canadian Dimension* for this time period.

[19] This is perhaps some consolation to Audrey McLaughlin, who went through a similar experience in 1989. Initially there were efforts to encourage other, supposedly stronger candidates. Even when a number of the 'star candidates' did not run, McLaughlin required four ballots to secure her victory and received an even lower percentage of the vote on the final ballot than did Broadbent a decade and half earlier.

[20] According to one party strategist, this ad was largely ineffective.

[21] Early in his leadership tenure Broadbent enquired as to the NDP's fifty best ridings. He was aghast that the NDP did not have such electoral information at its fingertips.

[22] Broadbent has suggested that it was his intention to defeat the Clark government as early as possible (interview, August 1991).

[23] This was a theme that he would reiterate later in preparation for the 1988 campaign (interview with Ed Broadbent, 1989).

[24] Gruending, 1990: 189-212. With hindsight, Blakeney's concerns over the charter seem even more sound. When interviewed in August 1991, Broadbent noted that early on he received a letter from Trudeau agreeing to address the resource question (Broadbent–Trudeau correspondence, 20-21 Oct. 1980).

[25] Interview with Broadent, 1989: see also Broadbent (1988: 137).

[26] Interview with Broadbent, 1989; see also Steed (273-4); Richards and Kerr (1984: 10).

[27] The reasons offered for this omission are multiple. Broadbent and his staff have suggested that a lack of funds and an impending crucial federal election were key reasons (interview with Broadbent, 1989). In addition, some party officials were not enamoured of the hybrid document. The fact that no single person could claim sole credit may have reduced the likelihood of anyone's promoting its distribution. It may be too that such blueprints for a better society are declining in importance in the TV age (see Chapter 3).

[28] Ironically, Laxer and Broadbent had previously tried (unsuccessfully) to interest the NDP in a new industrial strategy.

[29] A few years later, a number of these same journalists would be predicting an NDP federal government! Neither set of journalistic accounts was justified but both did sell more newspapers.

[30] It would be perhaps Broadbent's best campaign performance. See Penniman (1988: 175); Pammett, 'The 1988 Vote', in Frizzell et al. (1989: 120) and Clarke *et al.* (1991: 90).

[31] On left populism, see Richards (1988); Richards and Pratt (1979); Laycock (1990).

[32] Interview with Broadbent, 1989.

[33] The wording of the Meech Lake Accord was not finalized until June; hence there is some confusion over dates.

[34] BC New Democrat MP Ian Waddell, who expressed concern over the Accord's neglect of the rights of Native peoples and women and the scaling down of federal powers, voted against it; as a result, he lost his caucus responsibility (Steed: 302, 321). Similarly, Yukon MP Audrey McLaughlin, who had campaigned and was first elected in 1987 on an anti-Meech Lake platform, also voted against it, though in her case Broadbent excused the deviation. Time, however, would prove McLaughlin's position the more popular in NDP ranks.

[35] One close observer of Broadbent has suggested that over time he went from a standard British Fabian socialist emphasis on the powers of the central government to being more receptive to provincial (i.e., Quebec) authority/jurisdiction.

[36] Interview with Broadbent, 1989. See also his last formal speech as federal leader to the party's Federal Council, 4 March 1989. His conclusions were in part based on data found in the *Reid Report*, August 1987, vol. 2, no. 8, and March 1988, vol., 3, no. 3. Angus Reid, of course, did polling for the NDP in the run up to the 1988 election.

[37] Interview with Broadbent, 1989.

[38] Clarke and his colleagues (1991: 70) list free trade under the general heading of economic issues. Other scholars, however, including this one, suggest that by 1988 free trade was so highly charged as a social issue, a foreign-policy issue, and even a resource issue that it is a mistake to label it simply as an economic one.

[39] Broadbent has subsequently suggested that the collective rights of the French-speaking population in Quebec should be protected against the relatively minor individual rights of advertisers. For example, in a speech (11 Dec. 1990) at the National Conference on Human Rights and Solidarity he warned to 'beware' of 'those who [defend] the unequivocal right to advertise products for sale in English as a fundamental right equal . . . to freedom of speech in religion and politics . . .' (Broadbent, 1990: 6).

[40] Other westerners such as Douglas and Barrett, however, supported Broadbent on the constitution (Gruending, 1990: 204; Steed: 247).

[41] Curiously, a number of CCF-NDP federal leaders have been out of synchronization with their party or key portions of it from time to time on major issues. In 1939 it was Woodsworth regarding Canada's entry into the Second World War. In the 1950s it was Coldwell on a number of aspects of Canadian foreign policy (e.g., the creation of NATO, the Korean War and German rearmament).

[42] In a 1991 interview with the author, Broadbent suggested that he and Trudeau exchanged correspondence early on outlining possible changes to the constitutional package; see note 24 above. See also Broadbent (1988: 135-6, 147-50).

[43] For example, Quebec was the last province to grant women the vote, in 1940; it was also notorious for its padlock act (1937) limiting civil liberties, which was not overturned by the Supreme Court until 1957.

[44] Party members who went along with Broadbent sometimes did so out of loyalty rather than because they agreed with the policy.

[45] In the mid-1970s he did allow an excerpt of his book (1970) to be reprinted in a small Canadian publication (*Newsletter*) devoted to industrial democracy and published by Canadians for a Democratic Workplace (among the members of the editorial board was the present author).

[46] Interview with Broadbent, 1989.

[47] One notable exception is his effort towards the creation of councils of federal ridings in an attempt to increase membership participation in the federal wing of the party. See p. 204.

[48] By contrast, a significant number of works in the Marxist tradition have appeared.

[49] *Le Temps D'Agir* (Broadbent, 1988) has been excluded from this category as it is largely a journalistic question-and-answer volume.

[50] Curiously, Bradford (1989) does not cite this book in his major study of social democracy, the NDP, and intellectuals.

[51] His absence from the 1983 Vancouver meeting is likely attributable to the death of his mother and a serious back injury. That he was absent from the 1984 Edmonton meeting that spawned the second, more critical volume is not surprising.

[52] Interview with Broadbent, 1989. Steed (xiii, 336) quotes Broadbent as using the adjective 'abysmal' to describe Canadian social democratic thought; see also Rosenblum and Findlay (1991: iii).

[53] In the 1950s Frank Underhill led the attacks upon party bureaucratic thinking. In the 1960s Laxer and Watkins did so. In the 1980s the leaders have been Cy Gonick and Leo Panitch.

[54] Unfortunately, the League For Social Reconstruction, created in 1932 on the eve of the founding of the CCF, folded a decade later (Horn, 1980). In recent years the Douglas-Coldwell Foundation, created in 1971, has endeavoured to fill the intellectual void for social democrats.

[55] The volume *Le Temps D'Agir* (1988), an edited collection of questions and answers with Broadbent, was a part of the extensive work to build up Broadbent's and the NDP's presence in Quebec. A dramatic increase in spending on French-language election advertising and money for Quebec organizers were other components of what NDP officials thought was a carefully worked-out strategy.

[56] The NDP has achieved its highest profile and most dramatic electoral performances when stressing such left-populist themes as 'corporate welfare bums' (1972) and 'ordinary Canadians' (1984) rather than socialist phrases such as 'nationalization', 'public ownership' and 'state planning'.

[57] Here one wonders if Broadbent's original roots in the middle class made him more sensitive to the plight of the middle strata of 'ordinary Canadians'.

[58] This tactic was in part inspired by the Parti Québécois's electoral success following its promise not to proceed immediately on sovereignty-association.

[59] Contrary to public statements by some party officials at the time, the NDP's document on defence policy was not simply a clarification.

[60] In the period 1984-88, the caucus included several former professors. Despite their high levels of professional training, many in the caucus were excluded from the central election planning (interviews with several MPs). One notes, for example, the presence of the former prominent social scientist Lynn McDonald, who was capable of interpreting survey data as well as, if not better than, most others on the election planning committee. But her relationship, as a fervent non-smoking crusader, with the cigar-smoking Broadbent was cool at best and she had a reputation among many New Democrats of being difficult to work with. Clearly, her frank analysis was not always appreciated. Relatedly, the longer Broadbent was leader, the more his reputation and workload increased and the smaller became his inner circle of advisers (most notably the talented team of George Nakitsas, Bill Knight, and Anne Carroll). As a result, there emerged a curious estrangement between the high-profile leader and many activists in the party. This was particularly so in the west, in part because of disagreements over the constitution, NATO policy, and differing visions of social democracy and how it should be presented to the Canadian public.

[61] The rise of the Reform Party and the Bloc Québécois reinforces this perception.

EIGHT

The 1988 Federal Election: A Case Study of Party Organization and Strategy

INTRODUCTION

To the casual observer, the outcome of the 1988 election, in which the NDP emerged yet again with a third-place finish, might have suggested that there had been little change from the previous campaign. The events leading up to that election, and the campaign itself, however, were anything but a repetition of 1984. The 1988 campaign was a historic one both for the NDP and for the Canadian polity. The public was politicized and polarized on the issue of free trade, and electoral uncertainty confronted all three major parties. As late as August 1988, all three were over the 30% level in the polls,[1] and the outcome was very much in doubt, not only as to the winner, but even as to whether there would be a majority government.

From the perspective of left-wing reform movements and parties, there have been several key elections in Canadian federal politics. The election of 1921 saw the successful emergence in Parliament of third parties with the rise of the populist and reform-oriented Progressives, but by the end of the decade the movement, largely lacking in party discipline, had disintegrated.[2] While the CCF had been formed in 1932, it was not until the election of 1945 that the federal party offered a dramatic challenge to the Liberal and Conservative parties and the forces of capitalism. Having risen in strength to the point of leading the nation, albeit briefly and narrowly, in public-opinion polls in 1943, the CCF anticipated that after a close three-way race the 1945 election would provide the long-awaited breakthrough to national political power. Although the party's showing was its best ever in terms of both seats and percentage vote, the result was nevertheless disappointing. The CCF never again came close to challenging the Liberals or Conservatives for national political power. A newly refurbished social-democratic organization arose with the formation of the NDP in 1961, but when, a year later, the Canadian public was presented with an opportunity to judge the New Party, it responded with only enough seats for a fourth-place finish.[3] After so many setbacks, many in the left wondered whether another opening would emerge.

The election of 1988 seemed to present a fourth historic opportunity for an electoral breakthrough. Just over a year before the election, the NDP found itself leading in public-opinion polls, and many believed that at last the party had a chance of displacing the Liberals, who in the 1984 Conservative landslide had received their lowest percentage vote (28%) and number of seats (40) ever. With 18.8% of the vote and 30 seats (later increased to 32 as a result of several by-election victories in 1987), the NDP was closer than ever before to overtaking the Liberals (see Chapter 4); in the crucial province of Ontario alone, it had 13 seats to the Liberals' 14.

Nor was the Liberals' loss of seats the only reason for the growing belief that the NDP might finally displace them. First, Liberal leader John Turner was held in low esteem by much of the Canadian public; even many members of his own party and caucus were not enthusiastic about his leadership. In contrast, Ed Broadbent was seen by a substantial number of Canadians as the most and trustworthy leader; 'Honest Ed' was a refreshing change in a world of cynical politicians. For two straight years, from September 1986 to August 1988, he topped the polls as the leader the public would most like to see as prime minister. Remarkably, in September 1987 support for Broadbent even surpassed the combined total levels of Turner and Mulroney.

Second, the Liberal Party was seen as seriously divided as a result of repeated efforts by some of its members to remove Turner as leader. The NDP, on the other hand, was portrayed as a disciplined yet democratic organization with a leader firmly at the helm of both party affairs and the caucus.[4]

Third, the federal Liberal Party appeared to be undergoing a long-term decline in membership and income. The much-publicized financial woes of the party's national office in 1987-88 reinforced this impression. While the NDP's finances have never been its strength (Paltiel, 1970; Stanbury, 1986, 1989), its membership, public support, and income generally had been on the rise.

Finally, the Liberals, widely perceived as Canada's governing party for much of the twentieth century, were unaccustomed to the role of a small opposition party. By contrast, the CCF-NDP had fifty-five years of experience in that role, and its caucus and senior staff personnel seemed capable of performing the job better than their Liberal counterparts. The press accounts of the four years of the thirty-third Parliament frequently echoed this view, and as early as June 1985 polls were reporting that a larger number of Canadians saw the NDP as a more effective opposition than the Liberal Party.[5]

At the same time, senior NDP strategists believed that a historic opportunity now existed for the NDP in Quebec. The existence of the pro-separatist, nationalist Parti Québécois as a rival social-democratic party had in the past been yet another obstacle to the NDP in the province. However, the defeat of the PQ provincial government in 1985 reflected a decline in that party's organizational strength. Its membership and income had both dropped, and it had to contend with finding an adequate successor to the dynamic René Lévesque. In addition, the departure of the Quebec-born Trudeau as federal Liberal leader meant that some Quebec Liberals might now be more receptive to the NDP. The 1987 Montreal federal convention was the NDP's first ever in the province, and its success, both organizationally and in the media, offered yet another reason to believe that raised hopes might be justified. Certainly the NDP's Quebec membership had sky-rocketed from a paltry 500 in 1983 to 10,000 on the eve of the 1988 election.

Thus there were many reasons for optimism: a popular leader, growing support in the polls, and declines in the strength of rival political parties. However, there were also important reasons for scepticism and caution. In the euphoria of the 1987 pre-campaign period, the counter-arguments and possible reasons why the NDP might not make significant gains were for the most part ignored or downplayed by political pundits, party strategists, and the public at large. These obstacles would become more apparent as the 1988 campaign itself unfolded.

NDP ELECTION ORGANIZATION AND COMMITTEE STRUCTURE

The departure of federal secretary Dennis Young in 1987 and the resignation of Terry Grier, chair of the Strategy and Election Planning Committee (SEPC), just prior to the election created more senior personnel changes than would usually be the case before an election. Nevertheless, at the outset of the 1988 campaign the NDP organization looked solid.

Between NDP conventions, the party's principal decision-making bodies are normally the federal executive and the federal council. Technically, the SEPC is a committee of the federal executive. Immediately prior to an election campaign, however, the SEPC becomes the pre-eminent organ of the NDP. Operating closely with its steering and platform committees, the SEPC designs the strategic election plan, while day-to-day administration and execution of the plan are left to the federal secretary, who also serves as the campaign manager, along with his staff.[6]

In 1988 the SEPC was composed of the chairman (Terry Grier); the party leader (Ed Broadbent); the federal president (Johanna den Hertog); the federal treasurer (Clare Booker); the federal secretary (Bill Knight); the principal adviser to the leader (George Nakitsas); one representative each from the parliamentary caucus (Rod Murphy), the participation of women (POW) committee (Brenda O'Brien), and the Canadian Labour Congress (CLC; Pat Kerwin as co-chair); and one or two people from each of the provincial sections, for a total of 21 members. It was not unusual for certain key federal staff members to be in attendance as well. The composition of the committee was not dramatically different from that which operated in 1984 (Morley, 1988: 136), although its size had increased somewhat.

Since the election, the composition of the committee has come under some criticism. Several party strategists have suggested that, in its quest for greater regional representation, the SEPC had grown too large; while it gained in openness and democracy, it lost some of the efficiency it should have possessed as a small, semi-professional advisory group.[7] On the other hand, questions have also arisen over whether there was sufficient labour representation on the SEPC. Given the growth in numbers of provincial representatives, labour probably should have been granted greater representation. (This certainly would have helped to convey labour's concern about the need for greater emphasis on free trade in the campaign strategy; see p. 232 below.)

The CLC did, however, have a committee to deal with political education during the election and co-ordinate the labour movement's campaign action: the National Political Action Committee (NPAC). Composed of approximately 50 people, it included representatives from the provincial labour federations and affiliated unions, as well as key CLC officials. Usually several senior party personnel were also invited to attend. The NPAC was chaired by Bob White, president of the Canadian Auto Workers Union and a vice-president of the NDP. Since Pat Kerwin, co-chair of the SEPC, was in charge of co-ordinating political education in the CLC through the NPAC, his role in integrating the work of the two committees was crucial. The NPAC met on average three times a year to review the NDP's campaign strategy and endeavour to implement labour's part of the plan. The affiliated CLC unions made significant financial contributions to the party (estimated at over $1-million) and were active in a parallel political campaign of telephone canvassing and distribution of union flyers and publications.

The SEPC started preparing for the campaign at least three years before the election was called—earlier than in the past—usually meeting several times a year. But the full committee was too large, and its members too widely scattered, to meet quickly and often. Therefore a smaller body was also required. The SEPC Steering Committee[8] was composed of thirteen people, seven of them based in Ottawa. Roughly half were members of the SEPC proper; four others were key personnel from the party's federal office. Prior to the election call, the steering committee met several times a year apart from the meetings of the full SEPC. During the election campaign itself the steering committee met every Sunday in either Ottawa or Toronto to discuss the campaign's progress and plan any necessary shifts in tactics.

The thirteen-member election platform committee, another sub-committee of the SEPC, included the chair of the latter, the party president, the caucus research director, the federal secretary, the principal secretary to the leader, the deputy campaign director, the caucus chairman, and several representatives from key sections of the party.[9] Culling from the hundreds of resolutions passed at previous party conventions, the committee strove to draft a coherent policy platform that would maximize the party's electoral appeal. Among the publications emanating from the committee were, first, a 14-page printed pamphlet entitled 'A Fair Deal For Canada: New Democrats Speaking for Average Canadians', and later a 36-page typed document entitled 'Meeting the Challenge: Ed Broadbent and the New Democrats speak up for average Canadians'. The titles of these documents conveyed the main campaign message.

To oversee the increased efforts and expenditures involved in polling, a special opinion-research committee was also formed. Its members were Vic Fingerhut, the party's key polling consultant, Pat Kerwin of the CLC, and Brian McKee, the federal policy co-ordinator, although on occasion it accepted input from others.

During the campaign itself two key groups supervised and modified, where necessary, the application of the election strategy. At the pinnacle of the decision-making hierarchy was a very small inner circle of advisers to Broadbent.[10] George Nakitsas, travelling daily with him, was the tour director and the closest to Broadbent's ear; Bill Knight, the federal secretary and former principal adviser to Broadbent, was campaign director; Robin Sears, a former federal secretary, was deputy campaign director; and Arlene Wortsman, the only woman, was caucus research director. Each Saturday night they discussed the past week's events and endeavoured to anticipate the next week's.

Each Sunday, following the meeting of the inner circle, the steering committee (its membership slightly altered from the pre-campaign period) would meet for three to four hours to examine the details of the campaign in greater depth. Among the participants were the SEPC chairman and co-chairmen, the federal campaign director, the campaign co-director, the tour director, the tour logistics co-ordinator, the pollster, the director of polling, the director of organization, the media co-ordinator, the director of research, the chief speech-writer, two press-liaison personnel (one each for English and French journalists) and a media watch co-ordinator. The weekly agenda would include a campaign overview and a discussion of the main campaign message, polling, media coverage, labour's campaign, and the tour.

In the final weeks before election day, relations among the key decision-makers showed the strains of a very long campaign and declining prospects. The best of plans and organization, it seemed, were not enough.

NDP ELECTION FINANCES AND PARTY INCOME

Analysis of elections has increasingly focused on the party leaders, their television debates, media coverage, and advertising. However, to understand the NDP's 1988 campaign and the obstacles it faced, it is important to examine both the election budget and the sources of the party's funds—in large part, the contributions of tens of thousands of volunteer workers.

In the three previous federal elections, the NDP's campaign expenditures had been $2,190,000 (1979), $3,086,000 (1980), $4,731,000 (1984)[11]—considerably less, in each case, than the amounts spent by the Liberals and Conservatives.[12] Early projections for the NDP's 1988 federal campaign aimed at $4.7-million, virtually the same as in 1984. However, as the NDP started its dramatic rise in the opinion polls, and it began to seem possible both to achieve a breakthrough in Quebec and to displace the sagging federal Liberals,[13] the past practice of spending very little in Quebec would have to be reversed. Accordingly, Terry Grier, chairman of the SEPC, recommended to the 1987 NDP federal convention that the campaign budget be raised by 50%, to the $7-million range.[14]

For 1988, the NDP advertising budget was targeted at just over $3-million. The leader's tour, the second largest portion of the campaign budget after advertising, was projected to cost over $1.5 million. The remainder of the campaign expenditures were to be primarily for organization ($0.5-million), direct mail and fund-raising ($0.5-million), riding support materials ($0.3-million), opinion research ($0.3-million), and the pre-election campaign ($0.5-million).[15]

Increasingly, the largest election expense in modern democracies is mass advertising. Table 8.1 shows the amounts and allocations involved in recent NDP election advertising budgets.[16]

Table 8.1 NDP Election Advertising Budgets

	total	print	radio	TV
1979	$1.3-million	24%	19%	58%
1980	$1.8-million	23%	13%	64%
1984	$1.8-million	9%	27%	64%
1988	$3.1-million	5%	15%	80%

The 1988 campaign was the first in which the NDP attempted to be national in scope and to operate fully in two languages. This required far more money for production of separate French-language ads and purchase of Quebec media time. It was calculated that one-third of the advertising budget would go to Quebec[17]—a bold decision, given the party's past record in the province.

Almost half (46.8%) of these funds were to be raised from the various provincial sections, most notably Ontario, British Columbia and Saskatchewan, the provinces with the largest memberships (Whitehorn, 1985b; see also Chapter 1); the rest of the money was to come from the affiliated member unions of the Canadian Labour Congress, the largest proportion of which were based in Ontario (16%);[18] the growing funds derived from direct mail[19] (8.5%); interest from bank accounts (a modest 2%); and the anticipated government election rebate (an estimated 26.6%).

NDP POLLING ORGANIZATION AND SET-UP

There has been a tremendous rise in the number of polls, both public and private, conducted during election campaigns; the number of public polls alone doubled from 1984 to 1988.[20] Not surprisingly, the impact and coverage of polls have also increased.[21] The growing emphasis upon standings in the polls rather than discussion of policy content has been one target for criticism by those concerned about the trivialization of election coverage.[22]

By 1988 the NDP had joined the trend, and its use of polling had become far more professional and systematic. Over $200,000 was allocated for survey research during the campaign, and just over $100,000 more in the immediate pre-election period. The architect of the polling strategy was the Washington-based Vic Fingerhut. With a background working for the Democratic Party in the United States and trade unions on both sides of the border, Fingerhut had been brought in late in the 1984 campaign to reverse the party's rapidly deteriorating situation. He was credited with devising and testing the phrase 'ordinary Canadians' and making the slogan a key element in the NDP's relative success. For the next four years, Fingerhut continued to counsel the NDP on polling, and travelled to Toronto or Ottawa each weekend of the seven-week campaign, to help refine the polling strategy.

The bulk of NDP polling data was gathered by Access Survey Research, a Winnipeg-based company linked to pollster Angus Reid; however, the party opted to do its own in-house analysis of the data under the supervision of Brian McKee. Thus a computerized electronic triangle emerged in which data gathered in Winnipeg were analysed in Ottawa under the supervision of a polling specialist in Washington. Other pollsters sometimes used included Léger and Léger for Quebec and Viewpoints Research for selected area polls.

In the 1984 election, when NDP federal surveys had been confined to 40 or 50 key ridings with the focus on the seats where the party had incumbents, no ridings were polled east of the Ottawa River; its polling lacked not only breadth and depth, but continuity.[23] By contrast, in 1988 the NDP could draw upon a solid four years of surveys across the entire country. Quebec was not only included in the national sample, but was even the target of special surveys by Léger and Léger.

NDP polling from 1985 to 1988 fell into two categories. Prior to the campaign, surveys tended to be more detailed, designed to build a national data base from which comparisons could be made at a later time. Then, during the campaign itself, the party opted for shorter surveys of 8 to 15 minutes exploring such topics as voting intentions, party identification, perceptions of the three parties and their leaders on a range of issues, and the viability of party commercials and literature. The campaign surveys were conducted daily with a sample of 200 persons and were then combined into a weekly rolling sample of about 1,000. With the increases in both non-aligned voters and electoral volatility (Leduc, 1984; Dalton, 1988), such rolling surveys were deemed ideal for monitoring the ebbs and flows of a modern campaign.[24] While the core of the questions remained the same, the special committee on polling,[25] usually meeting over each weekend, was able to alter some questions as the needs of the campaign dictated.

In addition to conducting mass surveys, the NDP made greater use of small focus groups (e.g., women, unionists, non-unionists) in selected cities such as Windsor, Winnipeg, Montreal, and Quebec City. In each case, about a dozen people (chosen by pollsters according to demographic criteria) would be led in a group discussion designed to test party ads and possible reasons for and against voting NDP.

It was an irony of the 1988 campaign that, despite the great increase in polling, the party did not fare as well as expected. Some party members, both during the campaign and, even more, after it, believed that too much emphasis had been placed on technology rather than ideology, and that too much time and energy had been spent on packaging the leader rather than discussion of party policy. In the eyes of many, the party had locked itself into a strategy based on polling completed a year earlier, when public opinion of the NDP was much higher. Some felt that the survey research had led to excessive caution and dullness in the language employed. At the very least, crucial reaction time had been slowed. Still others suggested that the problem lay not in the polling itself, but in a tendency to ignore the polls' findings (Mason, 1990).

NDP STRATEGY
Pre-election

In 1984, when the NDP stood a distant third, at 11% in the polls, the NDP's campaign had been a defensive one that focused on merely trying to retain incumbent seats, the bulk of which were in the west. In contrast, by 1987 the party had soared to a commanding 41% in the polls, and party strategists believed that they could win an election and form Canada's first socialist federal government. Accordingly, a fully bilingual national campaign was planned with 144 ridings targeted for attention, triple the 1984 number. Of these, 59 were in the west, where the party had always been strong; 39 in Quebec, based on the party's lead in public-opinion polls in the province; 35 in Ontario, where the largest section of the affiliated trade-union movement was located; and 11 in Atlantic Canada.[26] What was striking was the very high number of seats deemed winnable, particularly in Quebec. Strategists recognized the danger that the party might overextend itself, with too few funds and experienced personnel for the large number of ridings targeted.[27] However, they assumed that for the NDP to stay above the 30% level in the national polls, it had to maintain its improved presence in Quebec. How viable such a plan would be if the party dropped in the polls would remain to be seen.[28]

Given the high levels of support for both Broadbent and the party in the 1987 polls, some strategists expected that the NDP would undergo unprecedented scrutiny and attack.[29] To lessen the negative impact of greater media and public attention, the NDP tried to defuse the effects of some of its more controversial policies in the pre-election period. Accordingly, in April the International Affairs Committee and the Policy Review Committee issued a report entitled 'Canada's Stake in Common Security' that effectively postponed for at least one term of office the NDP's past commitment to pull out of NATO. Similarly, in an effort to retain the new support in Quebec, party leaders endeavoured to dissuade critics of the Meech Lake Accord such as Manitoba NDP leader Gary Doer. In the case of British Columbia, the NDP provincial caucus voted for the Accord despite rank-and-file opposition at the provincial convention.

During the campaign itself, party spokespersons were advised to minimize references to controversial matters such as withdrawal from NATO, nationalization of private corporations, and abortion. Most notably, the terms 'socialism' and 'social democracy' were not mentioned in either of the two major election policy compendiums. In order to minimize adverse media coverage, the Broadbent itinerary stressed partisan NDP meetings or scripted photo-opportunity sessions, and scheduled few unstructured events such as talk shows. Instructions were given that fewer people were to talk to the press; it was hoped that this would limit the issuing of contradictory statements and the opportunity for the media to play one party spokesperson off against another. Apart from Ed Broadbent, the main official responsible for speaking to the press was to be Robin Sears, the party's chief media 'spin doctor'. Efforts were made to provide greater central direction to the campaign, and local and national campaigns were to be better co-ordinated.

In candidate selection, the NDP had two major aims. The first was to attract as many high-profile personalities as possible — people who would strengthen the NDP's image as a party that was indeed ready to govern. Such highly visible individuals would also partially compensate for organizational weaknesses in areas such as Quebec. Broadbent and his staff endeavoured to recruit a 'dream team' of four ex-premiers (Dave Barrett, Allan Blakeney, Ed Schreyer, and Howard Pawley) and the eloquent former UN ambassador Stephen Lewis, but only Barrett and Pawley accepted nomination.[30] At the same time, in an effort to reflect the official party policy of commitment to gender parity, the NDP sought a greater number of women candidates. In the end, although it nominated far more women than any other party (84), this number still fell well short of male/female parity.

Party strategists planning the 1988 campaign were confronted with at least three interrelated image problems. The first was that, according to the polls, too few people identified themselves as NDPers; even in targeted and incumbent ridings, identification with the NDP often ranked second or even third.[31] Second, socialism was still the least appealing of the three major ideologies in Canada, as it had been since the days of the CCF. Third, while both the Conservatives and the Liberals relied on financial contributions from private corporations (Stanbury, 1989), it was well-known that the NDP drew upon the support of the trade-union movement, which the general public tended to regard less favourably than it did the business community.[32]

In addition to these problems, of course, the NDP was operating with less money, and much less organizational expertise in the province of Quebec, than its rivals. Therefore it had to make extensive use of the one major asset it possessed: Ed Broadbent, who had proven to be the most popular political leader in Canada for most of the previous two years. The NDP's main campaign message became Broadbent, and he himself became the main vehicle to convey it. It was a vivid example of McLuhan's dictum 'the medium is the message'.

Campaign themes and slogans

NDP strategists did not initially expect a single theme to predominate. How wrong they would prove to be! Drawing on the likeable personality of their leader, they decided to run a populist programme. Instead of stressing socialist doctrine[33] about nationalization and public ownership, the campaign would emphasize 'fairness' for 'average Canadians'[34] and the 'average family'. Broadbent was to tell his listeners that only the NDP would protect the interests of average Canadians in the fields of taxation, pensions, and child care. The two election pamphlets, 'A Fair Deal for Canada' and 'Meeting the Challenge' (neither of which was widely distributed), took a similar approach. The first made no mention of the terms 'socialism' or 'social democracy', and although the second did mention withdrawal from

NATO and NORAD, both were silent on the questions of public ownership, nationalization, and abortion.

The themes of honesty and integrity were considered a strong suit for Broadbent. With the Liberals in organizational disarray and saddled with a vacillating and unpopular leader, the NDP perceived the Conservatives as the main target,[35] and chose to attack the Mulroney record of scandals and patronage. Accordingly, NDP strategy was to stress the party's positive election prospects in a close 'three-way race'.

The party approached the topic of free trade, the dominant issue of the campaign (Clarke et al., 1991), with some ambivalence. Although it had a solid record of nationalist concern about increased corporate integration into the US economic sphere,[36] had consistently called for greater controls on the amount of foreign ownership in Canada, and had been highly critical in Parliament of the Canada-US free-trade agreement,[37] key NDP strategists believed that free trade was not a particularly good issue for the party to stress.[38] There were several reasons for this perception. First, the party's pre-election polling suggested that the public saw free trade as a 'managing the economy' issue—an area in which the NDP was perceived as doing poorly.[39] Second, it was feared that too much emphasis on free trade would deflect public attention away from areas such as integrity, where the party and Broadbent would score much higher. Third, support for free trade was higher in Quebec, and the NDP would have difficulty improving its chances there by stressing its opposition to the deal.[40] Finally, the anti-free-trade vote was divided between two parties: thus if the public was roughly balanced for and against free trade, the Liberals and NDP would each end up with a smaller percentage of the vote than the solitary major party supporting it. This latter fear proved to be well founded. In order to minimize these problems, the party decided that when it did address free trade, it would link the issue to areas in which the NDP was seen as strong (e.g., protection of health-care services and the environment),[41] and—in the belief that many who favoured free trade in principle opposed this particular deal —would attempt to suggest negative connotations by referring to it as 'the Mulroney-Reagan deal'. The initial decision to downplay the free-trade issue was to give rise to some tension between the NDP and its trade-union affiliates in the CLC, which in the two years before and during the election campaign had spent considerable effort and money on criticizing the deal, even donating funds to the NDP specifically to publicize its flaws.

Any modern election campaign covering a relatively short seven-week period must be flexible enough to adapt to changing circumstances. The rise in stature of John Turner following the television debates and the phoenix-like rebirth of the Liberal Party midway through the campaign saw the Liberals surpass the NDP in the polls. To halt the decline in NDP support, strategists endeavoured to find a new campaign theme that would put the party back on track, but the best they could do was to urge Canadians to reject the corporate interests of Mulroney's Wall Street and Turner's Bay Street in favour of ordinary Canadians, Main Street, and the NDP. It was too little, too late, and too much a stale repeat of the 1984 slogan.

Having determined that the audience most receptive to the NDP would be soft Liberal voters, women[42] (especially those in the paid workforce), and unionists, and hoping that a significant number of PQ supporters could be won over in the province of Quebec, the party allocated $2-million for English advertising and $1-million for French. Working under the supervision of Julie Mason, the party's advertising co-ordinator, Michael Morgan and Associates of Vancouver created the English ads, while Société Nouvelle in Montreal drew up the French ones. In both sets of ads Broadbent's name was stressed. In contrast to past years, when either few ads were made in French, or those that were tended to be poor literal translations of English scripts, this time the campaign was designed with a Francophone audience in mind. To test the effectiveness of the party's message, the NDP chose to operate a six-week pre-election ad campaign focusing on the Montreal area.

Not wishing to appear too strident or ideological, the NDP opted for rel-atively soft ads dealing with the health-care system and the environment. One example was a TV ad that was quickly labelled 'On Golden Pond', showing an old man and his grandson walking together by a pristine lake and forest and expressing their concern about the deterioration of the envi-ronment. Though few could object to its content, its effectiveness in winning over undecided voters was questionable.[43] Both the Liberal and the Conservative campaigns used more negative advertising,[44] seemingly with more success, although budget sizes and free advertising time were also important factors working against the NDP.[45] The post-election conclusion drawn by several NDP strategists was that in future more negative advertis-ing would have to be used.

CAMPAIGN STRATEGY CRITIQUE

There were several weaknesses in this campaign strategy. Few would dis-agree that the party's main asset was Ed Broadbent—but how extensive a campaign could the NDP build around its leader? In June 1988, Broadbent was rated first (34%) among the party leaders as the one the public felt would make the best prime minister; by 10 November he had slipped to third (17%),[46] and as his popularity dropped so did the NDP's. Nor were Broadbent's ratings uniformly high across all areas surveyed: while he was regarded as being the most 'likeable' and 'trustworthy', he dropped to second place on questions concerning competence and ideas/policies.[47] Later, and quite significantly, he would be ranked least believable of the three party leaders on free trade.[48]

Another problem was the decision to soften the party's policies and public statements so as to appear less radical. Polling had helped the party to discern the safer message, but in the process the NDP's language had become excessively cautious, if not downright dull. Phrases like 'Ed Broadbent and more fairness, openness and honesty for the average Canadian' may not have offended anyone, but neither did they inspire voters the way the speeches (and pamphlets) of T.C. Douglas and David Lewis had.[49]

In a remarkable wave of politicization, the country became mobilized and divided over the issue of Canada-US free trade.[50] While the Conservatives suggested that the deal would create hundreds of thousands of jobs, and that failure to ratify it would jeopardize the Auto Pact and unleash a backlash of US protectionism, the NDP and the Liberals warned against loss of Canadian sovereignty and jobs, importation of market- and corporate-oriented values, and a significant erosion of our welfare and social services. Confused by these contradictory claims, the electorate oscillated in its opinions as the campaign progressed.[51] As noted above, opposition to free trade was a platform almost tailor-made for the NDP. Nevertheless, the party attempted to downplay the issue: it was not even mentioned in Broadbent's opening campaign speech. By contrast, Turner's pre-election request that the Liberal-dominated Senate delay approval of the deal and his success on the subject in the English-language television debates meant that as the importance of free trade grew,[52] the NDP continued to place third in the polls on the issue.[53] A more effective response to the public's concerns in this area would have enhanced both the NDP's stature and its election performance.

An immediate post-election Gallup poll (8 Dec. 1988) indicated that almost two-thirds of all Canadians wanted a referendum on free trade. Curiously, however, the NDP continued to oppose this populist mechanism of participatory democracy (see Chapters 7 and 9). Despite the election of a Conservative government, a referendum on the issue probably would have seen the anti-free-trade forces victorious.[54]

THE LEADER'S TOUR AND CAMPAIGN
Organizational Structure

The importance of the leader's tour has grown in recent years. According to one analyst, half the front-page newspaper stories during the 1984 campaign were based on leaders' statements (Fletcher, 1988: 173). Given Ed Broadbent's high profile and stature, it is not surprising that the leader's tour was perceived as the main vehicle for communicating the NDP's election message.

In any federal election, the party leader travels as widely and as often as possible in order to give the party the highest possible media profile in each region. Since the NDP's goal in the 1988 federal election was to make significant inroads in previously barren electoral regions such as

Quebec and Alberta, the 1988 tour was more ambitious in scope than ever before.

For about half a year prior to the campaign, Broadbent endeavoured to travel into each region once a month. Once the 51-day campaign had started he appeared in Ontario and Quebec on a weekly basis,[55] making five trips to the west and three to Atlantic Canada. By far the most time was spent in Ontario (54%). Toronto was the hub of his cross-Canada itinerary and the site of the television debate, and with 99 seats Ontario offered the greatest prize. The next largest amount of time (23%) went to the west (where the party had a successful electoral history), and the remainder was allocated to Quebec (15%) and the Maritimes (8%), in both cases an increase from 1984.

There was a weekly cycle to the campaign that would see the leader's tour return to either Toronto or Ottawa every Saturday. This allowed his four or five most senior strategy advisers to meet together on Saturday night. This meeting was then followed on Sunday by a larger and more formal meeting with key staff.

The $1.5-million leader's tour was co-ordinated by two groups. Travelling with Broadbent on his cross-Canada odyssey was a band of fifteen party personnel and three policemen. George Nakitsas, his principal adviser, acted as the tour director, while Anne Carroll, his executive secretary, supervised the on-site details of the itinerary arrangements. Along with her assistant, there were two press secretaries (one for English and one for French), a speech-writer, an events producer, three secretaries, and three technicians. The only staff member missing from the original plan was the party's research director[56]—an oversight that, given subsequent campaign developments, may have been significant.

Providing long-distance logistical support was the tour office staff based in Ottawa. This ten-person group consisted of Wayne Harding as tour co-ordinator, three day-planners including one exclusively focusing on Quebec, a secondary tours day-planner, a media monitor with his own network of persons tracking all media coverage, a media liaison assistant, and several secretaries. Although fax machines, cellular telephones, and computers made it easier than ever before to keep in touch, communication did not necessarily improve. As the tour progressed, tensions inevitably emerged between those wearied by combat on the front lines of the tour and those in the relative comfort of Ottawa and Toronto; the same pattern occurred in the 1984 campaign (Hills, 1984: 52), but was alleviated somewhat by an 8% rise in party support in the polls. In 1988 no such amelioration took place.

Pre-Debates Period

Leading into the election period, there had been some slippage in levels of support for the NDP. Still, many in the party saw this development as only minor and temporary. Citing the 8% increase in support in 1984,[57] they believed that the party would do exceptionally well in the actual campaign. While Turner's Senate gambit (19 July 1988) to block passage of free trade suggested there was still some skill and life left in the Liberal Party, continuing intrigue in the latter caucus by plotters wishing to dump Turner gave reason to believe that the Liberals might continue on their self-destructive path.

On 1 October the 51-day campaign commenced. The NDP was third in the polls, with an average standing of 25.5%[58]—a far cry from the lofty levels of the summer of 1987. But the historic endorsement of the NDP by Louis Laberge of the 450,000-member Quebec Federation of Labour,[59] combined with favourable press coverage, lulled many into thinking that NDP fortunes were on the upswing once more. One weak note, however, was Broadbent's failure to mention free trade as an issue in his opening remarks of the campaign; it was an omission to be regretted later.

Week two brought a rise to 27.7% support for the NDP, but also a somewhat controversial statement. In reply to a question about the Liberal Party's ongoing woes, Broadbent indicated his hope that Canada someday would see a two-party system and the demise of the Liberals. While the statement's impact would not be immediately felt, these comments prompted many life-long Liberals to rally behind their party with money and labour, whatever their misgivings about John Turner (Caplan et al., 1989: 122). The statement also conveyed, both to the public at large[60] and to the press corps, an uncharacteristic and unbecoming impression of arrogance on Broadbent's part.

NDP support peaked in week three at 29.5%—enough for second place, ahead of the Liberals. Dramatic reports of alleged attempts by senior Liberal strategists to dump Turner in the midst of the campaign fuelled NDP hopes that the rival camp would see further disorganization. The NDP ship appeared on course. Then came the television debates.

The French-Language Debate

Television debates have become increasingly important to the Canadian political process. Historically, as a smaller third party, the NDP has been delighted to be able to participate equally in a forum with the Liberals and Conservatives, and such parity in television status has certainly been a factor in the NDP's growth.

On the eve of the two three-hour debates, virtually all NDP strategists expected Broadbent to perform well overall. In years of tenure, he was the most experienced of the party leaders; he also had the most practice in television debates. While his French was weaker than his opponents',[61] he had performed respectably in the shorter 1984 French debate. Most assumed that on 24 October he would not lose too much ground, and that the next night, in English, he would excel.

Much of the recent rise in NDP support in Quebec rested on the stature of Ed Broadbent,[62] and the party's French-language campaign ads reflected this fact in stressing the leader's name, not the party label. Given the organizational weakness of the NDP in Quebec, it was more important than many realized that Broadbent's relative 'success' in the 1984 debate be surpassed. This was particularly so if the NDP strategy of staying above 30% in the national polls was to be viable.

The French debate was a fairly restrained and moderate affair; no doubt the participants were saving themselves for the more important English-language debate the next night. While Broadbent did not blunder, speaking in his second language, the fully bilingual Turner and Mulroney easily outperformed him, and he certainly won no new converts. An Environics poll of those watching the French debate reported that Turner was perceived to have edged out Mulroney 35% to 31%. Broadbent was a distant third with a mere 4%.[63]

During the first three weeks of the campaign, NDP support in Quebec had risen from 23% to 29%. Immediately after the debate, however,[64] the party began a steady decline, ending at 14% in the election itself.[65] While undoubtedly the English-language debate contributed to this fall, it is not unrealistic to assume that for many Francophones, Broadbent's poor performance in their language was a crucial factor. And, unfortunately, even if the French debate was not seen by many in the rest of the country, it set the mood for the English debate the following night.

The English-Language Debate

The English-language debate of 25 October was by far the more important in terms of audience size and impact. It was also far more polemical and heated than its French counterpart. NDP strategists generally expected that, as in 1984, Turner would not perform very well, that Mulroney would be handicapped with a government record to defend, and that Broadbent would prevail. Instead Broadbent was fatigued from the marathon session in French the night before; he looked haggard,[66] he erred in part of the attribution of an eight-year-old quotation, and his performance, while passable, contained little spark. Above all, however, his efforts were eclipsed by the electrifying exchange of patriotic fervour between Turner and Mulroney over the issue of free trade, in which Turner, appearing sincere and forceful, overcame months of negative media coverage.

While some of the initial political commentary suggested that the debate was indecisive, repeated replays of the dramatic Turner-Mulroney exchange, coupled with more detailed media analysis, soon helped to sway the public to a sweeping conclusion. Whatever the reality of the three-hour debate might have been, the impression was that Turner had won. Mulroney came second and Broadbent a distant last.[67] Broadbent and the NDP appeared to have become marginalized, and as a result, Turner and the Liberals clearly took over as the standard bearers of the growing opposition to free trade. One NDP official estimated that instead of claiming 60% of the anti-free-trade support, as was the case before the debate, the NDP dropped to about 30%.

The Post-Debates Period

As a consequence of the debates, support for the Liberals rose another 10%, while the NDP fell from 29.5% in week three to 26.4% in week four and 22.5% in week five. The Liberals temporarily displaced the Conservatives in first place, and the NDP was consigned to third. Four years as an effective opposition, it seemed, had been eclipsed by a one-minute television excerpt. Such is the power of the medium of television.

Soon there was more bad news. On 3 November, retired Supreme Court Justice Emmett Hall, regarded by many as the architect of Canada's national medicare system, categorically rejected NDP and Liberal assertions that free trade would jeopardize medicare. Then earlier efforts to make gains in Quebec by flirting with Quebec nationalism came back to haunt the NDP. Seven leading figures in the Quebec party, most notably Michel Agnaieff and Jean-Paul Harney, indicated their support for provincial use of the constitution's notwithstanding (i.e., exemption) clause over the federal Charter of Rights to ensure that provincial legislation requiring unilingual French signs in Quebec (Bill 101) prevailed. Press accounts also suggested that some Quebec NDP candidates believed the province's English minority was already 'overprivileged'.[68] While Broadbent tried to distance himself from such remarks, the damage was done. Belatedly catching on to the importance of free trade, the party began to suggest that the Liberals were in fact divided on the issue of free trade,[69] but this effort was over-shadowed by the massive intervention into the campaign by large corpo-rations. These private interest groups spent millions of dollars on political ads criticizing the opponents of free trade. In so doing, they overwhelmed the NDP's much smaller publicity campaign.

The Quebec language controversy continued to dog Broadbent in week six. When asked to comment on whether he would support Bill 101, he pleaded that it would be out of place for him, as a non-Quebecker, to comment. To many Canadians who had admired Broadbent's principled statements in the past, this seemed a particularly opportunistic stance. It would win him no seats in Quebec and no laurels elsewhere.[70] The NDP bottomed at 22.3% in the polls. Meanwhile the reaction of the business community to the Liberals' surge in support was reflected in drops in the Canadian dollar and the Toronto stock exchange.

Along with a continuing barrage of free-trade ads, the last week of the campaign saw interjections by two neo-conservative heads of government, Reagan and Thatcher,[71] on behalf of Mulroney. Broadbent, at last consent-ing to more unscripted encounters, continued to suggest that both Turner and Mulroney were peddling a similar corporate agenda. In a campaign that had seen such polarization between the Liberals and the Conservatives over free trade, this message seemed out of place: 1988 was not 1984.[72] The NDP ended the campaign at 22.5% in the polls and with 20.4% of the votes. Instead of making a giant leap forward for socialism, the NDP had lurched ahead by mere inches.

INTEREST GROUPS AND THEIR IMPACT ON THE NDP CAMPAIGN

Interest groups, allowed virtually free rein since the 1984 ruling by Alberta Justice Donald Medhurst (Paltiel, 1988: 144), were particularly important in the 1988 election. While several single-issue groups were active on such matters as abortion and capital punishment, the dominant issue of the 1988 campaign was free trade (Clarke et al., 1991).

Among the more notable of the pro-free-trade organizations were the government of Canada, through the External Affairs Department; the Canadian Alliance For Trade and Job Opportunities, an organization that included the Canadian Chamber of Commerce and the Business Council on National Issues; the National Citizens' Coalition,[73] an ultra-right and largely pro-Conservative lobby group; Canada Stand Proud; Farmers For Free Trade; Concerned Citizens of Canada; the Tourism Industry Association of Canada; a large number of individual private corporations operating under their own corporate names (e.g., Minto, Husky); and key newspapers such as *The Globe and Mail* (providing special pages of pro-free-trade editorials), and the major Montreal dailies.

The anti-free-trade groups included the Council of Canadians, led by the *Canadian Encyclopedia* publisher Mel Hurtig; the Pro Canada Network; the National Action Committee on the Status of Women; several labour federations, including the Canadian Labour Congress and the Ontario Federation of Labour; a number of individual trade unions, including the Canadian Auto Workers led by Bob White; and several newspapers, most notably *The Toronto Star*.

Although the latter groups had less money,[74] both sides spent millions of dollars on advertising, far outspending the political parties, and offered millions more in free services, with the result that both pro- and anti-free-trade pamphlets were distributed to virtually every household in the country. Special supplements inserted in daily newspapers became a common sight, as did scores of full-page ads. As early as June 1988, the *Globe and Mail* reported that the Department of External Affairs had spent $14-million on *domestic* advertising to promote free trade and planned to spend another $10-million.[75] The federal government mailed millions of pamphlets outlining in glowing terms the alleged advantages of the trade deal. None of the potential weaknesses of the deal were suggested in such government publications.

Of the non-governmental interest groups active in the federal election, the Pro Canada Network (PCN), spending about $650,000 in total,[76] got off the mark first with a colourful, highly entertaining 24-page pamphlet opposing free trade. Its expenditures were dwarfed, however, by those of the Canadian Alliance for Trade and Job Opportunities. Alarmed at the early success of the PCN booklet and the effectiveness of Turner's performance in the TV debate, the Alliance cranked up its organizational know-how and exercised its corporate muscle. According to newspaper accounts (*Toronto Star*, 19 Nov. 1988), having spent $2-million in the two years preceding the election campaign, the Alliance continued its efforts right through the crucial final days—even on election eve, when political parties are silenced —spending at least $1.5-million during the campaign proper; post-election reports suggest the amounts were even higher.[77] On two separate occasions during the election period the Alliance paid for a four-page insert entitled 'Straight Talk on Free Trade' and placed it in 35 Canadian daily newspapers. One NDP official suggested that one Toronto paper alone printed over $900,000 worth of pro-free-trade ads.[78]

Interest-group activity also involved personal contacts. While union activists telephoned fellow members about the dangers of the Mulroney-Reagan trade deal, employers sent around circulars on company stationery warning employees of dire job consequences if the deal were not implemented.[79]

Under normal circumstances, interest groups might have a marginal impact on the outcome of an election campaign. In a country so polarized over free trade and largely divided along the class lines of business vs. labour (Salutin, 1989) and their respective ideological differences (conservatism vs. reform liberalism and socialism), the weight of powerful interest groups was crucial in determining which political party would be victorious. In the words of prominent analyst Michael Kirby: 'the Conservatives had a virtually unlimited advertising budget once the business community decided to enter the campaign on behalf of free trade. Election rules prohibit outside advertising in support of a political party, but only one [major] party was backing the trade deal' (Caplan et al., 1989: 230).

The 1974 Election Expenses Act was intended to give all major parties a fair chance to be heard by the public in the limited time period of an election campaign. But in one solitary 1984 ruling, the Canadian courts nullified these reforms and thwarted all previous moves towards greater democratization of the political process. As Khayyam Paltiel, the architect of the 1974 election finance legislation, noted just before his death, 'Canadian election contests in the future may well be dominated by political action committees [interest groups] on the American model' (1988: 159).

The implications of unrestrained corporate intervention in Canadian elections are substantial. The NDP is a mass-based party (Duverger, 1963) which draws on small dues from hundreds of thousands of ordinary Canadians. If such a party has to compete financially with the huge budgets and professional advertising techniques of giant corporations, achieving election victory seems a herculean task. To publicly regulate and limit political parties as to spending and not do likewise to private interest groups seems analogous to tying the hands of one boxer but not his opponent's.[80] No wonder the Chief Electoral Officer at the time, Jean-Marc Hamel, warned of the collapse of our electoral system.[81]

OUTCOME

Vote

NDP expectations regarding the election outcome declined steadily as the campaign progressed. At the issuing of the writs there was confidence that an NDP government might actually be formed. A few weeks later the hope was for a second-place finish and the status of the official opposition. With the slide to third place after the debates, NDP activists began speculating about their possible role in a minority Parliament, and hoped at least to achieve a toehold in Quebec. None of these aspirations was to be realized.

Results from the west helped to propel the party, for the first time in the 56-year history of the federal CCF-NDP, past the 20% barrier, to 20.4% of the national vote.[82] Still, the increase was far less than most journalists had expected just a year earlier. As it had so often in the past, Saskatchewan gave the NDP its highest level of support (44.2%). British Columbia was next (37.0%), followed by the Yukon/Northwest Territories (36.8%), Manitoba (21.4%), and Ontario (20.1%). In the middle of the pack were Alberta (17.4%), Quebec (14.0%), Newfoundland (12.4%), and Nova Scotia (11.4%), and New Brunswick (9.3%), and Prince Edward Island (7.5%) came last (see Appendix Table 1). The party received its highest percentage of the federal vote ever[83] in British Columbia, Quebec, Prince Edward Island, and the Yukon/Northwest Territories. Alberta's support was its second highest, and Saskatchewan, continuing its remarkable pattern of support, recorded its third highest level. Overall, the 1988 NDP vote was greater than the party's 1962-84 average in eight regions; only in Manitoba and Nova Scotia was support for the party below average.

Seats

With 43 MPs in the enlarged House of Commons, the NDP came out of the election with a greater number and percentage of seats (14.6%) than ever before.[84] Still, as noted elsewhere (Cairns, 1968; Whitehorn, 1985b; see also Chapter 1), the single-member constituency system tends to award a third-place party a proportionately lower percentage of seats than votes. In 1988 the index of difference between the NDP's vote (20.4%) and seats (14.6%) was 5.8, less than the NDP's past average (7.9) (see Chapter 1 and Whitehorn, 1985b).

The party had 19 MPs from British Columbia (including Dave Barrett, Svend Robinson, Nelson Riis, Ian Waddell, Lynn Hunter, Joy Langan, Margaret Mitchell, John Brewin, and Bob Skelly), 10 from Saskatchewan (including Lorne Nystrom, Simon de Jong, and Les Benjamin), another 10 from Ontario (including Broadbent, Steven Langdon, Howard McCurdy, Dan Heap, and John Rodriguez), 2 from Manitoba (Rod Murphy and Bill Blaikie), and one each from Alberta (Ross Harvey) and the Yukon (Audrey McLaughlin); BC, Saskatchewan and Alberta posted gains while Ontario and Manitoba experienced losses.[85] However, until Phil Edmonston's by-election win in Chambly, Quebec, in 1990, the party had no elected members east of Oshawa, Ontario, despite the fact that it received a combined total of over 600,000 votes from Quebec and Atlantic Canada.

The electoral bias can be seen in the composition of the NDP caucus. An east/west regional breakdown of total 1988 NDP votes and seats is shown in Table 8.2.

Table 8.2 NDP Vote and Seats, 1988

	vote	seats
East	1,556,296	10
	58.0%	23.3%
West	1,129,012	33
	42.0%	76.7%
TOTAL	2,685,308	43
	100%	100%

As has been the case so often in the recent past,[86] a majority of the NDP's votes came from the more populous east, but the overwhelming majority of its caucus members were elected from the west. The obvious consequence of this pattern is that the NDP is more widely perceived than it should be as a western-based party. This perception hampers the party in its efforts to represent and make gains in the other regions of Canada. In addition, a preponderance of parliamentary members from the west can make the role of a non-western leader more difficult than it might otherwise be.[87]

Moreover, it is worth noting that, although it has been a long-term goal of the NDP to achieve gender parity, the 1988 election did little to alleviate the gross gender imbalance either in the NDP caucus or in the House of Commons. While the NDP did manage to offer more female candidates than any other party,[88] only five of them were elected.[89]

POST-ELECTION REACTION: THE
LABOUR BACKLASH

Over the months prior to the election, the NDP had moderated its policy positions in an effort to make electoral gains. Many party members who might have objected remained silent, believing that all would be justified, or rectified, with improved party standings. As the campaign itself progressed, however, many in the party and its allied organizations became particularly upset over the party's inability to focus on the key issue of the campaign: free trade.

The main vehicles of early post-election criticism were a pair of stinging letters from the heads of two of the largest unions affiliated with the NDP: a 7-page letter, dated 28 November 1988, from Canadian Auto Workers president Bob White, and a 12-page letter, dated 5 December, from Steelworkers executive officers Leo Gerard and Gerard Docquier.

Describing the election as 'disastrous', a 'disintegration of what should have been the New Democratic Party's finest hour', White observed the profound 'disappointment and anger' within the ranks and expressed dismay that labour's 'financial and people support is accepted gratefully, but its ideas and leadership are completely ignored'. He condemned the inadequate attention to free trade and questioned the wisdom of the 'small group running the campaign'—particularly the party's American pollster who had labelled free trade as merely an economic-management issue—and concluded: 'This party doesn't belong to a handful of people who ultimately think they have all the answers. . . .' Although White stopped short of criticizing Broadbent directly or asking for his resignation, he did call for a thorough post-mortem on the campaign.

The Steelworkers' letter, which described the election as perhaps the 'most important of this century'—and a 'watershed' regarding the Americanization of Canada — suggested that the party's lack of success was rooted in a 'highly suspect plan' filled with 'fundamental errors in tactics and strategy'. It questioned the NDP strategists who had believed that the Liberal Party would collapse, that the anti-free-trade position would not help the NDP, and that the issue could be given a low profile. Characterizing the central operations as dominated by paid employees of the party, Docquier and Gerard condemned the planners' 'betrayal' of principles and reliance on polls, which they allowed to 'dominate our strategy'. They criticized the planners' inability to adjust the strategy as events warranted and cited examples of 'ineptitude' that contributed to Broadbent's being 'unprepared' for the free-trade debate. Overall, they concluded that the 'link between the trade union movement and the party at the strategic level failed completely'; in short, 'Communication just wasn't there.'

Along with labour criticism of the campaign, comments surfaced from former party notables such as Stephen Lewis and Gerry Caplan urging the NDP not to forsake its principles in the quest for electoral success;[90] better, they suggested, to lose an election than a party's ideological soul or *raison d'être*. Several tense post-election sessions were held, including a joint CLC-NDP meeting, and lively discussions in the federal NDP executive and the parliamentary caucus. Formal internal reviews were conducted by special committees—including one by the caucus, chaired by Lorne Nystrom, which offered an interim report in January 1989. This was followed by the report of the party's own Election Review Committee (co-chaired by Nancy Riche and Gillian Sandeman), which was submitted later in the year to the Federal Council and was more widely disseminated than the caucus report. In addition, a post-election survey was mailed to key party officials in all federal ridings and all Federal Council members. Over a thousand questionnaires were distributed asking for feedback on the party's election campaign. Attention, however, was soon deflected to choosing a successor to Broadbent. Not surprisingly, even a year after the election, in the midst of the party's leadership race, NDP members continued to express frustration over the 1988 election campaign, and the leadership candidates often echoed this discontent in their campaign speeches.

CONCLUSION

The past decade has been a time of changing expectations for the NDP, which has gone from third place in the polls to first and then back to third. In 1983 the goal was simply to survive and retain official standing as a party in the House of Commons. In 1984 the aim was to regain traditional levels of support. In 1985 the party hoped to catch the Liberals and eventually become the official opposition. Then from 1987 to mid-1988, it believed it could form the next government. But it seems that (like the CCF in 1945), the NDP peaked too soon, and gave its rivals time to recover. In view of the heightened expectations, the third-place finish in 1988 was bound to be disappointing, and the prospects for displacing the Liberals, let alone forming a government, are not encouraging.

There are several reasons for the Liberal Party's continuing strength. One is that it still has important ties to the business community and the advertising industry—groups that can be mobilized swiftly and effectively during an election campaign to provide last-minute funds and services and partially compensate for the federal Liberals' financial difficulties and organizational woes in the 1980s. Second, Liberal Party identification is more enduring than many expected. Despite widespread personal antipathy towards leader John Turner, neither Liberal Party members nor the Canadian public wished to see the demise of a party that had contributed so much to Canadian history. While Jean Chrétien may not be the most dynamic leader the Liberals have had, as of late 1991 he has guided them back to first place in the polls, and seems more firmly at the helm of his party than did his predecessor. Third, while the federal Liberals were unusually weak during the 1984-88 period, there was a revival of Liberal strength at the provincial level, with the party forming governments in four provinces (most notably Quebec and Ontario in 1988). In contrast, the NDP went into the 1988 campaign without a single provincial government as a base from which to rally around the socialist banner.[91] It remains to be seen if the party's 1990 Ontario victory and 1991 successes in BC and Saskatchewan will alter the federal equation.

The NDP still has a number of problems. First, though much of the rise in its national standing in 1987 came from Quebec, the public-opinion data masked an important organizational weakness. Quebec party membership in 1983 was officially 500 persons; for decades, the Quebec NDP has depended on funds from outside the province to stay afloat. To make matters worse, many of the party's key federal leaders and staffers still lack fluency in French.

Second, while the federal NDP continues to be rated positively on issues such as integrity, protection of the environment, and maintaining the welfare system, in other areas it lags considerably (e.g., Canada-US relations, defence and foreign policy, federal-provincial affairs, French-English relations, and managing the economy).[92] In the words of former federal secretary Gerry Caplan, the party is loved for its heart but not its brain (1989: 147).[93] For the NDP to win any future federal election, it must be perceived as more competent on a wider range of policy areas. How this might be accomplished remains to be seen.

Third, after more than half a century of election contests, virtually none of the major privately owned daily newspapers has given either the federal CCF or the NDP sustained editorial support.[94] (One of the reasons for greater success of European social-democratic parties is that they receive greater press support.) Since, as a result, the NDP must rely entirely on costly paid advertisements, this lack of free editorial coverage is an enormous handicap.[95]

The Future

The fact that the dramatic increase in 1988 election expenditures produced the NDP's best-ever vote and seat total suggests that more money might solve a number of the party's organizational and electoral problems. However, post-election cutbacks in many federal and provincial NDP offices suggest that it may have spent more in 1988 than it could afford. Whether it spent the money in the most advantageous locations remains a subject for debate; certainly a lot was spent in Quebec with no seats in the general election to show for it. Given that most of the money for Quebec came from outside the province, it will be interesting to see if the other provincial sections will be as generous in the next federal election.

What seems significant about NDP election expenditures is that they have generally been lower than both the Conservatives' and the Liberals'.[96] As long as this is the case, it does not seem realistic to expect the NDP to displace either of the two other major parties. The stark lesson from the most recent federal elections is that the party that spent the most money also won the most seats: money, it seems, can buy political power.

Three major issues confront the NDP. The first is whether the party will ever be able to build a meaningful organizational structure in Quebec. Although the record NDP vote of 14% is a positive step, given our electoral system a great deal more would be needed. One area for further discussion and action is the requirement of joint provincial/federal party memberships, an arrangement that works well in other provinces. The Quebec situation is unique, however, in that there the NDP has a large and powerful social-democratic rival at the provincial level: the Parti Québécois. The 1989 Quebec provincial election, in which the PQ placed a strong second behind the Liberals while the NDP fell to a distant fifth place, suggests that the latter's prospects are bleak.

The second issue facing the NDP, and most social-democratic parties, is what policy direction to take in the 1990s. The 1988 strategy of moving towards the political centre largely failed, as New Left critics suggested it would.[97] A number of party members believe the NDP should now redirect its efforts back to the left and return to being the conscience of the nation. At the very least, debate is required about the future of socialism and the appropriate mechanisms to bring about social and economic change (see Wilson, 1985; Richards and Kerr, 1986; Rosenblum and Findlay 1991; Richards et al., 1991). If the 1980s were a decade largely lost to neo-conservatives, socialists hope the current one will be kinder. The recent election victories in Ontario, BC, and Saskatchewan suggest it may.

The final issue for the NDP is that of leadership. Although after the election a majority of Canadians felt that Broadbent should stay on as leader,[98] many in the party blamed him and his closest advisers for the NDP's disappointing showing[99] and some (e.g., MP John Rodriguez) demanded that he step down. In December 1989 Broadbent resigned both as party leader and as Member of Parliament. It was the end of an era for Canada's social-democratic party. The 1990s would open with a new party leader, Audrey McLaughlin, to lead the NDP into the next federal election.

NOTES

This chapter is a revised and expanded version of a chapter in A. Frizzell et al., *The Canadian General Election of 1988* (Ottawa: Carleton University Press, 1989). It was originally presented as a paper to the Center of Canadian Studies at the School of Advanced International Studies at Johns Hopkins University on 18 Nov. 1988. I am grateful for the forum provided by Professor Charles Doran and his colleagues at the Center.

[1] The Angus Reid poll conducted 17-23 Aug. had support for the Conservatives at 36%, for the Liberals at 32%, and for the NDP at 30%.

[2] For analysis of some of the differences between a movement and a party, see Chapter 2 and Whitehorn (1985a).

[3] The now largely defunct federal Social Credit party came third.

[4] In 1983 and 1984 journalists had portrayed a dramatically different image of the NDP as a party divided, with serious challenges to its leader, and on the brink of oblivion. Press coverage of the NDP in the 1980s seemed somewhat erratic.

[5] Reid poll, 20-25 June 1985.

[6] The federal office staff doubled to about thirty for the 1988 election.

[7] One member also suggested that too many party bureaucrats and too few politicians were appointed.

[8] Closely related to the SEPC steering committee in membership and function was an even smaller body called the election readiness core group. Seven of the ten committee members were based in Ottawa and a high percentage were senior party personnel.

[9] Interestingly, there was very little overlap in membership with the policy review committee.

[10] By far the most detailed account of these key figures and their relationship to Broadbent can be found in Judy Steed's biography of the latter (1988).

[11] In addition to the party's expenditures, NDP candidates' expenses were as follows: $2,665,000 (1979), $2,987,000 (1980), $4,479,000 (1984). They lagged well behind the candidates of the two other parties in both expenditures and income (Stanbury, 1986: 798-9; see also Paltiel, 1988: 153; and Wearing, 1991b).

[12] One should be cautious in comparing data on party election expenditures. The NDP, spending the least of the major parties in the past, has generally been below its allowable limits and therefore tends to try to claim as many expenditures as possible to maximize its financial reimbursement. Given that both the Liberals and Conservatives have tended to be quite near their allowable spending limits, these two parties are prone to underestimate their election expenditures (e.g., downplaying the cost of expensive media advertising consultants). As a result, the published data are inclined to overestimate the degree of parity between the NDP and the Liberals and Conservatives (Paltiel, 1988: 154; interviews with senior NDP officials; see also Stanbury, 1989 and note 96 below).

[13] Since public reporting began in 1974, the number of individuals donating to the federal NDP had exceeded that of those contributing to the Liberal Party (Stanbury, 1989).

[14] The Chief Electoral Officer set the NDP's 1988 spending limit at $8,005,799, the same as the Conservative Party's.

[15] Estimates provided by the NDP federal office at the completion of the campaign.

[16] Sources: Fletcher (1988: 164); Paltiel (1988: 153), and correspondence with the NDP federal secretary, Dick Proctor. Advertising data are final figures.

[17] About $2-million in total was earmarked for Quebec. Much would go to pay salaries of staff members hired to try to build a new party structure in the province.

[18] Whitehorn (1988). See also Archer (1987). It is interesting to note that as a source of funds for the NDP labour is usually less significant than corporations are for the Conservatives (Stanbury 1986, 1989). Union financial contributions to the NDP rise during election years. For example, in the period 1974 to 1984 donations from unions in non-election years accounted for 11.8% of NDP

income vs. 23.7% in election years (calculations based on data reported by Stanbury [1986: 803]). For earlier years see Paltiel (1970). Labour also assisted by loaning personnel and paying for at least one mailing to union members.

[19] In 1981-84 direct mail accounted for up to one-fifth of the party's income (Paltiel, 1988: 150). In 1987 the NDP sent out over 1.1 million pieces of direct mail, with a disproportionate amount going to targeted swing ridings, and raised $1.3-million with a 2% return rate.

[20] The *Globe and Mail* reported that 11 public polls were conducted in the 1984 campaign, vs. more than 25 in 1988 (25 Nov. 1988).

[21] Fletcher (1988: 170) reports that lines/air time devoted to the party/leader popularity race accounted for about 20% of coverage.

[22] See the conclusion of Chapter 3.

[23] Larry Ellis, a previous party pollster, had departed in controversy by the beginning of 1984 (Hills 1984).

[24] NDP polling data did prove to be accurate in this regard.

[25] Membership usually consisted of Vic Fingerhut, Pat Kerwin, and Brian McKee, and sometimes included Julie Mason and Anna-Rae Fishman.

[26] Subsequent success rates in targeted seats were as follows: 54% for the west, 29% for Ontario, and zero for Quebec and Atlantic Canada.

[27] This is doubly so given that Canada's electoral system does not reward a party with any seats for a close second-place finish. While the party continued to make use of its labour-intensive three-canvass technique, instead of placing the best canvassers in the polls in which the party had the highest level of support, it placed them in swing polls to maximize their effectiveness. Similarly, there was greater effort to put more trained personnel into ridings targeted for possible victory rather than in incumbent ridings.

[28] Gerry Caplan, former NDP federal secretary and now a political analyst, suggested that the strategy should have been revised as the party's popularity declined (Caplan et al., 1989: 221). In fact, party planners did seem to scale down their aspirations. Evidence for this can be seen in the shift in Broadbent's itinerary away from the initial emphasis upon new ridings to one stressing incumbent ridings that the NDP was trying to retain.

[29] In fact, as noted elsewhere in this book, there were similarities to the 1945 campaign; see Lewis (1981); Caplan (1973); and Read and Whitehorn (1991).

[30] Only Barrett was elected. In all likelihood, the party would have done better in both Manitoba and Ontario had more of these prominent figures chosen to run.

[31] Interview with NDP official. The CBC also reported (16 Oct. 1988) that the NDP was the party for which more Canadians said that they would never vote.

[32] In January 1988 Gallup reported that 32% of all Canadians saw big labour as the greatest threat; only 17% selected big business. See also Chapter 1 and Whitehorn (1985b).

[33] If Dukakis to the south was afraid to say the l-word of liberalism, so too many NDP officials did not seem eager to utter the s-word of socialism.

[34] Party surveys had shown that this theme still had strong appeal. However, by tinkering with 1984's 'ordinary Canadians' and substituting 'average Canadians' (in French 'le vrai monde'), the party weakened the repetitive value of the phrase, with the result that Canadians no longer linked it exclusively to the NDP.

[35] While the majority favoured this focus, there was some disagreement within the

SEPC. The Ontario provincial NDP, battling a Liberal provincial government, thought that greater attention should be paid to the Liberals. Morley (1988: 128) reports a similar lack of consensus as to the primary target in the 1984 campaign.

[36] Particularly on the part of Wafflers such as Jim Laxer in the late 1960s.

[37] The irony of the NDP's position in 1988 is that the CCF, in the 1933 Regina Manifesto, favoured free trade. See Chapter 3.

[38] Many saw an uneasy parallel to the polarized wage-and-price controls debate in the election of 1974, in which the NDP, as the third party, lost substantial ground.

[39] See, for example, an Environics poll in which the NDP placed third at 17% versus the Conservatives at 40% and the Liberals at 21% (*Globe and Mail*, 15 Oct. 1988). See also Morley (1988: 129). For a general discussion of how parties differ on issue areas in surveys of public attitudes, see Dalton (1988) and Keefe (1984).

[40] See, for example, an Environics poll conducted 2-10 Oct. 1988.

[41] In these areas the NDP topped all other parties (Environics poll, *Globe and Mail*, 15 Oct. 1988).

[42] Both Gallup and Environics reported in July that more women than men preferred the NDP (*Toronto Star*, 15 July 1988, and *Globe and Mail*, 29 July 1988).

[43] A Gallup poll on 15 Nov. found that Canadians rated NDP ads the least informative. See also Caplan (1989: 224).

[44] The Liberal ads suggested that Mulroney had sold out the country, while later Conservative ads called Turner a liar.

[45] In 1988 television time allocations, based on party seats and vote in the previous election, were a whopping 195 minutes for the Conservatives, 84 minutes for the Liberals, and 67 minutes for the NDP (only 16% of the available time) (*Globe and Mail*, 12 Oct. 1988). See also Fletcher (1988: 163). One mitigating force was the parity awarded to the NDP on the CBC's *The Journal*.

[46] CBC broadcast 10 Nov. 1988. Earlier CTV and Environics polls also reported Broadbent in third place.

[47] Environics survey, 13 Oct. 1988.

[48] Gallup polls 14-17 Nov. 1988, Gallup Reports 19 and 20 Nov. 1988. Believability on free trade was 36% for Mulroney, 19% for Turner, and a paltry 13% for Broadbent. Also significant were poll findings that the NDP ranked third in articulating Quebec's interests.

[49] Even less inspiring were the election platform booklets. The second of these, 'A Fair Deal For Canada', had the following section titles: A Fairer Tax Deal For Average Canadians, Fairness for Every Part of Canada, Fairness for Families, Fairness for Women, Fairness for Our Parents and Grandparents, Fairness for Young Canadians, Fairness for Rural Canadians, Fairness for Aboriginal Peoples, Fairness for Ethnocultural Communities and Visible Minorities, and Fairness for Small Business in Canada.

[50] Pollster Angus Reid reported that 63% of Canadians believed free trade was the key issue (*Toronto Star*, 29 Oct. 1988; see also Clarke et al., 1991). Since free trade attracted most of the attention, several other issues received less coverage than they perhaps warranted.

While the three federal party leaders reached a consensus on the Meech Lake constitutional accord, the western sections of the NDP exhibited clear signs of discontent. One area of concern was the perception that Meech Lake would significantly weaken the ability of any future socialist government in Ottawa to carry out national programmes. Many saw Meech and free trade as a two-pronged attack on the power of the federal government. Events immediately after the election confirmed that more debate on this issue was necessary both within the party and outside (e.g., as of early 1989 all western NDP provincial leaders opposed Meech Lake).

The Conservative government's programme of privatization, a likely area of continued activity in any second term for Mulroney, was also criticized by the NDP. The public, nevertheless, might have benefitted from greater discussion of this issue dividing the political right and left (Archer and Whitehorn, 1990, 1991).

The Mulroney government's proposed increase in defence expenditures and plan to purchase a costly fleet of nuclear-powered submarines were not well addressed during the campaign. Defence was seen by many NDP strategists as a topic to avoid, lest the public be reminded of the party's past and generally unpopular convention resolutions favouring withdrawal from NATO and NORAD.

It is interesting to note that the trade deal attracted little attention in the US election campaign during the same period.

[51] In May a Decima poll reported that 51% supported free trade; by October Environics reported that this had dropped to 44%; just after the leaders' debates Gallup reported that only a minority of 26% were in favour, and by election eve the figure was still only 34%.

[52] On 10 Nov. 1988, the CBC reported that in October 39% said free trade would affect how they voted, whereas by November the percentage had increased to 54%.

[53] As early as May, pollster Angus Reid found that when positing free trade as the decisive issue, 38% of respondents said they would vote for the Conservatives, 34% for the Liberals, and only 27% for the NDP (*Kingston Whig Standard*, 28 May 1988). In November, the CBC polled those opposed to free trade and asked which party was best on the issue: 60% answered in favour of the Liberals, while only 27% responded in favour of the NDP (10 Nov. 1988, CBC broadcast). An October Reid poll found similar results (*Toronto Star*, 29 Oct. 1988).

[54] See, for example, Environics (11 Nov. 1988) and Gallup (20 Nov. 1988). Another poll found that 20% of those intending to vote Conservative opposed free trade (mid-November CTV poll, cited in Caplan, 1989: 202).

[55] The increased forays into Quebec were draining, given Broadbent's lack of fluency in French, and may have contributed to the flatness of his performance in 1988. Some also noted that the absence of his wife Lucille and her calming influence may have contributed to his poor performance on the tour (*Toronto Star*, 17 Nov. 1988).

[56] As Nakitsas had previously served as research director, he may have felt that it was unnecessary to take the newly appointed research director along.

[57] The flaw in this argument is that it may be easier to win back former supporters and return to traditional levels of support, as in 1984, than to find new supporters, as in 1988.

[58] Since more than 25 national public polls were conducted during the campaign, a weekly average of all the polls has been calculated for this and subsequent weeks. Compiled from a larger sample, such an average provides a more stable base on which to compare developments from week to week.

[59] The QFL provided no money but did loan ten staff members for the campaign (*Toronto Star*, 10 Oct. 1988).

[60] Gallup subsequently reported that 78% of Canadians favoured a three-party system (*Kingston Whig Standard*, 10 Nov.).

[61] Given that the French debate was likely to be the most draining for Broadbent, NDP strategists sought (unsuccessfully) to have the sequence of the debates reversed.

[62] He was aided by the fact that the NDP caucus in the 1985-88 period contained the largest number of bilingual MPs in the party's history.

[63] *Globe and Mail*, 28 Oct. 1988. Broadbent had also rated 4% in 1984. The difference was that in that election he and his party were simply fighting to stay alive, not to achieve a breakthrough in Quebec.

[64] One should note that it is difficult to separate clearly the impacts of the various debates and the onset of political advertising.

[65] A similar pattern can be found in the decline in numbers selecting Broadbent as most likely to make the best prime minister. In early October, Broadbent's rating in Quebec was 24%; by mid-November it was 15% (Gallup Report, 14 Nov. 1988, and Environics polls, *Globe and Mail*, 13 Oct. 1988 and 11 Nov. 1988).

[66] It had been decided not to have a television rehearsal, but instead to go over a large and detailed briefing book.

[67] Poll results from four national surveys found that only 10-11% felt that Broadbent had won the debate, vs. 46-72% for Turner and 16-19% for Mulroney. By contrast, 29% felt that Broadbent had won the English debate in 1984 (second place, behind Mulroney).

[68] *Globe and Mail*, 5 Nov. 1988; *Toronto Star*, 5 Nov. 1988. In contrast, the French-language NDP press release stated that French was threatened ('menacée') in Quebec and Canada (correspondence with G. Nadeau, NDP leader, 18 July 1989). The alleged discrepancy was explained in one NDP interview as due to differences between the official text and statements made at the press conference.

[69] Empirical confirmation of this perception can be found in Perlin's 1984 survey of Liberal convention delegates. See for example Blake (1988) and Archer and Whitehorn (1990, 1991).

[70] There is some indication that NDP MP Mike Cassidy's loss in Ottawa South can in part be attributed to the NDP's language statements.

[71] Some partisans felt this was part of an international conservative conspiracy.

[72] In contrast, the Liberal phrase 'It's more than an election, it's your future' captured the mood of the national debate.

[73] Its estimated budget for the 1988 campaign was $0.5-million. An even larger amount was reported spent by this lobby group on advertising in the 1984 election (Paltiel, 1988: 144).

[74] The *Globe and Mail* (18 April 1989) reported that the ratio in spending was five to one. Given that a plurality of Canadians opposed the free-trade deal on the eve of voting day, it appears that the more affluent interests supported free trade, while the less affluent opposed it.

[75] *Globe and Mail*, 13 June 1988. This combined total of $24-million surpassed the amount spent on ads by all the political parties, let alone that spent by the NDP on opposing the deal.

[76] *Toronto Star*, 18 Nov. 1988

77 *Kingston Whig Standard* (1 Nov. 1988); *Toronto Star* 17 and 19 Nov. 1988). Subsequent reports suggest the ad campaign cost $5.2-million, more than either the Liberal or NDP advertising budgets (*Toronto Star*, 23 May 1989).

78 Some, it was suggested, were even paid for by US-owned corporations.

79 The parallel to the 1945 corporate-sponsored pro-free-enterprise campaign is striking. See Chapter 4; Lewis (1981); Read and Whitehorn (1991).

80 This seemed to be the basis for the public concern raised by Commissioner George Allen of the Chief Electoral Office in the closing days of the 1988 campaign (*Toronto Star*, 19 Nov. 1988).

81 *Kingston Whig Standard*, 18 April 1989.

82 Of course, the party had surpassed this level on a number of occasions in national public-opinion polls, most memorably in 1943 and in 1987, when it led the nation in popularity.

83 Data cover the entire CCF-NDP period from 1932 to 1988.

84 The CCF-NDP's other best years in percentage of seats were 1945 (11.4%) and 1980 (11.3%).

85 Provincial explanations for federal NDP results include the unpopularity of the Social Credit government in British Columbia and the Conservative government in Saskatchewan, the solid performance in opposition by the Alberta NDP, and the still lingering dissatisfaction with the former Manitoba NDP government of Howard Pawley.

86 For earlier data on this discrepancy between location of votes and of seats, see Whitehorn (1985b) and Chapter 1.

87 One notes that in 1983, when Broadbent was in conflict with a number of party members from the west over the constitution, he was in a similar position, with relatively few caucus members from the east.

88 The NDP ran 85 women in 295 ridings for a rate of 28.5% (data supplied by the Chief Electoral Officer, December 1988).

89 This is an increase from 1980 (two) and 1984 (three). See also Kome (1985).

90 *Kingston Whig Standard* 29 Nov. 1988, and *Globe and Mail*, 30 Nov. 1988.

91 The solitary NDP administration was Tony Penniket's Yukon territorial government.

92 Environics poll, *Globe and Mail*, 15 Oct. 1988.

93 See also *Reid Report* 2(8) (Aug. 1987); 3 (3) (March 1988).

94 Fletcher (1988: 167) also notes that in 1980 and 1984 the amount of press coverage on the NDP was less than that on the Liberals and Conservatives.

95 See also Fletcher's comments (1988: 168, 176) on the 1984 election.

96 In 1988 the NDP, with one more candidate than the Liberal Party, was officially allowed to spend more than the Liberals: data from the CEO suggest that the NDP did spend marginally more. (*Ottawa Citizen*, 26 May 1989). Since several of the parties have been very close to their legal election limits, however, significant under-reporting of expenditures was likely. Perhaps more reliably, the CEO listed party income for the 1988 election year as a whopping $24.5 million for the Conservatives, $13.2 million for the Liberals and $11.7 million for the NDP. This income discrepancy continues despite the fact that in 1988 far more individuals donated to the NDP alone (120,703) than to the two other parties combined (67,926 for the Conservatives and 37,911 for the Liberals). Clearly, as one would expect for a party claiming to representing the less affluent, NDP donations

on average are smaller than those for the Conservatives and Liberals and are far less likely to come from big business (Stanbury, 1989).

97 For a differing interpretation see Mason (1990).

98 Gallup reported (12 Dec. 1988) that 58% of Canadians believed Broadbent should stay on as leader, while 25% felt he should resign and 17% had no opinion.

99 Lynn McDonald (*Toronto Star* 23 Nov. 1988). Whereas in 1984 Broadbent ran an exceptional campaign that was praised by the public, the media, and party members alike, his performance in 1988 was lacklustre. Data cited by Fletcher (1988: 175) regarding the media's image of Broadbent's previous election performances in 1979, 1980, and 1984 suggest a somewhat inconsistent pattern. In 1979 overall media coverage was positive with a scoring of +12%. In 1980 a negative rating of -26% was recorded, while in 1984 the score was a positive +67%. These data may suggest a certain fickleness by the media towards political leaders. However, they also suggest that perhaps both party strategists and the media overgeneralized from the preceding campaign about Broadbent's election skills and largely ignored earlier press evaluations that were less glowing.

NINE

Future Prospects:
Social Democracy in the 1990s

AUDREY McLAUGHLIN, THE NDP, AND
THE NEXT FEDERAL ELECTION

While the next federal election may not be called until 1993, and is therefore beyond the detailed scope of this volume, several preliminary observations can be made regarding the relative strengths and weaknesses of the
NDP and its rivals.

The Conservatives seem vulnerable in a number of areas. Despite
employing some of the most expensive public-relations and polling experts
in the country, the Conservative party and its leader, Brian Mulroney, are
mired at very low levels in public-opinion polls. One reason for this is the
unpopularity of the policies they have pursued. In the midst of the 1984
election campaign, Mulroney promised that social programmes were a
'sacred trust', but the actions of his government have suggested otherwise.
To make matters worse, the Conservative Party's agenda has become more
ideologically rigid with the passage of time. Increasingly, public services are
earmarked for cutbacks and/or privatization. As the resolutions passed at
the August 1991 Conservative policy convention in Toronto revealed, the
red Tories (i.e., the genuine progressive conservatives) seem to be in
decline and the more hard-line neo-conservatives in the ascendancy.

Brian Mulroney also promised 'jobs, jobs, and jobs' in the 1984 campaign. As one New Democratic activist commented in 1991: 'Many Canadians are wondering "where, where, where?" and with the GST, all they see are taxes, taxes and more taxes.' The Conservative Party thus seems vulnerable in the area of economic competence, which was once regarded as its strength.

The proposal to expand the North American free-trade zone to include the Central American state of Mexico appears even less popular than the original agreement. Mexico lacks the strong civil-liberties tradition that is required for a fully democratic state, and its record on social and environmental legislation is similarly weak. Accordingly, many Canadians are sceptical about possible integration with such a country.

While the Canadian public continues to be concerned with the economy, Mulroney seems preoccupied with leaving his mark on history and surpassing the record of his Liberal predecessor Pierre Trudeau in constitutional affairs. Mulroney's constitutional ventures have helped to unleash anew the genie of Quebec separatism. Few doubt that the Meech Lake constitutional paralysis and the post-Meech malaise have adversely affected Canadian federalism. The man who in 1984 promised to heal the divisions of the Trudeau era has been anything but a peacemaker.

Finally, politics is not only a matter of ideology: it also involves leaders and their personalities. If a man is judged by his friends, the long list of Mulroney's former associates who have resigned in disgrace or been accused of corruption raises fundamental questions about his integrity. The public holds contemporary politicians as a group in low esteem, but Mulroney and his party are given an even lower rating. For many Canadians, he epitomizes what they dislike about politicians.

Among the NDP's rivals, the Conservative Party is not the only one with problems. Many Canadians believe that on two occasions, first in 1984 and most recently in 1990, the Liberal Party selected the wrong leader. Instead of choosing a voice for the future, they twice seem to have chosen one from the past. To what degree current leader Jean Chrétien can overcome this negative image remains to be seen. An additional concern is funding: in an age when money appears more crucial than ever to election prospects, the Liberal Party still needs to improve its record in raising funds. Finally, many believe that despite his Québécois roots, Chrétien is out of touch with current nationalist sentiments in Quebec. Certainly his image outside the province as a populist straight-shooter was tarnished during his 1990 leadership run, when he appeared to be ducking controversial issues. Nevertheless, the Liberals do seem to be recovering from the near-disaster of the 1984 election.

The NDP, for its part, possesses some handicaps as well. Given that Canadian politics is still largely dominated by male politicians and journalists, the NDP's first female federal leader faces a difficult task. To date,

Audrey McLaughlin has opted for a gentler and more consensual style of leadership. In the aftermath of the frustrating 1988 federal election, in which Broadbent was accused of insufficient consultation, this is a positive change. A consensual style can also help to soothe the egos of defeated rivals, and was probably a wise tactic for McLaughlin to pursue following the 1989 NDP leadership contest. However, many Canadians are searching for a strong and dynamic voice, and to them a consensual style may appear as a sign of weakness. Equally important, as this style is relatively time-consuming and undramatic, it risks failing to inspire either party activists or the electorate. Canadians who have had their fill of platitudes from Mulroney will not relish hearing still more speeches in the bland language derived from polling research. They want a clear, honest voice and expect such from the NDP. As a relative newcomer to Ottawa and its political intrigues, McLaughlin could still offer such a voice. But she will have to resist the continuing pressure by some to turn the New Democratic Party into a bland bureaucratic electoral machine. The CCF-NDP's roots were as a 'ginger group'; the party might do well to rediscover some of that ginger.

Another problem is that, coming from the sparsely populated Yukon, McLaughlin represents a region perceived by most Canadians as a minor player in constitutional negotiations. Her Conservative and Liberal opponents are both based in Quebec and profess to know it intimately at a time when strong spokespersons from that province seem crucial. Will the NDP and its leader appear irrelevant in debates on Quebec, particularly those conducted in French? On the other hand, a national leader from the far northwest could reinforce the NDP's traditionally strong presence on the Prairies and the Pacific coast and help to tap western alienation and discontent with central Canada. Certainly the 1991 provincial election successes in British Columbia and Saskatchewan are likely to assist in this regard.

As a social-democratic organization firmly identified with the building of the welfare state, the NDP is perceived by the public as strong on social issues and the environment, but much weaker on matters relating to the economy and international affairs. The challenge for New Democrats is either to change the priorities of the electorate or to alter its perception of the party's ability to manage the economy and conduct foreign policy.

In recent elections, the NDP has benefitted from the collapse of its main rival for third place, the Social Credit party. In the absence of a significant fourth-place party, in both the 1984 and 1988 elections the NDP was treated as one of the major players. If, however, the Reform Party and the regionally-based Bloc Québécois continue to grow, a five-party system is increasingly possible and will offer new challenges to the NDP. It could, for example, make the margin needed for victory both locally and nationally even lower than before. The Ontario 1990 NDP provincial election victory proved that in a multi-party election, less than 40 per cent of the vote can be sufficient for a majority government. In the next federal election, therefore, the NDP could do very well in total seats even if it still does not receive a majority of the national vote; for once, the bias in our national electoral system might benefit the party. Another possibility, of course, is that the NDP may be displaced as the third party in Parliament. Modern readers should be reminded that neither the NDP nor the CCF always held third place: at various times in the past, the right-populist Social Credit displaced the CCF-NDP, and the similarly inclined and increasingly well-funded Reform Party could do likewise in the future. Finally, a five-party election could produce a minority government, and—assuming that a third-place finish is still the most realistic prospect for the NDP—this could once again give the party the chance to play a major role in setting the legislative agenda.

In any event, the NDP should keep in mind the growing perception that it is no longer a new party; indeed, it is considerably older than the radical Green Party, the right-wing Reform Party, and the nationalist Bloc Québécois. With its roots in the first third of the twentieth century, the NDP might find it useful to re-examine some of its policies to see how well they will serve into the next century.

TOWARDS A NEW SOCIALIST AGENDA
Introduction

To appreciate the complexity of the path ahead, we need to understand the road we have already travelled. In the nineteenth century, socialism was not a static ideology; it evolved over time in response to new ideas, changing socio-economic conditions, and differing political circumstances. Comparing the socialism of the 1830s with that of the 1890s, one notes that under the influence of the utopian socialists, significant emphasis was placed upon decentralization and local communities. By the latter part of the nineteenth century, however, socialists under the influence of Karl Marx were putting greater stress upon central government ownership and state planning.

In the twentieth century, the Russian revolution fractured socialism into revolutionary and evolutionary wings (Cole, 1967; Laidler, 1968; Whitehorn, 1985c, 1991b). The revolutionary wing gravitated towards the labels Marxist-Leninism and communism, while the evolutionary stream opted for social democracy and democratic socialism as self-descriptions.[1]

The Canadian variant of evolutionary socialism coalesced in the 1930s through the organizational vehicle of the Co-operative Commonwealth Federation. Echoing the intertwined influences of the Fabian socialists in England and the League for Social Reconstruction in Canada (Horn, 1980), the CCF opted for a somewhat technocratic and élitist emphasis upon central planning, as evidenced in the pages of the LSR's *Social Planning For Canada*. In the floundering market conditions of the Great Depression, the state appeared to be a key component of the solution. Social reconstruction, it was suggested, would be fostered by government funds, programmes, and regulatory measures. Not surprisingly, significant emphasis was placed upon public (i.e., state) ownership. As noted elsewhere, the coalition of social-democratic labour parties and farmers' groups was heavily based in the west and somewhat indifferent to Quebec. Rooted in a society characterized by high levels of unemployment and poverty, the socialism of the 1930s was preoccupied with re-establishing economic growth and jobs. The global nature of the Great Depression also encouraged these socialists to see the solutions to their collective ills in a strong central state promoting welfare and employment programmes domestically and free trade internationally.

Just as the socialism of the latter part of the nineteenth century differed in a number of aspects from that of sixty years earlier, so too Canadian socialism of the 1990s shows signs of possessing different emphases from its counterpart in the 1930s. Contemporary demands for a more participatory political style in part reflect a better-educated population with a higher proportion of professionals who expect more consultation. In an age of scepticism about the integrity of politicians and increasing feelings of alienation and cynicism among the electorate, many have come to see the state not as the solution, but as a key part of the problem. In the age of the GST, the taxman is ever-present. The state is viewed as big brother, intruding too often and almost always in the wrong direction. Accordingly, social democrats have become more interested in decentralized forms of community involvement and ownership, such as co-operatives, workers' self-management, and self-help groups. In an age of mass production and consumption, the mounting problems of waste and pollution have heightened concerns about establishing a better ecological balance. While western social democrats' past indifference towards Quebec has not been overcome entirely, in recent decades the province has received significantly greater attention; however, this does not always reflect a willingness to accommodate fully Canada's Francophones. The internationalism of socialists in the 1930s has been tempered somewhat by today's socialists who, in English Canada at least, seek to link the two collectivist doctrines of socialism and nationalism together. Accordingly, such socialists are much more willing to support protectionist measures against foreign, particularly American, economic domination of Canada. In the eyes of these social democrats, the collective liberation of workers is inextricably linked with the liberation of the Canadian nation from American corporate interests.

To understand socialist programmes, it may be useful to examine two broad areas: increased public ownership and state services, and redistributive policies. Most citizens accept some element of public ownership and public service in their community. For example, we have municipal garbage collection, public utilities, public transit, public schooling, provincial hydro, government-funded medical care and pensions, special commissions and boards for key products (e.g., Atomic Energy Commission, Canadian Wheat Board), public funding for low-cost housing, government-run postal services, and publicly-supported roads, railroads, and airlines; even in the area of culture we have provincially-funded universities, public broadcasting, and government grants to the arts. Most of us have become so accustomed to such services that we often no longer even think of many of them as publicly owned, funded, and/or operated.[2] In many cases, we take the successes for granted. In a sense, all of us have now become socialists to some degree: we recognize that we are social beings.

Contrary to what many conservative and ultra-right-wing parties would have the public believe, social-democratic parties over the past two centuries have called for a mix of public ownership (collective rights and responsibilities) combined with private ownership (individual rights and responsibilities). Except for the extremists at either ideological pole, most people want some judicious mix of collective and individual ownership. The real debate concerns the proper ratio. Which areas in a changing world should a society keep in the public sector? How much ownership should be public, and how much private? Table 9.1 presents a rough outline of the preferred mix for each of the major ideological perspectives.

Table 9.1 Ownership patterns

public %	private %	ideological perspective
90	10	hardline communist
70	30	communist economic reformer
40	60	marxist humanist socialist
30	70	social democrat
20	80	reform liberal
15	85	classical liberal
10	90	contemporary neo-conservative
05	95	libertarian

The areas selected for public ownership will also vary depending on the nature of the society, the economy, and the historical era. Thus a small, isolated population in a largely traditional agrarian, self-sufficient community where labour productivity is based upon manual and animal power needs public funding for roads and railroads to tie together the isolated hamlets, villages, and emerging cities.

A society undergoing the profound shocks of modernization, urbanization, industrialization, and subsequent population growth will have different needs. A sizeable pool of unskilled labour working in large, noisy, and grimy factories filled with hazardous machinery and living in overcrowded and poorly serviced cities fosters calls for municipal ownership to ensure distribution of essential public services such as garbage collection, city lighting, pipelines for water and gas, and public transit.

In a modern, highly urban society in which skilled and relatively affluent labour works with advanced technological equipment, demands are often heard for national public ownership of scarce and strategic commodities such as oil, gas, and uranium.

Today in a society, such as Canada's, that is geared to the production and distribution of mass consumer goods and services, there is growing concern about excessive waste, toxic chemicals, and the destruction of our fragile ecosystem. Increasingly, calls are heard to reassert public ownership and control over forests and lakes to preserve the quality of public life. The water we drink and the air we breathe are no longer taken for granted but are seen as vital parts of our common wealth.

Historically, the social services promoted in socialist programmes have been less controversial than the areas selected for public ownership, but no less important. Socialist policies are usually of a redistributive nature, endeavouring to take excessive wealth from the rich and give these funds to the needy and poor. The programmes pursued by social democrats have included a graduated income tax; insurance against unemployment, accidents, and ill health; pensions for the aged and sick; and public funding for schools, universities, and low-cost housing. These specific measures make up the intertwined social safety net that helps to foster a sense of community and shared collective fate. These socialist programmes aim to lessen the excessive concentration of social, economic, and political power in the hands of a few corporate executives, and instead to create more of a balance between the mass public and the powerful élites (Mills, 1956); the goal is to alleviate the sense of powerlessness and alienation felt by members of the lower socio-economic classes and strata. At the same time, social democrats want to expand political rights so as to include social, economic, and, increasingly, ecological rights.[3] In this way, the single dimension of political democracy is widened and strengthened by the addition of economic and social democracy.

To a reasonable extent, we understand the path that we have travelled. But what is the course for socialists approaching a new century? Will it be the dawn of a new and better civilization, or something far less pleasant? Any speculation on the future course of socialism is less likely to be a set of solutions than a preliminary outline of some of the key issues that a new socialist agenda will need to address. The challenges, of course, are not unique to socialists. But the specific nature of the social-democratic reply will need to be so.

Ideology

The CCF in the 1930s was strongly internationalist. In the 1950s, however, socialism in Canada took a nationalist turn.[4] Why? Was this shift justified? More important, is nationalism today a positive or a negative force, as we are crowded into one global village? Has social democracy succumbed too much to the lure and perhaps false consciousness of nationalism? Can humanity still afford such parochial ethnic and tribal orientations? Instead of nationalism, do we need a new ideology of internationalism? Could Canadian socialists, coming from a country that is a respected middle power, play a leading role in such developments?

In the nineteenth century and most of the twentieth, socialist collectivism challenged the excesses of individualism and private property. The great French sociologist and socialist Émile Durkheim warned of the dangers of excessive individualism in two pioneering works, *Socialism* (1958) and *Suicide* (1951). For Durkheim, public constraints on egoism were necessary for the health of both the community and the individual.

At the end of the twentieth century, environmental collectivism confronts the excesses of greedy individualism and private ownership of property (Gorz, 1980; Milbrath, 1984; Porritt, 1984; Hulsberg, 1988; Kemp and Wall, 1990). Concerns about our shared environment can serve perhaps as a means to rediscover collectivism. Will the old political left and the new Greens bond to form a stronger progressive collectivism for the twenty-first century? Given the overlap of the two collectivist doctrines in theory and practice (Inglehart, 1977; Milbrath, 1984), such a progressive alliance seems possible. Certainly across Western Europe we have witnessed the greening of the social-democratic parties; in recent years, the emphasis has been less upon socialist red, and more upon environmentalist green. Thus the socialism of the 1990s is likely to urge the theme of 'sustainable growth' raised in the Bruntland Report (World Commission, 1987). The emphasis will be not so much on indiscriminately producing more wealth, but on conserving it.

As women have entered the paid workforce in increasing numbers, their collective economic and political power has increased. Have women become less traditional and, if so, more receptive to social-democratic programmes of reform? Female respondents in recent mass public surveys and electoral campaigns indicate that they do have strong concerns about social-welfare issues, and thus could be attracted to a social-democratic party. Will feminists unite inside or outside leftist parties such as the NDP? Will they reject existing political parties, even the NDP, as excessively patriarchal, and rely more on their own organizations? How well will the demands for gender parity be received by the NDP-affiliated unions in which the membership and leadership are predominantly male?

Socialists have been eager to point out the need for a social charter of rights. Would such a charter include key planks for feminists? Equal pay for equal work sounds reasonable, but how does one decide which tasks are equal in value? Is universal state-funded day care to be a rallying cry of the 1990s? Is it as appealing to men as to women? Should the emphasis be on upholding women's right to control their own bodies and ending centuries of collective powerlessness in this regard? Should the right to have an abortion be expanded and be available as an option at any time? If not, when should such a right cease? How does the community balance its responsibility to protect the rights of the helpless fetus and child, on the one hand, and those of the individual mother, on the other? Where does the line between the responsibilities of the community and the rights of the individual fall? Who makes these decisions? What sort of due process is required?

Social democracy and reform liberalism share a commitment to a roughly compatible blend of individualism and collectivism, along with a desire to use the power of the state to aid the 'have-nots' in society. Indeed, the two doctrines together largely built the contemporary welfare state. Following a decade of mean-spirited cutbacks by neo-conservative governments, is it time for new alliances by the moderate and democratic left against the new right? If new avenues for co-operation are not explored, the centre-left may be divided and vanquished. Perhaps the time has come in Canada to consider more seriously coalition government, particularly if a five-party Parliament looms on the horizon.

With hindsight, the latter half of the 1960s and the early 1970s seem to have been golden years for social democracy. The much earlier victories for public schools, public utilities, government-sponsored pensions, unemployment insurance, and public housing were capped in 1968 by the introduction of state-run medicare. All of these key political victories appeared secure, to the point that some scholars and activists were even asking what remained to be done. But how firmly entrenched were the gains? A series of neo-conservative victories in Great Britain (from 1979), the United States (from 1980), West Germany (from 1982) and eventually Canada (from 1984) showed how swiftly social programmes could be eroded. Just as political democracy needs vigilance if it is to be maintained, so too it appears that social and economic democracy must be continually reinforced. Without such sustenance, a number of these precious programmes can wither.

Unfortunately, we live in an age in which private pollsters counsel conservative politicians to say that social programmes are a sacred trust, yet at the same time encourage them to dismantle such programmes. The methods include slashing budgets and staff and even redefining and weakening the mandates of key public agencies. Thus the Foreign Investment Review Agency (FIRA) becomes Investment Canada, and Canadian sovereignty is sacrificed to the Mammon of large foreign corporations.

Still, social democrats should not be smug about the intertwined issues of privatization and reducing budgets. They would be well-advised to question more rigorously whether in fact there are areas that no longer need a catalyst from the public sector. For example, in the 1930s passenger airlines were new and potentially risky ventures—but how necessary is state funding of such enterprises today? Social democrats ought to explore where public expenditures can be reduced and state involvement diminished. In so doing, socialist governments could concentrate funds and services where they are most desperately needed. Decisions on redirection of public-spending priorities may be particularly painful for socialists to initiate. But they are too important to be left by default to neo-conservatives. No government, conservative nor socialist, is omniscient. Public funding and power are, and should be, limited by definition, and social democrats would do well to remind themselves of this fact. At times, they should endeavour to do less—but to do it far better. The persistence of class stratification (Porter, 1965; Curtis and Scott, 1973; Forcese, 1975; Clement, 1975; Harp and Hofley, 1980; Hunter, 1981: Veltmeyer, 1986) is a reminder that to date the successes have been limited.

Groups

Political scientists and politicians alike have noted the rise of political alienation and the decline of party allegiance. Moreover, the state has come to be seen as a key part of the problem. To address these developments, a social-democratic party must be willing to explore new and less alienating forms of political participation. Too often, Canadian politics has resembled a beer ad in which John A. and the boys, or Pierre and the boys, or most recently Brian and the boys, get together over a few drinks to thrash out our constitution. Like the beer ads, our political culture is sexist, élitist, and exclusionary.

In 1867, when the literacy rate was low and most of the population lived in isolated villages and farms, a traditional élitist culture made reasonable sense. Today, with mass communications and high literacy rates, it makes little sense to maintain a political style born in an era when women were prohibited from voting and when slavery was still a pattern of social relations in some regions of the world. It may be that higher levels of education have contributed to the greater scepticism about politics and politicians. No doubt the more bureaucratic nature of modern society has also accentuated the sense of alienation and powerlessness. In any case, the challenge of politics in our age is to find ways to empower people.

To progress as a 'new democratic party', the NDP must establish new forms of democracy both within the party itself and in society at large. Historically, at the outset of this century, before the birth of the NDP, federal party leaders were selected by a caucus of MPs. Today they are chosen by election at a national convention. Perhaps in the future we will see more use of nation-wide referenda of all party members. Should the NDP pursue a more participatory mechanism for the crucial task of leadership selection

(Hayward and Whitehorn, 1991)? Greater use of membership referenda on key political issues might also be explored as a means to increase citizen involvement.

As a party endeavouring to make Canadian society more democratic, the NDP must make a stronger commitment to industrial democracy and workers' self-management and demand greater public accounting from all major corporations. Social democrats must also fight to establish public scrutiny of the activities of private interest groups, to ensure that if massive interventions occur in federal elections, as they did in 1988, they do so with full disclosure of all funding sources. Similarly, a social-democratic party should insist on open accounting by all political parties, whether they choose their leaders at conventions or by other means (Whitehorn and Hayward, 1991). On extraordinary issues facing the nation, such as constitutional changes and new major treaties (e.g., free trade or, earlier, NATO), a social-democratic party should encourage the use of referenda—a mechanism of which even Britain, a polity supposedly rooted in an élitist culture and strongly committed to parliamentary procedures, has made better use. The electoral system also needs modification to ensure that our federal Parliament is more representative and responsive to the public at large. Introduction of certain elements of proportional representation would facilitate some improvements.

Finally, reform of the Senate is long overdue. Perhaps the ideal second chamber would be one consisting of ordinary Canadians chosen by a lottery that could be based on social insurance numbers; few Canadians, however, would be likely to favour such a radical egalitarian measure (even though we use a similar system already for questions of life and death in jury selection). Certainly most current proposals for Senate reform involve greater provincial input and seem unlikely to alleviate our strong parochial tendencies and inter-regional tensions. In any case, the institution needs a dramatic change in its composition, to reduce the number of males, lawyers, and wealthy businessmen occupying its seats. Somehow we must increase the numbers of women, minorities, scientists, and other citizens too infrequently heard in the halls of political power.

Historically, social-democratic parties have often forged important links with the labour movement (Horowitz, 1968; Archer, 1991). How will these ties be maintained or strengthened in the years ahead? As trade unions evolve, will they be diverted from their efforts for political change and focus more exclusively on economic matters (Babcock, 1974)? As large factories and mines diminish in their importance to a modern economy, will there be a corresponding decline in the more militant and politically-organized unions? As the shift continues towards a service economy characterized by increasing numbers of part-time and unskilled workers, will rates of unionization and affiliation to a social-democratic party decline? Clearly the rate of unionization in the United States has dropped dramatically in recent decades (Goldfield, 1987; Richards et al., 1991: 108).

In the 1930s and 1940s, industrial unions were formed in Canada with strong ties to the United States (Abella, 1973). In the 1960s, these American-dominated international unions were challenged by increasingly loud calls for national trade unions in Canada, and eventually these nationalist appeals carried the day. However, with the increased emphasis on free trade, is it now time to reconsider the emphasis upon national rather than international unions? A contest between a multinational corporation and a national union can hardly be equitable. Not to re-evaluate methods of trade-union organization would seem a futile attempt to defy the economic determinism that the socialist movement has outlined over the years.

Technological advances are now such that computers can calculate infinitely complicated problems and mechanical robots can perform increasingly complex tasks. The synthesis of the two is likely to be revolutionary. As a result, the role, not to mention the power, of blue-collar workers will be challenged. Just as the photocopier eclipsed the typing pool, will robots displace a group of workers that has been a key component of the politically active labour movement?

Despite all the talk about the end of the Protestant work ethic and the emergence of the leisure society, the reality is that a powerful stratum of overworked professionals and managers continues to exist in conjunction with multitudes of unemployed and underemployed persons. The so-called hidden unemployment of the latter group is not so invisible during the periodic recessions that we still experience. Not surprisingly, a society of individuals nurtured on a belief in the power of big brother has been conditioned to expect the state to find jobs for the tens, if not hundreds, of thousands of unemployed. Yet at the same time many of these same citizens want lower taxes. Such is the seemingly contradictory nature of the public's aspirations, and of the tasks demanded of governments today.

The pioneering volume on Canadian social democracy was a 1950 study by Seymour Lipset entitled *Agrarian Socialism* (1968). Today Canada is largely an urban society. Nevertheless, there is a crisis in agriculture, and it is not unimportant. The financial plight of the farmer is grave. The loss of a family farm is not just the loss of a job and a business property, but the loss of a home. Just as the high cost of land for houses in urban areas is becoming an insurmountable obstacle for many young families, so too the cost of farm land and equipment is making the prospect of embarking on farming as a career increasingly difficult. Should land banks be used to enable young families to carry on in the vocation of farming?

The latter half of the twentieth century has seen a dramatic rise in the number of women in the paid workforce. Are women expected to combine two careers, one in the home and one in the office? Is this an example of the continuing proletarianization of women and the intensification of their labour? At the same time, the growing demands for and commitment to pay equity means that women increasingly have access to greater economic power. How will they exercise it?

Along with more economic power, women still seek greater physical emancipation. From the 1960s onwards, women began to acquire more control over their own bodies through birth control and access to clinical abortions. In the 1990s, however, it is perhaps more difficult than ever for women to travel safely in urban streets at night. What remedies, if any, do social democrats propose to halt the continuing violence against women? Where do socialists stand on the related issues of pornography and censorship? Does the community have a right to restrain certain individual actions when half the population is adversely affected?

Social democrats have often prided themselves on being the wave of the future and offering an ideology that is potentially the most attractive to the youth of the country. But is this necessarily so? Culturally, the generation brought up on music videos and hanging out at suburban malls does not seem to be an ideal recruiting ground for socialist parties. In the past decade, many young people have seemed to be more at home chasing the commercialized vision proposed by big business and neo-conservatives. Among those who dare to rebel, the extreme individualism of the punkers seems equally unlikely to usher in the proletarian revolution. Still, more of the young do seem alarmed about our environment, and this concern may introduce them to the need for positive collective action.

With modernization, important and fundamental demographic shifts occur in the make-up of society. One clear pattern is the aging of the population (Foot, 1982; McDaniel, 1986). Does this mark the end of the youth culture that followed the Second World War? As a result, will the types of social services demanded shift? Will less money be needed for schooling the young? Already, the traumatic issue of school closings and their implications for small communities has caused considerable grief in several locales. With the aging of the population will we see more emphasis upon adult education? Will there need to be a major reallocation of funds from schools to nursing homes? Will the growing numbers of elderly flex their muscles and resist the calls for greater state expenditures on public schools? In the competition for scarce funding, will generational conflict increase? Will class conflict in the future involve middle-class pensioners calling for greater police protection of their property and demanding less public spending in areas deemed essential by younger workers? With the aging of the population, the future radical call may well be 'grey power'.[5] More affluent pensioners will likely continue the great trek to Florida in search of sun and recreation. Among those less fortunate, however, the declining value of pensions will generate a new group of poor.

One of the consequences of the aging of the Canadian population will be a rise in the numbers of persons who are physically vulnerable in urban streets and ethnic ghettos. How progressive and tolerant will this aging demographic group be? Will they lead the demands for greater law and order? How will elderly persons from European stock react to new waves of non-white immigration from Asia and Africa?

Advances in medical sciences will continue to raise the perplexing moral dilemma of how long doctors and nurses should prolong individual life. Should the community have the right to set limits on the public cost of such medical services for the elderly? Should families as collective units have a right to say when there has been enough personal pain for an individual's life-support to be withdrawn?

Social democrats have usually taken pride in thinking that they are truly citizens of the world. In practice, though, how well have workers reacted to the complex cultural and ethnic mosaics of large metropolitan areas? Have workers and socialists always been among the most tolerant in our population (Lipset, 1960, 1981)? Or have they been among the first to feel threatened, and thus to strike out in frustration and even, on occasion, anger? Instead of class conflict in the cities, do we see increasing signs of ethnic clashes? With increasing waves of immigration, Toronto, Montreal, and Vancouver seem to be microcosms of the global village (McLuhan, 1968), and at times no more peaceful.

In recent years, social-democratic parties and trade unions have often called for greater foreign aid and improved conditions for immigrants. Yet at the same time socialists have also frequently urged the imposition of protectionist economic measures. How appropriate are such measures in a world with so much poverty? Surely no country as large and rich as Canada can remain an isolated island in the sea of impoverished and overcrowded humanity. Perhaps social democrats need to rechart and renew with greater vigour their internationalist vision—to be better prepared to sacrifice for the collective good not only on the domestic scene but also to a far greater degree in the international sphere.

Issue Areas

Despite their philosophical differences, in practice social democrats, reform liberals, and communists alike have favoured an expanded governmental role. But do we expect too much from government? Is there a danger in concentrating too many tasks and powers in an all-powerful government Leviathan? Socialist George Orwell warned of the spectre of Big Brother.

In Canada, recent discussions about the state have been intertwined with the debate on the constitutional make-up of the federal system. Should the powers of the provinces be expanded and those of the federal government diminished? What about municipal government? Should it be given formal recognition and greater scope in our constitutional division of powers?

For over a century, socialists have called for greater use of state planning to moderate the boom-and-bust fluctuations of the market cycle. Along with public ownership, state planning was seen as one of the twin pillars of the socialist edifice. In the 1990s, however, the confident belief in the healing power of central planning has been shaken, particularly with the discrediting of communist regimes in Eastern Europe. Perhaps socialists in the 1990s will wish to explore further the ideas of market socialism (Lange and Taylor, 1938; Sik, 1967; Selucky, 1979; Horvat, 1982).

Neo-conservatives have placed great stress on the creation of wealth. What Canadians like about the NDP is its repudiation of the single-minded pursuit of money, and its stress instead upon compassionate concern for the health and well-being of all.[6] Today, owners and senior managers of factories still earnestly strive to maximize private corporate profits and take a short-run view while producing wastes that will need to be stored at public expense for hundreds or even thousands of years. In such cases, it is hard to see where the net community benefit is. The motto of far too many corporate executives seems to be 'private gain at public expense'. Too often we see the desire to make a quick buck and let the community figure out later how to finance the clean-up. This pattern of irresponsible corporate behaviour[7] is far too wasteful, expensive, and, above all, dangerous to continue. Our health and that of future generations must not be so recklessly ignored.

With the rise of the service economy, in addition to producing millions of automobiles we are now producing billions of hamburgers. Instead of full-time jobs and relatively strong unions, we see a growing trend to part-time work and, in some countries, fewer unions. Instead of working adults, we see poorly paid teenagers putting on a happy face at fast-food stands. Under that corporate smile, has the workforce been transformed into a sub-proletariat?

The twentieth century has seen a tremendous explosion in the number and size of cities (Breese, 1966; World Bank, 1972). How far will the urban sprawl spread? How much congestion will occur? The golden horseshoe of southern Ontario doesn't look very golden any more, with its grey haze of pollution and its traffic snarls verging at times on gridlock. The larger cities have become, the more impersonal and dangerous they seem. 'How safe are our streets?' is a question posed not only by conservative law-and-order advocates.

In today's cities, with skyscrapers climbing ever higher and escalating land costs, who can still afford a house? In large metropolitan areas, public land banks may be needed to assemble plots for affordable housing. The individual private home may have to rest on collective land tenure.

How can governments encourage affordable housing and still provide mechanisms and incentives to build decent new housing? The lesson from Eastern Europe is that state-sponsored low rents are not a panacea. Indeed, in time such government policies, no matter how well-intentioned, may aggravate the problem.

One problem that mounts day by day is that of urban garbage. As cities use up every available piece of land, where are the future garbage sites going to be? Is the remedy to ship the mountains of urban refuse to less-populated and poorer regions of the country? In effect, poorer regions would be compensated by inter-regional garbage transfer payments. Instead of passengers, our neglected railway lines would transport garbage. At the same time, as the environmental crisis gains momentum we are likely to hear greater demands for public lands for parks, forests, and protection of water sources.

The pledge of universality in key social services is one that most socialists over the decades have cherished. Today, questions are posed as to whether we can still afford free services for all. Should there be deterrent fees? Should the rich pay a modest amount for social services? Is there any danger that unrestricted free services for all will result in insufficient funds to sustain the programmes in the long run? The first crisis of medical care was the lack of a publicly-run system offering affordable treatment for each individual patient. The second may well be over whether our society can afford all the escalating medical bills. Draconian efforts by governments to impose freezes on medical salaries may please the taxpayer and the voter in the short run, but hardly contribute to the long-term health of our medical care system. It certainly does little to stop the trend towards the proletarianization of our least well-paid medical workers. Why can a baseball player earn millions of dollars per year but a nurse labouring long hours caring for the sick and elderly earn only between $35,000 and $50,000? How is it that utility hockey players can be paid more than many family doctors?[8] Surely skilled surgeons should be paid amounts commensurate with their crucial social responsibilities.

Many parents wonder if we are in the midst of a schooling crisis. In our commitment to mass education, have we inadvertently produced miseducation? In our stress on the technological, have we lost our sense of values? In our desire to avoid ethnocentrism, have we fostered a generation with too few coherent social norms (Bibby, 1990)? How well have we overcome sexist and racist stereotypes? In our stress on the rights of the individual child, have we ignored those of the collective? The ideal solution would be to integrate the child with special needs into a small class. However, all school boards are suffering from inadequate funds for ideal teacher-student ratios. Thus in reality the child requiring special attention is often placed in a class that is already too large, adding to the burden of the overworked teacher. Too often the result is teacher burnout and/or too little time with the teacher for the rest of the class. Our schools, and even our society, seem beset with problems of discipline. In our reluctance to take harsh disciplinary measures we may preserve the disruptive child's rights, but perhaps in so doing we sacrifice the right of the class collective to a hospitable learning environment. Increasingly, parents pose the disconcerting questions 'How much is learned in school?' and 'How safe is our child's school?'. Is there not a better way of combining individual and collective needs?

To most observers the judicial system seems neither swift nor just. Protecting the individual rights of the drunk driver, the break-in burglar, or the rapist too often seems to mean that those of the victims or the collective are ignored. How well have we protected the community? Have socialists lost their sense of community and become too individualistic in their analysis and prescriptions? Perhaps it is time to reconsider and re-emphasize collective rights.

'Workers of the world unite' is no doubt one of the most famous and moving phrases of the international socialist movement. If it was timely in the nineteenth century, today it is crucial. As the globalization of the world economy continues apace, international trade becomes a greater part of each national economy. As a result, international division of labour becomes more important than ever. What are the attitudes of socialists, trade unionists, and workers to national tariffs versus free-trade zones? The economic realm is dominated by powerful multinational corporations that have resources and manpower rivalling those of many states. Can organized labour keep up with such economic giants? Will labour's hard-won gains in building the welfare state be eroded as corporations move jobs to non-unionized and low-paid labour forces elsewhere in the world? How should labour and social-democratic parties respond to such corporate threats and actions?

In recent years, communist regimes have been falling one after the other—as if to prove a communist domino theory in reverse. The pace of events has led analysts to wonder where all the communists have gone. The East may still be the East, but the West seems everywhere.

If the East-West rift has lessened, however, the North-South cleavage is as wide as ever. The history of the world is characterized not only by class stratification but also by regional domination and conflict. How long will the billions of poor people in the Third World continue to suffer? Will they rise and overturn the old order? Already we have seen signs that Third World states are willing to challenge the major modern powers. A few years ago, Argentina took on Britain; more recently Iraq confronted the United States. Both Argentina and Iraq lost these rounds, but their actions suggest new ambitions among some leaders of Third World states. Such states will not always be pre-nuclear in weaponry. The old ways of international politics are not enough to see us through the near future. The US/USSR arms race has been dramatically altered by the fragmentation of the Soviet Union. But how big will the peace dividend be? Why have not more of the weapons been turned into ploughshares? Who now controls many of the weapons? Has the break-up of the Soviet communist bloc unleashed the genie of nationalism? Some of the roots of both the First and Second World Wars can be found in Eastern Europe. Is much of Eastern Europe still a powder-keg? Or is the militarization of the Third World the new threat to global peace?

Even if we survive the dangers of war, other forces now at work have the potential to engulf us. In 8,000 BC, approximately 10 million persons inhabited the entire globe. As late as 1650 AD, the world population was only 600 million. Today we are over 5 billion persons occupying the same land mass—a more than eight-fold increase in just over three centuries. Some suggest a total of over eight billion by the year 2025 (World Commission, 1987). Others speculate that the number may go as high as 10 billion by the end of the twenty-second century (Kurian, 1984). Can the world sustain such a population at reasonable standards of living? We may have the potential to keep expanding our numbers towards infinity, but the world we inhabit is all too finite. To make matters worse, the numbers are not distributed equally over the globe. China and India alone account for approximately 40 per cent of the world's population. How long will it be before such states demand a greater share of the world's wealth?

On the eve of the new century, it is appropriate to ask anew what has happened to socialist internationalism. Surely we need to impose greater limits upon the nation-state. Instead of contributing to the ongoing squabbling over federal versus provincial jurisdictions and constitutional powers, Canadian socialists should focus upon the desperately poor and militarily dangerous world that surrounds us. The era of 1867 is long over. While redistribution of constitutional power is urgently needed, the recipient should be neither the provinces nor the Canadian government, but a struggling world government. In all our parochial discussions of amending the Canadian constitution and enacting our charter of rights, not one mention has been made of the United Nations.

Canadians have considerable technological know-how and international good will. Yet we seem to lack the vision and the determination to pursue a more dynamic and rigorous policy for peace and justice in the world we inhabit. Canadians should be at the forefront of building a better world. We play a key role in UN peacekeeping, but we could do much more.[9] The UN desperately needs better funding, organization, and leadership. Canadian socialists could encourage greater support for our nascent world government. It would mean going beyond the preoccupation with provincial rights and Canadian sovereignty, and would require a more resolute commitment to internationalism. It would involve a new collectivism combined with much-needed altruism to build a co-operative commonwealth in a global community.

In the end, however, whatever positions social democrats take, no ideology alone, no one political party, nor any single leader will be sufficient to preserve our unique planet. It will take a much greater effort. To rephrase and update the earlier socialist plea to all of humanity: 'People of the world unite . . . tomorrow may be too late.'

NOTES

[1] Both groups, however, would continue to employ the term 'socialism' in their own limited way.

[2] For analysis of Canada's Crown corporations, see Ashley and Smails (1965);

Stewart (1987); Laux and Molot (1988: 62).

[3] Speech by Audrey McLaughlin, Kingston, Ont., 10 April 1991.

[4] Even David Lewis fell under the spell of the nationalist linkage from the 1950s onwards. Of course, his support for nationalist measures was not sufficient for the Waffle New Leftists in the 1960s.

[5] Ironically, the demands for grey power in the 1990s and beyond will be articulated in part by the 1960s generation of student radicals—the ones who once said 'never trust anyone over thirty'.

[6] In the words of one early socialist, J.W. Kneeshaw, 'Instead of the rule of gold, we seek that of the golden rule.'

[7] This is a variant of the 'corporate welfare bums' theme raised by former NDP leader David Lewis (1972).

[8] In 1991 it is estimated that the gross income of a family doctor's business is about $115,000 per year, less about 30% to 40% ($35,000 to $46,000) for rent, staff, and equipment; this leaves a doctor with a real disposable income before taxes of between $69,000 and $80,000 per year. This may still seem like a lot, but when one considers that doctors require many more years of education and thus enter the labour force and start to earn money quite late in life, and that as they are self-employed they receive no employee pensions, their annual income seems inadequate for the essential work they perform.

[9] Canadians are in the midst of a debate about the role of our armed forces. Perhaps it is time to give our soldiers a more challenging set of tasks than the token political efforts that have too often been asked of them. Let's equip our armed forces to do more of the peacekeeping that is desperately needed in this war-torn world. The role of peacekeeper is one in which Canadians could be proud to serve, and it could inspire our youth and reinvigorate the idealism of an older generation.

Appendix: Table 1 CCF-NDP Federal Vote and Seats By Province/Territory: 1935-1988

	BC	Alta.	Sask.	Man.	Ont.	Que.	NB	NS	PEI	Nfld.	NWT/Yukon	TOTAL
						CCF						
						1935						
vote	97,015	30,921	69,376	54,491	127,927	7,326	—	—	—	—	—	387,056
%	33.6	13.0	20.1	19.4	8.0	0.6	—	—	—	—	—	8.8
seats	3		2	2								7
						1940						
vote	103,181	35,082	106,267	61,448	61,166	7,160	761	17,715	—	—	—	393,230
%	28.4	13.0	28.6	19.4	3.8	0.6	0.4	6.3	—	—	—	8.5
seats	1		5	1				1				8
						1945						
vote	125,945	57,077	167,233	101,892	260,502	33,450	14,999	51,892	2,685	—	584[a]	816,259
%	29.4	18.4	44.4	31.6	14.4	2.4	7.4	16.7	4.2	—	27.5	15.6
seats	4		18	5	1			1				28
						1949						
vote	145,442	31,329	152,399	83,176	306,551	17,767	9,450	33,333	1,626	197	1,140	782,410
%	31.5	9.3	40.9	25.9	15.2	1.1	4.2	9.9	2.4	0.2	17.0	13.4
seats	3		5	3	1			1				13
						1953						
vote	125,487	23,573	156,406	64,402	212,224	23,833	6,769	22,357	552	707	—	636,310
%	26.6	6.9	44.2	23.6	11.1	1.5	3.0	6.7	0.8	0.6	—	11.3
seats	7		11	3	1			1				23
						1957						
vote	131,873	27,127	140,293	82,398	274,069	31,780	2,001	17,117	680	321	—	707,659
%	22.3	6.3	36.0	23.7	12.1	1.8	0.9	4.4	1.0	0.3	—	10.7
seats	7		10	5	3							25

	BC	Alta.	Sask.	Man.	Ont.	Que.	NB	NS	PEI	Nfld	NWT/Yukon	TOTAL
						1958						
vote	153,405	19,666	112,800	74,906	262,120	45,594	4,541	18,911	215	240	—	692,398
%	24.5	4.4	28.4	19.6	10.5	2.3	1.8	4.5	0.3	0.2	—	9.5
seats	4		1	3	3							8

CCF AVERAGE VOTE AND TOTAL SEATS

	BC	Alta.	Sask.	Man.	Ont.	Que.	NB	NS	PEI	Nfld	NWT/Yukon	TOTAL
%	28.0	10.2	34.7	23.3	10.7	1.5	3.0[b]	8.1[b]	1.7[b]	0.3[b]	22.3[b]	11.1
N	29	0	52	19	8	0	0	4	0	0	0	112

NDP

	BC	Alta.	Sask.	Man.	Ont.	Que.	NB	NS	PEI	Nfld	NWT/Yukon	TOTAL
						1962						
vote	212,035	42,305	93,444	76,514	456,459	91,795	13,200	39,689	3,802	7,590	—	1,036,853
%	30.9	8.4	22.1	19.7	17.0	4.4	5.3	9.4	5.2	4.9	—	13.5
seats	10		0	2	6			1				19
						1963						
vote	222,883	35,775	76,126	66,652	442,340	151,061	8,899	26,617	1,140	6,364	—	1,037,857
%	30.3	6.5	18.2	16.7	15.9	7.1	3.7	6.4	1.6	4.2	—	13.1
seats	9		0	2	6							17
						1965						
vote	239,132	43,818	104,626	91,193	594,112	244,339	22,759	38,043	1,463	1,742	431	1,381,658
%	32.9	8.3	26.0	24.0	21.7	12.0	9.4	9.1	2.0	1.2	2.9	17.9
seats	9		0	3	9							21
						1968						
vote	260,989	52,720	147,941	99,974	607,011	164,466	12,277	22,676	1,636	7,042	1,528	1,378,260
%	32.7	9.4	35.7	25.0	20.6	7.5	4.9	6.7	3.2	4.4	9.6	17.0
seats	7		6	3	6							22
						1972						
vote	332,345	89,811	155,195	116,474	768,076	168,910	16,703	47,072	4,229	8,165	6,548	1,713,528
%	35.0	12.6	35.9	26.3	21.5	6.4	5.7	12.3	7.5	4.7	29.5	17.7
seats	11		5	3	11						1	31

	BC	Alta.	Sask.	Man.	Ont.	Que.	NB	NS	PEI	Nfld	NWT/Yukon	TOTAL
1974												
vote	232,547	63,310	130,391	104,829	680,113	162,080	24,869	43,470	2,666	16,445	7,028	1,467,748
%	23.0	9.3	31.5	23.5	19.1	6.6	8.7	11.2	4.6	9.5	33.2	15.4
seats	2		2	2	8			1			1	16
1979												
vote	381,678	84,236	175,011	167,850	873,182	163,492	51,642	79,603	4,181	59,978	7,926	2,048,779
%	31.9	9.9	35.8	32.7	21.1	5.1	15.3	18.7	6.5	29.7	29.4	17.9
seats	8		4	5	6			1		1	1	26
1980												
vote	426,858	81,755	165,308	159,434	874,229	268,409	54,517	88,052	4,339	33,943	8,143	2,164,987
%	35.3	10.3	36.3	33.5	21.9	9.1	16.2	20.9	6.6	16.7	31.5	19.8
seats	12		7	7	5						1	32
1984												
vote	502,331	143,588	200,918	139,999	921,504	301,928	53,332	70,190	4,737	13,993	7,395	2,359,947
%	35.1	14.1	38.4	27.2	20.8	8.8	14.1	15.2	6.5	5.8	23.7	18.8
seats	8		5	4	13							30
1988												
vote	566,582	202,847	231,358	115,638	939,928	488,633	35,790	54,515	5,661	31,769	12,587	2,685,308
%	37.0	17.4	44.2	21.3	20.1	14.0	9.3	11.4	7.5	12.4	37.0	20.4
seats	19	1	10	2	10					1	1	43
NDP AVERAGE VOTE AND TOTAL SEATS (1988 INCLUSIVE)												
%	32.4	10.6	32.4	25.0	20.0	8.1	9.3	12.1	5.1	9.4	24.6[b]	17.2
N	95	1	39	33	80	0	0	3	0	1	5	257

[a] Yukon only
[b] reduced number of cases; average based only on elections contested.
N: total seats won over all years
SOURCES: Data derived from Beck (1968), Penniman (1975, 1981, 1988), Report of the Chief Electoral Officer (various years).

Appendix: Table 2 CCF/NDP Provincial and Territorial Governments

Province	Years	Premier
British Columbia	1972-75	Dave Barrett
	1991-	Mike Harcourt
Saskatchewan	1944-61	T.C. Douglas
	1961-64	Woodrow Lloyd
	1971-82	Allan Blakeney
	1991-	Roy Romanow
Manitoba	1969-77	Ed Schreyer
	1981-88	Howard Pawley
Ontario	1990-	Bob Rae
Yukon Territory	1985-	Tony Penikett

BIBLIOGRAPHY

Abella, I.
  1973 *Nationalism, Communism, and Canadian Labour: The* CIO, *the Communist Party, and the Canadian Congress of Labour, 1935-1956.* Toronto: University of Toronto Press.
  1974 *On Strike: Six Key Labour Struggles in Canada 1919-1949.* Toronto: Lewis and Samuel.

Abella, I., and H. Troper
  1982 *None is Too Many: Canada and the Jews of Europe, 1933-1948.* Toronto: Lester and Orpen Dennys.

Abbott, E., ed.
  1990 *Chronicle of Canada.* Montreal: Chronicle.

Allen, R.
  1973 *The Social Passion: Religion and Social Reform in Canada 1914-1928.* Toronto: University of Toronto Press.

Allen, R., ed.
  1975 *The Social Gospel in Canada.* Ottawa: National Museums of Canada.

Anderson, D.
  1987 *To Change the World: A Biography of Pauline Jewett.* Richmond Hill, Ont.: Irwin.

Archer, K.
  1985 'The Failure of the New Democratic Party: Unions, Unionists, and Politics in Canada'. *Canadian Journal of Political Science* 18, 2.
  1987 'Canadian Unions, the New Democratic Party, and the Problems of Collective Action'. *Labour/Le Travail* 20.
  1990 *Political Choices and Electoral Consequences: A Study of Organized Labour and the New Democratic Party.* Montreal: McGill-Queen's University Press.
  1991 'The Process of Leadership Selection in the New Democratic Party'. Research paper submitted to the Royal Commission on Electoral Reform and Party Financing.

Archer, K., and A. Whitehorn
  1990 'Opinion Structure Among New Democratic Party Activists: A Comparison With Liberals and Conservatives'. *Canadian Journal of Political Science* 23, 1 (March).
  1991 'Opinion Structure of New Democrat, Liberal and Conservative Activists'. In Thorburn (1991).

Archer, M.
  1975 *Canada's Economic Problems and Policies.* Toronto: Macmillan.

Ashley, C., and R. Smails
1965 *Canadian Crown Corporations*. Toronto: Macmillan.
Avakumovic, I.
1978 *Socialism in Canada: A Study of the* CCF-NDP *in Federal and Provincial Politics*. Toronto: McClelland and Stewart.
Babcock, R.
1974 *Gompers in Canada: A Study in American Continentalism Before the First World War*. Toronto: University of Toronto Press.
Badgley, R., and S. Wolfe
1967 *Doctors' Strike: Medical Care and Conflict in Saskatchewan*. Toronto: Macmillan.
Bakker, I.
1990 'The Size and Scope of Government: Robin Hood Sent Packing?'. In M. Whittington and G. Williams, eds, *Canadian Politics in the 1990s*. Scarborough, Ont.: Nelson.
Bashevkin, S.
1985 'Women's Participation in the Ontario Political Parties'. In Bashevkin, ed., *Canadian Political Behaviour: Introductory Readings*. Toronto: Methuen.
Baum, G.
1980 *Catholics and Canadian Socialism: Political Thought in the Thirties and Forties*. Toronto: Lorimer.
BC NDP
1979 *Policies For People: Policies of the British Columbia New Democratic Party 1961-1978*. Vancouver: n.p.
Beaulieu, P.
1977 *Ed Schreyer: A Social Democrat in Power*. Winnipeg: Queenston House.
Beck, J.M.
1968 *Pendulum of Power: Canada's Federal Elections*. Toronto: Prentice-Hall.
Bell, D.
1962 *The End of Ideology: On the Exhaustion of Political Ideas in the Fifties*. New York: Free Press.
Berger, T.
1981 *Fragile Freedoms: Human Rights and Dissent in Canada*. Toronto: Clarke, Irwin.
Berlin, I.
1970 *The Hedgehog and the Fox*. New York: Simon and Schuster.
Bibby, R.
1990 *Mosaic Madness: The Poverty and Potential of Life in Canada*. Toronto: Stoddart.
Black, D.
1984 *Winners and Losers: The Book of Canadian Political Lists*. Toronto: Methuen.
Black, E.
1983 'What's Left? The NDP After Regina'. *Canadian Dimension*, November.
Blake, D.
1988 'Division and Cohesion: The Major Parties'. In Perlin (1988).
Blake, D., K. Carty, and L. Erickson
1991 *Grassroots Politicians: Party Activists in British Columbia*. Vancouver: University of British Columbia Press.

Blevins, L.
1974   *The Young Voter's Manual*. Tottawa, NJ: Littlefield, Adams.
Bothwell, R., and J. Granatstein
n.d.   *The Gouzenko Transcripts: The Evidence Presented to the Kellock-Taschereau Royal Commission of 1946*. Ottawa: Deneau.
Boyle, P.
1982   *Elections British Columbia*. Vancouver: Lions Gate.
Bradford, N.
1989   'Ideas, Intellectuals, and Social Democracy in Canada'. In Gagnon and Tanguay (1989).
Bradley, M.
1985   *Crisis of Clarity: The New Democratic Party and the Quest for the Holy Grail*. Toronto: Summerhill.
Breese, G.
1966   *Urbanization in Newly Developing Countries*. Englewood Cliffs, NJ: Prentice-Hall.
Brennan, W., ed.
1985   *Building the Co-operative Commonwealth: Essays on the Democratic Socialist Tradition in Canada*. Regina: Canadian Plains Research Center.
Broadbent, E.
1970   *The Liberal Rip-off: Trudeauism vs. the Politics of Equality*. Toronto: New Press.
1988   *Le Temps d'Agir*. Montreal: Guérin.
1990   'Collective Rights in the Canadian Tradition'. Paper presented to the National Conference on Human Rights and Canadian Solidarity, Ottawa.
Brodie, J.
1985   'From Waffles to Grits: A Decade in the Life of the New Democratic Party'. In Thorburn (1985).
1988   'The Gender Factor and National Leadership Conventions in Canada'. In Perlin (1988).
1990   *The Political Economy of Canadian Regionalism*. Toronto: Harcourt Brace Jovanovich.
Brodie, J., and J. Jenson
1980   *Crisis, Challenge and Change: Party and Class in Canada*. Toronto: Methuen.
1988   *Crisis, Challenge and Change: Party and Class in Canada Revisited*. Toronto: Methuen.
Brown, L.
1973   'The Progressive Tradition in Saskatchewan'. In Roussopoulos (1973).
Brown, R.
1989   *Being Brown: A Very Public Life*. Toronto: Random House.
Brownstone, M.
1971   'The Douglas-Lloyd Governments: Innovation and Bureaucratic Adaptation'. In Lapierre (1971).
Bullen, J.
1983   'The Ontario Waffle and the Struggle For an Independent Socialist Canada: Conflict Within the NDP'. *Canadian Historical Review* 64 (June).
Burnham, J.
1941   *The Managerial Revolution*. Harmondsworth: Penguin.

Butler, D., and A. Ranney, eds
1978 *Referendums*. Washington, DC: American Enterprise Institute.
Cairns, A.
1968 'The Electoral System and the Party System in Canada, 1921-1965'. *Canadian Journal of Political Science* 1, 1. (Reprinted in Fox and White [1987]).
Caplan, G.
1973 *The Dilemma of Canadian Socialism: The CCF in Ontario*. Toronto: McClelland and Stewart.
1975 'The Failure of Canadian Socialism: The Ontario Experience, 1932-1945'. In Clark (1975).
Caplan, G., et al.
1989 *Election: The Issues, the Strategies, the Aftermath*. Scarborough, Ont.: Prentice-Hall.
Caplan, U.
1982 *Like One That Dreamed: A Portrait of A.M. Klein*. Toronto: McGraw-Hill Ryerson.
Carpenter, L.P.
1973 *G.D.H. Cole*. Cambridge: Cambridge University Press.
Carrigan, D.O.
1968 *Canadian Party Platforms 1867-1968*. Urbana: University of Illinois Press.
Carty, K., et al.
1991 *Leaders and Parties in Canadian Politics: The Experience of the Provinces*. Toronto: Harcourt Brace Jovanovich
Casgrain, T.
1972 *A Woman in a Man's World*. Toronto: McClelland and Stewart.
Cassidy, H.
1943 *Social Security and Reconstruction in Canada*. Toronto: Ryerson.
CBC Research
1985 *CBC Election 84: 1984 Election Survey*. Toronto: CBC.
Chi, N.
1976 'Class Cleavage'. In Winn and McNemeny (1976).
Chi, N., and G. Perlin
1979 'The New Democratic Party: A Party in Transition'. In Thorburn (1979).
Chrétien, J.
1985 *Straight From the Heart*. Toronto: Key Porter.
Christian, W., and C. Campbell
1974, *Political Parties and Ideologies in Canada*. Toronto: McGraw-Hill Ryerson.
1990
Clark, S., et al.
1975 *Prophecy and Protest: Social Movements in Twentieth Century Canada*. Toronto: Gage.
Clarke, H., et al.
1979, *Political Choice in Canada*. Toronto: McGraw-Hill.
1980
Clarke, H., et al.
1984, *Absent Mandate*. Toronto: Gage.
1991

Clarkson, S., and C. McCall
1990   *Trudeau and Our Times*. Toronto: McClelland and Stewart.
Clement, W.
1975   *The Canadian Corporate Elite: An Analysis of Economic Power*. Toronto: McClelland and Stewart.
Coldwell, M.J.
1945   *Left-Turn Canada*. Toronto: Duell, Sloan and Pearce.
Cole, G.D.H.
1918,   *Self-Government in Industry*. London: Bell and Sons.
1920
1967   *A History of Socialist Thought*. London: Macmillan.
Colombo, J.
1976   *Colombo's Concise Canadian Quotations*. Edmonton: Hurtig.
Courtney, J.
1973   *The Selection of National Party Leaders in Canada*. Toronto: Macmillan.
Crosland, C.A.R.
1963   *The Future of Socialism*. London: Jonathan Cape.
Cross, M.
1974   *The Decline and Fall of A Good Idea: CCF-NDP Manifestoes, 1932 to 1969*. Toronto: New Hogtown.
Crossman, R.
1949,   *The God that Failed*. New York: Bantam.
1965
Crowley, T.
1990   *Agnes Macphail and the Politics of Equality*. Toronto: Lorimer.
Curtis, J., and W. Scott
1973   *Social Stratification in Canada*. Scarborough, Ont.: Prentice-Hall.
Dahl, R., and E. Tufte
1973   *Size and Democracy*. Stanford: Stanford University Press.
Dalton, R.
1988   *Citizen Politics in Western Democracies*. Chatham: Chatham House.
Dalton, R., et al.
1984   *Electoral Change in Advanced Industrial Democracies: Realignment or Dealignment?* Princeton: Princeton University Press.
Daniel, C., ed.
1987   *Chronicle of the 20th Century*. Mount Kisco, NY: Chronicle.
Davis, A.
1973   'The Saskatchewan CCF'. In Roussopoulos (1973).
de Grazia, A.
1964   'Party'. In J. Gould and W. Kolb, eds. *A Dictionary of the Social Sciences*. New York: Free Press.
Dewey, J.
1939   *Intelligence in the Modern World: John Dewey's Philosophy*. New York: Random House.
Djwa, S.
1987   *The Politics of Imagination: A Life of F.R. Scott*. Toronto: McClelland and Stewart.

Djwa, S., and R. Macdonald, eds
  1983   *On F.R. Scott: Essays on His Contribution to Law, Literature and Politics.*
          Kingston: McGill-Queen's University Press.
Doern, R.
  1981   *The Battle Over Bilingualism: The Manitoba Language Question 1983-1985.*
          Winnipeg: Cambridge.
Durkheim, E.
  1951   *Suicide.* New York: Free Press.
  1958   *Socialism.* New York: Collier.
Duverger, M.
  1963   *Political Parties.* New York: John Wiley.
Dyck, B.
  1988   *Running to Beat Hell: A Biography of A.M. (Sandy) Nicholson.* Regina:
          Canadian Plains Research Center.
Dyck, R.
  1986   *Provincial Politics in Canada.* Scarborough, Ont.: Prentice-Hall.
Eager, E.
  1980   *Saskatchewan Government: Politics and Pragmatism.* Saskatoon: Western
          Producer Prairie Books.
Earle, M., and C. Gamberg
  1989   *Workers and the State in Twentieth Century Nova Scotia.* Fredericton, NB:
          Gorsebrook Research Institute.
Easton, D.
  1965   *A Systems Analysis of Political Life.* New York: John Wiley and Sons.
Engelmann, F.
  1954   'The Cooperative Commonwealth Federation of Canada: A Study of
          Membership Participation in Party Policy-Making'. PhD dissertation, Yale
          University.
  1956   'Membership Participation in Policy-making in the C.C.F.'. *Canadian
          Journal of Economics and Political Science* 22, 2 (May).
Epstein, L.
  1975   'Political Parties'. In *Handbook of Political Science*, vol. 4. Reading, Mass.:
          Addison Wesley.
Erickson, L.
  1988   'CCF-NDP Popularity and the Economy'. *Canadian Journal of Political Science*
          21 (March).
Feigert, F.
  1989   *Canada Votes 1935-1988.* Durham, NC: Duke University Press.
Finifter, A., ed.
  1972   *Alienation and the Social System.* New York: John Wiley and Sons.
Fletcher, F.
  1988   'The Media and the 1984 Landslide'. In Penniman (1988).
Fletcher, F., and R. Drummond
  1979   *Canadian Attitude Trends 1960-1978.* Montreal: Institute for Research on
          Public Policy.
Foot, D.
  1982   *Canada's Population Outlook: Demographic Futures and Economic Chal-
          lenges.* Toronto: Lorimer.

Forcese, D.
  1975   *The Canadian Class Structure*. Toronto: McGraw-Hill.
Forsey, E.
  1974   *Freedom and Order*. Toronto: McClelland and Stewart.
  1982   *Trade Unions in Canada 1812-1902*. Toronto: University of Toronto.
  1990   *A Life on the Fringe: The Memoirs of Eugene Forsey*. Toronto: Oxford University Press.
Fowke, E., ed.
  1948   *Towards Socialism: Selections From the Writings of J.S. Woodsworth*. Toronto: Ontario Woodsworth Memorial Foundation.
Fox, P., ed.
  1966,   *Politics: Canada*. Toronto: McGraw-Hill.
  1977,
  1982
Fox, P., and G. White, eds
  1987,   *Politics: Canada*. Toronto: McGraw-Hill Ryerson.
  1991
Francis, D.
  1986   *Frank H. Underhill: Intellectual Provocateur*. Toronto: University of Toronto Press.
Fraser, G.
  1989   *Playing For Keeps: The Making of the Prime Minister, 1988*. Toronto: McClelland and Stewart.
Frizzell, A., et al.
  1984   *The Canadian General Election of 1984: Politicians, Parties, Press and Polls*. Ottawa: Carleton University Press.
  1989   *The Canadian General Election of 1988*. Ottawa: Carleton University Press.
Fry, J., ed.
  1979   *Economy, Class and Social Reality: Issues in Contemporary Canadian Society*. Toronto: Butterworths.
Gagnon, A., and A.B. Tanguay, eds
  1989   *Canadian Parties in Transition: Discourse, Organization and Representation*. Scarborough, Ont.: Nelson.
Garson, D.
  1976   *Political Science Methods*. Boston: Holbrook.
Garson, D., ed.
  1977   *Worker Self-Management in Industry: The West European Experience*. New York: Praeger.
Gellner, J.
  1974   *Bayonets in the Streets: Urban Guerrilla at Home and Abroad*. Don Mills, Ont.: Collier-Macmillan.
Geyer, R.F., and D. Schweitzer, eds
  1976   *Theories of Alienation: Critical Perspectives in Philosophy and the Social Sciences*. Leiden: Martinus Nijhoff.
  1981   *Alienation: Problems of Meaning, Theory and Method*. Routledge and Kegan Paul.
Gibbins, R.
  1980   *Prairie Politics and Society*. Toronto: Butterworths.
  1982   *Regionalism: Territorial Politics in Canada and the United States*. Toronto: Butterworths.

Godfrey, D., and M. Watkins, eds
  1970 *Gordon to Watkins to You: A Documentary: the Battle for Control of Our Economy.* Toronto: New Press.
Goldfarb, M., and T. Axworthy
  1988 *Marching To a Different Drummer.* Toronto: Stoddart.
Goldfield, M.
  1987 *The Decline of Organized Labor in the United States.* Chicago: University of Chicago Press.
Goldthorpe, J.
  1968a *The Affluent Worker: Industrial Attitudes and Behaviour.* Cambridge: Cambridge University Press.
  1968b *The Affluent Worker: Political Attributes and Behaviour.* Cambridge: Cambridge University Press.
  1969 *The Affluent Worker in the Class Structure.* Cambridge: Cambridge University Press.
Good, W.C.
  1958 *Farmer Citizen: My Fifty Years in the Canadian Farmers' Movement.* Toronto: Ryerson.
Gorz, A.
  1980 *Ecology as Politics.* Montreal: Black Rose.
Gregg, A., and M. Posner
  1990 *The Big Picture: What Canadians Think About Almost Everything.* Toronto: Macfarlane, Walter and Ross.
Groome, A.
  1967 'M.J. Coldwell and CCF Foreign Policy, 1932-1950'. MA thesis. Regina: University of Saskatchewan.
Gruending, D.
  1990 *Promises to Keep: A Political Biography of Allan Blakeney.* Saskatoon: Western Producer Prairie Books.
Grun, B.
  1975 *The Timetables of History: A Horizontal Linkage of People and Events.* New York: Simon and Schuster.
Guest, D.
  1980 *The Emergence of Social Security in Canada.* Vancouver: University of British Columbia Press.
Hackett, R.
  1979 'The Waffle Conflict in the NDP'. In Thorburn (1979).
  1980 'Pie in the Sky: A History of the Ontario Waffle'. *Canadian Dimension,* special edition, October-November.
Haggart, R., and A. Golden
  1979 *Rumours of War.* Toronto: Lorimer.
Hammond, T.
  1975 *The Anatomy of Communist Takeovers.* New Haven: Yale University Press.
Harp, J., and J. Hofley
  1980 *Structured Inequality in Canada.* Scarborough, Ont.: Prentice-Hall.
Harrop, G.
  1984 *Advocate of Compassion: Stanley Knowles in the Political Process.* Hantsport, NS: Lancelot.
  1987 *Clarie Gillis, M.P. 1940-1957.* Hantsport, NS: Lancelot.

Hayward, S., and A. Whitehorn
 1991 'Leadership Selection: Which Method?' Paper presented to the Douglas-Coldwell Foundation, April.
Heaps, L.
 1970 *The Rebel in the House: The Life and Times of A.A. Heaps MP*. London: Niccolo.
Heaps, L., ed.
 1991 *Our Canada*. Toronto: Lorimer.
Higginbotham, C.
 1968 *Off the Record: The CCF in Saskatchewan*. Toronto: McClelland and Stewart.
Hills, N.
 1984 'The NDP Survivors'. In Frizzell et al. (1984).
Hodgson, M.
 1976 *The Squire of Kootenay West: A Biography of Bert Herridge*. Saanichton, BC: Hancock House.
Hoffer, E.
 1951 *The True Believer*. New York: Mentor.
Hoffman, G.
 1975 'The Saskatchewan Farmer-Labor Party, 1932-1934: How Radical Was It At Its Origin?' *Saskatchewan History* 28, 2 (Spring).
 1977 'The Entry of the United Farmers of Canada, Saskatchewan Section into Politics: A Reassessment'. *Saskatchewan History* 30, 3 (Autumn)
 1983 'The 1934 Saskatchewan Provincial Election Campaign'. *Saskatchewan History*, Spring.
Horn, M.
 1973 'Frank Underhill's Early Drafts of the Regina Manifesto 1933'. *Canadian Historical Review* 54 (December).
 1980 *The League For Social Reconstruction: Intellectual Origins of the Democratic Left in Canada 1930-1942*. Toronto: University of Toronto Press.
Horn, M., ed.
 1972 *The Dirty Thirties: Canadians in the Great Depression*. [Toronto:] Copp Clark.
Horowitz, G.
 1968 *Canadian Labour in Politics*. Toronto: University of Toronto.
Horvat, B.
 1982 *The Political Economy of Socialism: A Marxist Social Theory*. Armonk, NY: Sharpe.
Hulsberg, W.
 1988 *The German Greens: A Social and Political Profile*. London: Verso.
Hunnius, G., ed.
 1970 *Industrial Democracy and Canadian Labour*. Montreal: Black Rose.
 1971 *Participatory Democracy For Canadians*. Montreal: Black Rose.
Hunnius, G., et al., eds
 1973 *Workers Control: A Reader on Labor and Social Change*. New York: Vintage.
Hunter, A.
 1981 *Class Tells: On Social Inequality in Canada*. Toronto: Butterworths.

Huntington, S.
 1968 *Political Order in Changing Societies*. New Haven: Yale University Press.
Inglehart, R.
 1977 *The Silent Revolution: Changing Values and Political Styles Among Western Publics*. Princeton: Princeton University Press.
Irvine, W.
 (1920) *The Farmers in Politics*. Toronto: McClelland and Stewart.
 1976
Irving, J.
 1959 *The Social Credit Movement in Alberta*. Toronto: University of Toronto Press.
Kalbach, W., and W. McVey
 1971 *The Demographic Basis of Canadian Society*. Toronto: McGraw-Hill.
Katsiaficas, G.
 1987 *The Imagination of the New Left: A Global Analysis of 1968*. Boston: South End Press.
Kavic, L., and G. Nixon
 1978, *The 1200 Days*. Coquitlam, BC: Kaen.
 1979
Kealey, L., and J. Sangster, eds
 1989 *Beyond the Vote: Canadian Women and Politics*. Toronto: University of Toronto Press.
Keefe, W.
 1984 *Parties, Politics, and Public Policy in America*. New York: Holt, Rinehart and Winston.
Kemp, P., and D. Wall
 1990 *A Green Manifesto For the 1990s*. London: Penguin.
Kerr, D., ed.
 1981 *Western Canadian Politics: The Radical Tradition*. Edmonton: NeWest.
King, W.
 1956 *Social Movements in the United States*. New York: Random House.
Knowles, S.
 1961 *The New Party*. Toronto: McClelland and Stewart.
Kolakowski, L.
 1968 *Toward A Marxist Humanism: Essays on the Left Today*. New York: Grove.
Kome, P., ed.
 1985 *Women of Influence: Canadian Women and Politics*. Toronto: Doubleday.
Kurian, G.
 1984 *The New Book of World Rankings*. New York: Facts on File.
Laidler, H.
 1968 *History of Socialism*. New York: Thomas Y. Crowell.
Lamoureux, A.
 1985 *Le NDP et le Québec 1958-1985*. Montreal: Editions du Parc.
Landes, R.
 1983 *The Canadian Polity: A Comparative Introduction*. Scarborough, Ont.: Prentice-Hall.
Lange, O., and F. Taylor
 1938 *On the Economic Theory of Socialism*. New York: McGraw-Hill.

LaPalombara, J.
1974 *Politics Within Nations*. Englewood Cliffs, NJ: Prentice-Hall.
LaPalombara, J., and M. Weiner, eds
1966 *Political Parties and Political Development*. Princeton: Princeton University Press.
Lapierre, L., et al., eds
1971 *Essays on the Left: Essays in Honour of T.C. Douglas*. Toronto: McClelland and Stewart.
Larmour, J.
1985 'The Douglas Government's Changing Emphasis on Public, Private and Co-operative Development in Saskatchewan 1944-1961'. In Brennan (1985).
Latouche, D.
1991 'Universal Democracy and Effective Leadership: Lessons From the Parti Québécois Experience'. In Carty et al. (1991).
Laux, J., and M. Molot
1988 *State Capitalism: Public Enterprise in Canada*. Ithaca, NY: Cornell University Press.
Laxer, J.
1970 *The Energy Poker Game: The Politics of the Continental Resources Deal*. Toronto: New Press.
1984 *Rethinking the Economy: The Laxer Report on Canadian Economic Problems and Policies*. Toronto: NC Press.
Laxer, R., ed.
1973 *(Canada) Ltd.: The Political Economy of Dependency*. Toronto: McClelland and Stewart.
Laycock, D.
1990 *Populist and Democratic Thought in the Canadian Prairies 1910 to 1945*. Toronto: University of Toronto Press.
Lazarus, M.
1977a *The Long Winding Road: Canadian Labour in Politics*. Vancouver: Boag.
1977b *Up From the Ranks: Trade Union VIP's Past and Present*. n.p. Co-operative Press Associates.
1980 *The Pension Story*. Ottawa: Co-operative Press.
Lele, J., G. Perlin, and H. Thorburn
1979 'The National Party Convention'. In Thorburn (1979).
Levitt, K.
1970 *Silent Surrender: The Multinational Corporation in Canada*. Toronto: Macmillan.
Lewis, D.
1972 *Louder Voices: The Corporate Welfare Bums*. Toronto: James Lewis and Samuel.
1981 *The Good Fight: Political Memoirs 1909-1958*. Toronto: Macmillan.
Lewis, D., and F.R. Scott
1943 *Make This Your Canada: A Review of C.C.F. History and Policy*. Toronto: Central Canada Publishing.
Lifton, R.J.
1963 *Thought Reform and the Psychology of Totalism*. New York: Norton.

Lipset, S.
1950, *Agrarian Socialism: The Cooperative Commonwealth Federation in*
1968 *Saskatchewan, A Study in Political Sociology* Berkeley: University of California Press.
1960, *Political Man: The Social Bases of Politics.* Garden City, NY: Doubleday
1981 (1960); Baltimore: Johns Hopkin (1981).
Lloyd, D.
1979 *Woodrow: A Biography of W.S. Lloyd.* n.p. Woodrow Lloyd Memorial Fund.
Lovick, L.D.
1979 *Till Power is Brought to Pooling: Tommy Douglas Speaks.* Lantzville, BC: Oolichan.
League For Social Reconstruction
(1935) *Social Planning For Canada.* Toronto: Nelson/University of Toronto.
1975
Lynch, C.
1983 *You Can't Print That! Memoirs of a Political Voyeur.* Toronto: Totem.
McAllister, J.
1984 *The Government of Edward Schreyer.* Kingston, Ont.: McGill-Queen's University Press.
McCall, C.
1982 *Grits: An Intimate Portrait of the Liberal Party.* Toronto: Macmillan.
McDaniel, S.
1986 *Canada's Aging Population.* Toronto: Butterworths.
MacDonald, D.
1988 *The Happy Warrior: Political Memoirs.* Markham, Ont.: Fitzhenry and Whiteside.
MacDonald, D., ed.
1980, *The Government and Politics of Ontario.* Toronto: Van Nostrand/Nelson.
1985
McDonald, L.
1987 *The Party That Changed Canada: The New Democratic Party Then and Now.* Toronto: Macmillan.
MacEwan, P.
1976 *Miners and Steelworkers: Labour in Cape Breton.* Toronto: Samuel Stevens Hakkert.
1980 *The Akerman Years.* Antigonish, NS: Formac.
McHenry, D.
1950 *The Third Force in Canada: The Cooperative Commonwealth Federation 1932-1948.* Berkeley: University of California Press.
MacInnis, G.
1953 *J.S. Woodsworth: A Man to Remember.* Toronto: Macmillan.
MacInnis, G., and C. Woodsworth, eds
c. 1935 *Canada Through C.C.F. Glasses.* Vancouver.
McLeod, J.
1988 *The Oxford Book of Canadian Political Anecdotes.* Toronto: Oxford University Press.
McLeod, T., and I. McLeod

1987   *Tommy Douglas: The Road to Jerusalem*. Edmonton: Hurtig.

McLuhan, M.
1968   *War and Peace in the Global Village*. New York: Bantam.

McNaught, K.
1959   *A Prophet in Politics: A Biography of J.S. Woodsworth*. Toronto: University of Toronto Press.
1980   *J.S. Woodsworth*. Toronto: Fitzhenry and Whiteside.

Macpherson, C.B.
1953   *Democracy in Alberta: Social Credit and The Party System*. Toronto: University of Toronto Press.
1962   *The Political Theory of Possessive Individualism: Hobbes to Locke*. London: Oxford University Press.

MacPherson, I.
1985   'The CCF and the Co-operative Movement in The Douglas Years: An Uneasy Alliance'. In Brennan (1985).

Manitoba NDP
1979   *Manitoba NDP Convention Resolutions: 1961-1978*. Winnipeg.

Mardiros, A.
1979   *William Irvine: The Life of a Prairie Radical*. Toronto: Lorimer.

Marsh, J., ed.
1985,   *The Canadian Encyclopedia*. Edmonton: Hurtig.
1988

Mason, J.
1990   'Courting the Ordinary Canadian'. *Canadian Forum*, October.

Mather, B.
n. d.   *Prominent Portraits*. Vancouver: Boag Foundation.

Mathews, R., and J. Steele, eds
1969   *The Struggle For Canadian Universities: A Dossier*. Toronto: New Press.

Meisel, J.
1962   *The Canadian General Election of 1957*. Toronto: University of Toronto Press.
1975   *Working Papers on Canadian Politics*. Montreal: McGill-Queen's University Press.

Meisel, J., ed.
1964   *Papers on the 1962 Election*. Toronto: University of Toronto.

Melnyk, O.
1989   *Remembering the CCF: No Bankers in Heaven*. Toronto: McGraw-Hill Ryerson.

Michalos, A.
1980   *North American Social Report: A Comparative Study of the Quality of Life in Canada and the USA from 1964-1974*. Dordrecht, Netherlands: Reidel.

Michels, R.
1962   *Political Parties: A Sociological Study of the Oligarchic Tendencies of Modern Democracy*. New York: Free Press.

Mickiewicz, E.
1973   *Handbook of Soviet Social Science Data*. New York: Free Press.

Milbrath, L.
1984 *Environmentalists: Vanguard For a New Society*. Albany: University of New York Press.
Miller, R., and F. Isbester
1971 *Canadian Labour in Transition*. Scarborough, Ont: Prentice-Hall.
Mills, A.
1991 *Fool For Christ: The Political Thought of J.S. Woodsworth*. Toronto: University of Toronto Press.
Mills, C.B.
1956 *The Power Elite*. New York: Oxford University Press.
Morf, G.
1970 *Terror in Quebec: Case Studies of the FLQ*. Vancouver: Clarke Irwin.
Morley, T.
1984 *Secular Socialists: the CCF/NDP in Ontario, A Biography*. Kingston, Ont.: McGill-Queen's University Press.
1888 'The New Democratic Party in the 1984 Federal General Election'. In Penniman (1988).
Morton, D.
1974 *NDP: The Dream of Power*. Toronto: Hakkert.
1977 *NDP: Social Democracy in Canada*. Toronto: Hakkert.
1986 *The New Democrats 1961-1986: The Politics of Change*. Toronto: Copp Clark Pitman.
Morton, W.
1967 *The Progressive Party in Canada*. Toronto: University of Toronto Press.
Mosca, G.
1939 *The Ruling Class*. New York: McGraw-Hill.
Myers, J.
1986 *The Fitzhenry and Whiteside Book of Canadian Facts and Dates*. Toronto: Fitzhenry and Whiteside.
Naylor, C.D.
1986 *Private Practice, Public Payments: Canadian Medicine and the Politics of Health Insurance 1911-1986*. Kingston: McGill-Queen's University Press.
New Democrats
1986 *Resolutions Reference*. Ottawa.
Nightingale, D.
1982 *Workplace Democracy: An Inquiry Into Employee Participation in Canadian Working Organizations*. Toronto: University of Toronto Press.
Oliver, M., ed.
1961 *Social Purpose For Canada*. Toronto: University of Toronto Press.
Ontario CCF
1944 *Planning For Freedom*. Toronto: Thistle.
Ontario NDP
c.1983 *Programme: Policies of the Ontario New Democrats*. Toronto.
Osgood, C.
1957 *The Measurement of Meaning*. Urbana: University of Illinois Press.
1979 'From Yin and Yang to And or But in Cross Cultural Perspective'. *International Journal of Psychology* 4, 1.

Paltiel, K.
  1970 *Political Party Financing in Canada*. Toronto: McGraw-Hill.
  1988 'The 1984 Federal General Election and Developments in Canadian Party Finances'. In Penniman (1988).
Pammett, J.
  1991 'Class Voting and Class Consciousness in Canada'. In Wearing (1991a).
Pateman, C.
  1970 *Participation and Democratic Theory*. Cambridge: Cambridge University Press.
Penner, N.
  1977 *The Canadian Left: A Critical Analysis*. Toronto: Prentice-Hall.
  1988 *Canadian Communism: The Stalin Years and Beyond*. Toronto: Methuen.
Penniman, H., ed.
  1975 *Canada at the Polls: The General Election of 1974*. Washington,DC: American Enterprise Institute.
  1981 *Canada at the Polls: 1979 and 1980: A Study of the General Elections*. Washington, DC American Enterprise Institute.
  1988 *Canada at the Polls, 1984: A Study of the Federal General Elections*. Durham, NC: Duke University Press.
Pennington, D.
  1989, *Agnes Macphail: Reformer, Canada's First Female M.P.* Toronto: Simon and
  1990   Pierre.
Perlin, G.
  1980 *The Tory Syndrome*. Montreal: McGill-Queen's University Press.
Perlin, G., ed.
  1988 *Party Democracy in Canada*. Scarborough, Ont.: Prentice-Hall.
Pitsula, J., and K. Rasmussen
  1990 *Privatizing A Province: The New Right in Saskatchewan*. Vancouver: New Star.
Porritt, J.
  1984 *Seeing Green: The Politics of Ecology Explained*. Oxford: Basil Blackwell.
Porter, J.
  1965 *The Vertical Mosaic: An Analysis of Social Class and Power in Canada*. Toronto: University of Toronto Press.
  1967 *Canadian Social Structure: A Statistical Profile*. Toronto: McClelland and Stewart.
Pratt, L., ed.
  1986 *Socialism and Democracy in Alberta: Essays in Honour of Grant Notley*. Edmonton: NeWest.
Rands, S.
  1981 'The CCF in Saskatchewan'. In Kerr (1981).
Read, E., and A. Whitehorn
  1991 'Social Democracy Thwarted: A Case Study of the 1945 and 1988 Federal Elections'. Paper presented to the Canadian Political Science Association annual meetings, June.
Reid, T., and J. Reid
  1969 *Student Power and the Canadian Campus*. Toronto: Peter Martin Associates.

Richards, J.
1983 'Social Democracy and the Unions: What's Left?' Paper presented to the Quebec Political Science Society annual meeting.
1988 'Populism'. In Marsh (1988).

Richards, J., and D. Kerr
1986 *Canada, What's Left? A New Social Contract Pro and Con.* Edmonton: NeWest.

Richards, J., and L. Pratt
1979 *Prairie Capitalism: Power and Influence in the New West.* Toronto: McClelland and Stewart.

Richards, J., et al., eds.
1991 *Social Democracy Without Illusions: Renewal of the Canadian Left.* Toronto: McClelland and Stewart.

Roberts, B.
1988 *Whence They Came! Deportations From Canada 1901-1935.* Altona: University of Ottawa Press.

Rosenblum, S., and P. Findlay, eds
1991 *Debating Canada's Future: Views From the Left.* Toronto: Lorimer.

Ross, D.
1980 *The Canadian Fact Book on Income Distribution.* Ottawa: Canadian Council on Social Development.

Roussopoulos, D., ed.
1970 *The New Left in Canada.* Montreal: Our Generation.
1973 *Canada and Radical Social Change.* Montreal: Black Rose.

Salutin, R.
1989 *Waiting For Democracy: A Citizen's Journey.* Markham, Ont.: Viking.

Sangster, J.
1989 *Dreams of Equality: Women On the Canadian Left, 1920-1950.* Toronto: McClelland and Stewart.

Sargent, L.
1972 *New Left Thought: An Introduction.* Homewood, Ill.: Dorsey.

Saywell, J.
1970, *Quebec 70: A Documentary Narrative.* Toronto: University of Toronto Press.
1971

Scarrow, H.
1962 *Canada Votes: A Handbook of Federal and Provincial Election Data.* New Orleans: Hauser.

Schacht, R.
1971 *Alienation.* Garden City, NJ: Anchor.

Schweitzer, D., and R.F. Geyer, eds
1989 *Alienation Theories and De-Alienation Strategies.* Northwood, UK: Science Reviews.

Scotton, A., ed.
1977 *New Democratic Policies 1961-1976.* Ottawa: Mutual Press.

Seidle, F.L., and K. Paltiel
1981 'Party Finance, the Election Expenses Act, and Campaign Spending in 1979 and 1980'. In Penniman (1981).

Selucky, R.
1979 *Marxism, Socialism, Freedom.* London: Macmillan.

Shackleton, D.
1975 *Tommy Douglas*. Toronto: McClelland and Stewart.
Sherwood, D.
1966 'The N.D.P. and French Canada, 1961-1965'. MA thesis. McGill University.
Shulman, M.
1979 *Member of the Legislature*. Toronto: Fitzhenry and Whiteside.
Sik, O.
1967 *Plan and Market Under Socialism*. White Plains, NY: International Arts and Sciences Press.
Sims, R.
1977 'Conceptions of War: The Co-operative Commonwealth Federation of Canada: 1932-1940'. MA thesis. Carleton University.
Sinclair, P.
1973 'The Saskatchewan CCF: Ascent to Power and the Decline of Socialism'. *Canadian Historical Review*, December. Reprinted in S. Clark et al. (1975).
Sivard, R.
1987 *World Military and Social Expenditures 1987-88*. Washington, DC: World Priorities.
Smallwood, F.
1983 *The Other Candidates: Third Parties in Presidential Elections*. Hanover, NH: University Press of New England.
Smart, J.
1973 'Populist and Socialist Movements in Canadian History'. In R. Laxer (1973).
Smith, C.
1989 *Unfinished Journey: the Lewis Family*. Toronto: Summerhill.
Stanbury, W.T.
1986 'The Mother's Milk of Politics: Political Contributions to Federal Parties in Canada, 1974-1984'. *Canadian Journal of Political Science* 19, 4.
1989 'Financing Federal Political Parties in Canada, 1974-1986'. In Gagnon and Tanguay (1989).
Steed, J.
1988 *Ed Broadbent: The Pursuit of Power*. Markham, Ont.: Penguin.
Steeves, D.
1960 *The Compassionate Rebel: Ernest E. Winch and His Times*. Vancouver: Evergreen.
Stirling, R., and D. Kouri
1979 'Unempoyment Indexes—The Canadian Context'. In Fry (1979).
Stewart, M., and D. French
1959 *Ask No Quarter: A Biography of Agnes Macphail*. Toronto: Longmans, Green.
Stewart, W.
1987 *Uneasy Lies the Head: The Truth About Canada's Crown Corporations*. Toronto: Collins.
Stinson, L.
1975 *Political Warriors: Recollections of a Social Democrat*. Winnipeg: Queenston.

Struthers, J.
1983   No Fault of Their Own: Unemployment and the Canadian Welfare State 1914-1941. Toronto: University of Toronto Press.
Surich, J.
1975   'Purists and Pragmatists: Canadian Democratic Socialism at the Crossroads'. In Penniman (1975).
Swayze, C.
1987   Hard Choices: A Life of Tom Berger. Vancouver: Douglas and McIntryre.
Taylor, C.
1970   The Pattern of Politics. Toronto: McClelland and Stewart.
Teeple, G.
1972   '"Liberals in a Hurry": Socialism and the CCF-NDP'. In Teeple, ed., Capitalism and the National Question in Canada. Toronto: University of Toronto Press.
Thomas, L.
1981   'The CCF Victory in Saskatchewan, 1944'. Saskatchewan History, Winter.
1982   The Making of a Socialist: The Recollections of Tommy Douglas. Edmonton: University of Alberta Press.
Thomas, L., ed.
1977   William Aberhart and Social Credit in Alberta. Vancouver: Copp Clark.
Thorburn, H.
1986   'The New Democratic Party and National Defence'. In N. Orvik, ed., Semi-Alignment and Western Security. London: Croom Helm.
Thorburn, H., ed.
1979,   Party Politics in Canada. 4th, 5th, 6th ed. Scarborough, Ont.: Prentice-Hall.
1985,
1991
Toennies, F.
1963   Community and Society. New York: Harper and Row.
Toffler, A.
1970   Future Shock. New York: Bantam.
Tollefson, E.
1963   Bitter Medicine. Saskatoon: Modern Press.
Townsend, J.
1969   Political Participation in Communist China. Berkeley: University of California Press.
Trofimenkoff, S.
1982   Stanley Knowles: The Man from Winnipeg North Centre. Saskatoon: Western Producer Prairie Books.
1989   'Thérèse Casgrain and the CCF in Quebec'. In Kealey and Sangster (1989).
Trotsky, L.
1959   The Russian Revolution. Garden City, NJ: Doubleday Anchor.
Trudeau, M.
1979   Beyond Reason. New York: Pocket Books.
Trudeau, P.
1968   Federalism and the French Canadians. Toronto: Macmillan.
Tyre, R.
1962   Douglas in Saskatchewan. Vancouver: Mitchell.

Underhill, F.
1944   *James Shaver Woodsworth: Untypical Canadian.* Toronto: Ontario Woodsworth Memorial Foundation.
1961   *In Search of Canadian Liberalism.* Toronto: Macmillan.
Urlanis, B.
1971   *Wars and Population.* Moscow: Progress.
Van Loon, R., and M. Whittington
1987   *The Canadian Political System: Environment, Structure and Process.* Toronto: McGraw-Hill Ryerson.
Veltmeyer, H.
1986   *Canadian Class Structure.* Toronto: Garamond.
Walden, D.
1980   ' "When Monopoly Capital Took Fright. . . .": The Anti-CCF Campaign of 1943-45'. Paper presented to the annual meeting of the Canadian Political Science Association, Montreal, June.
Wearing, J.
1988   *Strained Relations.* Toronto: McClelland and Stewart.
1991a 'Regulating Federal Election Spending'. In Fox and White (1991).
Wearing, J., ed.
1991b *The Ballot and Its Message: Voting in Canada.* Toronto: Copp Clark Pitman.
Weber, M.
1964   *The Theory of Social and Economic Organization.* New York: Free Press.
Webster, D.
(n.d.) *Growth of the N.D.P. in B.C. 1900-1970: 81 Political Biographies.* [Vancouver]: Broadway Publishers.
Weinrich, P.
1982   *Social Protest From the Left in Canada: 1870-1970: A Bibliography.* Toronto: University of Toronto Press.
Whelan, E. and P.
1990   *Touched By Tommy.* Regina: Whelan.
Whitehorn, A.
1974   'Alienation and Workers' Self-Management'. *Canadian Slavonic Papers* 14, 2.
1978   'Yugoslav Workers' Self-Management: A Blueprint for Industrial Democracy?'. *Canadian Slavonic Papers*, September.
1979a 'Alienation and Industrial Society: A Case Study of Workers' Self-Management'. *Canadian Review of Sociology and Anthropology*, May.
1979b 'Yugoslavia: A Case Study of Self-Managing Socialism?'. In Andre Liebich, ed, *The Future of Socialism in Europe.* Montreal: InterUniversity Centre for European Studies.
1985a 'An Analysis of the Historiography of the CCF-NDP: The Protest Movement Becalmed Tradition'. In Brennan (1985).
1985b 'The CCF-NDP: Fifty Years After' In Thorburn (1985).
1985c 'Social Democracy'. In Marsh (1985, 1988).
1985d 'New Democratic Party'. In Marsh (1985, 1988).
1987   'Douglas and the Historians'. *NeWest*, May.
1988   'The New Democratic Party in Convention'. In Perlin (1988).
1989   'The New Democratic Party Election Campaign: Dashed Hopes'. In Frizzell et al. (1989).

1991a   'The CCF-NDP and the End of the Broadbent Era'. In Thorburn (1991).
1991b   'The Communist Party of Canada'. In Thorburn (1991).
1991c   'David Lewis'. In Heaps (1991).
1991d   'In Search of a Praxis for Alienation Research'. In A. Oldenquist and M. Rosner, eds, *Alienation, Community and Work*.Westport, Conn.: Greenwood.
Whitehorn, A., and K. Archer
1989   'The New Democratic Party and Territoriality'. Paper presented to the Canadian Political Science Association meeting, June.
Whitehorn, A., and S. Hayward
1990   Unpublished submission to the Royal Commission on Electoral Reform and Party Financing.
Whiteley, P.
1983   *The Labour Party in Crisis*. London: Methuen.
Wilkinson, P.
1971   *Social Movement*. London: Macmillan.
Wilson, D., ed.
1985   *Democratic Socialism: The Challenge of the Eighties and Beyond*. Vancouver: New Star.
Winn, C., and J. McNenemy
1976   *Political Parties in Canada*. Toronto: McGraw-Hill.
Wiseman, N.
1983   *Social Democracy in Manitoba*. Winnipeg: University of Manitoba Press.
Wood, N.
1959   *Communism and British Intellectuals*. London: Victor Gollancz.
Woolstencroft, P.
1991   '"Tories Kick Machine to Bits": Leadership Selection and the Ontario Progressive Conservative Party'. In Carty et al. (1991).
World Bank
1972   *Urbanization*. Washington, DC: World Bank.
World Commission on Environment and Development
1987   *Our Common Future*. Oxford: Oxford University Press.
Wright, J.F.C.
1965   *The Louise Lucas Story: This Time Tomorrow*. Montreal: Harvest House.
Young, W.
1969   *The Anatomy of a Party: The National CCF 1932-1961*. Toronto: University of Toronto Press.
1971   'A Profile of Activists in the British Columbia NDP'. *Journal of Canadian Studies* 5, 1.
Zakuta, L.
1964   *A Protest Movement Becalmed*. Toronto: University of Toronto Press.
Ziegler, O.
1934   *Woodsworth: Social Pioneer*. Toronto: Ontario Publishing.
Zolf, L.
1973   *Dance of the Dialectic*. Toronto: James Lewis and Samuel.

INDEX

abortion, 128, 221, 251; delegate positions, 134, 135
advertising: in election (1988), 192, 216-17, 222; interest-group, 12, 27-8, 44, 227, 228-30, 253
Agnaieff, Michel, 227
agriculture, 39, 40; *see also* farmers
Alberta: and CCF, 8; federal vote/seats, 3, 4, 5, 262-4; provincial NDP, 8; *see also* elections
alienation, 63; political, 127, 252; regional, 11, 13, 91, 108, 127; worker, 136
Althouse, Vic, 97
Anguish, Doug, 11, 97
anti-socialist campaigns, 75, 163, 178n.37, 197-8
Argue, Hazen, 11, 16n.14, 46, 76, 77, 80, 82; as CCF leader, 115, 116-17; defection, 83; and Douglas, 150
Atlantic provinces, 61; alienation, 108, 127; voting patterns, 103n.34
Auto Pact, 223

Bacher, John, 16n.15
Barrett, Dave, 7, 90, 115, 220, 231
Benjamin, Les, 89, 93, 231
Berger, Tom, 84, 102n.30
Berlin, Isaiah, xi
bilingualism, 51, 81, 83, 159; delegate positions, 127, 134, 135; in manifestos, 59, 61
bill of rights, 47, 87
Blackburn, Derek, 91, 93
Blaikie, Bill, 95, 100, 231
Blakeney, Allan, 7, 90, 98, 220; and constitution, 193-4; and New Regina Manifesto, 62
Bloc Québécois, 210n.61, 245, 246
Booker, Clare, 214
Bradley, Michael, 145, 171-2
Brewin, Andrew, 20, 46, 52, 84, 87, 91, 93, 170
Brewin, John, 170, 231

British Columbia: federal vote/seats, 3, 4, 5, 262-4; provincial NDP, 7, 9, 75; Socialist Fellowship, 13; *see also* elections
British North America (BNA) Act, 39, 41
Broadbent, Ed, 11, 62, 91, 120, 214, 231; advisers, 215; background, 188; and Bill 101, 227; and Blakeney, 193-4; and coalition offer, 193, 198-9; and constitution, 11, 14, 193, 195-6, 199; and councils of federal ridings, 204; and elections (1979) 192, (1984) 195, (1988) 196-8, 199, 212, 214, 215, 219, 220-8; and free trade, 197, 199; and gender parity, 204; and industrial democracy, 200; influences, 188-9; and middle class, 203, 205; in minority Parliament (1972-74), 191; and NATO, 203; as NDP leader, 115, 116, 117, 191-2; personality, 189, 205; and polling, 203-4, 219; popularity, 12, 189-90, 212, 220, 222; and Laxer, 194; on Liberal Party, 197; and New Left, 190; and New Regina Manifesto, 62, 194; and Quebec, 195-6, 197, 199, 202; and proportional representation, 9; and referenda, 200; resignation, 12, 198; and socialist theory, 201; in TV debates (1979) 192, (1988) 189, 225-7; and Waffle, 190; and workers' self-management, 200
Brown, Rosemary, 115, 117, 191
Bund, Jewish Labour, 153, 154, 155
business: 'big', 15, 121; small, 55-6, 60, 62, 64
Business Council on National Issues, 228

Calgary Programme (1932), 13, 36-8; content analysis, 37, 38, 43
Cameron, Colin, 85